Josephine Baker in Art and Life

Josephine Baker

in Art and Life

THE ICON AND THE IMAGE

Bennetta Jules-Rosette

University of Illinois Press
Urbana and Chicago

Library of Congress Cataloging-in-Publication Data

Jules-Rosette, Bennetta.
Josephine Baker in art and life : the icon and the image /
Bennetta Jules-Rosette, Simon Njami.
p.   cm.
Includes bibliographical references and index.
ISBN-13: 978-0-252-03157-1 (cloth : alk. paper)
ISBN-10: 0-252-03157-1 (cloth : alk. paper)
ISBN-13: 978-0-252-07412-7 (pbk. : alk. paper)
ISBN-10: 0-252-07412-2 (pbk. : alk. paper)
1. Baker, Josephine, 1906–1975.
2. Dancers—France—Biography.
3. African American entertainers—France—Biography.
I. Simon, Njami.
II. Title.
GV1785.B3J85   2007
792.8'028'092—dc22   2006006965

Quotations by Josephine Baker from Josephine Baker and Jo Bouillon,
Josephine (English translation by Mariana Fitzpatrick © Harper and
Row, 1977), and excerpts from Erving Goffman, *Frame Analysis*
(Harper and Row, 1974, © Erving Goffman), appear with permission
of HarperCollins Publishers. Excerpts from the introduction to Paul
Colin's *Le Tumulte noir* are reprinted from *Josephine Baker and La
Revue Nègre: Paul Colin's Lithographs of Le Tumulte noir in Paris, 1927*,
by Henry Louis Gates Jr. and Karen C. C. Dalton (New York: Harry N.
Abrams, Inc., 1998), all rights reserved.

To Josephine Baker
and the performers, artists, scholars,
and international audiences that she inspired
and
to the memory of my parents,
Walter Edward Washington and
Bennetta Bullock Washington

Contents

Illustrations

Foreword: A Luminous Humanism
Simon Njami

The image that most people hold of Josephine Baker is that of an ingénue who danced wearing only a skimpy banana skirt. But Baker must be seen beyond the banana skirt syndrome. It is the fate of mythic figures, in particular those emerging from show business, to be frozen in collective memory and to project images that may have become exaggerated, stereotyped, or outmoded. In a consumer society where the cult of the image is a form of thought, public personalities have no freedom. Thus, Marilyn Monroe will always be remembered as that young woman with the white dress swirling around her thighs above a subway vent, and Sidney Poitier will always be the noble black man fighting for justice and representing an entire race in the Hollywood productions of the 1950s and 1960s.

In reading Bennetta Jules-Rosette's *Josephine Baker in Art and Life,* I was fascinated by the duality inherent in every individual, which became a thread weaving together the fabric of Josephine Baker's story. Baker was a woman torn between multiple identities and multiple loves. She lived for her loves and, in a certain sense, died as a result of them. It seems to me that as a key to understanding her destiny, nothing is more important than the song "I Have Two Loves," which became her theme song and was associated with her throughout her life. In my opinion, everything is contained in the song's assertion, "I have two loves, my country and Paris," which goes far beyond its apparent simplicity. In these few words, Baker transcends herself and reaches out to the destiny of an entire generation. It is in this far-reaching influence that we can see the startling modernity of this woman, who resembled and even surpassed Colette and Georges Sand. She wished to be free all her life, and she was always guided by that passion and commitment.

Many forces pushed this young woman to leave her native land in 1925. In the north of the United States, black Americans initiated the vibrant Harlem Renaissance, but racial tension was escalating, and the specter of violence lurked on every street corner. The young Baker could never forget any of this. The suffering of an entire people was her suffering. When she adopted

Paris as her new home, it was because of the sudden burst of freedom that she experienced there. This freedom expressed itself symbolically through the nude body. Baker triumphed first in *La Revue nègre,* the stage show that became the craze of the city, performed by the troupe of the same name, and then in Parisian cabarets. At the moment that Baker began her new life of liberty and became a star on stage and screen, French women did not have the right to vote. Baker was able to transcend societal restrictions and convey a universal message. She belonged to no one. What her audience saw had little to do with the real drama. Under the stage lights, it was the drama of exile that actually unfolded. Baker's persona and performances presented the existential dilemma of the self and the other.

Young people today, expressing their malaise as they cruise the streets of Paris, pigeon-holed by the impossibility of double nationalities that have suddenly become problematic, should be inspired by Baker's ability to meld the fragments of her complex identity. Her consciousness of being privileged as a celebrity created a sense of obligation that she could not escape, even as a famous star. Her sense of responsibility led her to believe that she should share the fruits of her success by helping others. That was the result of having been brought up in a large family, for Josephine's family is enormous. It includes all of the black people that she left in the United States and everyone around the world who suffered. She was not born with a silver spoon in her mouth, and she would never forget that. She was able to unite glamour and political consciousness, fame and justice, freedom and commitment.

What intuition inspired Baker to build her Rainbow Tribe at the end of World War II, if not the piercing lucidity with which certain pure spirits are endowed. The Rainbow Tribe was a family in search of its roots, torn between inhabiting a world apart and being in the world. Beyond race, color, religion, and social class, this was an ideal world tailored to human proportions. Baker undertook this experiment to give back to the world and to prepare a new future where the pain of poverty and racism that plagued her while growing up would vanish.

Josephine could have shut herself off in the egotism of those who have achieved great success, but this would not have been true to her character, as the end of her life illustrated. She gave without limit because she believed that life is nothing if one does not imbue it with true meaning. So it is with those figures who have contributed in full measure to our humanity. Did Nelson Mandela, after leaving prison on Robben Island to become president of South Africa, realize that the rainbow nation that he proposed to build had already been forecast by a black American woman living in France many years earlier? Perhaps not. But what a beautiful turn of fate. What a wonderful legacy.

At the beginning of the twenty-first century, when our world is faced with the worst identity crisis of its history, and global chaos places human beings in stifling conflict with each other, the life of Josephine Baker, as analyzed by Bennetta Jules-Rosette, offers a reminder, and a useful lesson, for today and for the future. It is the lesson of a luminous humanism.

Preface

On the hot and muggy day of August 28, 1963, I first encountered Josephine Baker. Wearing her French air force uniform, she appeared on stage at the March on Washington. At the time, her foreign military attire contrasted strangely with the dress of the other civil rights activists. I never knew Josephine Baker personally. I was a young student in a crowd of thousands, but the power of her presence moved me, and I never forgot it. Years later, while I was conducting research on black Paris at the Musée de l'Homme in Paris, Baker's image resurfaced in connection with my study of the museum curator Georges-Henri Rivière and the journal *Présence Africaine*. I carefully preserved a record of the museum images and, with the permission of the museum's photothèque, published one photo of Baker in my 1998 book *Black Paris*.

In that context, I viewed Baker as an antecedent of *négritude* and the cultural and literary movements of the 1940s and 1950s. Her role in the 1925 show with La Revue nègre was well known. Nonetheless, I found the early photograph of her wearing a banana skirt to be both fascinating and unsettling. I circle around and return to this image throughout the present book because it is both provocative and profoundly disturbing. Why had Baker remained in France? What history lay between the banana skirt and the military uniform? How had someone who played such a crucial role in supporting the Musée de l'Homme and shaping the intellectual and cultural movements of black Paris come to be remembered primarily as a "savage" dancer? These contradictions intrigued me as I filed my notes on Baker for later review.

Out of curiosity, while living in Bordeaux in 1997, I made a trip to the Château des Milandes, Baker's dream castle in the Dordogne. My interest in both Baker and the study of tourism had inspired the trip, which became a turning point in my perceptions of Baker and in my research. Once again, I was confronted by the banana-skirt image and the contradictions between Baker's humanitarian political activism and her primal performative persona. The life story presented in the château's wax museum raised many unanswered questions.

Baker's images began to haunt me, and I felt compelled to write an article on the topic. I immediately planned to move on to another study of the artistic history of black Paris, but Baker's image would not go away. I continued to pursue research on Baker in Parisian archives. At the Bibliothèque Nationale, the Bibliothèque de l'Arsenal, and the Bibliothèque Richelieu, I read as many primary and secondary sources about her life as I could find. I am grateful to the librarians at the Bibliothèque Nationale and the Bibliothèque de l'Arsenal for the press books, photographic images, video clips, and musical recordings that they have assembled to document Baker's life and for their help in guiding me through them and identifying primary source materials.

The bulk of the research for this book was conducted in France in a social atmosphere where Baker's example is still critical. The present study focuses on Baker's career there, although, ironically, my first encounter was with Baker the civil rights activist in the United States. It is my hope that this book will offer a new way of framing future works on Baker. New research on Baker in the Americas and around the world will constitute a welcome addition to the vast body of scholarship about her. As I reviewed Baker's life and learned more about the obstacles that she confronted, I began to see my own decisions to study and live for a time in France in a different light. Anyone inspired by Baker cannot resist her appeal. There is a sense in which she adopts everyone who studies her. My book on Baker has emerged as the story of one woman's struggle against all odds to live her dream and, by extension, of everyone's promise to do so.

It became clear to me that Baker stood at the intersection of the major artistic and cultural movements of the mid-twentieth century and that her image brought to a head critical questions about race, gender, and postcolonial history. My obsession with Baker led friends and colleagues to send me postcards and posters of her that contributed to, and often duplicated, my growing collection of images of Baker. I began to realize that the postcards and popular images also constituted data that needed to be incorporated into my unfolding research. This research has resulted in the present critical cultural study of images of Baker in performance, art, literature, tourism, film, and politics. Although the tone of the book is often elegiac, the topics covered are drawn together by a biographically inflected cultural analysis. I do not restrict myself to Baker's early history and images but, instead, cover her entire life's path, as well as her influence on postmodern cultural forms.

Acknowledgments

Many people and institutions have contributed directly and indirectly to the development of this research. The Academic Senate of the University of California, San Diego, provided support for four research trips to Paris and southwestern France, in 1999, 2000, 2001, and 2004. Mylène Ribadeniera served as a graduate research assistant on this project in 2001 and 2002, in France and in California. Through her lively questions, enthusiasm about Baker, and attention to archival detail, she made an invaluable contribution to this work. My colleague Bernard Traimond, professor of anthropology at the Université de Bordeaux II, accompanied me on trips to the Château des Milandes and offered constant encouragement as well as valuable insights on the war years and the Resistance in France. I cannot thank him enough for his patience, good humor, and confidence in this project. Serge A. Tornay, former director of the Musée de l'Homme in Paris, provided me with letters of affiliation and support, as well as critical commentaries on the project. Denis-Constant Martin of the Fondation Nationale de Sciences Politiques in Paris and an expert on the history of jazz in France shared his research insights with me and made incisive comments on my manuscript. I appreciate his willingness to listen to my stories about Josephine Baker.

Gerald M. Platt of the University of Massachusetts, Amherst, commented on chapter summaries, provided pertinent insights on Baker's role in the U.S. civil rights movement, and raised challenging questions about Baker's political history and images of her. I am indebted to him for his perceptive comments and ongoing encouragement. Teshome Gabriel of the University of California, Los Angeles, read early versions of my work on Baker and made helpful comments on the article that I published on Baker in the 2000 issue of *Emergences.* Dean MacCannell of the University of California, Davis, offered constructive comments on my work at various stages of its development and shared with me his insights on tourism, postmodern icons, film theory, and Marilyn Monroe. Peter J. Bloom of the University of California, Santa Barbara, my former collaborator in the research on black Paris, shared his knowledge of French colonial cinema and the history of Paris in the 1920s with me.

Other colleagues in many fields who encouraged this research and made useful comments and suggestions along the way include the novelists and cultural critics Simon Njami and Bolya Baenga in Paris; the poet, actor, and director Jean-Baptiste Tiémélé in Paris; the author, filmmaker, and former director of the Théâtre Noir de Paris, Benjamin Jules-Rosette; the historian Bogumil Jewsiewicki of the Université Laval; the anthropologist Filip De Boeck of the University of Leuven; the dance theorist Francesca Castaldi; the literary theorist Françoise Naudillon of Concordia University; the historian and cultural critic George Lipsitz of the University of California, Santa Barbara; and the historian Didier Gondola of Indiana University, Purdue and Indianapolis. The anthropologists Richard Werbner of the University of Manchester and Pnina Werbner at the University of Keele offered valuable insights on Baker in the context of the postcolonial era and gender issues.

I would like to thank Olivia Lahs-Gonzales, director of the Sheldon Art Galleries in St. Louis, for inspiring me to see Baker's images from a new perspective as part of our research collaboration on the art catalog *Josephine Baker: Image and Icon*. I am grateful to Angélique de Saint-Exupéry for her encouragement and her hospitality at the Château des Milandes. In addition I appreciate the supportive comments on my work from Akio Bouillon, Josephine Baker's eldest son. I am also grateful to Albert Jaton and Juliette Pallas Jaton for granting me an interview about their years working with Josephine Baker and Jo Bouillon at the Château des Milandes and to the late Stephen Papich, Baker's former manager and friend, for his encouraging words toward the end of this project. The Baker scholar Bryan Hammond also provided valuable feedback and historical and photographic advice, and Ivory Moss, a Baker enthusiast, offered new data and insights on Josephine Baker's interviews and performances.

The seminar on the sociology of art, culture, and knowledge (ACK Group), which is part of the Focused Research Group on Popular Art and Music of the African and African-American Studies Research Project at the University of California, San Diego, has played an important role in the development of ideas for this book. This group has included, at various times, J. R. Osborn, whose help with the images in this book has been invaluable; Gordon Chang, who assisted with the final proofing and cross-checking of references; Lea Marie Ruiz-Ade, who read and commented on the manuscript; Ricardo Guthrie; Jonathan Markovitz; Cristin McVey; Mylène Ribadeniera; Paula Marie Seniors, and Jonathan Stern. They have voiced opinions on chapter summaries, reviewed Baker's images with me, and served as a sounding board for the research as it has evolved.

Special thanks are due to my late father, Walter E. Washington, who consistently provided encouragement and support for this project and for many others over the years. Both of my parents witnessed my reactions to a first encounter with Baker, and my late mother, Bennetta Bullock Washington, served as an inspiration and a role model whose cultural influence in many ways mirrored that of Josephine Baker. Mary B. Washington and Maxine Thomas listened patiently to my accounts of Baker's life. Members of my family, Violaine Jules-Rosette Thompson, Fred Thompson, and Monica Thompson, played Baker's musical recordings with me and have been supportive as I became increasingly absorbed in this project. Sylvia Moeller provided critical, editorial, and technical support during several stages of this work. Her energy and her insights on Baker's images and cultural influence have stimulated this research. My friend and colleague Sallie Bayless has listened to innumerable stories about Baker and has offered critical commentaries on the later versions of the manuscript. I appreciate the help of Benjamin Jules-Rosette and the photographer and filmmaker Franz Kennedy with the photographic images in Paris. My thanks are extended to John Wakeman and Gary Agliata for their careful and diligent work on the production of the photographic images. Kathi Menard helped with the editorial changes on the manuscript. Special thanks are also due to Joan Catapano, Carol Bolton Betts, and the outstanding editorial and production staff at the University of Illinois Press for their hard work and faith in this project.

Primary source data for this research have been made available through representatives of the Association Joséphine Baker of Castelnaud-la-Chapelle, the Château des Milandes, the Bibliothèque Nationale, the Bibliothèque de l'Arsenal, and the Bibliothèque Richelieu in Paris; the Moorland-Spingarn Research Center of Howard University in Washington, D.C.; the New York Public Library; and the Art and Music Library of the University of California, San Diego. The sources of images used in the text are credited in the illustration captions. Permission to quote from Josephine Baker's published letters and speeches has been obtained through her biographer and former manager, Stephen Papich, who also provided lively anecdotes and reminiscences about Baker. Daphne Muse, author and critic, first brought to my attention Josephine Baker's children's book *La Tribu arc-en-ciel*. Permission to quote from this source has been granted by Piet Worm. Previous comprehensive biographies of Josephine Baker by Jean-Claude Baker and Chris Chase, Emmanuel Bonini, Lynn Haney, Bryan Hammond and Patrick O'Connor, Phyllis Rose, and Ean Wood have also been helpful resources and guideposts for cross-checking data on her life.

An early version of chapter 1 was presented as "Touristic Simulations in the African Diaspora" in the lecture series on popular culture in Africa sponsored by the Center for African Studies at the University of California, Berkeley/Stanford University, September 17, 2002. I revised a later version of this chapter for presentation as "The Aesthetics of Morality and the Commodification of Emotions" at the Annual Meeting of the American Anthropological Association in New Orleans, November 20, 2002. I published portions of chapter 2 in an article entitled "Two Loves: Josephine Baker as Icon and Image," *Emergences* 10, no. 1 (2000): 55–77; they appear here with the permission of Carfax Publishing (http://tandf.co.uk). An abridged version of chapter 6, entitled "Hues of the Rainbow in a Global Village," was presented at the Forty-seventh Annual Meeting of the African Studies Association, November 12, 2004, in New Orleans. Portions of chapters 4 and 6 were presented at the Black Paris Conference organized by Samantha Haigh and Nicki Hitchcott on May 1, 2004, at the University of London and published in the conference proceedings as "Josephine Baker and Utopian Visions of Black Paris," *Journal of Romance Studies* 5, no. 3 (2005): 33–50. They appear here with permission of that journal. Using data I gathered for chapters 2 and 4 of the present book, I wrote the lead essay for the art catalog *Josephine Baker: Image and Icon* (Sheldon Art Galleries, 2006), edited by Olivia Lahs-Gonazales.

I appreciatively acknowledge permission to quote from the following previously published texts: direct quotes by Josephine Baker about her life and experiences, from Josephine Baker and Jo Bouillon, *Josephine* (English translation by Mariana Fitzpatrick © Harper and Row, 1977); excerpts from Félix de la Camara and Pepito Abatino, *Mon sang dans tes veines* (1931), from the Bibliothèque Nationale, Paris; excerpts from Lynn Haney, *Naked at the Feast* (Chrysalis Books and Dodd, Mead, and Company, 1981); excerpts from Jean-Claude Baker and Chris Chase, *Josephine: The Hungry Heart* (Random House, 1993); excerpts from Bryan Hammond and Patrick O'Connor, *Josephine* (Jonathan Cape, 1988), courtesy of Random House, London; excerpts from the introduction to Paul Colin's *Le Tumulte noir,* reprinted from *Josephine Baker and La Revue Nègre: Paul Colin's Lithographs of Le Tumulte noir in Paris, 1927,* by Henry Louis Gates and Karen C. C. Dalton (New York: Harry N.

Abrams, Inc.); excerpt from Dana Farcaros and Michael Pauls, *Dordogone and the Lot* (2001), a tourist guidebook, courtesy of Globe Pequot Press, Guilford, Connecticut; excerpts from *Remembering Josephine* (Bobbs-Merrill Press, 1976), with permission from the author, Stephen Papich; excerpts from Erving Goffman, *Frame Analysis* (Harper and Row, 1974, © Erving Goffman); excerpts from Marcel Sauvage, *Les Mémoires de Joséphine Baker* (Éditions Kra, 1927), from the Bibliothèque Nationale, Paris. I would also like to express appreciation for the information provided in an interview in Paris with Albert Jaton and Juliette Pallas Jaton and personal communications by Stephen Papich in Los Angeles, which have been quoted with permission.

Song lyrics from the following publishers are gratefully acknowledged: excerpt from "J'ai deux amours" (1930), by Géo Koger, Henri Varna, and Vincent Scotto, courtesy of Éditions Salabert S.A. and BMG Music Publishing; excerpts from "C'est lui" (1934), by R. Bernstein and Georges Van Parys, courtesy of Éditions Salabert S.A. and BMG Music Publishing; excerpt from "Dans mon village" (1953), by Henri Lemarchand and Francis Lopez, courtesy of Éditions Salabert S.A. and BMG Music Publishing; excerpts from "Sous le ciel d'Afrique" (Neath the Tropic Blue Skies), courtesy of Éditions Choudens, Paris, and ASCAP.

Permission to quote from the following screenplays and film texts is gratefully acknowledged: Kino International for *Zouzou* (1934) and *Princesse Tam-Tam* (1935) (now in the public domain); Mick Csáky and Channel 4, Britain, for *Chasing a Rainbow: The Life of Josephine Baker* (1986), directed by Christopher Ralling; and Home Box Office, Inc., for *The Josephine Baker Story* (1991), directed by Brian Gibson. Excerpts from these screenplays have been used to illustrate the development of images of Josephine Baker during different historical periods.

The photographic images, biographical materials, and song texts highlight reflections about Baker across generations and diverse historical epochs. I have made every effort to acquire permission for copyright materials. If there are any inadvertent omissions, I offer my apologies and will include those citations in future editions of the book. I extend my sincere appreciation to the sources of all photographic, archival, and textual materials.

Prologue

Josephine Baker's cultural legacy is still alive beyond the hundredth anniversary of her birth in 1906. It exists in live performances, art, photography, fashion, film, literature, and social activism. Baker mesmerized audiences during her lifetime and continues to attract and mystify biographers. Much recent scholarship on Baker has placed her in a pantheon of black feminist heroines, which often has produced a larger-than-life, one-dimensional image. Regardless of the reasons for such depictions, there is a need to remove Baker from reductive stereotypes and to humanize her legacy. This book explores the complex construction of Baker's multiple images in art and life. It is concerned with how art transforms social life, and how life imitates art. Although it presents and evaluates carefully researched biographical facts, it is not a biography. Rather, it offers critical reflections on the symbolic Baker and the images that she and her collaborators constructed during the era of modernity and for the postmodern future.

On a bright spring day in 1997, I first visited the Château des Milandes, Josephine Baker's medieval castle in southwestern France. While climbing the château's labyrinthine staircases, I was struck by the ways in which the narrative of Baker's life had been transformed into a tourist attraction. Baker's story, which began with her move from the United States to Paris in 1925, extended through her meteoric rise to fame in the Parisian music halls of the late 1920s and ended with the sobering moment of her eviction from the château in 1969. Yet, Baker's presence still permeates the château and, like an underground spring, provides it with a source of survival and renewal. Spectacular wax dioramas I saw at the château made her seem more real than ever and reinforced her status as a cult icon. When Baker lost the château in 1969, parts of the original Jorama—a wax museum that she had organized to represent her career—were lost or destroyed, but they were recreated for the new display. The château's owner and the Association Joséphine Baker of Castelnaud-la-Chapelle joined forces to revive and maintain Baker's dream, but the carefully crafted touristic narrative left many research questions unanswered.

Constructed Images and Nested Narratives

Driven by curiosity about my new subject, I returned to Paris to explore archives containing copious records of Baker's life. Spread across three major archives, the Bibliothèque Nationale, the Bibliothèque de l'Arsenal, and the Bibliothèque Richelieu, the voluminous records form the rich fabric of Baker's life. I waited for hours as the librarians delivered to me fragments of a life on crumbling yellowed paper and microfilm. As I pored over stacks of faded press clippings, theater programs, novels, and obscure biographies, I realized that the narrative was far more complex than the story outlined by panoramas in wax at Les Milandes. As early as 1927, when Baker was only twenty-one years old, she collaborated with Marcel Sauvage on her first biography, *Les Mémoires de Joséphine Baker*. It was as though destiny had a plan for her that would be illustrated by an archetypal tale.

Born Freda Josephine McDonald to an impoverished family in St. Louis, Missouri, on June 3, 1906, Josephine Baker escaped to France in the fall of 1925 as a dancer with the black American vaudeville troupe called La Revue nègre. Its first show opened on October 2, 1925, for a three-month run at the Théâtre des Champs-Elysées. Baker was an instant success with her *danse sauvage,* which she performed first in feathers and later in a banana belt. Within two years, she rose to fame in Paris and became the toast of the worlds of art and musical theater. She resided in France for the rest of her life, and, in her later years, she became a humanitarian with a unique vision of Paris and the world.

The heyday of Baker's early performance career lasted from 1925 to 1935. Under the guidance of her companion and manager Giuseppe (Pepito) Abatino, Baker achieved status as a music-hall, recording, and film star and a model for France's "new woman," a position that was consolidated during the 1930s. Afterwards, while continuing to perform, she became a militant, a political activist, and a philanthropist. Disparate forces from the worlds of avant-garde art, museum culture, politics, and commerce would coalesce to make her a household name in France and throughout the world. With Pepito, she was able to purchase a mansion, Beau-Chêne, and to live her Cinderella dream. The fairy-tale narrative mapped a pathway to assimilation and social success. This master trope was crosscut by sensationalistic images of the primal Baker as a savage dancer and as the Black Venus. In most biographies of Baker, and in her own accounts, these images are treated as external constructions, which she nonetheless readily accepted and learned to manipulate. How much control did the young Baker have over the image-making process and what was her role, her agency, in making the dream come true? While music-hall impresarios, managers, fashion cartels, artists, photographers, and biographers all contributed to the construction of the primal Baker, and later the mature star ("La Bakaire"), Baker cleverly took advantage of and responded to these forces in creating her public persona and the narrative of her life.

Colonial discourse and anthropometric theories of race lay behind the primal image of Fatou, the character made famous in Baker's danse sauvage. These theories created a climate in which the sexualized figure of an exotic black woman released atavistic fantasies repressed by modernism's mechanical rationality. The character of Fatou was modeled on Fatou-gaye, the bewitching African mistress of the French explorer Jean Peyral, known as *le spahi*, in Pierre Loti's popular 1881 novel *Le Roman d'un spahi*, which was made into a film in 1936.[1] Loti's novel had been serialized, and the image of Fatou was still well known to popular audiences in the 1920s. Black Venus, which was a subtle permutation of the primal Fatou, embodied neoclassical aesthetics; French literary narratives drawn from Baudelaire, Flaubert, and Zola; and the fascination for African art in cubist and surrealist circles.

Although the primal dancer and the Black Venus are closely related images relying on exoticism, they are distinct in Baker's case and have different implications as nested narratives and strategies of representation for her in literature, criticism, photography, and film. The core meanings of these images persist over time, but their surface manifestations were subject to constant and frequent manipulation by Baker and her collaborators. The primal dancer was based on raw eroticism and sexuality, while the Black Venus was a sophisticated and seductive exotic goddess. The first image is "hot," and the second is "cool." While the surrealist Jean Cocteau is credited with dreaming up the banana skirt Paul Colin created for Baker's 1926 performance at the Folies-Bergère, George Hoyningen-Huene, a *Vogue* editor, popularized the statuesque Black Venus image in a 1929 photograph. Both of these images subtly undermine the Cinderella story by casting the fairyland princess back into the empire of nature, creating what the literary theorist Gérard Genette has called an entangled narrative structure with multiple dimensions.[2] At key turning points, Baker responded to and modified her own images by imbuing them with a sense of pathos, joy, irony, and ecstasy. Baker's early audience

in France was in the music hall, but she expanded and exploded these stereotypical images through recordings, film, photography, and fashion. Baker
inspired audiences not so much in single performances as through her magical
ability to communicate her ideas and transform herself with the creation of
each image.

Another narrative recurring throughout Baker's life is that of the Marian,
or Madonna, motif. In her 1931 novella *Mon sang dans tes veines* (My Blood
in Your Veins), recounted to and adapted by Félix de la Camara and Pepito
Abatino, Josephine devises the character of Joan (also called Jô), a young
mulatto girl whose mother is the maid in the home of a Boston millionaire, Ira
Cushman Barclay, and his son, Fred. Joan selflessly saves Fred's life through a
blood transfusion. The primal Baker and the new saintly image meld in *Mon
sang dans tes veines*. Baker continued to develop this image as part of her humanitarian self-sacrifice in World War II and in the domestic experiment with
her adopted Rainbow Tribe at Les Milandes. The Marian motif also became
part of Baker's public persona through statues, photographs, and paintings.
Transcending the Cinderella trope, she moved to a larger humanitarian and
religious narrative of sacred devotion and sacrifice. This narrative also involves issues of race since the ultimate goal of her sacrifice was to pave the
way for an egalitarian, interracial society. According to the Baker biographer
Lynn Haney, one of Josephine's friends stated, "Josephine thought of herself
as a member of the Holy family . . . , but it was not always clear which role
she thought she was playing. Sometimes she pictured herself as the black
Madonna, other times as the child of God, and the Virgin Mary."[3]

All of these narratives culminate at Les Milandes, both in life and in
touristic simulation. At Les Milandes, Baker reconstructed the experiences
of her Parisian youth in lavish dioramas and created a symbolic representation of her rise to fame in a world apart from the rest of France. While much
recent scholarship on Baker's primal images considers a period that ends in
1935, the roots for the later Marian motif of Sainte Joséphine were already
established by 1931 and can be seen as a proleptic anticipation of what was to
come decades later.[4] This complex interplay and layering of images and narratives provides a palette from which the picture of Baker's life may be painted.
French and international audiences have developed contrasting responses to
these narratives over the years, contributing to a further cross-cultural and
cross-generational layering of Baker's images. I argue that the search for the
true Baker (*la véritable Joséphine*), while compelling, is less fecund than an

exploration of the constructed images and nested narratives that constitute her persona and the social strategies that she used to bring these images to life. The various permutations of primal, glamour, political, and everyday images propel the master performances and narratives of Baker's life.

Semiography as a Method

Biographies assemble the fragments of a life—historical documents, relics, and archival materials—into a unified narrative. Every biographer, including the autobiographer, has a point of view, a goal, and even an ax to grind. Biographies consist of signifying profiles that situate subjects in terms of their lived experiences. In recounting their narratives, some biographers try to tell seamless stories, which, while they may include ruptures and the counterpoints of a subject's successes and failures, end with a clear moral message about the impact of a life. There is another genre of biography that may be labeled more broadly as analytic. Jean-Paul Sartre used an analytic study in his biography of Jean Genet and in his own self-analysis in *Les Mots*. In both cases, he attempted to show how social forces of marginalization influenced individual psychology. In his studies of Martin Luther and Mahatma Gandhi, the psychologist Erik Erikson also employed analytic biography to illustrate phases of the identity cycle during a life's course. These analytic biographies use the subject's life as a template for theories of the life cycle and accounts of socialization in a historical and political context. Frantz Fanon also drew on autobiographical elements of description to illustrate the clinical aspects of racial consciousness and how it affects the individual.[5]

In contrast, semiography is a research method that uses the tools of sociosemiotics to excavate the narratives, images, and representations that constitute the public and private lives of biographical subjects. It traces the story of a life through signs, symbols, and images. Although it shares much in common with biography, semiography offers a special approach to rereading Baker's art and life in sociological and cultural terms. While documentation of a life is essential to semiography, as it is to biography, semiography's focus is to interpret how the pieces of the puzzle fit together as a cultural production rather than a chronology. Semiography explores the ideal images of a performer, the public performances in which those images appear, and the responses of diverse audiences to the performer's decisions, actions, and experimentation. The main questions that semiographers pose are, how do subjects blend into the era in which they live through their cultural productions, and how and when do their lives transcend their times? Semiographers deal with symbols. Events, press clippings, notes, and historical traces represent something more than mere artifacts. They are, in fact, examples of artifice, or the strategies of representation used by the subjects and those around them to construct the narrative of a life. This thick description, or deep analysis, of a life relies on a study of the signs and symbols that make sense of the events, trends, decisions, and patterns in that life.[6]

Key events in Baker's life may be reviewed in several ways: as biographical descriptions, literary constructions, touristic markers, performances, and filmic signs made to appeal to diverse real and diegetic audiences. The biographical subject coalesces these signs, providing the source of their meaning and the sense of their continuity. In other words, semiography is a hermeneutic exploration of a life story that treats the interplay of its multiple meanings as a series of interconnected representations interpreted in social and historical context. Semiography also includes a subjective dimension. One Baker biographer, Phyllis Rose, states that she identified with her subject's spontaneity, energy, and sense of sexual freedom and abandon, while Jean-Claude Baker admits to being enthralled, emotionally consumed, and angered by her blinding heat and energy.[7] This emotional connection between authors and Baker as a biographical subject cannot be overlooked. Semiography searches for the symbolic roots of these connections in the interpretation of cultural signs.

Contradictions in the multiple, nested narratives of a life provide opportunities for exploring the worldviews, conflicts, and values of an era. In many respects, the semiographer's responsibilities extend beyond those of the biographer to an analysis of the social forces and trends that create meaning in the narrative of a life. Ultimately, the semiographer's work discloses the meaning of a life narrative and series of performances within the subject's historical setting and in relationship to dominant discourses of the period. Semiography requires an archaeology of knowledge that unearths images, subjective impressions, and social facts. I have pursued this method in my account of the images and master narratives of Josephine Baker in art and life as part of a series of cultural discourses.

Biographers differ considerably in their interpretations of the cultural meanings of Baker's primal images and the successes or failures of her Rainbow Tribe and the brotherhood experiments. Many biographers question whether Baker was reality-oriented in her goals, strategies, and obsessions. Here again, I am less concerned with the rationality of her actions than I am with understanding the rationale of those actions as everyday practices and techniques of image construction. Facts about Baker's life shift from some of the primary sources, which contradict each other, to secondary sources, which compound the contradictions in data and descriptions. A close reading of Baker biographies reveals a kaleidoscope of contradictory facts extending from accounts of her birth to descriptions of the time and circumstances of her death and the identities of her adopted children. In some cases, Baker's own myth-making competes with known biographical facts, overshadowing and contradicting them. I have attempted to resolve some of these problems by documenting the first appearance of most images and by matching images and narratives with concrete events, as well as with published interviews, wherever possible.[8] I also draw on Baker's first-person accounts and self-writing as a way of gaining access to the subjective dimension of these narratives.

Plan of the Book

The three parts of this book reflect different styles and phases of image creation in the life of Josephine Baker. Part 1 deals with the making of a cultural icon through tourism, performance, and film. It documents and firmly establishes Baker's rise to stardom in terms of a series of iconic images and nested narratives. Chapter 1 takes a retrospective look at the tourist attractions that Baker inspired and constructed. It provides a point of entry into Baker's life through surviving artifacts and edifices that have come to represent her. By beginning with an exploration of tourism, I set the stage for the rest of the book by establishing the importance of Baker's persona and enduring images for interpreting the meaning of specific events in her life. We move from the traces of her life memorialized in touristic sites to an account of her career. In this chapter, the Château des Milandes surfaces as the totalizing symbol of Baker's master narratives—the Cinderella story and the Marian motif. Here I also chronicle the salience of Baker's touristic images as reflections of different stages of her career.

Chapter 2 provides an overview of Baker's life and its narratives of miraculous success and struggle. It addresses the essential images that become the building blocks for her early career and the ways in which Baker consciously used these narratives and scripts as retrospective justifications for her life choices. Chapter 3 continues with a focus on Baker's early years by analyzing three of her four feature-length films—*Sirène des tropiques* (1928), *Zouzou* (1934), and *Princesse Tam-Tam* (1935). Now being digitally remastered and rediscovered internationally as landmarks of musical comedy, Baker's films from the 1930s received scant attention in the United States when they were released. Deploying nested narratives, the films are both moralistic and mythic. Almost more than any other medium, cinema emphasizes the importance of memory work in the creation of new roles and identities. I examine the double articulation of Baker's primal image with the Cinderella and escape narratives through a detailed analysis of film clips and dialogue (in the cases of *Zouzou* and *Princesse Tam-Tam*). I demonstrate how the discourse of art deco musicals interfaces with neoprimitivism in film. I then contrast the narrative structure of these films with two films about Baker's life, Christopher Ralling and Mick Csáky's 1986 documentary *Chasing a Rainbow: The Life of Josephine Baker* and Brian Gibson's 1991 Home Box Office television docudrama *The Josephine Baker Story*. By contrasting these films semiotically, I delve deeper into Baker's cultural meanings as a motion picture icon. In addition, I demonstrate how a biographical narrative is constructed by the filmic subject and modified by contemporary filmmakers and their audiences in the documentary and docudrama modes.

Part 2 deals with the historic Baker as her images emerged in the worlds of art, performance, and humanitarianism. I discuss in detail how Baker carved out new pathways for her increasingly complex and sophisticated performative and political images. The fourth chapter examines art and style in Baker's work. Here I analyze the influence of avant-garde art, fashion, and architecture on Baker's image construction and look at the relationship between Baker and the art world of the late 1920s and the 1930s. Paul Colin and Miguel Covarrubias's designs, Paul Poiret's fashions, and Adolf Loos's architectural visions inspired and helped to construct Baker's new images, and she, in turn, exploited the world of art in scaffolding the images used in her music-hall career. Chapter 5 explores Baker's scripts of self-writing as the conscious framing of social life through narrative, biographies, and performance. I examine how Baker inscribed her images in public and private life through autobiographical narratives of success and escape. This chapter addresses Baker as the author, not only of her own biographies, but of her multiple roles and life choices as a performer, a war hero, a public figure, and a mother. Chapter 6 rounds out the discussion of the historic Baker's living her dream with an exploration of her public projection of the maternal and Madonna images as the founder of a utopian world village at Les Milandes with the Rainbow Tribe. Here I explore the sociological contradictions involved in fabricating a utopian community by using the cultural metaphor of a family.

The concluding part of the book assesses Baker's goal of changing the world by linking social and political activism to her performances. I address the dialectic of art and life and the ways in which private choices and manufactured public images redouble in Baker's life as she performed politics to create new narratives with a strong social impact. Chapter 7 focuses on Baker's social activism and the narrative of universal brotherhood. Here I examine the obstacles that she confronted in realizing her dream of multiculturalism with the Rainbow Tribe and discuss the local and international problems that she faced. The FBI files on Baker's life that were declassified on September 2, 1982, provide a fascinating data source reflecting the responses to Baker's activism and the limitations placed on her political goals. In chapter 8, I turn my attention to the echoes and influences of Baker's images and narratives in contemporary popular culture. From Grace Jones to Madonna and La Toya Jackson, Baker inspired cross-racial and gender-bending strategies of performance and popular presentation. Postmodernism also standardizes and stereotypes aspects of racial and gender images through television, film, and computerized media. I discuss these strategies as part of Baker's iconic, symbolic, and political legacy. The book concludes in chapter 9 with the review of a life in the eternal comeback, in which all of the images taken together are reassessed for their global impact.

Josephine Baker was truly a cultural phenomenon. Her life provides a vibrant source from which to draw in the sociology of culture and the arts. But Baker's life narrative makes an important contribution far beyond these scholarly concerns, helping us to understand the problems surrounding race and gender issues in modern society. Her strategies foreshadowed postmodern techniques of image building. Her dreams of universalism and egalitarian achievement were timeless. Striving to understand Baker is crucial to interpreting modernism's legacies, for through her persona and narratives, she provides a way to understand the strengths and pitfalls of contemporary popular culture.

Part One

Creating the Image

1 Touring with Baker's Image

While we could retain the common-sense notion that fostered
appearances can be discredited by a discrepant reality, there is
often no reason for claiming that the facts discrepant with the
fostered impression are any more real reality than is the reality
they embarrass.

—Erving Goffman, 1959

Imagine taking a tour inspired by the sights and sounds of Josephine Baker's life. Baker's presence pervades the costumes she wore, the objects she touched, and the buildings she occupied. The terrain on which Baker's monumental images have been created and displayed is part of her enduring legacy. Tourism encapsulates the memories of that terrain and of the people and places that are part of Baker's history. It is a mutable terrain that changes to fit the times and provides a flashback into Baker's past. My first extended encounter with Baker's images took place through tourism. After winding through the hills of the Dordogne in southwestern France, I found the Château des Milandes, Baker's hidden treasure, where she lived for more than two decades.

The Château des Milandes remains a tribute to Baker and to the Rainbow Tribe, her twelve adopted children of different cultural backgrounds and ethnicities. A 1992 publicity brochure for the château contains a poignant black-and-white photo of a wax diorama with life-sized figures (fig. 1).[1] The allegorical imagery of the diorama implies that Josephine, surrounded by her children, is a saint who has reached the end of her pilgrimage.

In this diorama, Baker is at Les Milandes standing at the top of Mount José, where she faces a large cross. Clad in a simple print dress, she is accompanied by nine of the twelve children from her Rainbow Tribe, who have climbed with her to the hilltop. The caption reads, "Josephine Baker et sa tribu arc-en-ciel." The muted overhead lighting evokes the traces of a rainbow. Seven of the children are holding hands, and Josephine, in the center, clutches the hands of two children, one on either side of her. The two smallest members of the tribe lag behind as they struggle up the hillside toward the site of salvation. In the far right of the picture lurks a faceless, shadowy figure, perhaps the representation of temptation or a harbinger of doom. The theme of the diorama is echoed in a sculpture that Baker commissioned of herself in a biblical costume standing before the Rainbow Tribe in what Phyllis Rose terms "the posture of St. Francis of Assisi" and in the madonna that was sculpted in her image for Place Joséphine Baker at Les Milandes.[2] The diorama recalls the moralistic preambles of Josephine's later songs, such as "Dans mon village," in which she solemnly defends the home of her Rainbow children.[3] This theme also appears in the statue of Josephine holding her eldest son, Akio, that was unveiled at the Château des Milandes in 2006 to commemorate the centennial of Baker's birth. The sculpture is the work of Anne Dominique Marichol, known as Chouski. (See figure 43 in chapter 6 for this image.) Although these images of Sainte Joséphine superficially have little in common with Baker's early archetypal poses from her days with *La Revue nègre,* both sets of images construe her as a legend. The diorama and the Chouski statue, however, add to the narrative the dimensions of a sacred journey and a Marian quest.

Constructing Baker's Touristic Image

Touring with Baker's image in many respects resembles the pilgrimage depicted in the diorama of Sainte Joséphine, a cathartic journey in which the artistic subject's identity is magically transformed. This simulated pilgrimage is also a dramatically staged experience. Pilgrimages have an ancient history, but their form and content changed with the advent of modern tourism.[4] No longer is the devotee necessarily a religious mystic, and the object of the

Figure 1. Wax rendering of Josephine Baker and her Rainbow Tribe at the top of Mount José. From the publicity brochure *Château des Milandes: Ancienne demeure de Joséphine Baker* (Dordogne: Château des Milandes, 1992).

pilgrimage may itself be a simulation or an escapade. But even contemporary pilgrims, whose quest is secular rather than strictly religious, seek to be close to icons and glorified objects of value so that some of the magical power will rub off on them. Legends surround the sacred icons of pilgrimage, imbuing them with special meanings larger than life. These legends are part of the common culture and narratives that establish the authenticity of sacred sights (which are both physical and symbolic locales), and they linger even when the sights lose their initial religious appeal.

An integral part of the contemporary touristic pilgrimage is the symbolic construction of the tourist attraction. Touristic images consist of fragments of place, space, and personal identity preserved in memory through souvenirs. Dean MacCannell refers to this process of preservation as the "domination of the touristic sight by its markers"—the signs and images demarcating the sight's uniqueness and sacrilization.[5] Tourist guidebooks, popular histories, and biographies reinforce legends that bolster the authenticity of the tourist sight and help to construct its relics as objects of value. Postcards, photographs, and paintings take this process a step further by adding a layer of illusion and mystification to the sight.[6] These images allude to concepts of nation, ethnicity, and history that are meaningful to tourists and reflect their desired identities. Sacred and secular sights often coexist in the same space and draw on overlapping images. Tourism and pilgrimages are linked by sight involvement, a sense of adoration in religious terms that turns into secular sightseeing in contemporary tourism. Background information and touristic markers create sight involvement that clues tourists in to the relevance of what they are seeing.[7] Even when these markers are readily available, tourists may reject them as insufficient or uninteresting. Instead, they search for further signs of authentication to make the sight meaningful. In the case of touring with Baker's image, biographical narratives and photographs contribute to this authentication process, or the creation of the illusion of authenticity.

The first phase of our journey begins in Montmartre, a section of Paris in which Josephine Baker once lived, performed in the music hall, and opened her own cabaret, Chez Joséphine. Montmartre was the home of expatriate black American musicians and artists during the 1920s and 1930s. In 1925, the cast of La Revue nègre lived at the Hôtel Fournet on boulevard des Batignolles in Montmartre.[8] Today, Montmartre remains a popular tourist destination. The quarter, which became an official part of the city of Paris in 1860, contains two compelling landmarks with controversial histories—the basilica of Sacré-

Coeur and the Moulin Rouge music hall. During France's Third Republic, both the Sacré-Coeur and the music halls of Montmartre elicited the attention of politicians and urban planners because of the large number of outsiders they drew into the community. Sacré-Coeur is a Byzantine-style structure built to fulfill a vow of penitence made by French Catholics after the Franco-Prussian war in 1870. Early pilgrims came to the church to expiate guilt and have their prayers answered. Many of them believed that France could be restored only by the return of the Bourbon monarchy.[9] Counterposed against this upsurge of religiosity was the rise of a new Parisian working class and a bohemian subculture centering around the music halls and cabarets. The objects of citizens' complaints, political surveillance, and numerous cleanup campaigns, the cabarets nonetheless flourished. Political satirists, cartoonists, painters, poets, and novelists, including Henri Toulouse-Lautrec and Émile Zola, depicted the vibrant night life that became part of Montmartre's signature at the end of the nineteenth century. In 1908, the city of Paris assumed control of the Sacré-Coeur basilica, and the structure acquired the status of a renowned monument and a tourist sight. Meanwhile, although the popularity of music halls declined after the rise of cinema, these institutions survived, becoming "high temples of kitsch."[10]

Turn-of-the-century Montmartre boasted other touristic attractions. The quarter was the home of Alfred Grévin, the caricaturist and neorealist sculptor who popularized the wax museum in the 1880s.[11] Arthur Meyer, an entrepreneur and Parisian newspaper publisher, came up with the idea of representing historical settings and current events realistically in wax tableaux. He hired Grévin to execute his ideas and gathered considerable support for this venture from wealthy businessmen and cultural figures of the day.[12] The Musée Grévin, which was decorated with lavish colonnades and gilt fixtures, opened its doors to an eager and curious public on June 5, 1882, at 10, boulevard Montmartre, on the far limits of the quarter. The tableaux represented political and historical figures, fictional icons, artists, actors, and ordinary people. Early wax museums, which were popular in eighteenth- and nineteenth-century London, were curiosity cabinets in which anthropological renditions of anatomical abnormalities were displayed.[13] Although other wax museums had existed in Paris before Grévin's, such as that of the Swiss anatomist Philippe Curtius—the ancestor of Madame Tussaud's establishment—no project before the Musée Grévin had involved such an incredible dedication to what has come to be known as spectacular realism. Tableaux included rehearsals at the Comédie Française, a papal cortège, exotic scenes of colonial Africa, and dramatic settings from novels such as Zola's *Germinal*.

When competition with the silent cinema emerged in the early 1900s, the Musée Grévin introduced a wax *journal lumineux* (illuminated documentary) complete with a sound-and-light display that was the forerunner of movie newsreels. Grévin displays were cleverly organized so that spectators walking through and witnessing them from various angles had the sense of being present at an event as it unfolded. As a result of the Grévin's success, wax museums flourished all over Paris during the 1890s, and one was even established in the basement of the Olympia Theater. From the music hall, museum exhibitors could draw on a massive array of costumes and stage sets for their dioramas. It is no accident that Grévin's approach to display was later adopted to fill Josephine Baker's touristic museum at the Château des Milandes with spectacles in wax, occupying an intermediary space between the popular culture of the boulevard and the high culture of the official museum.

Today, religious and secular forces no longer battle for dominance in Montmartre. The cathedral, the music halls, the peep shows, and the Musée Grévin all remain exotic curiosities in a touristic pilgrimage. The discourse and narratives of tourism have transformed these locales into sights that reflect memories of the religious and artistic exuberance of turn-of-the-century France.

Postcards and Pastiche

As with pilgrimage, tourism involves the traffic in symbolic relics. From the Crusades to Canterbury, medieval travelers returned with amulets, bells, badges, and souvenirs.[14] According to Turner and Turner, these objects and images "became fetishes operating by principles of sympathetic and contagious magic, rather than serving as vehicles of religious and ethical ideas."[15] When Nancy Holloway, an ardent Josephine Baker fan, purchased one of the performer's dresses at a 1976 antiques fair in Paris, she vowed in tears to preserve it as "a true relic."[16] Baker costumes, dolls, puppets, posters, and postcards may be viewed as relics that function as affective symbols of a multifaceted ideal fueled by the metanarrative of Baker's life.

Postcards demarcate borders crossed in the touristic encounter. They preserve icons and landmarks as authentic souvenirs. These freeze-frame images are personalized by the inclusion of the touristic subject, or an individual with whom the subject identifies, in the photograph and by the addition of supplemental texts and inscriptions.[17] As souvenirs, postcards fit into frames that people use to organize the flow and memory of their travel experiences. The typical monument photograph with standardized inscriptions marks the borders crossed, distancing the sender from the receiver. Barbara Kirshenblatt-Gimblett illustrates the extreme flattening of this type of touristic discourse to the point of absurdity in the generic postcard provided by some tourist companies in which the traveler fills in the destination and checks off one of several standard messages: "Wish you were here"; "Having a wonderful time"; "Running out of money"; and so forth. In the generic card, the photographic image is removed, and the minimalist logic of touristic escape is deprived of all substance save its frame.[18]

Baker's primal image appeared on postcards circulating around Paris. Paul Colin's famous 1925 poster for *La Revue nègre* was miniaturized as a postcard and still remains the most readily available commercial image of Josephine. The signature banana-skirt image of Josephine, also appearing in Paul Colin's *Le Tumulte noir,* is another postcard reduction. A classic photograph in Roger-Viollet's collection showing Baker dancing in the spiked banana skirt from *La Folie du jour* (1926–27) has been transformed into a postcard. The early postcards include a photograph from the Folies-Bergère (1926–27) in which Josephine is posed on top of a mirror lake in a grass skirt just after having descended from a giant crystal ball. (A postcard from the Collection Cinémathèque Suisse in Lausanne labels this pose as one from *La Sirène des tropiques.*) The pose is reproduced as the spectacular wax-figure centerpiece at the Château des Milandes and appears on a 1995 postcard advertising Les Milandes that shows a young tourist taking a photograph of the wax figure (fig. 2).[19] There are multiple frames in this intriguing publicity postcard, as both the child taking the photograph and Josephine are reflected in the mirror, and both look outward at the spectator. This double-mirrored image reflexively references its own touristic construction.

Several images from 1925–27 appear in posters, cards, and photographs. They include another poster for the 1926–27 Folies-Bergère show, which also traveled to the Lutetia Palace in Brussels. The Lutetia Palace image shows Josephine in a beaded halter top and long earrings. The photograph on which the poster is based includes a full-body shot of Josephine in the same outfit, complete with ostrich feathers. Two postcards thematically round out this

Figure 2. Postcard advertising the Château des Milandes as a touristic site. Photo by J.-L. Chedal entitled "Scène de Musée Grévin" (Dordogne: Château des Milandes, 1995).

early sequence. One shows the now famous photograph of Josephine in a reclining lioness pose, ready to pounce, nude except for a small piece of fabric around her waist. This feline posture carries the exotic, savage-animal imagery to its extreme point. The postcard lists this photograph in the Viollet collection as well. It contrasts with another widely circulating Viollet photograph, published on a postcard circa 1925, in which Josephine appears on the roof of the Théâtre des Champs-Elysées in a short, black leotard with a tank top. Standing with arms akimbo and knees bent, Josephine displays the cross-eyed clown face characteristic of her early vaudeville numbers.

In biographies of Baker, these images are presented as traces of her early performances. They have in common an erotic, sexualized image, and in all examples, with the exception of the Colin posters and the clown face, Baker stares seductively at her audience. While the lioness image conveys a wild energy, the other photographs are subtly seductive and passive. They are geared toward a male gaze and suggest the photographic subject's desire to be adored, manipulated, and dominated. Although they are relics of the 1920s, these photographs are still in circulation as postcards and constitute the first, and often the only, contact that many people have with Baker's image.

A central feature of this primal image production is its reduplication in mass quantities. The primal image freezes the young and nubile Baker in a stereotypical and controlled relationship to her audience. This image of her subjugation is blatantly underscored in the film *Zouzou* (1934), which concludes with Baker in plumes, perched in a large birdcage and singing a tune about Haiti. In fact, the cage might be viewed as a metaphor for the music-hall stage and its restricted ideological space. Race plays an important role in this primal imagery because it both inscribes the savage persona and provides a reason for its entrapment.

The show *Paris qui remue* (Swinging Paris), which ran during 1930–31, marks a critical point in Baker's self-presentation, both on stage and in touristic imagery. Haim (Boris) Lipnitzki's 1930 photograph of Baker in her dressing room in the Casino de Paris before the show, sold at Les Milandes as a souvenir, presents a double reflection of Baker. She applies makeup and is reflected in two mirrors, a large rectangular stage mirror and a small oval easel-backed one (fig. 3). The clock by her side reads 5:50, presumably the early evening before the show. The subject's self-confidence is projected through the shadowy reflections in these double mirrors. Behind Baker, an unidentified man (probably Henri Varna) observes her from the hallway, providing the third gaze from the spectator's viewpoint. There also exists, in the uncut photograph, a third person in the room, probably a maid, whose gaze is invisible, as well as the unseen photographer, creating a triple play on voyeurism. Counting Baker's own image, there are six gazes at Baker in this photograph.

Previous publications and analyses of this famous photograph are incomplete.[20] Bryan Hammond's and Phyllis Rose's reproductions of the photograph (and even the cover of the present book) crop out the male spectator at the door, making it seem as though Josephine's smile is a vain response to the reflections of her own image.[21] Born in Odessa in 1887, Boris Lipnitzki migrated to Paris where he became a portrait photographer. During the interwar years, he took thousands of portrait shots, including several series on Baker. The original 1930 photograph backstage by Lipnitzki in the H. Roger-Viollet collection has been reproduced in several of Baker's biographies. It always appears in the cropped form, presumably because the glaring backstage light above Baker's dresser obstructs the view of her in the photo. But cropping out the light also removes the male figure, whose presence completes the visual logic of the picture. The presence of the spectator brings into view, and therefore into consciousness, the male gaze critical to the poses in Baker's early photographs. In the 1926–27 Folies-Bergère photograph and the related wax rendering, the mirror is used to reflect an erotic body. Baker is treated as an object of desire and an exotic pinup girl, while Lipnitzki presents her with more depth and complexity. Although Boris Lipnitzki did make a series of coquettish nude photographs of Baker during the late 1920s, he also photographed her in lavish costumes at the Casino de Paris (1930) and with Georges-Henri Rivière at the Musée de l'Homme (1933). Lipnitzki breaks through Baker's archetypal primal image to reveal another side of her persona, which is both sassy and pensive.

Between 1928 and 1930, Baker's image was captured in classic art photography. In Berlin, she posed nude for the famous German art photographer Madame d'Ora. In this series of photographs, Josephine suggestively holds a long, silky fabric and wears jewelry by the designer Jean Dunand.[22] She was also photographed by George Hoyningen-Huene in 1929 in a statuesque nude pose, as the Black Venus, in which she clutches a lustrous veil that cascades around her feet (fig. 4).[23] A Russian-born American expatriate, Hoyningen-Huene was the chief photographer for the French edition of *Vogue* during the late 1920s. His photograph of a statuesque nude Baker became a classic erotic image that contrasted with the depiction of the savage dancer. In her thesis on Baker and modernism, Jackie Barshak effectively summarizes the artistic effect of Hoyningen-Huene's image when she states that his "use of pastiche gives greater authority to the expression of idealized beauty encoded in the image."[24] This image draws on cubist abstraction, African art, and neoclassical sources that Josephine actually used in decorating her mansion at Le Vésinet.

Figure 3. Josephine Baker backstage at the Casino de Paris, 1930. Photo by Haim (Boris) Lipnitzki, from the collection of Lipnitzki-Viollet, courtesy of Documentation Photographique Roger-Viollet.

Figure 4. Josephine
Baker as Black Venus,
1929. Photo by
George Hoyningen-
Huene, courtesy of
AKG-Images, London.

These images contrast with a series of postcards and photographs from
the late 1940s and the 1950s in which Baker wears flowing designer gowns
and elaborate foot-high hairstyles (chignons and ponytails), coiffed by the
stylist Jean Clement with his crew of assistants. She is in profile, with her
haughty gaze turned away from the viewer, conveying a feeling that she is

untouchable and out of reach as a superstar and fashion icon. During the late 1940s and early 1950s, Baker's costumes became more elaborate. Long gowns, feathers, glittering jewelry, and wigs embellished her glamorous image. In her 1949 return to the Folies-Bergère, Baker appeared as a medieval princess, complete with a diaphanous gown and pointed headdress, as part of the ballet *Beauty and the Beast*. She also dressed in a Renaissance costume as Mary Stuart in a stunning and memorable number in which she performed "Ave Maria."

Josephine's public fashions outside of the music hall changed to Dior and Balenciaga. Although many photographs and sketches survive from this period, there are only a few postcards. They include a 1951 postcard image of Josephine from the Michael Ochs Archives. Posing in profile in an evening gown with a long train, she wears an elaborate, three-tiered chignon with a flowing ponytail styled by Jean Clement (fig. 5). This is the new look that Baker promoted for her 1951 tour to the United States, Cuba, and South America. Her Columbia Records cover for *Joséphine* from the same period, also reproduced as a postcard, shows her with a puffy-sleeved gown, long earrings, and the same tiered chignon. Her glance is frosty and distant on the record cover, her eyes half-closed. Through this remote image, Josephine establishes her sense of dominance as she samples the accouterments of class and style in fashion poses.

In her public fashions, Baker also appeared in matching green and rose gowns, capes, and furs, including a ten-pound pink fox fur. The costume designer Lucien Bertaux sketched a series of these gowns in which Baker herself became a virtual fashion gallery.[25] Baker often hosted fashion shows for tourists and special guests at the Château des Milandes. One of the best known shows took place on May 30, 1959, when she invited some of the most popular models from the Maison Boussac to pose under the arched entryways of the château.[26] Jo (Joseph Jean Étienne) Bouillon, Baker's husband, who was then in his last days at the château, described this event: "During the summer a group of mannequins was brought to Les Milandes to model the latest fashions. 'I want you girls to absolutely *sparkle*,' ordered Josephine. 'Wear your most elaborate gowns and plenty of jewelry.' It was a colorful sight to see those exquisite young women in evening dress parading before our tourists in their stout shoes and casual clothes. On days when we had no such 'added attractions,' Josephine performed alone."[27]

The stage costumes that Baker designed and wore became even more extravagant and elaborate in the 1960s and 70s. She added facial rhinestones,

Figure 5. Josephine Baker in a glamorous gown for her 1951 Havana tour. Photo by Armando (Armand Hernandez), 1951, from the collection of Jean Clement, courtesy of the Michael Ochs Archives, postcard ref. 2891 (Rohnert, Calif.: Pomegranate Publications).

long eyelashes, more makeup, and heavier headdresses. Ironically, during this period, Josephine's domestic dress became more maternal, consisting of cotton house shifts, woven headwraps, and heavy walking shoes. During the 1960s, she also often appeared at official functions, without makeup, in her air force uniform. Thus, she developed touristic images that juxtaposed the simple and the ornate, the private and the public selves. Describing Baker at Les Milandes, Bouillon explained, "Our visitors were delighted after battling summer heat, sudden storms, and dusty roads, to enjoy Josephine first as a star, then a half-hour later, stripped of her finery, as a barmaid serving them drinks."[28] The contrast between stage front and backstage exemplified by Josephine's role switching is a form of staged authenticity, in which tourists acquire a sense of the reality and genuineness of an icon or sight by glimpsing its backstage construction. Fan magazines and television talk shows thrive on this backstage glimpse, revealing that superstars are, after all, just human. But it is their stardom and status as icons that makes their ordinariness interesting.

At the Château des Milandes visitors can buy an unusual postcard that is difficult to find elsewhere. It depicts Baker at age sixty-three, wearing a feathered headdress in rainbow colors and a jeweled, long-sleeved gown (fig. 6). Heavily made up, her face is sprinkled with rhinestones, and she holds a microphone in her right hand while making a thumbs-up sign with her left. The caption reads, "Joséphine Baker—Les adieux à Bobino—Paris 1970," and gives the address of the Château des Milandes.[29] There are several photographs of Baker dressed in the same costume for her 1968 comeback performance at the Olympia.[30] The original photograph upon which this postcard was based appears to date from this show. This performance was filmed and reproduced in a 1987 documentary film entitled *Olympia Story,* by François Reichenbach. Since the postcard is in question here, I will use the date listed on the back of the card (1970), which also nostalgically evokes the site of Baker's last performance at the Théâtre Bobino in 1975, although this costume was not actually used there.

One balmy summer afternoon when I was at Les Milandes, elderly women swarmed through the château's gift shop to purchase the postcard. By the end of that day, very few copies were left. This postcard was far more popular with the older set than were renditions of a young and nubile Josephine in her Revue nègre days. One of the sources of appeal of the 1970 image, in contrast to the more widely available copies of Paul Colin's images of blackface, scantily

Figure 6. Postcard entitled "Les Adieux à Bobino, Paris, 1970," showing Josephine Baker at her 1968 Olympia Theater performance. The feather headdress was
tinged with the colors of the rainbow. Postcard ref. M15, Château des Milandes,
Dordogne.

clad figures, is its portrayal of Josephine as a successful survivor, confident in herself, "bien dans sa peau"—comfortable in her skin. This image is the flip side of the pure and asexual saintly Baker seeking redemption in her pilgrimage to the hilltop with the Rainbow Tribe. It is also an extension of her glamorous persona with some crucial exceptions—her gaze is warm, inviting, and direct, and her maternal smile suggests a sense of comfort beneath the glitter. Playing upon and manipulating classic stereotypes, Josephine's contrasting images crystallized the "whore-madonna complex."

Baker's Buildings

The homes that Baker designed and in which she lived externalize contrasting aspects of her public persona in the form of tourist sights. Josephine's homes were large-scale cultural productions.[31] Two properties, in particular, were organized to meet the touristic gaze—Le Beau-Chêne, in the Paris suburb of Le Vésinet, and the Château des Milandes. Baker also lived in and owned other properties, including an apartment building on avenue Bugeaud in the sixteenth arrondissement of Paris that was used as a model by the architect Adolf Loos. But Le Beau-Chêne and Les Milandes were the most grandiose of her homes, and they have received the most public attention.[32] In tourism, markers are metonymic representations of sights. For example, the Eiffel Tower is a metonymic representation of France, and its image may in turn be represented as a marker in the form of a postcard, a miniature replica, a t-shirt, or an advertisement. In the case of Baker's buildings, Baker intended key symbols within each sight as markers evoking emotional responses and memories for tourists.

Beautiful Oak

Pepito Abatino and Josephine Baker purchased their residence at 52, avenue Georges Clémenceau, Le Vésinet, in 1929 (fig. 7). They called their home first the Villa Joséphine, then Le Beau-Chêne (Beautiful Oak), the latter because of the lush trees on the property. Beau-Chêne was Baker's residence on and off until 1947. Her stays there overlapped with some of the time that she spent at Les Milandes, from 1938 to 1947. But her memorable years at Le Beau-Chêne ended with Abatino's death after her return to Paris in 1936. Jo Bouillon also resided there briefly with Baker in the 1940s.

Figure 7. Le Beau-Chêne, residence of Baker and Abatino in Le Vesinet, west of Paris. Photo from Lynn Haney, *Naked at the Feast* (New York: Dodd, Mead, 1981), 169.

While it is not currently a tourist site, Beau-Chêne was used to welcome many visitors and tourists when Baker lived there during the height of her success in the 1930s. Outside were several artificial ponds, including a lily pond in which Baker swam nude. On the enormous grounds, she kept a menagerie of exotic animals—monkeys, cockatoos, game fowl, geese, and her pet leopard, Chiquita.[33] Baker enjoyed spending time outdoors tending to her garden and animals, a pattern that continued amid much more publicity at Les Milandes. The front lawn of Beau-Chêne featured Josephine's Temple of Love, an imitation Greco-Roman pantheon surrounded by marble columns with carvings of Venus, Diana, and Circe that resembled in form and presentation Baker's appearance as the Black Venus in Hoyningen-Huene's photograph. Baker hired an electrician from the Galeries Lafayette department store to illuminate each statue with a spotlight and to place her name in lights on a giant flowered sign in the front yard. The statues encircled yet another lily pond. The Temple of Love was visible from the street, and tourists could occasionally glimpse an illuminated Baker in the lily pond—or imagine that they did.

Although the exterior of the building resembled a seventeenth-century hunting lodge for French nobles, Baker turned the interior into an eclectic combination of artistic contrasts. Haney describes Beau-Chêne's interior spaces:

> There was no overall decorating plan, but the mixture was undeniably charming. A Louis XIV room, swimming in gilt; an East Indian room, complete with temple bells; little salons, big salons, a billiard room, a studio for Josephine to practice her singing and dancing. All these came together to make a home that was both luxurious and warm. Dozens of life-size portraits of Josephine dominated the walls of the first and second floors, her compelling eyes blazing out from every turn and landing. The enclosed sunporch, one of the most handsome rooms in the house, painted robin's-egg blue, served as Pepito's office, where he spent long days poring over the business aspects of Josephine's career and filing her clippings.[34]

As she did later at Les Milandes, which was based on Le Vésinet's pattern of glamour and comfort, Josephine devoted considerable attention to her bathroom (fig. 8). The bathroom at Le Vésinet contained a bank of mirrors as well as a silver-plated bathtub that mirrored her image. The abundant portraits and redoubled reflections at Beau-Chêne were part of Josephine's image construction. It is as though by looking at herself, Josephine would finally fit in and assimilate to the various image-ideals that she was trying to create. The combination of multiple mirrors and antiques from various periods gave Beau-Chêne an atmosphere that was at once homey, kitsch, and theatrical.

During their time together at Beau-Chêne, Pepito and Josephine worked on building her new stage image, which was to emerge in *Paris qui remue*. This refurbished image was bolstered by the composition of Josephine's 1931 novella as told to Pepito and Félix de la Camara—*Mon sang dans tes veines* (My Blood in Your Veins) (fig. 9). The book's allegorical tale about race, universalism, salvation, and altruistic love foreshadows the saintly image of Josephine and the Rainbow Tribe before the cross. The novella also introduces the recurrent theme of Josephine's self-sacrifice in the face of prejudice and racist ideologies, a theme that motivates her iconic representations in tourism, her stage performances, and her humanitarian work.

Figure 8. Baker in one of her famous bathing poses adapted from *La Sirène des tropiques*. Image from a postcard entitled "When the Party's Over," postcard ref. B67, courtesy of AKG-Images, London.

Mon sang dans tes veines describes the troubled life of Joan (Jô), the tragic mulatto daughter of a black maid who works for the family of a self-made millionaire, Ira Cushman Barclay. The millionaire's fortune results from the clever exportation of American chewing gum to Europe during World War I. With this fortune, Barclay purchases a mansion on a large estate coincidentally known as Oaks, located in a Boston suburb.[35] Upon Barclay's death from a cerebral hemorrhage, his fortune goes to his wife and his young son, Fred,

Figure 9. Advertisement for *Mon Sang dans tes veines*, the novella inspired by Josephine Baker. Photo by George Hoyningen-Huene, 1927, from the original program for *Paris qui remue*, 1930–31 season, collection of Mary Strauss, St. Louis.

who has recently returned from the war in Europe. Although Joan and Fred were close as children and were frequently photographed together as part of an extended family, Fred scarcely acknowledges Joan's existence after he returns from the war. In the meantime, she has begun to idolize him, dreaming of an idyllic life by his side. Her adoration is combined with a fervent religiosity in which she identifies with both the Virgin Mary and Christ. In order to establish her religious ardor as a motivating drive in the narrative, the authors devise a scene in which Joan sees the Virgin as black, or at least bronze, and subsequently learns that there are black madonnas in Europe:

> Joan fut élevée dans la religion catholique. Aussi sa première idée, en arrivant à la vieille chapelle, fut de remplacer les fleurs devant l'image dont elle ne pouvait reconnaître le dessin tant l'icone était couverte de poussière et de toiles d'araignées.
>
> Après quelques essais, elle avait réussi, très adroitement, à ouvrir la petite grille, et pieusement, ayant enlevé les araignées et les fleurs fanées, elle s'approcha pour contempler la peinture.
>
> Surprise, elle laissa échapper un cri étouffé . . .

Dans la petite chapelle, de son cadre doré la Madone la regardait.

Mais, est-ce que Joan voit bien?

Ne se trompe-t-elle pas? . . .

Le Mère de l'Univers est d'une couleur sombre . . . est-elle brunie par le temps, ou . . .

Joan n'ose même pas espérer.[36]

[Joan was raised in the Catholic religion. Also, her first idea, in arriving at the old chapel, was to replace the flowers in front of the image whose form she couldn't recognize since the icon was covered with so much dust and so many spiders' webs.

After a few tries, she very adroitly succeeded in opening the small gate and piously, having removed the spiders and dead flowers, approached to contemplate the painting.

Shocked, she let forth a stifled cry . . .

In the small chapel, from her golden frame, the Madonna looked straight at her.

But, was Joan seeing clearly?

Wasn't she mistaken? . . .

The Mother of the Universe was of a dark color . . . was she bronzed by time, or . . .

Joan didn't even dare to hope.][37]

Based on this early experience, Joan is transfigured and realizes the saintly goodness within herself. Meanwhile, Fred grows even more arrogant and becomes engaged to a young flapper, Clarence Clifton, who hates Joan and all black people. Shortly after a spat with his fiancée, Fred has an automobile accident in which his Rolls Royce is overturned. Joan comes to the rescue, providing him with a lifesaving blood transfusion. When Fred eventually finds out the source of the transfusion, he panics. "No, certainly not! Clarence would never permit that any other blood than hers mix with that of her husband."[38]

Ideologies of racial purity and images of contamination enter the picture when Fred decides to break his engagement to Clarence, having discovered that Dr. Anderson has allowed Joan to be the blood donor. Embarrassed and frightened, Joan leaves the Oaks and runs away to a far destination (*une forêt lointaine*) where she can be close to nature.[39] When Fred confesses the entire ordeal to Clarence, she closes the narrative by saying, "Poor Mr. Barclay, so having discovered her blood in your veins, you have become *un nègre blanc*."[40]

Prejudice, the book concludes, makes true happiness impossible. This narrative, developed at Beau-Chêne, is a metaphor for both the place and the cultural space it represents. The savage Joan becomes a saint by virtue of her return to a state of nature. The narrative, which is superficially about Joan's devotion to Fred, is also about Josephine's devotion to Pepito as filtered through a tale that he coauthors. Thus, the mirror effects of Beau-Chêne continue to redouble in the novel. While the book received little public recognition when it first appeared, and the scenario was never enacted on film, *Mon sang dans tes veines* is a key to understanding Baker's mythic narrative and the touristic imagery of the Oaks (Beau-Chêne). Phyllis Rose asserts, "*My Blood in Your Veins* is little more than a curiosity in the history of fiction. As a publishing event it was of no importance at all."[41] While Rose's remark may well describe the reception of the book in 1931, a reexamination of this important text shows that it is crucial to developing the Marian motif that recurs in Baker's master narrative.

The enchanted tale initiated at Beau-Chêne reached its culmination for Baker at Les Milandes. There Baker conducted her work for the French underground, experienced the peak of her career, married Jo Bouillon, adopted the Rainbow Tribe, and waged her campaign for universal brotherhood. As with Joan's idealism, Baker's dream at Les Milandes was thwarted. Yet, Les Milandes stands as a touristic simulation of Baker's multiple private and public images, her idyllic narratives, and her life.

Château Les Milandes

Built in 1489 around the ruins of a thirteenth-century castle by François de Caumont, Lord of Castelnaud, the medieval-Renaissance castle, under the name Les Mirandes de Castelnaud, was occupied by the Caumont family and its descendants until the French Revolution. It then became the property of the state, a status maintained until it was purchased first by a wealthy industrialist in 1870 and then a doctor in 1920. Baker and Jo Bouillon bought the castle with its six-hundred-acre lot from Dr. Henri Males on June 8, 1947. It became the home of the Rainbow Tribe and a nightclub and resort. Baker also began construction of the Milandes theme park, the vestiges of which still exist (fig. 10). The current owner, Angélique de Saint-Exupéry, maintains the château as a touristic attraction.

When Baker first saw the château in 1930, it was boarded up and partially vacant. She rented the property in 1938, and after purchasing it in 1947, she spent millions of francs on the restoration of the estate. She designed an

Figure 10. The Château des Milandes, southern exposure. Courtesy of Château des Milandes, Dordogne, France, 2006.

African village for her workers on the property, which also contained its own postal service, complete with Baker postcards and stamps, and an experimental farm (fig. 11). The project included a three-star hotel, La Chartreuse, run by her husband and his friends. Les Milandes opened its doors to the public with an inaugural celebration held at La Chartreuse on September 4, 1949. In 1950 alone, 140,000 tourists visited the château and resort, and records show that between 1954 and 1959, more than 500,000 tourists came to the château each summer.[42] As ideologically loaded as the banana skirt was for her youth, Les Milandes became the totalizing symbol of the successes and struggles of Josephine Baker's later life.

Billboards advertising "this splendid site that seduced Josephine Baker" line the highway between Bordeaux and the Dordogne. Pamphlets at cafés and tourist stops along the way beckon travelers to visit the famous château and its wax museum, formerly the Jorama. One guidebook to the châteaux of the central Dordogne describes Les Milandes in terms of the narrative of Josephine's life:

Figure 11. Josephine Baker's African village at Les Milandes. From the publicity brochure *Château des Milandes: Ancienne demeure de Joséphine Baker* (Dordogne: Château des Milandes, 1992).

In the 1930s, while she was on holiday in the Dordogne, Les Milandes cast a spell on Josephine Baker almost as powerful as the spell Josephine had cast over Paris with her joyful, exuberant versions of the Charleston and Black Bottom, performed in a costume made of nothing but bananas. Of all of the black Americans who came to France to escape racism at home, Josephine was the most successful, becoming the highest paid performer in Europe—not bad for someone who was born in a cardboard box in St. Louis. She purchased her dream castle and 600 acres to go with it, and used it during the war to hide people wanted by the Nazis, earning a medal for her work in the Resistance. In the late 1940s, after spending millions on the restoration of Les Milandes, she adopted 13 [*sic*] children of every race and creed, her "Rainbow Tribe," and hosted anti-racism conferences. But her ambitions (which included a 120-acre pleasure garden and amusement park) were unfortunately bigger than her purse.[43]

The guidebook qualifies the tourist attractions at Les Milandes as "more National Trust than interracial trust."[44] The authors then outline some of the key attractions not to be missed by any dedicated tourist—the Gothic chapel of the château, the grotto near the house containing Place Joséphine Baker, and a statue of the Virgin Mary carved in Josephine's image. The notion that Baker was born in a cardboard box and came from humble origins embeds this religious imagery in an account of mythic proportions.

The Jorama memorialized the key events of her life as twelve stations of the cross. The first scene portrayed a forlorn little girl in ill-fitting clothes dancing for her siblings in a St. Louis basement. Bouillon describes the original display as one of the finishing touches on Les Milandes:

> The Jorama Wax Museum traced Josephine's life from the days when she put on shows for her brother and sisters to a scene portraying her scaling nearby Mount José with her seven children (they had rushed things a bit, but we were convinced that our little Indian would soon be with us). Other events captured in wax included our audience with a surprisingly lifelike Pius XII. Close by, a glass cabinet displayed Josephine's war mementos: the flag of the Twenty-fourth Colonial Infantry Regiment, her air force field jacket, an inscribed photograph of Général de Gaulle.[45]

The wax museum, now recreated at Les Milandes, preserves the narrative structure and feeling of the old Jorama and recreates Josephine's mythic biography.

Since Baker's departure from Les Milandes in 1969, private ownership of the château has changed hands many times. The owners are responsible for the upkeep of the château, and the Association Joséphine Baker, headed by Mäité Jardin, has organized special exhibits in the chapel. Angélique de Saint-Exupéry, owner of the château in 2006, organized the Baker centennial celebration at Les Milandes in concert with a group known as the Association "Opération Joséphine." Angélique's parents, Henry and Claude de Labarre, and her husband, Bruno de Saint-Exupéry, have also been actively involved in remodeling and upgrading the château and its grounds. The guided tour of the château was restructured for the 2006 centennial and certain aspects of the interior of the château were redesigned for visitors. For the 2006 guided tour, a new foyer with a billiard table was opened to receive visitors. In the 2004 guided tour, one entered instead through the vast dining room, which exuded the history of its medieval walls and heavy oak furniture. In the 1996 and 1997 tours, one then moved to a narrow winding staircase leading to the Rainbow children's rooms and the music chamber. This section of the tour was cordoned off in 2006. Instead, one passes through the costume room as well as a room filled with photographs of Baker from various periods of her life. On the wall, a photograph of Baker at the 1963 March on Washington and an image of Dr. Martin Luther King Jr. have been added to underscore Baker's commitment to the civil rights movement. These photographs also send a special message to American tourists.

Each year, the tour has been modified and expanded by a change of format and the addition of new Grévin wax figures. In 2004, the first wax diorama presented Josephine in an evening gown and a slick hairstyle from the late 1920s. She welcomed visitors into her official living room. Tourists then moved into the commemorative hall featuring Josephine's work with the secret service and the Resistance. There was a wax figure of Josephine, dressed in the original French air force sublieutenant's uniform, receiving her 1961 Legion of Honor from General Valin, also a wax figure. Photographic memorabilia of the Resistance and war medals decorate the walls, and a life-sized wax figure of Charles de Gaulle loomed in the hallway. The next room contained images of Josephine's early performances at the Théâtre des Champs-Elysées and the Folies-Bergère. The centerpiece of this room was a wax reproduction of George Hoyningen-Huene's photograph of a bejeweled Black Venus holding a long diaphanous fabric that drapes across a pedestal. Music-hall tunes play in the background, creating a theatrical ambiance. In what was probably a ballroom and reception area in the old château, Josephine's Salle des Robes (Costume Room) displayed a dozen of her most fashionable costumes, dresses, and headpieces bathed in glowing light. This room remains intact in the 2006 tour of the château. In the spirit of the original Jorama, this dramatic room commemorates Josephine's image as a fashion icon.

At the end of the costume gallery is a long staircase leading past the Rainbow children's nursery and the music room. The nursery contains uniform, hospital-style beds placed in a row against the wall. The 2006 tour eliminates this room and replaces it with a large photo of the children's quarters. In describing Adolf Loos's design for Baker's unbuilt Parisian house, Beatriz Colomina states that it is "a house that excludes family life."[46] In contrast, Les Milandes converts family life into a touristic mystification and Josephine's maternal image into a myth larger than life. Photographs show the children at mealtimes and on holidays in ritualistic embraces, along with a few candid shots of them at play.

After leaving the nursery area with a blast of Baker tunes, one takes another winding staircase. In the 1996, 1997, and 2004 tours, this staircase led to a landing that displayed the publicity centerpiece of Les Milandes. Here was a life-sized wax figure of Josephine, bare-breasted in a grass skirt and resting on a large mirror. The figure was illuminated by strobe lights. This figure was copied meticulously from the signature photograph of Josephine in her 1926–27 Folies-Bergère performance of *La Folie du jour.* Although the Grévin figure on the crystalline lake was used to advertise the museum for several years, many tourists found the scene difficult to watch. The strobe lights cut the spectator's gaze, causing one to blink, and they heightened the anomalous and anachronistic effect of this scene in a classic château. Nevertheless, this centerpiece figure, which was moved to the room immediately behind the foyer in 2006 and is no longer illuminated by strobe lights, was dramatic and compelling in its presentation.

Considered from a historical perspective, the illuminated centerpiece image employed the Musée Grévin's technique of the *journal lumineux,* in which mirrors were rotated and lights were flashed to create the illusion of cinematic movement.[47] This illuminated scene produced the effect of a live theatrical performance. Viewed in this way, the mirrored panorama at Les Milandes is not only an example of touristic kitsch but also a replica of the popular forms of entertainment during Baker's early music-hall years in Montmartre. The strobe lights preserved Grévin's technique and highlighted the longevity of Josephine's career in the public eye, but they also demarcated two different phases of her life. That is, they reinforced the trajectory of the touristic pilgrimage by impelling viewers to take a break from her primal image before they proceeded to the Rainbow children's area where Josephine is reconfigured as a mother. Displaying the wax figure in this way reminded viewers of its importance to Baker's narrative while forcing them to close their eyes to the outdated image.

Yet another winding staircase leads to a short hallway plastered with photographs of Josephine and her Rainbow Tribe. Her voice lilts over a loudspeaker the familiar refrain, "J'ai deux amours, mon pays et Paris," which is followed by a medley of her favorite tunes. The omniscient narrator then instructs tourists to proceed to a small chamber around the corner. Innocent viewers feel trapped inside a labyrinth and are transformed into pilgrims caught up in the intricacies of Baker's myth. The ambivalent message about two loves is reinforced by the spectator's total sense of spatial disorientation.

In all versions of the tour, Josephine's bedroom culminates the labyrinthine journey. The chamber is relatively small and square, with windows on two sides. The present bed is not the antique *lit de Marie Antoinette* in which Josephine took so much pride, but the silk and satin bedcovers simulate the original. An armoire contains Baker's comb, brush, feathers, and makeup pots. Next to the bedroom is a luxurious full bathroom with black mirrors and gold-plated fixtures, which were installed in the 1950s and were vastly ahead of their time for the French plumbing of the era.

Stephen Papich, one of Baker's managers, described his guided tour of the château with Josephine in 1960, ending with the bedroom:

> On and on it went. Finally the tour reached Josephine's bedroom. By the standards of the other rooms in the château, it bordered on the severe. It was rather small—she liked it that way—but there were huge windows that would let in the morning sun. By this time Josephine had become a Catholic. On her little writing desk was a large crucifix, and on either side were two paintings of the Virgin on plaster; one was the Virgin of Guadalupe. They had been given to her by the President of Mexico long ago.
>
> There were a chaise, the usual carpets on the floor, and two tiny reading lamps with tulip shades. Commanding the entire room was the famous bed of Marie Antoinette. Its canopy rose almost nine feet high, and the spread was a striped silk. It was in this bed that Josephine did most of her thinking.
>
> "I just love this little bed of mine. When I am in it, I can really think. Sometimes I rest here looking out of first one window and then the other, and I try to get my thoughts together like I used to. It seems it doesn't come as easy to me as it did, though. When I was younger, I could think it all out very quickly and understand it, too. Now it is a little different. I guess maybe I'm getting old."[48]

In the pre-2006 tours, down the hall from Josephine's room were Jo Bouillon's room and study, lined with photographs of Josephine throughout her career in France. This small suite, literally an apartment unto itself, was clearly the emotional centerpiece of the authentic backstage tour, in a way that the illuminated Grévin statue is not. The sitting room contained the famous banana skirt and photographs of Josephine in the music hall, with Jo Bouillon, and with President de Gaulle and other French dignitaries. One felt her presence in the sitting room so strongly that it seemed as though she might emerge at any moment to greet her visitors, or perhaps to chastise them for trespassing on her private territory. Jo Bouillon's room has been transformed into the bedroom of Baker's eldest son, Akio, in the 2006 tour. Akio's collaboration in the restructuring of the tour partially explains this change, which has the overall effect of normalizing the Rainbow Tribe as a nuclear family and erasing the vestiges of Baker and Bouillon's volatile relationship.

The final stop on all versions of the tour is the large kitchen where the Rainbow Tribe took its breakfast. The long kitchen table, often depicted in documentary films and Baker's publicity photos for her Rainbow family, has been replaced by a facsimile. The kitchen walls are lined with photographs of Baker, her mother, and the children, culminating with a photograph of Baker in her "nightgown of misery" locked out of the château on the morning of her eviction on September 22, 1969. Without further explanation of the fate and fortunes of the family, the spectator is ejected into the courtyard behind the château.

The Château des Milandes tells the superficial story of a life sketched by fragmentary recollections, much in the same way that family photographs frame our memories, creating the mnemonic ruins that reflect an indexical identity. As a touristic simulation, Les Milandes pushes us to reflect on larger questions of identity, nationality, gender, and the cultural politics of exile.[49] Situated in the château region of the Dordogne, Château des Milandes is not the largest or the most impressive castle in the area. It is one tourist site among many, but its distinctiveness derives from its association with Baker's history and her ideas. As a touristic artifact, the château points to the ways in which Baker molded herself into a folk icon, a virtual edifice, and a social movement. Les Milandes also introduces many unanswered questions about Baker's incomplete projects—the College of Universal Brotherhood, the theme park, the experimental farm, and her Rainbow Tribe. The constant rearrangement of the château's tour reflects the protean and ambivalent aspects of Baker's image. For a short time, the family was on stage with Baker, providing their own personal tour of the world. Yet, even the family life on display at Les Milandes was a simulation, a larger-than-life touristic replica of a perfect extended family in an ideal world in which all nations, ethnicities, and backgrounds blend. MacCannell refers to tourism as "an enormous deferral of the question of the acceptance of otherness."[50] Seen in this light, Baker's ideal of universalism and harmony was a dream deferred and a simulation that could not be achieved as a sustained reality. Following this logic of cultural deferral, we can understand why holding onto Les Milandes as both a home and a touristic sight enthralled Baker.

Josephine Baker as Art and Artifice

The dynamic of Baker's life may be viewed as what Jean Baudrillard has termed a "scenodrama," or a form of collective dramaturgy performed on the stage of social life. Baudrillard's emphasis on the links between the "scenario," or narrative, and mediated cultural productions provides an effective point of departure for analyzing touristic sights in relationship to the larger biographical and cultural narratives that frame them.[51] Yet, this drama also originated and was enacted in the theater, the music hall, and film. The touristic staging of Baker's life draws on the theatrical elements of her scripts, narratives, performances, and poses, transforming each of them into a touristic landmark. Thus, the primal, grass-skirted figure is converted into a wax sound-and-light spectacle that evokes the image of the original performance. In Baker's case, each touristic simulation builds upon a foundational image that is itself a simulation. Beau-Chêne and Les Milandes were Baker's dream castles onto which she projected the Cinderella narrative of her public life. They also became tourist sights in which elements of this narrative were externalized and woven into collective fantasies. These fantasies are, in the literal sense, spectacular and render the search for the real (*véritable*) Baker not only impossible, but in many respects far less intriguing than a pursuit of the fantasies themselves.[52]

When one is touring with Baker's image, several issues emerge that pertain to the worlds of art history and museum culture. In her work on African art and artifacts, Susan Vogel notes that, from an institutional perspective, once African sculpture entered the art museum in the early twentieth century, "it became necessary to determine which objects were properly art and should be displayed in art museums, and which were artifacts that belonged in natural history museums."[53] In its evolution, the wax museum was linked to both the natural history museum and the tradition of documentary reportage. Wax techniques were also appropriated by the music hall and the world of popular art. The museum artifact is a second-order semioconstruction, a representation based on performative artifice. During her lifetime, both as the primal dancer and Black Venus, and through her memorialization in wax, Baker became an artifact, and she did so through her own artifice as a performer.

Touring with Baker's image differs from seeing a live performance or a film. Theater audiences have expectations based on the verisimilitude of the characters and scenes and their privileged knowledge about what is taking place. Erving Goffman refers to the audience's privilege as "a peculiar form of eavesdropping that provides the spectators with special information to which they cannot openly respond."[54] Goffman elaborates:

> As with those who watch a sport, those who watch a play are disattended by the actor-in-character and yet they are fully privy to what is happening onstage in frame. However, . . . the staged interaction is opened up, slowed down, and focused so that the audience's peculiar form of eavesdropping is maximally facilitated, a fact that marks theatrical audiences off from other kinds. Theatrical audiences have only restricted rights to reply to the show they watch and are allowed only a restricted role, but unlike the onlookers at excavation sites, they do have *some* expectations in that regard.[55]

Front regions of touristic sights operate in a manner similar to the theatrical stage. Once the props are set up, the audience has restricted rights of response. Nevertheless, tourists attempt to penetrate the proscenium and unearth the authentic information and experiences. In touring with Baker's image, one achieves this process of authentication via constant biographical references to the narrative of a life and the search for gossip and untold stories. Relics, postcards, photographs, and real edifices create this sense of authenticity amid a sea of glitter, greasepaint, and wax, for there is a story to be told. The visible part of this story is made available through the encoding of signs of a life and symbols, such as the banana skirt, that have become so familiar that they speak for themselves.

Touristic Signs of a Life

The permutations of Baker's life narrative are essential to understanding the touristic displays based on her image. In his *Morphology of the Folktale*, Vladimir Propp outlines the basic narrative functions in the structure of Russian fairy tales.[56] Of the nine narrative functions analyzed by Propp, one of the most important is the hero's transformation through absence and departure from home. A. J. Greimas, a semiotician, condenses Propp's narrative schema into four basic movements: the qualifying test, the main test, the glorifying test (or confrontation and mastery of the narrative problem), and final attribution.[57] Baker's Cinderella story, which constitutes her master narrative, involves departure from home with vaudeville troupes (qualifying test), leaving for France with its struggles and successes (main test), eventual stardom (glorifying test), and her legacy as an icon (final attribution). Propp points out that the hero's departure on a foreordained quest, whether by dispatch or request, sets in motion the wheels of destiny and forces far beyond the hero's control.[58] It is these forces that transform the folktale into a legend and proffer the moral of the story.

Baker's narrative recycles with various iterations. Gérard Genette writes, "Every iterative narrative is a synthetic narrating of the events that occur and reoccur in the course of an iterative series."[59] For Baker, this iterative series involves transformations through travel, escape, and "exile."[60] Her initial departure from home brings moderate success in New York. Her embarkation to France ushers in the success of the glorifying test, marked along the way by various struggles, the arrival of a helper (Pepito Abatino), and the breaking point of the 1928–29 European tour. Early primal images of Baker stop at the first iteration of the Cinderella story in the form of music-hall fame. Colin's lithographs and the related postcards and relics render iconic this part of the narrative in Baker's biographies and in touristic displays.

Once Baker moved to Beau-Chêne in 1929, she was installed in Cinderella's castle and began to develop a larger and more challenging narrative—the Marian chronicle, which appears in Joan's self-sacrifice in *Mon sang dans tes veines.* The early versions of this narrative, which also surface in her films *Sirène des tropiques* and *Princesse Tam-Tam,* send the heroine back to nature and her primal origins after the glorifying test. In spite of Joan's momentary victory over racism, she too returns to nature. The expanded version of the Marian motif includes the Rainbow Tribe and, in fact, all of humanity, in the glorifying test of self-sacrifice. Cinderella's achievements pale by comparison, for the true touchstone of success, as Baker wrote in one of her poems, is not material but spiritual. The Marian narrative returns us to the diorama image of Baker before the cross as the culmination of her suffering and redemption. In many respects, this image closes the fairy tale of Les Milandes. The loss of Les Milandes begins Baker's cycle of struggles and tests anew, with poverty, age, and idealism as the adversaries. This cycle of nested narratives creates the endless stream of Baker's images within a life course of struggles and successes.

The theme of departure and return that transects all of Baker's imbricated narratives is identical with the narrative of escape in the touristic voyage.[61] The tourist leaves home for exotic locales and, after a series of good and bad experiences, returns home as a changed person. The identity transformations of pilgrimage and tourism are mirrored in the various symbols of Baker's departures and returns (the banana skirt, the air force uniform, the glamorous gowns, and the house dresses). Combined with Baker's fairy-tale edifices at Beau-Chêne and Les Milandes, these symbols embellish the powerful iterative narrative of touring with Baker's image. These symbols and traces of the past become more meaningful when we return to Baker's early years and her efforts to create the public images that she would use throughout her life.

2   Opening Nights

I never took the easy path, always the rough one. Even in the
theatre, I don't know *why* I'm rehearsing myself to death. But,
you know, when I took the rough path, I wanted to make it a
little easier for those who followed me.

　　—Josephine Baker, 1963

The curtain rose at 9:30 P.M. on October 2, 1925, revealing a
dimly lit stage with a bold cartoon-like sketch of a New York
skyscraper as a backdrop. Magical clarinet music resembling the melodies of
a snake charmer wafted through the air. It was the opening night of *La Revue
nègre* at the Théâtre des Champs-Elysées in Paris. The revue's cast of twenty-
five artists and musicians performed seven vaudeville-style tableaux: "New
York Skyscraper," "Mississippi Steamboat Race," "Louisiana Camp Meeting,"
"Les Strutting Babies," "Darkey Impressions," "Les Pieds qui parlent," and
"Charleston Cabaret." The highlight of the show was a wildly erotic dance,
referred to in the press as a Dionysian spectacle, performed by Josephine
Baker. It was a reenactment of Pierre Loti's popular nineteenth-century novel
about the seductive native girl Fatou-gaye and the French explorer Jean
Peyral. Suddenly Baker appeared as Fatou, carried onto the stage upside
down by her Antillian partner, Joe Alex (fig. 12). The atmosphere was tense.
Clad only in beads and a belt of feathers, with glaring spotlights focused on
her, Baker began to gyrate. No one knew what to expect. Baker described

Figure 12. Baker's danse sauvage, performed with Joe Alex, 1925. Photo courtesy of AKG-Images, London.

the scene: "Driven by dark forces I didn't recognize, I improvised, crazed by the music, the overheated theater filled to the bursting point, the scorching eye of the spotlights. Even my teeth and eyes burned with fever. Each time I leaped I seemed to touch the sky and when I regained earth it seemed to be mine alone. I felt . . . intoxicated."[1] The image of the frenetic savage dancer and her "stomach dance" followed Baker throughout her life. She used it as a challenge, a key to fame, and a memory of past glory.

Image and Invention

Josephine Baker fashioned herself as an icon through performance and ultimately transformed her theatrical performances into social and political statements. Baker's early appeal was based on an exotic performative image that used the primitive, non-Western "other" as a point of reference and a source of fantasy.[2] More broadly, Baker has come to be seen as a "pop icon" whose achievements and celebrity are self-referential, standing as signifiers of her historical importance. In this context, performance may be defined both as the dramatic display of art in culture and discourse, and, more specifically, as the enactment of culture by individual actors in theater, exhibits, festivals, and media.[3] Baker's iconic performative imagery eventually transcended—and attempted to negate—barriers of race, class, and gender in Euro-American society. She constantly reinvented herself to suit the purposes of her projects. Homi Bhabha has referred to this reinvention process, which he calls doubling, as a performance in which the self as subject becomes its own object.[4] Bhabha elaborates: "We are no longer confronted with an ontological problem of being but with the discursive strategy of the moment of interrogation, a moment in which the demand for identification becomes, primarily, a response to other questions of signification and desire, culture, and politics."[5] In other words, the personal construction of identity not only reflects but also restructures the subject's social world.

Key transitions in Josephine Baker's life course reveal the role of image construction and reinvention in the social and cultural production of identity discourses. As ways of speaking about one's perceived and desired location in the social world, identity discourses express virtual states of existence.[6] These discourses are affirmations, rather than statements of fact, that link individuals to larger collective identities. Baker worked within the genre of the French music hall while developing practices that would make her unique. In complicity with her promoters and audiences, Baker employed five performative strategies of image and identity construction: (1) exoticizing race and gender; (2) reversing racial and cultural codes and meanings; (3) displaying difference through nudity, cross-dressing, song, and dance; (4) exploiting the images of difference; and (5) universalizing the outcomes to allow the performative messages to reach a larger audience. These strategies emerged gradually and with varying degrees of sophistication.

The epigraph for this chapter, excerpted from Baker's speech at the 1963 March on Washington, suggests that she saw herself as an image-creator. Early in her career, Baker's role in her own image construction was greatly influenced by her managers and promoters, but later it became more forceful and autonomous. This image-making process may be traced through the evolution of the famous banana skirt, at first an idea concocted by Jean Coc-

teau and Paul Colin, who drew on Covarrubias's caricatures for his sketches
of Baker. The skirt's modifications reflect the evolution of artistic agency
within a framework of social control. The original skirt was a collection
of realistic-looking bananas, as shown in figure 13. The early designs were
used as templates for advertisements for Bakerfix pomade and on postcards.
The banana skirt first appeared in two scenes of the 1926 production of *La
Folie du jour.* By 1927, as seen in figure 14, the bananas had become pointed
spikes—a parody of the original skirt and a humorous design innovation in
which Baker took part. These photographs indicate that in just one year, Baker
began to take control of and modify her primal image through costuming.
In 1936 for the Ziegfeld Follies, the bananas were transformed into a series
of horizontal spikes worn with a pointed headdress that made a visual allu-

Figure 13. During just one year, Baker's banana skirt was transformed from a basic design to a more abstract pattern. Original banana skirt, circa 1926. Photo courtesy of the Billy Rose Theatre Collection, New York Public Library at Lincoln Center, Astor, Lenox, and Tilden Foundation.

Figure 14. Josephine Baker in *La Folie du jour,* 1927. Photo courtesy of the Billy Rose Theatre Collection, New York Public Library at Lincoln Center, Astor, Lenox, and Tilden Foundation.

sion to the original costume without any bananas at all (fig. 15). During the course of Baker's later life, younger female and male dancers played her part in banana skirts in theatrical retrospectives, some of which were staged and choreographed by Baker herself. Through the skirt's evolution and its place in Baker's narratives and performances, the changing character and extent of her agency are revealed. Even more critical to an understanding of this agency is Baker's self-writing through autobiographies, correspondence, and recorded performances.

The line between history and myth is blurred by Baker's own statements about her deprived youth in St. Louis and her move to France, as well as by

Figure 15. Another variation of the banana skirt designed by Vincente Minnelli for the 1936 Ziegfeld Follies. Photo © Bettmann/Corbis.

the factual and counterfactual reworkings of her numerous biographers.[7] Although they vary in terms of sophistication and complexity, these biographies are based on a narrative of exile that interfaces with the story of a black Cinderella.[8] While many of the biographers juxtapose the "real Josephine" (Emmanuel Bonini entitles his biography *La Véritable Joséphine*) and the icon, most of them shy away from the ongoing construction of race, gender, and nationality in her life in relationship to late twentieth-century society. These biographies, including Baker's own collaborations with Marcel Sauvage and André Rivollet, may be treated as data that reflect and are redundant to social discourse.[9] Sociologically speaking, these biographies offer a perfect arena for examining the interaction between social constraints and personal identity construction through classic narratives.[10]

Baker's early life has assumed the dimensions of a legend, in part because of her numerous, and often contradictory, reworkings of the story, which frequently lacked coherence. Her childhood assumed mythological proportions in her own autobiographical accounts. Her impoverished childhood in St. Louis fueled her dream to escape and provided her with an unconventional exposure to performance. Allegedly born in a cardboard box, Baker first resided at 212 Targee Street in one of the worst slums of St. Louis. Freda Josephine was the first child of Carrie McDonald and, as far as official records indicate, Eddie Carson, former vaudeville performers. Her early childhood was transient and unstable. Some sources suggest that Carson was not actually Baker's father. The mystery is compounded by Carrie's occasionally harsh criticism and apparent resentment toward her daughter during the early years.

Carrie later married a day laborer, Arthur Martin, and they moved from 212 Targee Street to nearby Gratiot Street in downtown St. Louis.[11] Carrie had three more children with Martin—Richard, Margaret, and Willie Mae. As a child, Josephine scavenged in the train yards around Union Station and in local markets. Carrie also sent her out to work as a child domestic in order to supplement her own meager income as a laundress. Josephine attended Lincoln Elementary School in St. Louis but found little inspiration in her studies. By all accounts, even her own, Josephine could read and write only haltingly when she arrived in Paris. Her early signatures on Parisian photographs were primitive scrawls. Throughout her life, her English remained simpler and more colloquial than her evolving literary French. But in the area of performance, she quickly picked up everything to which she was exposed. George Lipsitz remarks, "No one could have predicted that this skinny, buck-toothed, impoverished black child would one day become an international sex symbol receiving over forty thousand love letters and some two thousand marriage proposals before her twenty-first birthday."[12]

But this is jumping ahead of the story. Frustrated by her family life in St. Louis, Josephine made repeated attempts to run away from home and was eventually sent to live in a slightly better neighborhood with her grandmother, Elvira McDonald, and her aunt, Caroline, whose late husband's army pension strengthened the family's resources. Josephine began to work as a waitress in a nightspot known as the Old Chauffeur's Club in Chestnut Valley. She carefully watched the musicians and imitated their routines. On Sundays, she would attend the vaudeville shows at the Booker T. Washington Theater, where she eventually encountered the Jones Family Band, a local vaudeville team that included her in its act to dance and perform comic routines on the sidewalks of St. Louis. While working at the Old Chauffeur's Club, she also met and married a local foundry worker, Willie Wells. She is said to have been thirteen years old at the time but claimed that she was fifteen. The marriage was brief and stormy. Willie left in a huff after a heated argument, and Josephine began to throw herself into her performances with the Jones family.

Josephine learned quickly, picking up the trumpet, banjo, and fiddle with Mrs. Dyer Jones's instruction. The troupe walked through the streets of St. Louis performing on sidewalks for spare change and in front of the Booker T. Washington Theater, where Red Bennett, the manager, noticed them. Bennett was fascinated by Josephine and seized the opportunity to put her on stage when a vaudeville act know as the Dixie Steppers came to town. The Steppers decided to hire the entire Jones Family Band to supplement their act. For comic relief, Josephine was placed at the end of the chorus line. Opening night with the Dixie Steppers was a learning experience for Josephine. She deftly mastered the vaudeville routines and was eventually given a solo spot. Josephine's performance career was launched by a combination of her native talent, luck, and skill. Her family experiences and early performance history would later serve her well in France as part of her narrative as a self-made Cinderella.

The road was Baker's training ground. She traveled across the south with the Dixie Steppers, then to Chicago and Philadelphia. The work was arduous, and the living conditions were substandard and even frightening. As a minstrel show, the Steppers endured racial threats and taunts that Josephine claimed never to forget. In Philadelphia, Josephine met and married a railway porter, William Howard Baker, whose surname she adopted for life. This relationship too was short-lived, and Baker continued to look for work on the vaudeville circuit, dreaming of becoming part of the cast of a popular new musical, *Shuffle Along*. At this point, Baker had already mastered a considerable repertoire of vaudeville song-and-dance routines and had developed a unique comic style, but she was still searching for steady employment and an audience. A review of Baker's early years highlights the themes of race, class, and gender as formative forces that would eventually become integral to her performances. Her autobiography, published posthumously with Jo Bouillon, opens with a description of the 1917 race riots in St. Louis. Baker, who would have been eleven years old at the time, dramatically recalled this experience: "'A white woman was raped,' someone shouted, and although I didn't understand the meaning of his words, I knew that they described the ultimate catastrophe. The flames drew nearer. As the choking stench of ashes filled the air, I was overcome with panic. Mama threw us to the ground and covered us with her body."[13]

The St. Louis episode symbolically sets the tone for the transformation of "Tumpy" (short for Humpty Dumpty), the impoverished young girl traumatized by racism, into a runaway performer. Rebuilding herself through escape, travel, and performance, Josephine established a strategy of image creation that she used throughout her life. She tried on identities like costumes, adding an element from each new fitting to her persona. In *Naked at the Feast*, Lynn Haney characterizes Baker as emotionally volatile: "Josephine had trouble differentiating between manufactured emotions and her true emotions. She wanted to know the intoxication of love, the joys of motherhood, of tears and laughter, but most of all she did not want to be bored."[14]

Racial themes played out in Baker's primal imagery of Fatou may be linked to the stereotypes of minstrelsy, not only in their exaggeration and distortion of cultural images, but also in the songs and dances that Baker adapted from the minstrel repertoire. These performances and recordings firmly root Baker in an American theatrical tradition that she modified and transformed in France. Her comic performances in the French music hall through the 1930s included blackface parodies, and she continued to use vaudeville routines and techniques of comic timing in combination with her new exotic primitivism. Baker employed her body, attire, dances, and song lyrics as elements from which to mold her multiple symbolic images. As she began to reflect and write about herself, she drew on the Cinderella narrative as a way of framing her obstacles and the permeability of social class. In her 1934 film *Zouzou*, she even plays a laundress, mirroring her early years with Carrie. Aouina (or Alwina), the heroine of her 1935 film *Princesse Tam-Tam,* is a street urchin who steals oranges from a café, much as Baker had scavenged in the markets of downtown St. Louis. Her move from the primal erotic dancer to the sophisticated Black Venus also reflects her own biographical trajectory through performance. Part of Baker's unique talent lies in her ability to use, embellish, and transform her life story as an aspect of both public performance and personal identity construction.

Baker's emotional volatility may also be seen as a source of her motivations and reactions. This perspective is highlighted in Brian Gibson's 1991 Home Box Office television special. Scenes of the 1917 race riots in St. Louis appear early in the film and are redeployed in several darkly lit flashbacks. Emotional escape from the terrors of racism in St. Louis pushes the filmic Josephine to make key decisions in her life. She is presented as a passive subject, driven by irrational fears and later manipulated by music-hall agents and entrepreneurs. When persuading her to accept the unconventional aspects of her new Parisian persona, the musician Sidney Bechet, played by Kene Holliday in the film, simply states, "Ain't you a long way from East St. Louis?" In the film, Josephine's fear of returning to the United States is repeatedly linked to racism, a fear that was also popularly used to mask and explain away the complex motivations of African American expatriates who chose to live and work in Europe. This interpretation allowed Baker and other artistic expatriates, such as Richard Wright and James Baldwin, to be reclaimed as American icons who devoted their lives to remedying a crucial and unexplored flaw in American society.

Blacking Down and Lightening Up

In 1922, Josephine joined the cast of Noble Sissle and Eubie Blake's vaudeville musical *Shuffle Along.* Sissle and Blake were comedians, musicians, and trained composers who worked the vaudeville circuit in the tradition of the minstrel show. Minstrelsy is tragicomic performance based on the hegemonic dialectic of race relations. It may be interpreted as an intersection of racial desires based on mutual imitation of the dominated population by the racially dominant performers and is particularly characteristic of societies where racial barriers are rigid (e.g., the United States and South Africa). Eventually, black as well as white comedians performed in blackface. Sissle and Blake were influenced by this tradition but moved away from it by using light-skinned black chorus girls in their performances, along with blackface comedians. In collaboration with the writers F. E. Miller and Aubrey Lyles, they produced several musicals. According to Bryan Hammond and Patrick O'Connor, "Sissle and Blake had fallen to blacking-up in order to get engagements in better-paid, white-owned theaters, where it was the convention. . . . If the performers were blacked-up, the audience assumed they were white men."[15]

Initially, because of her clowning and lack of discipline, Josephine had difficulty staying with the cast and was threatened with dismissal. When the show had a chance to go to New York, Josephine was re-auditioned by Sissle and Blake and described the experience in racial terms. She reminisced,

Soon afterward I found myself face to face with Mr. Sissle, a thin man with a small mustache and a full head of hair. Mr. Blake, plump and bald-headed, sat at the piano, his nose buried in his music. He never once opened his mouth. Nor did Mr. Sissle waste words. "Too young," he snapped. I began my usual routine. "But I'm seventeen . . ." "Sorry. Too small, too thin, too dark." By the time I rejoined Wilsie at the stage door I was boiling with rage. "Too *dark?* Mr. Russell says I'm too *light!*" Wilsie tried to explain. Mr. Sissle wanted his chorus to look like the Tillers, a highly successful white company, so he was hiring only the lightest-skinned dancers. "He's ashamed of his kind," I sniffed. "Not at all, Josephine. It's just the opposite. He's hoping to beat the whites at their own game. Since they prefer blackface shows to real black performers, he's decided to give them white black folks. *Shuffle Along* isn't variety or burlesque. It's a real musical comedy with a plot."[16]

This incident appears to have reinforced Josephine's consciousness of color, which became a psychological and theatrical aspect of her early performances. Blacking up and lightening are strategies that call into question the phenotypical aspects of race and suggest that transcending apparent difference unmasks a fundamental human ingenuity. Although Baker's comic performances and primal dances in France drew on different paradigms of racialization, they used the minstrel-vaudeville blackface tradition as a resource (fig. 16).

Baker had auditioned for weeks without success for a part in *Shuffle Along*. The stage manager, Al Mayer, finally gave her a part in the road company as a

Figure 16. Josephine
Baker as a clown
in blackface, Paris,
1927. Photo ©
Bettmann/Corbis.

mascot, intended to provide comic relief at the end of the chorus line. Because
of her complexion and comic faces, other members of the cast referred to her
as "the monkey." By the end of the road tour, however, Baker's reputation as
a dancer and a comedian was established, and Sissle and Blake hired her for
their next show, *Chocolate Dandies*. In 1924, Baker performed comic routines
in that production, including her famous eye-crossing in blackface and wearing a clown costume (fig. 17). She received rave reviews. At the end of the
show's run, she went to work at the Plantation Club, a segregated nightclub
on West Fiftieth Street in New York that featured black performers for white

Figure 17. Baker as a vaudeville clown in a performance of *Chocolate Dandies*,
1924. Photo courtesy of the Billy Rose Theatre Collection, New York Public Library
at Lincoln Center, Astor, Lenox, and Tilden Foundation.

audiences in the style of the Cotton Club. Ethel Waters was the lead singer at the club, and Baker performed in the chorus. It was here that Baker was "discovered" by Caroline Dudley Regan, wife of a commercial attaché at the American embassy in Paris.[17] Caroline Regan was organizing a traveling version of *Shuffle Along* in order to revive the failing fortunes of the Théâtre des Champs-Elysées in Paris and bring it in tune with the jazz era and the negrophilia craze in France. She hired Josephine at $250 a week as part of the traveling troupe, which was dubbed La Revue nègre.

Spencer Williams, an African American composer with roots in New Orleans jazz, had already acquired a considerable reputation as a musical producer. Although he was later known by many in the role of Andy in the 1950s television sitcom *Amos 'n' Andy*, Williams actually had a far more varied and extensive career. He lived on and off in London and Paris and worked as a screenplay writer and director in Hollywood before becoming a television star. But it was in 1925 that he helped Carolyn Dudley Regan to assemble the twenty-five-person Revue nègre troupe, which included musicians who would later rise to fame in international jazz and expatriate art communities.

Spencer Williams became the troupe's composer, and Claude Hopkins, a musician trained at Howard University, was selected to lead the revue's eight-piece band. Hopkins had already toured Europe, as had Sidney Bechet, a band member and virtuoso clarinetist. Louis Douglas, who had resided in London since 1915, became the troupe's choreographer. Maude de Forest, a blues singer from the vaudeville circuit, was selected to play the lead in the show but was too ill to perform on opening night. Baker therefore became the star of that evening. Although several other black vaudeville troupes had already toured Europe, La Revue nègre was an unconditional smash hit during its three-month run at the Théâtre des Champs-Élysées.

The Paris that Baker encountered had already experienced an influx of black performers following World War I, most notably James Reese Europe and his 369th Infantry, the Harlem Hellfighters squadron, credited with introducing key elements of ragtime and jazz to Paris. The city was infused with black culture in the form of African art, jazz music, and boxing, all of which became exotic sources of inspiration for the literati and artists of the day. Primitivism existed as a discourse at the moment when one culture encountered another. Although the black population of France was negligible during the 1920s, images of the African colonies had permeated Paris through the Universal Expositions, the artistic forays of cubism, a new anthropology, and works such as Blaise Cendrar's 1921 *Anthologie nègre* and the Guyanese author René Maran's 1921 Prix Goncourt winner *Batoula*, about his impressions of life in Central Africa.

Along with Hottentots and other "specimens" of African cultures, the Universal Exposition of 1900 in Paris featured two black American vaudeville performers, Bert Williams and George Walker, who performed in blackface and first demonstrated the popular cakewalk to an enthralled French audience.[18] Williams and Walker foreshadowed what was to come: the adaptation of minstrelsy to the French music hall and, by extension, to the world of jazz. Montmartre and Pigalle in the ninth arrondissement became the new homes and cultural centers for the early black American entertainers and performers. Initially, Baker and members of La Revue nègre were integrated into this vibrant culture. While Baker performed with the revue at the Théâtre de Champs-Elysées in the third arrondissement, black musicians met after hours at the Grand Duc, a cabaret run by the African American entrepreneur Eugene Bullard at the corner of rue Pigalle and rue Fontaine. Ada Smith, a young black woman who was called Bricktop, was the lead singer at the Grand Duc and became one of Josephine's closest friends during her early years in Paris.[19]

Opening night of *La Revue nègre* introduced Baker's newly fabricated exoticism to France against the backdrop of sketchy surrealist scenery by the Mexican painter and set designer Miguel Covarrubias and the artist Paul Colin. André Daven, an impresario and theater producer, had added to the show an "African" dance choreographed by Jacques-Charles that was meant to intrigue the French audience. This performance shaped the indelible image of the savage dancer that launched Josephine's Parisian career. Daven described the opening night: "As she danced, quivering with intensity, the entire room felt the raw force of her passion, the excitement of her rhythm. She was eroticism personified. The simplicity of her emotions, her savage grace, were deeply moving. She laughed, she cried, then from her supple throat came a song, crystal clear at first, then with a hoarseness that caught at the heart."[20] Recalling this night, Baker described herself as consumed in a trance-like state of ecstatic improvisation.[21] She thus abdicated conscious responsibility for the creation of her racialized image and would later manipulate that image to her advantage and profit.

By all accounts, Josephine participated fully in the new racial, sexual, and personal freedom that Paris offered.[22] Within two years of her arrival in France, she was an established music-hall star, moving freely in the after-hours circles of the French glitterati, international artists, socialites, and politicians of the day. In 1926, she met Giuseppe (Pepito) Abatino. The Sicilian-born Abatino held a clerical job at the Ministry of Finance in Rome and commuted frequently to Paris for upscale social events. He encountered Baker during one of his trips, and by the end of 1926, they had become personal and business partners. As her social network broadened through Pepito's contacts and her own flourishing career, Josephine added an accent aigü to her name and began to withdraw from the confines of black Paris. According to Tyler Stovall, within only three years after her arrival in France, Josephine had distanced herself from the emerging black community of Paris.[23] Stovall asserts that once Josephine moved from her own club, Chez Joséphine, on rue Fontaine in Montmartre in 1928 to a new club on rue François 1er in a "luxurious" neighborhood "light years removed" from her original habitat, she also distanced herself from many of the black performers and artists in Paris, although Josephine denies this in her autobiographies.[24]

Much transpired, however, before Josephine Baker abandoned her close ties to black Paris. Her activities were deeply rooted in cultural ambivalence and the re-envisioning of racial identity. Her life poses the questions of how and whether the émigré artist or intellectual is different from any other immigrant. There is a broad consensus among Baker biographers and scholars that changes in Baker's persona and an increase in her artistic autonomy may be traced to 1934–35 when she appeared in the opera *La Créole* and completed her second film, *Zouzou*. Nevertheless, descriptions of her 1928–29 world tour suggest that crucial personal changes began then and became more evident to the public during the course of the 1930s. From 1930 to 1932, Baker performed in extravagant shows at the Casino de Paris. Her performances coincided with the 1931 Universal Colonial Exposition and fed into the quest for exoticism undertaken by the exposition's organizers and French anthropologists.

At the Casino de Paris, Josephine performed "La Petite Tonkinoise," a song written by Vincent Scotto, Pepito's brother. In this musical tableau, she played the Vietnamese consort of a French colonist in Tonkin, and it is out of this experience that the idea for her signature song, "J'ai deux amours," developed. Scotto wrote "Deux amours" with Henri Varna and Géo Koger for the 1930 Casino de Paris presentation of *Paris qui remue* and the song was produced as a record by Columbia in October of that year. While the original 1925 performances of La Revue nègre were never recorded, "J'ai deux amours" sold over 300,000 copies.[25]

Although the song was purportedly about Josephine's two loves—her natal country and Paris—it was initially inspired by a reference in "La Petite Tonkinoise" to Vietnam and France under colonialism. Interestingly, as early as the mid-1930s, Josephine began to change the concluding refrain of the song from "J'ai deux amours, mon pays et Paris" to "mon pays c'est Paris" (my country is Paris). Although Phyllis Rose argues that Baker made this change toward the end of her life, Baker actually began to sing this variation only two years after the record was released.[26] This tune, which itself illustrates Baker's biculturalism and ambivalence, also forecasts her resolution of this ambivalence in its modified refrain.

While at the Casino de Paris, Baker performed in *La Joie de Paris*, opening in December 1932. She sang a signature tune entitled "Si j'étais blanche!" (If I Were White!), which had been recorded one month earlier with her own orchestra. In this number, Baker wore a blonde wig, and she had lightened her skin with milk and lemon juice (fig. 18). The song opens with the line "I would like to be white. How happy I would be!" Some music-hall critics and socialites, such as Nancy Cunard, were shocked and revolted by this ironic white-face performance, which they considered a parody that destroyed Josephine's authenticity as a primal performer. In fact, the blonde wig represents a break with what Erving Goffman has termed the "expressive coherence" of a performance because it challenged Josephine's primal exotic persona.[27] It pointed to the colonial subject's denial of difference and to a double consciousness. This performance also made an ironic visual swipe at Josephine's Belgian-born music-hall rival, Mistinguett, who had opposed Josephine's headlining role at the Casino on the grounds that she was incompetent and inexperienced. The Baker biographers Haney, Hammond, and O'Connor consider the song to be a controversial challenge to Baker's primitivist image, while Borshuk interprets it as a reference to the 1920s fad of suntanning for beauty and health among Europeans, with ironic references to the transcoding of racial images.[28]

The lyrics of the "Si j'étais blanche!" recorded by Columbia in 1932, are accompanied by my translation:

Si j'étais blanche!
Moi si j'étais blanche
Sachez qu'mon bonheur
Qui près de vous s'épanche
Gardr' ait sa couleur
Au soleil, c'est par l'extérieur
Que l'on se dore
Moi c'est la flamme de mon coeur
Qui me colore

If I Were White!
Me, if I were white,
Know that my happiness
Which explodes near you,
Would guard its color
Under the sun, it's by one's exterior
That one tans
But for me, it's the flame of my heart
By which I am colored.][29]

In a filmed interview following *La Joie de Paris* (Joy of Paris), Baker tried on a series of hats and hairpieces, including the famous blonde wig, and pronounced, "To be beautiful, you must take plenty of fresh air and light, but not too much sunshine. . . . I use milk as well, as a lotion, it keeps me lighter."[30] During the early years, Baker was ambivalent about her skin color and publicly promoted the natural skin-lightening formulas and body creams that she used to enhance her appeal, although French audiences wanted to see a darker and more "primal" look, marketed by Pepito as "Bakerskin." Some of the photographs from this period also show Josephine's nose as thinner, probably doctored by makeup and photographic retouching. Although Baker may not be a genuine precursor of chameleon performers such as Michael Jackson and Madonna, there are undoubtedly parallels in the processes of performative image invention and racialized gender transcoding. Three of the film roles in which Baker played—*La Sirène des tropiques, Zouzou,* and *Princesse Tam-Tam*—between 1927 and 1935, present her, respectively, as Antillian (Martinican and Haitian), Tunisian, and mixed black. In press clippings, she is occasionally referred to as Spanish.[31] She never appears as either a sub-Saharan African or an African American in any filmic representations. Instead, she is an ambiguous exotic "other" who interweaves nuances of pri-

Figure 18. Josephine
Baker in a blonde
wig in the December
1932 production of
La Joie de Paris at
the Casino de Paris.
Photo courtesy of
Bryan Hammond
Collection.

mal native earthiness with European sophistication. This racial transcoding
precisely marks the moment of Josephine's reflection upon herself in terms
of her mirror image as a blonde.

Describing the sense of "crushing objecthood" that results from the racialized gaze, the Martinican psychiatrist Frantz Fanon writes, "The attitudes, the
glances of the other fixed me there, in a sense in which a chemical solution
is fixed by a dye. I was indignant; I demanded an explanation. Nothing happened. I burst apart. Now the fragments have been put together by another

self."[32] This process of fragmentation and reconstruction of identity is a commonplace experience for marginalized minorities. In the case of Josephine Baker, however, this experience is refracted by the prism of performance and the reconstruction of identity and appearance (body, skin tone, and hair) under the public gaze. The theatrical persona wraps around the private person and projects a new identity onto a public stage. The stereotype of the exotic banana dancer as animal-like contrasts with the all-too-human sophistication of a worldly Princesse Tam-Tam in Paris. Sidestepping Fanon's modernist imprisonment by colonialist categories of race through her performances, Baker transformed race into a series of costume changes that foreshadowed the desire to be postmodern.

Cross-Dressing and Nudity

During Josephine's heyday, cross-dressing was the flip side of titillating nudity. The writer and artist Colette, Josephine's close friend, was among the first to appear seminude in the music hall and was also a champion of cross-dressing. Coco Chanel later adopted cross-dressing as an influence on high-fashion style. Both cross-dressing and nudity challenged conventional restrictions on the autonomy and comportment of women in bourgeois society. Removing clothing and dressing as a male were sources of feminine empowerment that carried a shock value. In an apparent contradiction, nudity was also a mask that Baker donned as part of her primal image. By 1930, however, Baker had already begun to move away from this image. In the 1932 production of La Joie de Paris, Josephine appeared as a bandleader dressed in a tuxedo and top hat (fig. 19). In publicity displays, she frequently used photographs of herself in this sophisticated role, which, on the surface, contrasts starkly with the image of her as a banana-clad savage. In her final performance at the Théâtre Bobino in Paris, in 1975, the sixty-eight-year-old Baker, wearing a white beaded motorcycle outfit, complete with cap and gloves, roared onto the stage astride an old-fashioned Harley for her number on New York and Chicago. This gender-bending imagery influenced Baker's musical and stage personas throughout her life. Her practice of cross-dressing was continued by the female impersonators to whom she gave her clothes during the 1970s.

Shari Benstock argues that cross-dressing, such as that of Colette during the 1920s, was essentially experimental and intended for its shock value rather than signifying the presence of a bisexual subculture.[33] Others disagree. Jean-Claude Baker, Josephine's biographer and protégé, describes the

JOSÉPHINE BAKER

Figure 19. Josephine Baker in cross-dress as a bandleader in the December 1932 production of *La Joie de Paris* at the Casino de Paris. Photo by Studio Piaz, courtesy of Anna Ulrich Collection, Fotofolio, New York.

banana dance as a phallic display. "Only Josephine," he argues, "would dare to strategically fashion herself as a substitute phallus."[34] In this remark, which appeared almost casually in a photographic caption, Jean-Claude Baker and Chris Chase, his coauthor, have touched upon the link between cross-dressing and nudity in gender politics and the reconstruction of self.

As described by Fanon, nudity bursts the self apart by baring the external persona down to its essentials, while cross-dressing pulls the fragments together again by constituting an alternatively empowered self. As is typical with Josephine, empowerment entails adopting the accoutrements of "the other"—blonde wigs, lighter skin, and masculine clothing. Both the tradition of minstrelsy and the conventions of cross-dressing reinforce cultural stereotypes and then blur the boundaries by traversing them through performance. As a means of breaking through conventional barriers, nudity in stage performance is also a source of empowerment. Josephine further complicates the matter by her pan-sexuality and private love of nudity as a youth. When

Baker lived in Beau-Chêne, she was not above using her nude swimming as a strategy to surprise and disarm stuffy journalists and intrusive tourists. In her gender politics, Josephine vacillated between extremes in establishing an identity discourse of destabilization and female empowerment. These strategies are evident in both her alternating styles of dress and her moralistic yet seductive music (fig. 20).[35]

The 1991 Home Box Office production *The Josephine Baker Story* provides a window for viewing the popular reconfiguration of gender issues beyond questions of dress and fashion. In the television special, Josephine is depicted as obstinate, undisciplined, extravagant, and emotionally unstable. Tears and hysterical tantrums are her most common responses to difficult situations. She cries as a child after the St. Louis race riots and as an adult after being rebuffed for racial reasons during her two unsuccessful return visits to the United States. Even her coming of age as a woman is depicted as a reactive outburst triggered by the artist Paul Colin. Playing Baker, Lynne Whitfield asserts after one of their artistic sessions, "His eyes approved of me. To him, I wasn't just a woman or a colored woman. I was all women."

The film does not consider Baker as a rational, autonomous subject whose life choices were part of a conscious performative project rather than a complex of passive and negative reactions. Yet, Baker learned to drive a car and fly a plane, at a time when many women did not. She handled complicated financial transactions in a foreign language and culture, running the affairs of Les Milandes and remortgaging the property on her own, even while Bouillon was still present. While the film depicts Baker as childlike, irrational, and a stereotypical "shrew," Bouillon describes her in their joint biography as an intelligent, informed, and energetic decision-maker. He summarizes her daily routine on a trip to New York: "At bedtime she said her prayers, her head in her hands, but Josephine actually slept very little. She would soon be out of bed, preparing her lectures, checking through notes, writing letters, reading (she read constantly). Her speaking engagements invariably seemed to take her to the far ends of the city and since she made a point of answering all her audience's questions, it was usually a mad dash to the theater."[36]

Traversing Real and Imaginary Borders

As with race and gender, Baker pushed the limits of virtuality, and therefore of identity discourse, by situating nationality in a performative space. During her years with Abatino in the late 1920s and early 30s, Baker's French linguistic

Figure 20. Baker's imitation of Pavlova frames her in a hyper-feminine mode. Photo by Studio Piaz, 1932, courtesy of Bryan Hammond Collection.

skills had improved, and her attachment to France increased. In 1937, Baker married a Jewish French industrialist, Jean Lion, and became a French citizen. This marriage, which ended in 1942, is often glossed over in American biographies and films of Baker. Throughout World War II, she worked as a courier and counterespionage agent for the French underground, using her home at Les Milandes as an operating base before her transfer to Morocco. Although Les Milandes was ransacked during the war, Baker continued to hold a lease on the property and was able to regain and purchase it after the war.

Josephine had just returned from a tour in Argentina when war was declared in France on September 3, 1939. During the last two seasons before her tour of Argentina, Baker had participated in a series of revues organized by Colette and later in a music-hall series with Maurice Chevalier. While France was occupied, Josephine was barred from the stage and left for the south of France with her close friend and Resistance accomplice, Jacques Abtey, an undercover agent.[37] Under suspicion because of her fame and the failure of her marriage to Lion (during which she had studied for conversion to Judaism), Josephine was a triple threat.[38] She and Abtey worked tirelessly for de Gaulle's exiled government as part of the intelligence wing of the French secret service, both in France and North Africa. When Baker performed for the U.S. soldiers' Liberty Club in Casablanca in 1943 and followed the Allied Forces across North Africa in a campaign to integrate the U.S. Army, her commitment to France was positive and her relationship to the United States was supportive, although critical. She returned to Les Milandes in 1944 and received the Medal of Resistance with the grade of officer in 1946.

In 1951, Josephine toured the United States with Jo Bouillon, whom she had married in 1947. During her tour, Josephine insisted that all audiences for her shows be integrated. Threatening lawsuits against recalcitrant theaters and cabarets, she was initially successful with her integration campaign. Josephine miraculously revived several old theaters on the vaudeville circuit. The tour hit a roadblock on October 16, 1951, with the now famous Stork Club incident, in which Baker was refused service at the club and then called upon the conservative journalist Walter Winchell, another club patron, as a public witness of discrimination. (This key incident and its fallout is discussed further in chapter 7.) Winchell retorted with a blistering media attack, accusing Baker of being anti-American and a Communist sympathizer and sending the information to J. Edgar Hoover and the Federal Bureau of Investigation (FBI). This attack triggered FBI surveillance of Baker's activities over a seventeen-year period.

Baker escalated her criticisms of the United States. In 1952, she went on a goodwill tour of Argentina in blind support of Juan Péron, with whom she later became disillusioned. Although Baker returned briefly to the United States for performances in 1960 and the early 1970s, participated in the March on Washington in 1963, and wrote letters of support to Martin Luther King, she never again attempted to settle in the United States.

In 1961, Baker was named Chevalier de la Légion d'Honneur by the French government. She marched down the Champs-Elysées with President de Gaulle in May 1968. Flaunting a peace sign in counterprotest against student and worker activists, she left behind the costumes and postures of her militant past. She had become "more French than the French," a stalwart supporter of the postwar status quo. But Baker's trajectory in performing politics was much more complex than her patriotic images suggest. Her national histories and political education are replete with contradictions and ambivalent turns. At once a nationalist and a transnational citizen of the world, a follower of the political left and the right, a Protestant, a student of both Judaism and Islam, and a devout, although atypical, Catholic, she manipulated nationality as she did race, gender, religion, and social class.

Icon and Image

Josephine Baker combined the folkloric narrative of her rise to fame with powerful images of exoticism and freedom in a modern, mechanistic society. The virtual identity discourses that she engendered are part of a conscious and repeated process of identity reconstruction. Through parody and innuendo, she molded stereotypical roles that she was commissioned to play into a form of social criticism. Baker's life is a microcosm and a laboratory test case for the study of assimilation, acculturation, and identity invention. As a celebrity, Baker intensified and focused these processes by performing her identity transformations in public spaces. Her stage, filmic, and social personas are unified in the icon. Often overlooked, however, is her clever use of the performative strategies of assimilation and image construction to surmount cultural barriers. There are photographs and public records of each identity change and of the mass of contradictions and symbolic strategies that coalesced to create the image and the icon of Josephine Baker.[39] Her mediated identity and simulated reality are models for the "fifteen minutes of fame" sought by many popular cultural legends and ordinary people.

3 Celluloid Projections

Our taverns and our metropolitan streets, our offices and our furnished rooms, our railroad stations, and our factories appeared to have us locked up hopelessly. Then came the film and burst this prison world asunder by the dynamite of a tenth of a second, so that now, in the midst of its far-flung ruins and debris, we calmly and adventurously go traveling.

—Walter Benjamin, 1972

In October 1927, a large crowd assembled at the Théâtre Mogador in Paris.[1] "Lights, camera, action!" exclaimed Henri Etiévant as he took his place on stage with his codirector, Mario Nalpas. As the loud and creaky cameras roared, Etiévant instructed the crowd to applaud. Jacques Natanson, the artistic director, checked the set. Not satisfied with the first round of applause, Etiévant signaled the audience to start up again. Then, with characteristic panache, Josephine Baker burst onto the stage. She performed her savage dance and the crowd went wild. When she finished, they needed no encouragement to continue with the applause, throwing flowers onto the stage. Etiévant sighed with relief. He had just pushed silent film technology to the limit when he shot the most complex crowd scene of *La Sirène des tropiques*, Josephine Baker's first feature film.[2]

Maurice Dekobra, who published the novel *La Madone des sleepings*, which was adapted as a feature film released by Paramount France in 1928, was known for his romantic and melodramatic narratives.[3] Dekobra had written the scenario for *La Sirène des tropiques* in French, and it was too complicated for Josephine to read at that time. She claimed that no one bothered to translate the script into English for her.[4] Using all of the skills she had learned in the music hall, she mimed and improvised her way through each scene with melodramatic grimaces and comic routines that matched the filmmaker's sense of hyperbole. To be melodramatic in silent film was a positive attribute, for it was through exaggeration that emotions could be conveyed visually. Etiévant was pleased with the results, and Josephine received rave notices from many quarters when the film finally opened to a real (as opposed to a staged) audience in Paris on December 30, 1927.

From Music Hall to Movie Palace

The *cinématographe* invented in 1895 by Louis Lumière and his colleague Jules Carpentier, an engineer, was destined to transform French popular culture.[5] First used by Lumière to record everyday activities—workers leaving their factories, activity at railroad stations, street scenes, and children at play—cinema provided snippets that were integrated into the dioramas of the wax museums and rapidly surpassed the old exhibits in popularity. The Universal Colonial Exposition of 1900 in Paris included a *cinéorama* in which the audience experienced a simulated hot-air balloon ride around the world.[6] As a vehicle for fantastic voyages, film was also used to record specimens of France's colonies and to transform aspects of familiar everyday life into exotic adventures.[7]

At the turn of the century, short films were screened at music halls, concert cafés, and fairgrounds. The owners of the Olympia Theater in Paris were so besieged by moviegoers that they even entered the film distribution business, strengthening the ties between cabaret culture and new forms of entertainment. The popularity of the medium grew as the technology improved, and film audiences required larger spaces for regular screenings. In 1911, the Gaumont-Palace opened in Paris, with 3,400 seats for movie spectators.[8] Paris had become the movie capital of the world long before Hollywood assumed that role. The appearance of increasingly elaborate and entertaining narrative films made it possible for the new movie theaters to stay open most of the day with continuous screenings. Although World War I represented a hiatus in the volume production, by the 1920s the French film industry was firmly established, and cinema overshadowed the wax museum, the cabaret, and the music hall as a popular entertainment form.

Between 1927 and 1940, Josephine Baker appeared in a series of short film clips released by the Folies-Bergère (1927–28) and in four feature films: *La Sirène des tropiques* (1927), *Zouzou* (1934), *Princesse Tam-Tam* (1935), and *Fausse alerte* (1940, called *The French Way* in its English-language release) (see table). Pepito Abatino worked on the scenario and served as the artistic director for two of these films, *Zouzou* and *Princesse Tam-Tam*. He also masterminded Baker's film career, developing new versions of the iterative Cinderella and Pygmalion narratives that Josephine would deploy throughout her life. Music-hall sequences were incorporated into each film to show off Josephine's talents. She played character roles that only thinly disguised her theatrical persona and her real life. Abatino carefully crafted the narratives to appeal to what he perceived as French tastes, making sure that the exotic heroine would return to the empire of nature, retain the ties to her primal trappings, and exhibit self-sacrifice amid the glamour. The connection of cinema to the representation of colonial exotica was perfect for Baker, who portrayed seductive natives caught up in civilizing dramas with romantic twists. These narratives depicted a noble savage exposed to, but not corrupted by, civilization. Abatino was quick to capitalize on the dramatic and entrepreneurial possibilities of cinema for the advancement of Baker's career. He mounted expensive publicity campaigns to promote Baker's film image. Although their first attempt to use the medium in 1927, with *La Sirène des tropiques,* appears fragmentary and crude today, the film was popular, and Baker was praised in the press as a natural actress.[9] The continued popularity of Baker's films *La Sirène des tropiques, Zouzou,* and *Princesse Tam-Tam* is evidenced by the fact that Kino International, a film distribution company, reissued them on video to an eager audience in 1989 and upgraded them in digital format in 2005.

The growing links between the French and Italian film industries, represented by Cinéromans and Arys Nissotti Productions, respectively, allowed Abatino to draw on a familiar network of associates to promote Baker's career in the late 1920s. He moved from being a pushy bystander during the production of *Sirène des tropiques* to taking on the roles of producer, screenplay writer, and artistic director for *Zouzou* and *Princesse Tam-Tam*. Film allowed

Films of Josephine Baker, Their Narratives and Primary Images, 1927–40

Film	Filmmakers & Producers	Narrative	Images & Characters	Baker's Cultural Identification
La Sirène des tropiques (1927) Limited European distribution; remastered by Kino Int'l, 2005	Henri Etiévant, Mario Nalpas, and Luis Buñuel; Centrale Cinémato-graphique	Cinderella and sacrifice	Primal and glamour Baker's character: Papitou	Antillian
Le Pompier des Folies-Bergère (1928) Limited distribution in France; remastered by Kino Int'l, 2005	Les Folies-Bergère	Erotic escape	Working-class and music-hall street person and performer Baker's character: unnamed	Parisian
Zouzou (1934) International distribution; revived 1989; remastered by Kino Int'l, 2005	Marc Allégret; artistic direction, Pepito Abatino; produced by Arys Nisotti Productions	Cinderella and sacrifice	Working-class and glamour Baker's character: Zouzou	Mixed Antillian
Princesse Tam-Tam (1935) International distribution; revived 1989; remastered by Kino Int'l, 2005	Edmond T. Gréville; artistic direction, Pepito Abatino produced by Arys Nisotti Productions	Pygmalion and return to nature	Primal and glamour Baker's character: Aouina	North African, Indian
Fausse Alerte (1940) Distributed as *The French Way* by Manor Films, 1952	Jacques de Baroncelli; produced by Flag Films	Cinderella and sacrifice	Working-class and glamour Baker's character: Zazu Clairon	Antillian

Baker to combine song, dance, and drama in a modern medium. Nevertheless, Baker's film career was short-lived (1927–40) and did not garner the international recognition of her live stage performances and musical recordings. Her relative lack of success in film resulted in part from the diluted impact of her iterative narrative when translated into that medium and from the restricted cultural scope of the stereotypical exotic and racialized roles that she was compelled to play. In addition, her films were in competition with Hollywood film extravaganzas. In his discussion of black film as genre, the film historian Thomas Cripps describes Baker's work in cinema as "a string of exotic primitive roles" that were not thoughtfully chosen.[10] Baker's film roles, however, may be analyzed more productively in the context of the archetypal images and narratives that she developed as a performer and successfully promoted in France with Abatino and Arys Nissotti Productions. These film roles skew the interpretation of Baker toward the mythic story (Pygmalion/Galatea) and the colonized image (primitive/tamed). Baker is presented as a helpless female shaped by male desires and civilized by colonial means. She often balked at these stereotypical roles but performed them with her own creative flair.

Silent Cinderella

La Sirène des tropiques (1927), written by Maurice Dekobra, was directed by Henri Etiévant and Mario Nalpas, with the acclaimed Spanish filmmaker Luis Buñuel working for a short time as the assistant director. Only fragments of the 2,060-meter original film survive, in relatively poor condition, but the story is complete. In its 2005 remaster of *Sirène des tropiques,* Kino International restored some of the damaged footage and highlighted the use of blue and sepia tones for a contemporary audience.

Josephine plays Papitou (fig. 21), a young Antillian Creole who becomes the love interest of André Berval, a French engineer played by Pierre Batcheff, a well-known silent film actor and a handsome romantic lead.[11] In the story, Berval had been dispatched to the Antilles by the scheming Marquis de Severo (George Melchior) in order to separate him from his fiancée, Denise (Régina Thomas). Denise is not only Severo's godchild but also his love interest, in spite of the watchfulness of his wife, the Marquise de Severo (Régina Dalton). The marquis hires an unscrupulous local named Alvarez (Kiranine), who works as a corrupt colonial lackey, to dispose of Berval. Alvarez does so by staging a series of accidents and setting traps for Berval, who falls from a faulty

Figure 21. Josephine Baker
as Papitou, 1927. Photo
courtesy of Bryan Hammond
Collection.

rope ladder. Papitou meets Berval after the fall and rescues him. This act elicits Berval's deep gratitude and Papitou's unswerving devotion. In turn, Berval rescues Papitou from Alvarez's lechery. With Papitou's help, Berval unmasks Alvarez's treachery through a series of misadventures. Meanwhile, Denise and the Marquise de Severo, who have been concerned about Berval's welfare, arrive on the island and persuade him to return to Paris with them.

Crushed and dejected, Papitou can no longer live without Berval and, leaving her alcoholic French father and her dog behind, stows away on a ship to France. On board, she is chased by crew members and shocks society matrons by falling into a coal bin, turning black, and then into a flour bin, turning white. These slapstick scenes give Baker a chance to use her old vaudeville sketches of clowning and of doubling race. The shipboard segment includes an erotic mirrored bathing scene in the captain's chambers in which Josephine returns to her sepia tone.

Once in Paris, Papitou manages to obtain a job in a music hall where she performs uninhibited savage dances for a high-society audience, which features Pepito Abatino as her manager. With Pepito's help, she tracks down Berval at a party and once again attempts to save his life by taking his side in a duel provoked by Severo. She climbs a tree and shoots Severo, who falls to the ground. Berval feels compromised by this incident and argues with Papitou, who realizes that she must relinquish him. At this point, Denise gives Berval's prayer book to Papitou in thanks. Inside the book, the moral of the story is inscribed: "Sacrifice is the purest form of joy on earth." The film concludes with Papitou's act of self-sacrifice for unrequited love. In many respects, Dekobra's script resembles the scenario of *Mon sang dans tes veines* that would be composed by Josephine, Pepito, and Félix de la Camara four years later.

Sirène contains a Cinderella story crosscut by the wild dancer image of Papitou, who also ultimately becomes a "noble savage." The story reflects one version of Baker's iterative master narrative. Papitou arrives in Paris from exotic and humble origins and is transformed by her success in the music hall. Nonetheless, with all of her newfound sophistication, Papitou cannot control her passions and primal instincts. Berval and Denise push her to repent, renounce her emotions, and accept self-control and sacrifice as a sign of civilization.

Biographers' accounts suggest that Baker did not like the film's contrived ending and did not enjoy working on the project because of problems with scheduling, lighting, makeup, costumes, and dangerous stunts.[12] Nevertheless, *Sirène* provided Baker with media exposure and launched her film career. It also contributed to the elaboration of her nested escape-success narratives and the crystallization of her savage dancer and glamorous images. These two images conflict with each other in the film. A resolution is achieved through devoted self-sacrifice and the renunciation of love. In a classical sense, this moralized narrative might be considered to be Josephine Baker's "passion play" as a silent Cinderella.

Baker made another film in 1927, *Le Pompier des Folies-Bergère,* a short film based on her performance entitled *Un Vent des folies* at the Folies-Bergère. This film, which has been preserved in video format at the Bibliothèque Nationale in Paris and digitally upgraded by Kino International, documents the erotic fantasies of a fireman, with Josephine Baker appearing scantily dressed as an unnamed, seductive showgirl in two scenes. Although this film would be considered softcore pornography today, it is difficult to determine the extent of its distribution and the responses of its audience when it was released in 1928. The publicity for the repentant Papitou in *Sirène* far outweighed the provocative imagery of this seductive detour into erotica, which contemporary audiences still find amusing.

Carnivalesque Images in *Zouzou*

After the return from her 1928–29 world tour, Josephine and Pepito began to work relentlessly. Pepito pushed her to polish her talents in dance with tutoring in ballet from George Balanchine. She also worked on her French-speaking skills and vocal abilities while preparing the comic opera *La Créole* by Jacques Offenbach, adapted by Albert Willemetz. With Josephine's collaboration, Pepito wrote novels and screenplays. *Zouzou* is a poignant musical comedy written by Pepito and adapted for the screen by Carlo Rim. It contains the iterative Cinderella narrative with a new twist on issues of race, class, nationality, and exoticism. The protagonists, Zouzou and Jean, are adopted orphans, one black and one white, who spend their youth playing freaks of nature—interracial fraternal twins in the sideshow of the Cirque Romarin. When they grow up, they remain close, and the black Zouzou's passion for her white adopted brother evolves into an impossible triangle of unrequited love played out against the backdrop of the Parisian music hall.

To promote the film, Pepito launched an ambitious and very clever publicity campaign with the support of the producer Arys Nissotti. Dresses based on Zouzou's costumes were marketed to create the "Zouzou look" (figs. 22, 23). Pepito also made labels for bananas imprinted with the message "Josephine Baker is Zouzou."[13] He encouraged shopkeepers throughout Paris to display these bananas, and he also developed an internationally distributed Zouzou newsletter containing advice on love, fashion, and daily life.

Part of the film's appeal is the connection established to the French working class. Zouzou becomes a laundress for the French music hall, and it is from this position that she is able to learn the music-hall routines and, through luck, secure a leading role. This Cinderella narrative involves a figure unlike the purely primal Baker image and is based on an earthy plot with characters that are more credible and complex than those in *Sirène*. The film, however,

Figure 22. Publicity
for Josephine Baker's
1934 film *Zouzou*.
Photo courtesy of
Bryan Hammond
Collection.

is not without its melodramatic moments and stereotypical characters. The
ubiquitous Baker performs a music-hall number, "Haïti," scantily dressed as
a caged bird.

Baker claimed to have enjoyed Zouzou more than any of her other film
roles. In a 1934 article in the newspaper *Le Jour*, she said, "In *Zouzou*, they
give me a real opportunity [*une chance*]. My role has some comic passages,
and some sentimental ones. I'm able to show that I can play both kinds of
parts. In addition, I show that I can still dance in revue tableaux that have
a rather sensational character." The positive press response to *Zouzou* provoked Baker to remark, "Who could ask for more?"[14] A breadth of dramatic
possibilities makes *Zouzou*, now a cult classic, arguably Baker's best personal
and professional achievement in film.

Marc Allégret, *Zouzou*'s director, crafted the film to stand apart from the burgeoning Hollywood musical extravaganzas of the 1930s by using the musical sequences as filmic signs. He stated that he did not want to make a musical "à l'Américaine."[15] Although Parisian press reviews did not reach a large international audience, they hailed Allégret's masterful direction of the film at the Pathé-Nathan Studios in Joinville and praised the performances by Baker and the rising new French stars Jean Gabin (Jean Marchand), Pierre Larquey (Papa Mélé), and Madeleine Guitty (Josette, the chamber maid). The film editing was smooth, and the overall package was appealing. Pepito's publicity campaign became a resounding success.[16] *Zouzou* opened to a packed house at the Moulin Rouge movie theater in Paris on December 14, 1934.

The film begins with a sideshow scene of the Cirque Romarin with Papa Mélé (Father Mixture). I have used poetic license in this translation of the name, since "to mix" in French is *mêler,* but a "mixture" is a *mélange.* Papa Mélé is a circus barker who introduces the anomalous twins (*les phénomènes*) to a curious and incredulous audience. A band of young boys peeks into the sideshow trailer to glimpse Zouzou looking in the mirror. "Elle a une drôle de tête" (she's really funny looking), one of them exclaims. After an off-camera scuffle with Jean, the boys join the rest of the audience and listen to Papa Mélé's spiel. In the extracts below, I have translated the dialogue from the film, and I have added a brief description of the action that appears on screen.[17]

> PAPA MÉLÉ: Come in, ladies and gentlemen, come in! We're starting in just a few minutes. Children and soldiers can have half-price tickets. Come in if you want to see these extraordinary children. We'll begin in five minutes. You'll see Mademoiselle Zouzou and Monsieur Jean, who I'm honored to present to you immediately. Immediately, that is right away. [*Papa Mélé looks around flustered.*] Eh bien, where are they?
>
> CIRCUS CLOWN: I don't know, sir.
>
> PAPA MÉLÉ: [*To the clown*] Go and find them right away. [*To the audience*] Don't be impatient, ladies and gentlemen. The phenomena [sideshow freaks] have a right to arrive late from time to time. Heh, heh, heh, they're not like us. You mustn't try to understand them. These mysteries aren't meant to be understood.
>
> [*The children arrive.*]
>
> Ladies and gentlemen, I present to you a true miracle of nature. The two twins, the twins Mademoiselle Zouzou, who is here with Monsieur Jean. [*Shot of the twins and pan to the crowd.*] The most eminent scientists have

lost their Latin. These twins came into the world ten years ago on an island in the Polynesian archipelago. Their parents were a Chinese woman and an Indian, who didn't want to accept them because they did not have the same color as them. Ladies and gentlemen—a little bow, children. Voilà! . . .

Now ladies and gentlemen, you will see our own ballet corps, who the most famous Argentinian impresarios tried to steal from us by offering top prices. Let the music begin! [*Song "Les Cigognes" (The Storks) follows.*]

This fabrication sets in motion a nested narrative of fictitious parentage, racial hybridity, and curiosity. Interracial mixing is viewed as freakish, and the result is an outlandish carnivalesque curiosity. The tune "Les Cigognes" highlights the narrative by describing how the storks mistakenly delivered two siblings of different colors. While the chorus sings "Les Cigognes," Zouzou escapes to a dressing room in the circus tent, where she puts on the white powder of the trapeze artist in front of a large mirror. This sequence is one of many mirror scenes in *Zouzou* where Baker's skin tone becomes an important signifier.[18] The scene also echoes the flour bin segment in *Sirène* and Baker's famous song from *La Joie de Paris*, "Si j'étais blanche!" The circus performer scolds young Zouzou and chases her from the tent. The camera then cuts to the trailer where Papa Mélé, Zouzou, and Jean live.

Shot in shadowy lighting within the trailer's cramped quarters, the next scene concerns the children's paternity with a dialogue that advances the nested narratives of the film and parallels the metanarrative of Baker's life. The stork, later transmogrified into bird imagery, recurs as a filmic sign of cross-racial paternity in this scene as Zouzou and Jean question Papa Mélé about their parentage. The scene opens as Papa Mélé enters the room to put the children to bed.

PAPA MÉLÉ: What's wrong with you two? You're not yet in bed.
JEAN: Papa Mélé, Zouzou doesn't want to believe that we're twins.
PAPA MÉLÉ: Heh, heh, . . .
ZOUZOU: Did the same stork bring both of us?
PAPA MÉLÉ: But, of course, the same stork. Yes, only the big clumsy fellow let you fall into a sooty chimney. Heh, heh, heh . . .

Figure 23. Josephine Baker and Jean Gabin in a publicity pose for *Zouzou*. Photo courtesy of AKG-Images, London.

ZOUZOU: Why didn't the stork make two trips?

JEAN: Are you really our father, huh?

PAPA MÉLÉ: Well, certainly I'm your papa.

JEAN: But then, Zouzou's father, is he the same as my father?

PAPA MÉLÉ: Well, your father, that's not the same thing. You see, my little ones, a father is a papa one has never known.

JEAN: Then, can you have *two* fathers?

PAPA MÉLÉ: Ah, two fathers . . . ?

JEAN: What did my father say to you when he died?

PAPA MÉLÉ: I've told you that a hundred times, yes.

JEAN: Oooh . . . What did he say?

PAPA MÉLÉ: He said I can be only his father, but you, you will be his papa.

ZOUZOU: And mine, . . . what did he say to you?

PAPA MÉLÉ: Yours said the same thing, only with his eyes, because the poor thing, he couldn't speak anymore. He could speak only with his eyes. When he rolled his eyes like that, he made the whole circus laugh. I can see him now with his red suit, his silk pants, and his lady's stockings. He was so famous that he always came at the end of the show, even after the equestrian number.

JEAN: And mine too, he came at the end?

PAPA MÉLÉ: Yes, yes, little one. Just their names on a poster, your two fathers, and that was enough to pack the circus. Oh, I remember one time in Amsterdam . . . [*Papa Mélé's voice trails off in nostalgia.*]

Papa Mélé's attempt to explain the children's paternity and his own role is a curious mixture of fantasy and nostalgia. The evolving message of the unity of humanity, so central to Baker's narratives about race, is muted for the audience by the carnivalesque character of the scene and the equation of hybridity with deformity and exoticism. In her analysis of Papa Mélé's exchange with the children, Elizabeth Ezra argues that the two types of father-hood are allegories for a discourse of colonial dependency and assimilation in which the biological father represents the native lands of the children and the adoptive father stands for France as a colonial empire embracing all of its dependent subjects.[19] Zouzou's dubious origins also resonate with Baker's own biography. In its narrative function, Papa Mélé's scene with the children establishes the familial bond shared by Zouzou and Jean across cultures and the basis for the emotional entanglement of their relationship. It also sets the stage for yet another altruistic self-sacrifice on Baker's part.

At the end of the paternity sequence, Jean announces that he intends to become a sailor when he grows up, and, therefore, he'll have to leave Zouzou because "no women are allowed on the boats." The scene cuts to an adult Jean Marchand shipboard and then at a seaport café in Polynesia, where he witnesses an exotic dance by a native woman and writes a postcard to Zouzou about his projected return to Toulon. The adult Zouzou, living in Toulon with Papa Mélé, receives the card and begins to count the days until Jean's return. When Jean eventually arrives, he jumps ship without an official military discharge. Jean surprises Zouzou and Papa Mélé at home in Toulon. A joyous encounter ensues, full of lively banter, as Zouzou and Papa Mélé welcome the long-lost Jean. During this exchange, Zouzou notices that Jean bears the tattoo of a nude woman on his forearm and jealously asks him, "Who is that woman?" Jean replies, "Oh, no one in particular [n'importe laquelle]. For the same price I could have had a crocodile." Ezra interprets this scene as Zouzou's realization of one of the racial barriers that she must overcome in expressing her love for Jean because the tattoo on Jean's arm represents a woman of his color.[20] Zouzou, however, soon forgets this episode and spends a carefree day walking through the streets of Toulon with her adopted brother. This part of the film was shot on location in Toulon and contains the now famous bird-freeing sequence.

Zouzou and Jean walk through the *marché aux oiseau* (bird market), where Zouzou frees the caged birds behind the shopkeeper's back. Baker reportedly adored this scene and recounts it in the posthumous autobiography compiled by Jo Bouillon: "I'll never forget the scene where I set the bird free. I had hoped to rehearse it again and again, giving a new bird its liberty with every take, but the original bird wouldn't budge from its perch. He liked it where he was. The director was furious; in the film world, every minute has its price."[21]

The bird-freeing sequence contains multiple symbolic messages. It alludes analeptically to the birth myth with the stork; in the present, to Zouzou's and Jean's restricted social and racial situations; and proleptically, to Zouzou's entrapment in the music hall where she appears as a caged bird. It also refers to Jean's entrapment in the military and subsequently by the police after he is falsely accused of murder. The limitations of social class, race, and convention are represented by the birdcage, which places restrictions on both Zouzou and Jean from which they both wish to be free. Jean's weak attempt to stop Zouzou from freeing the birds also suggests his ambivalence about breaking

away from convention. The birdcage introduces a new twist into the iterative Cinderella narrative. Although Zouzou aspires to music-hall success,
she also wishes to free herself from the iron cage of fame. The bird-freeing
scene presages Zouzou's release from the domestic sphere with Papa Mélé
and Jean's final release from the confines of the ship and jail. Both Zouzou
and Jean recycle their entangled narratives of capture and release throughout
the film.

The two major nested narratives in *Zouzou* are the story of unrequited
love and the tale of success of the rising music-hall starlet. Rose compares
Zouzou to a modified version of the 1954 film *A Star Is Born*, emphasizing the
career success story.[22] The film, however, foregrounds the love story with the
Cinderella-like narrative as a subtheme. In Baker's films, musical performances
serve not so much to advance the film's plot in Hollywood style as they do
to punctuate it, as filmic signs that give deeper meaning to the plot.[23] Unlike
Busby Berkeley's Hollywood musical extravaganzas of the 1930s, Baker's films
featured closely intertwined music, choreography, and plot. The film's signature torch song, "C'est lui" (He's the One), one of Baker's most popular hits,
is a leitmotif throughout the production (fig. 24). Baker first sings the second
verse of the song while she is working at the laundry, the Blanchisserie Vallée,
in Paris, where the family has relocated. She is preparing to deliver a basket
of laundry to the music hall when the other women begin to question her:
"Zouzou, do you know the star of the show? Can you get us complimentary
tickets?" Zouzou shrugs; then the women in unison beg her to perform one of
the music-hall star's numbers. To egg Zouzou on, they chant the star's name,
"Barbara, Barbara, Barbara," and Zouzou begins by singing the second verse of
"C'est lui," intercut with Miss Barbara singing the first verse and the refrain.

> Twenty times a day by the dozens
> Some very passionate gentlemen
> Offer me the life of a queen
> For me to give myself to them.
> There's only one of them
> Who pleases me.
> He's naughty, and he doesn't have a cent.
> His stories, between us, are not clear.
> I know it well, but I don't care.

This sequence lasts just over two minutes and then cuts to Miss Barbara,

Figure 24. Cover for the sheet music of Josephine Baker's 1934 hit "C'est lui." Courtesy of Éditions Salabert and BMG Music Publishing, Paris.

who stumbles through the refrain and the first verse of the song in the music hall, in a minute-long sequence.

Refrain
For me, there's only one man
In Paris, and it's him.
I can't do anything about it.
My heart is taken by him.
I think I'm losing my mind.
He's so dumb.
He hasn't understood a thing.
For me, there's only one man in Paris.
And it's him.

French refrain

Pour moi, il n'y a qu'un homme dans Paris
Et c'est lui
Je ne peux rien y faire
mon coeur est pris pas lui
Je crois que je perd la tête
Il est si bête
Il n'a rien compris
Pour moi, il n'y a qu'un homme dans Paris
Et c'est lui.

Verse 1

I'd crawl through a mouse hole
for him.
Everyday, I adore him.
There's even more.
For me, there's only one man in Paris,
And it's him.

This song sets in motion the multiple love stories that complicate the film's plot: Zouzou and Jean; Miss Barbara and the music-hall owner, Saint-Lévy; Barbara and her Brazilian lover; and Claire Vallée, daughter of the laundry owner, and Jean Marchand. These subplots work to both the benefit and detriment of Zouzou. Aspects of the "C'est lui" torch song reflect the basic semiotic motif of jealousy in which the excluded person becomes a spectator who occupies the spatiotemporal position of a powerless observer who cannot affect the action in the scene. Zouzou's observations of the emerging affair between Claire and Jean reflect her exclusion and powerlessness both as a woman and as a marginal cultural outsider in France.

Aided by Jean, now a stage manager at the music hall, Barbara elopes with her Brazilian lover. Desolate and furious, Saint-Lévy joins forces with his colleague Monsieur Trompe and they struggle in a panic to replace Barbara. Having seen Zouzou, who has crept on stage to perform after a rehearsal, they ask her, but she initially turns them down. Only after Papa Mélé's death and Jean's false arrest the same night does Zouzou return to beg Monsieur Trompe for a job in order to bail out Jean. With the primary love-sacrifice narrative set in motion, the music-hall story begins.

A good deal of Baker's performance during the second half of *Zouzou* is based on song. Although her unique American accent passes well for that of an untutored Martinican laundress, the musical numbers require more sophistication. By playing off Zouzou's delivery against Miss Barbara's thick Eastern European accent and the various nonstandard French inflections of Saint-Lévy (portrayed as a Jewish immigrant) and of Jean and Claire, the latter rooted in the Parisian working class, Baker's vocal performances emerge as ideal. They are even iconically symbolized by a morning dance number set in a bedroom (in which she is absent) and featuring a giant telephone as a prop.[24]

On the evening of her debut, Zouzou performs two musical numbers—the extravagant "Haïti," for 3:56 minutes, and the signature song with all three verses, "C'est lui," for 6:10 minutes. In both of these musical scenes, there is a double articulation of the gazes of the male spectators in the diegetic and real audiences. Zouzou is framed by both the theatrical stage and the camera, emphasizing the simultaneous presence of entangled narratives and a doubled performative persona.

When performing "C'est lui," Baker wears a sumptuous feather-collared satin evening gown and a tiara in a fully glamorous image. "C'est lui" is filmed in a two-part take comprised of verse 1, with a long refrain and an improvised scat tune, for approximately 2:30 minutes, and verses 2 and 3, with a shorter refrain and a cutaway to the audience ovation, for approximately 3:40 minutes, followed by a second curtain call. "Haïti" and "C'est lui" may be viewed in performative, diegetic, and musical opposition.[25] The first number uses Baker's primal image, while the second builds on the glamour and glitter of the music hall. "Haïti" contains an operatic aria, while "C'est lui" is an earthy song with jazz interludes. Zouzou performs "Haïti" dressed as a skimpily clad bird in a large trapeze-like cage and "C'est lui" as a vamp.

At the end of her first performance of "Haïti," Zouzou jumps from the cage into the arms of the male chorus, performing a dramatic somersault. For a moment, the caged bird is free. She returns to her dressing room, where she reads a newspaper containing the photograph of the real murderer in whose place Jean has been arrested. She then informs the chamber maid, Josette, that she intends to report the matter to the police immediately.

> ZOUZOU: Jean is saved! Jean is saved!
> JOSETTE: What's wrong with you? Are you crazy?
> ZOUZOU: But look at this. Look. It's the man who killed Julot.
> JOSETTE: It's not possible . . . ugh . . . what are you doing?
> ZOUZOU: I'm leaving.

JOSETTE: What do you mean, you're leaving?

ZOUZOU: Quick, quick. My coat!

JOSETTE: You'll go another day—tomorrow or the day after when you have time. But now, your act is ready to start.

ZOUZOU: Josette, my shoes!

JOSETTE: I can't give you your shoes. That's *impossible*. Stop and think. All of Paris is in the theater. There are ministers, ambassadors.

ZOUZOU: I don't give a hoot.

JOSETTE: You won't go. You won't go. Over my dead body. Oh, what are we going to do. The curtain is ready to rise. Zouzou is gone. She's gone . . .

This scene establishes the emotional tension between Zouzou's ardor for Jean and her devotion to her music-hall career. She manages to rush to the police station during the intermission, identify the real murderer, arrange for Jean's release, and return before she is due on stage. At this point, she makes a dramatic entrance and performs "C'est lui" in the full two-part take, concluding with the third, betrayal verse.

> He runs after all the girls.
> They are all at his mercy.
> His look undresses them.
> His hands sometimes do, as well.
> I do nothing for him to love me.
> To others, he brings happiness,
> But he's mine anyway
> Because he's in my heart.
> (La la la—refrain)

A long tracking shot cuts to Zouzou walking to the jail, where she sees Jean exit and embrace Claire. Devastated, she returns to the music hall, passing posters of herself advertising the hundredth performance of her show. The melody for "Haïti" begins with a slow pan over the music hall's exterior. The closing suture shot zooms in on Zouzou in the birdcage in a soft closeup as she sings "Haïti" for another 1:28 minutes (fig. 25).

Verse 1
My desire, my love song
Who will give me back my country, Haïti?
Yes, you're my only country, Haïti.

Figure 25. Josephine Baker singing as a caged bird in the performance of "Haïti" from the film *Zouzou*, 1934. Photo courtesy of AKG-Images, London.

> When I remember the forests so beautiful,
> And the wide horizons far from your shores,
> The most beautiful cage is nothing but a jail.
> Yes, my desire, my love song, Haïti.

Although the narrative structure of *Zouzou* is complex when compared with that of the silent film *Sirène,* the heroine's self-sacrifice is similar in both films. Sacrifice is the price of civilization and of taming the caged bird. The music-hall success story contains within it the kernel of the primal Baker (an exotic bird) surrounded by a multilayered narrative of longing. Exile, betrayal, and loss form the backdrop against which Zouzou's stardom is achieved. In a 1934 article in *Le Jour,* Baker stated, "I'm enchanted by the film. Everyone seems very happy with what I've done, and I myself am very optimistic . . . and everything seems to me so real, so true, that I sometimes think that it's my own life that's unfolding on the set."[26]

African Aphrodite

The film *Princesse Tam-Tam* is a mythic allegory as well as a spoof on French colonial cinema. Directed by Edmond T. Gréville, with a scenario by Pepito Abatino and Yves Mirande, the film is replete with puns and ironic references to the colonial condition. English subtitles for the 2005 release of the film have been modified and updated to reflect some of these nuances. As with *Zouzou,* I will provide my own translations of the French dialogue. I will also note some of the subtitling changes when they are pertinent to the discussion.

In a Greek myth, Pygmalion, the king of Cyprus, falls in love with a statue of his own making, which is brought to life by the goddess Aphrodite. Galatea, the living statue, is in this sense a daughter of Aphrodite (Venus), who has created an irresolvable dilemma. In the narrative of *Princesse Tam-Tam,* Aouina (also translated from Arabic as Alwina in both versions of the English subtitles) becomes the African daughter of Aphrodite, remolded by the novelist Max de Mirecourt (Albert Préjean). To revive his flagging literary career and conjugal life, the novelist decides to travel to Africa with his assistant and collaborator Coton (Robert Arnoux). There he meets the peasant waif Aouina when she is begging in the bazaar.

Inspired by her natural naïveté, Max attempts to tame and civilize Aouina. He writes a novel in one night based on his fantasies about what would happen if he took Aouina to Paris and introduced her to high society as a princess. This archetypal narrative allows Baker to play her primal role as Aouina and to appear in glamorous costumes as the Princess of Parador. In the end, the fabricated princess reverts to type, performing primal dances (the Charleston and the conga) at a sailors' bar and a high-society party. Baker's seductive transformation from a Bedouin beggar girl into an exotic princess reflects the colonial stereotypes of the era. It is on the basis of this scene that Oliver Todd, in the 1986 documentary *Chasing a Rainbow: The Life of Josephine Baker,* describes *Princesse Tam-Tam* as "an attempt to emulate the sumptuous musicals that were beginning to come out of Hollywood" characterized by "fast cutting and synthetic commercialism."[27]

The verisimilitude of *Zouzou* is left behind in the fantastic fable of *Princesse Tam-Tam*. Stereotypical characters and a thin, although double-framed, narrative typify this spoof on colonial cinema. *Princesse Tam-Tam* premiered at the Moulin Rouge Cinema in Paris on November 8, 1935 (fig. 26). The scenario by Abatino and Mirande is witty and abounds with intertextual references to both *Sirène* and *Zouzou*. In fact, it might be argued that *Princesse* cannot be fully appreciated without some knowledge of the two earlier films. Certainly all three films were developed as vehicles to showcase Baker's evolving image. While *Zouzou* is about assimilation and its perils, *Princesse* is about the impossibility of acculturation. The heroine Aouina cannot adjust to France in spite of her superficial changes in dress and comportment.

Princesse Tam-Tam is based on a series of oppositions within a multiframed narrative. In the entangled framing narrative, Aouina never actually goes to Paris at all, and the entire adventure is a figment of the novelist/narrator's imagination. The opposing root images of civilized versus savage are paralleled by oppositions of master/servant, culture/nature, wife/mistress, and male/female. Each image set involves its own subplot embellished by the novelist Max de Mirecourt's fantasies about Aouina. If one views all of the images as the novelist's constructions within the master narrative, the irony of the representations is intensified.[28]

The film opens with an argument between de Mirecourt and his wife, Lucie, who accuses him of being a dried-up failure. Having spent the night on the living room sofa to escape his wife's constant haranguing, Max is awakened by his assistant and collaborator, Coton, who has just ghost-written an article on fashion and elegance for him. Note that Coton's name may be viewed as a double pun on the French word for cotton (*coton*) and the word for colonizer (*colon*), making him an enigmatic figure who is both slave and master. Later, Coton will refer to himself using the French colloquial term for ghostwriter—*nègre*—thereby complicating both the master/slave and racial metaphors used in the film's nested narratives.[29] The ghostwriter as *nègre* is both the "master" of the narrative and the unacknowledged "slave." When Aouina asks him about his constant notetaking, Coton replies, "Je suis nègre telque tu me vois, ma petite." In the 1989 subtitles, this sentence is translated, "I am a negro, my dear." It is modified in the 2005 subtitles to

Figure 26. Publicity poster for *Princesse Tam-Tam*, 1935, considered by some critics to be Baker's most ambitious screen performance. Photo courtesy of Bryan Hammond Collection.

read, "A ghostwriter is a slave, my dear." The multilayered fantasy of Aouina's transformation is as much Coton's creation as it is Max's.

Together, Max and Coton cook up a scheme of leaving Paris to write in Africa.

> COTON: You've got to go far away. If not, your wife will catch up with you, and she'll start up everything all over again. If you go far away, that will teach your wife a lesson. Not to upset you, but she's right. You're all washed up [*vidé*].
> MAX: Eh, you think so?
> LUCIE [*from the bedroom*]: Failure! Imbecile!
> MAX: Just listen to that, my friend. We'll go to the land of the savages, the real savages. Yes! To Africa! To Africa! [On va partir chez les sauvages, chez les vrais sauvages. Oui! En Afrique, en Afrique!]

Max's decision launches the North African adventure that leads to Aouina's discovery. The exteriors for the film were shot in Tunisia, and Aouina is depicted as both North African and a generalized exotic "other" (Indian, sub-Saharan African, even a bit of a gypsy). The opening shot brings the culture/nature opposition into play as Aouina peers out from behind a large cactus plant and then emerges to frolic with a herd of sheep. Pseudo-oriental music plays in the background, embellishing the film's exotic ambiance. The music uses melodies and scale variations influenced by Arabian music, although its origin is difficult to identify.[30] Max first encounters Aouina in a local café where she steals oranges from a tray. He buys the whole tray for her. In this scene, the waiter complains in Arabic in the background but his comments are not translated in the scenario or the subtitles.

> MAX: Why do you steal oranges?
> AOUINA: Because I don't have any money to buy them.
> MAX: What's your name?
> AOUINA: Aouina.
> MAX: Aouina.
> AOUINA: Yes, Aouina.
> COTON: That means a small spring [*source*], but I have the impression that she's the source of trouble.

Aouina then reappears, chased by a band of local street urchins. She drops the tray of oranges, and pandemonium ensues. This episode amuses

Max and initiates his *désir/plaisir* cycle and his longing to capture, possess, and tame this savage creature. Throughout the film, Aouina is referred to as a wild animal (*bête sauvage*), full of energy but in need of domestication. Aouina represents not only Max's own primal desires, but also his unharnessed fantasies, untamed imagination, and lack of literary discipline. She is the proverbial colonial id underlying Max's superficially civilized superego. On the level of colonial discourse, Aouina is also the elusive native woman whose primal erotic energy and naïveté both fascinate and repel the colonial master. Interestingly, she is the only adult "North African" woman to be featured in the Tunisian portion of the film. Max is obsessed by the thought of Aouina and next encounters her on a touristic trip to the ruins of Dougga, an ancient Roman amphitheater just outside of Tunis.

The establishing shot of the ruins sequence opens Baker's first musical performance in the film. Aouina runs up the steps of the ruins, followed by the ubiquitous gang of local street children. In front of the Roman columns, she performs an exotic dance, choreographed by Floyd Du Pont, that combines modern ballet, an oriental belly dance, the cakewalk, and an imitation of a chicken. This bizarre chicken strut lasts just over three minutes and foreshadows the other two savage dances that Baker performs later in the film. The chicken strut reinforces the civilized/savage and culture/nature oppositions within the film's nested narratives. Rose asserts, "Predictably, the film's best moments are the dance sequences, especially one in which, imitating a chicken, Baker dances on the steps of a ruined Roman amphitheater."[31] This *mise en scène* brings together East and West, savage and civilized, in a dialectic of unresolved contradictions. As Roman relics, the ruins of Dougga also represent the decline of the French colonial empire and the internal challenges of social class within France.[32] This interpretation is further supported by the association of Aouina's savage dancing with the carnival and the sailors' bar.

Aouina encounters the tourists at Dougga and pulls pranks on them such as substituting sand for salt in their picnic lunches. Tourism here symbolizes the thwarted encounter between two cultures. Afterwards, Max realizes that Aouina is his inspiration and searches for her everywhere. Running away from the authorities trying to arrest her for begging in town, Aouina arrives at Max's villa riding on the bumper of his car. Once at the villa, Aouina jumps off the car and begins to wander around the grounds, following animals and chasing a monkey up a tree in a scene reminiscent of her Folies-Bergère routines. She is spotted by Tahar, or Dar in the 2005 subtitles (Georges Péclet), Max's stoic

Arab servant, who grabs Aouina, strips off her blouse, and prepares to lash her. Max spies the violent scene from his living room window and commands Tahar to bring Aouina to him. Max's removal of Aouina from Tahar's lashing is not a reprieve. She is delivered into another form of domination when Tahar takes her to Max. The handing over of Aouina recalls the inability of dominated colonial subjects to protect their women from the desires of the dominators. This scene sets in motion another colonialist subplot, complete with the multiple master/slave and civilized/savage stereotypes. Tahar is stern, authoritarian, and abusive, while the colonial master is benign and giving. The master domesticates and harnesses the savagery of the colonial slave and the wild woman.

Max invites Aouina to stay at the villa with him but he has the ulterior motive of observing her behavior for his novel, which he calls "une histoire de race," a very trendy interracial story.

Reluctantly, Coton goes along with this plan as the ethnographic scribe. He follows Max and Aouina, pad and pencil in hand, transcribing every conversation. Frustrated with being treated as an anthropological specimen, Aouina finally protests.

> AOUINA: Why is he always with us, that one with the pencil?
> MAX: He's my slave, do you understand?
> AOUINA: I didn't know that you people had slaves.
> COTON: I myself am a *nègre* [pun intended], as you see me, little one.
> AOUINA: You, I don't like you because you're always making fun of me.
> [*Aouina sticks her tongue out at Coton.*]

This scene benefits from Baker's vaudevillesque improvisational skills, Robert Arnoux's impeccable comic timing, and the bond that appears to be established between both actors. It also sutures the multilayered master/slave colonial narrative already discussed and emphasizes the ways in which Max, as the creative artist, has been enslaved by his own muse. As Aouina storms off, Max and Coton lament the slow progress of both the novel and the civilizing of Aouina. Coton suggests that the only way to civilize Aouina is to teach her how to be a princess. Meanwhile, Tahar (or Dar), whose Arabic name means "land" or "place," concerned about Aouina's welfare, stations himself outside the window of her room. The servant constantly observes and judges the master's actions. These observations are symbolized by Tahar's frequent presence near windows and portals in the film.

After a brief cutaway to Lucie and the Maharajah of Daetane, who initiate a flirtation in Paris, the scene shifts back to Tahar and Aouina. As with the dyads in *Zouzou,* these two couples are part of the love triangle that consummates the "histoire de race." Both oriental men are presented as stoic and somewhat harsh. While the maharajah is suave, wealthy, and assimilated, Tahar is an earthy servant who produces natural gems of wisdom. He takes Aouina sailing on the bay so that she can escape from the rigors of her new education. When Aouina praises the master for his kindness and intelligence, Tahar issues a word of warning: "If the free birds of the sky take their food from the hands of men, they no longer have their freedom." This philosophical and moralistic discourse spurs Aouina into song. Her first vocal number of the film, "Le Chemin de Bonheur," lasts just over three minutes. Performed with operatic-style arias in the refrains, "Le Chemin" describes the pleasures of nature and the simple life. Translated by the composer-arranger Spencer Williams as "Dream Ship," this song was one of Baker's biggest hits of the 1930s in both France and the United States.[33]

The vocal complexity of "Le Chemin" contrasts with the simplicity of its message and with the image of Aouina as wild and uncivilized. Baker is shot in soft closeups in this scene, underscoring her erotic appeal. Sharpley-Whiting notes that "the attention of the French spectator is drawn to Baker/Aouina's 'exotic' beauty, highlighted by the camera's soft-filtered long takes of a youthful Baker with pencil-thin eyebrows, heavily made-up doe eyes and long, false eyelashes, and a smiling or childishly pouting mouth."[34] This scene is a prelude to Baker's glamorous appeal as the transformed Parisian Princess of Parador, yet it retains the naïve simplicity of the primal vixen.

While Tahar and Aouina are sailing, Max receives more news about Lucie and the maharajah. He resolves that the book must be completed immediately and decides to stay up all night and polish off the project on his own in order to return to his wife in Paris. The nested narrative within a narrative unfolds as Max's dreams of productivity and glory are fulfilled. Aouina learns to read, do multiplication tables, dress fashionably, and wear high-heeled shoes as Coton and Tahar watch helplessly. Finally, she is ready for her initiatory trip to Paris. "I would like to take a long trip with the white man" (Je voudrais faire un long voyage avec le monsieur blanc), exclaims Aouina. Then the film cuts to the Mediterranean crossing and the inevitable trip to the metropole.

When Aouina arrives at the apartment that Max has rented for her in Paris, she is shocked by its small size and artificiality. Looking at the silk flowers and glass fish that decorate the room, Aouina comments on the "fake things" (*choses fausses*) that are everywhere. Max responds knowingly, "There are many fake things that are more beautiful than the real ones." This exchange foreshadows the ultimate reacceptance of primal roots and return to nature that is characteristic of Baker's iterative narratives.

Coton takes on the responsibility of informing Lucie that Aouina has arrived in Paris, describing her as the Princess of Parador from a central Indian kingdom. Max and Coton organize a press conference for Aouina and prepare to present her to high society at the opera. Lucie immediately seeks the maharajah's advice.

> LUCIE: The Princess of Parador. That must be a neighbor of your country. Have you ever heard of her in India?
> MAHARAJAH: Oh, it's been such a long time that I've been in Europe. Besides, it's impossible to know everyone of one's own race.
> LUCIE: I want to know exactly who this princess is. To think that my husband is associated with her.
> MAHARAJAH: Is he going to produce her in high society?
> LUCIE: In a circus, perhaps.

This circus reference intertextually recalls *Zouzou* and highlights the impossibility of accepting an exotic foreigner into Parisian society. After her appearance at the opera, Aouina joins Max in a round of social events including a day at the races, art openings, and chic parties. In spite of the watchfulness of Max, Coton, and Tahar, Aouina repeatedly transgresses norms by showing too much exuberance, eating with her hands, and complaining about Parisian apartment life.[35] Finally, she asks Max for an evening off, feigning fatigue. Accompanied by Tahar, she heads out of the apartment to explore the places "where people can really enjoy themselves, live, and do everything they want." The camera pans to Aouina at a carnival sideshow and then entering a sailors' bar with Tahar—locations that are reminiscent of scenes from *Zouzou*.

At the bar, Baker performs her second key musical number, "Sous le ciel d'Afrique" (Neath the Tropic Blue Skies). As with "Le Chemin de bonheur," "Le Ciel" is a nostalgic lament about the beauty of nature and Africa. Ironically, however, it is also accompanied by a "savage dance" combining a tap routine with acrobatics and the Charleston. The soft-focus closeups of Baker singing "Le Ciel" contrast with her wild abandon and clowning while performing the savage dance.

The scene opens with an Afro-Antillian band singing the first two verses of "Sous le ciel d'Afrique."

Verse 1
Under the gray skies
of our gray cities
That break our poor hearts
Never any hope
Never any joy.

Verse 2
Our souls groan
with pain
Closing our eyes
to the space
that becomes blue
In the infinity of
the sun of Africa
over the gray tropics.

Refrain (by Aouina)
Under African skies
Each moment seems better
Than anywhere else.
And for us all is
desire/pleasure [*désir/plaisir*]
In the bewitching land [*au pays ensorcelleur*]

Verse 3 (by Aouina)
Its magic call
Rises before our eyes
And we will always
Perform dances of love
to rhythms filled
with fire.
Once a month comes
The moment to say
You should search for your dream
Far from the skies of your country
Neath the tropic blue skies.

Aouina concludes with one more refrain of "Le Ciel" before breaking into the wild dance. Odette (Viviane Romance), Lucie's close friend and confidante, has come to the bar slumming with a group of her high-society companions. Also in the bar are several drunken sailors and a mysterious and sullen white prostitute in blackface, mirroring Aouina's new status as a *fille* (loose woman) of ambiguous racial identity. The next morning, Odette reports the entire episode to Lucie by telephone.

ODETTE: Ha! If you had only seen that dance, my friend.

LUCIE: Really?

ODETTE: A savage dance [*danse de sauvage*] in a sailors' bar. If everyone who disputes [the authenticity of] the princess could have seen her.

LUCIE: Oh, you've just given me an idea. Everyone *must* see that dance. I want her to dance in front of the whole town. I want to make a fool of my husband. I'm going to organize something. I'll talk to the maharajah. I'm sure he'll help.

The maharajah agrees to organize an extravagant society party at his villa. He invites Aouina, Max, and Coton. Aouina appears bedecked with jewels in a stunning evening gown. The maharajah entertains the guests with a full music-hall show consisting of elaborate dance numbers, Chinese plate twirlers, an African drummer resembling Baker's partner Joe Alex, magicians, and hypnotic animation. Shot in Hollywood style from several angles with lavish special effects, the show conveys all of the excitement of a music-hall extravaganza. During the course of the evening, Odette plies Aouina with drinks and encourages her to dance. As the number "Ahé Conga" begins, Aouina jumps up, goes onto the stage, throws off her glamorous gown, and appears in an upscale, sequined version of her original peasant dress. She dances an improvised conga with abandon, to the shock and delight of the audience. Once again, a musical scene sutures the climactic moment of the film. Baker appears in several full-body shots with the camera lingering on her in front of an anonymous chorus.

Baker was particularly fond of the conga scene and viewed it as the high point of her performance in the film. In her autobiography with Bouillon, she remarked, "One of the things I particularly enjoyed about filming *Princess Tam-Tam* [sic] was the chance it gave me to introduce the conga to France. Not that the conga had anything to do with Tunisia; it was a dance enjoyed by the slaves after their work was done. We were all convinced that it would be the rage in Paris that winter. What better way to keep warm?"[36]

Following the peak dance performance, an exuberant audience mobs Aouina, who manages to escape to the maharajah's private quarters. He firmly warns her to return to her native land immediately before her real identity is discovered and more trouble ensues. To dramatize the gravity of her choice, he shows her two ornately grilled windows behind which even he is a prisoner. One faces east, and the other opens onto the west. Outside the window to the Occident, Aouina spies Max and Lucie in a fervent embrace of reconciliation. Beyond the window to the Orient, Tahar awaits her. She flees in haste to him.

Max completes his novel, entitled *Civilisation,* which is a grand success. Coton remarks that he wishes Aouina were there to share the glory, to which Max responds "Aouina is fine where she is." The camera then cuts to the closing scene at Max's former villa in Tunisia. Aouina holds a baby in her arms, and Tahar is in the background. The villa is overrun by chickens, geese, and goats. Books and papers are strewn everywhere. Among the books lying on the ground is a copy of Max's bestseller. A donkey slowly tears off and chews the cover page as the film comes to a close.

Princesse Tam-Tam, which has received more critical attention and commentary than the other films by Baker, leaves everyone in fixed and conventional social positions. It is a perfect example of Bhabha's notion of doubling through which colonial roles are reinforced. All stereotypes are intact, and order is imposed on the chaos of primal dreams and drives. Transgressing the barriers of race, class, and nationality is acceptable for an evening of slumming and fantastic storytelling. But in the light of day, the characters return to their original social and cultural places, and the cycle of nested narratives closes. This exotic adventure provides a moment of cathartic filmic release from the repetitive routines of modernity and the constraints of civilization. Ironically, it is through this reassertion of colonialist fantasies that Baker achieves her stardom.

Documentary Reflections

The 1980s saw a revival of interest in Josephine Baker as part of a new black renaissance in the arts. Baker was resurrected as an icon, a legend, and an emblem of a new era of globalization. Auctions of Baker's memorabilia were held in Paris and New York, and the Château des Milandes was refurbished for public viewing. Kino International restored and released *Zouzou* and *Princesse Tam-Tam* in video format, and another Baker revival was in full swing. In this atmosphere, the provocative and ambitious 1986 documentary film *Chasing a Rainbow: The Life of Josephine Baker*, directed by Christopher Ralling and produced by Mick Csáky and Channel Four, was released in Britain. Oliver Todd's narration for the film circumlocutes Baker's life, framing it in terms of key world events and public problems. This documentary strategy features Baker as a prime mover and participant in historic political events that shaped the twentieth century.

Although the classic master trope of the Cinderella story frames the film, several image oppositions are deployed to convince the viewer that Baker is both a larger-than-life legend and a real person with foibles, weaknesses, and obstacles to overcome. While Baker's own films situate her as what Kaja Silverman terms "the exceptional woman" who is an untouchable object of desire, *Chasing a Rainbow* depersonalizes and desexualizes Baker by treating her as a historical force whose life narrative and personal traits reflect the eras and cultures in which she lives.[37] The film opens with a shot of Baker's 1975 state funeral in Paris. The rest of the film follows a straight chronological line from Baker's youth in St. Louis to her final performance at the Théâtre Bobino in Paris. Following this chronological sequence, the film may be divided into four parts depicting Josephine's early life in St. Louis and New York, her rise to stardom in Paris, her gains and losses during the war and postwar years, and her final comeback. Each sequence is intertwined with a dual narrative that demonstrates Josephine's role in and reactions to the world around her through an artfully reconstructed narrative point of view. Bryan Hammond, a Baker biographer, served as the historical consultant for the film and provided many of the still images, which are intercut in the form of photographic montages throughout the film. These classic photographs are reinforced by rare and very valuable footage from Baker's performances, films, and travels.

Multiple narrative voices, including those of historical experts, Baker's friends, and her Rainbow children, create the film's sense of realism, along with the intercutting of historical footage about Baker and her times. These documentary techniques parallel the strategies used in most written biographies on Baker with two important exceptions: there is a heavy emphasis on the historical framing of events and a tendency to mute Baker's own intentionality and agency in favor of the opinions of expert observers. These experts are used to distinguish the realm of documentary fact from fiction and to establish Baker's legendary persona. Music creates the ambiance of each period and marks key turning points in Baker's life in conjunction, and often on a dual audiotrack, with verbal narration.[38]

After describing Baker's state funeral and the many honors that she received in France, Todd qualifies her status, noting that in spite of these accomplishments, "Josephine Baker was not French. Her roots lay in the very heart of black America." Jazz music plays in the background as the film cuts to found footage of black soldiers returning to the United States from World War I and a long shot of the 1917 St. Louis race riots. Todd continues:

> In the summer of 1917, an illegitimate black girl known to her family as Tumpy witnessed a scene she never forgot. In Josephine's hometown of St. Louis, the rumor spread that a white girl had been raped. A mob descended on the Negro quarter of the town, clamoring for revenge. Within hours, fifty people lay dead. In the pall of smoke lying over the city, one terrified little girl thought she saw the white-clothed figure of God watching over her. There were reasons enough to be afraid. Everywhere in America where there was a black community of any size an atmosphere of terror prevailed, carefully nurtured by the Ku Klux Klan. Lynchings were frequent, the local police did little to prevent them. There were even some who wore their police uniforms by day, and the uniform of the Klan by night.
>
> If the Negro community kept in its place, if a long day's work in the cotton field was followed by the simple pleasures of singing and dancing, then there need be no trouble. But heaven help the black man who wanted more than this. Appalled by the prospect of a life spent in her hometown, Josephine began to look for a way of escape. She quickly found one. Up and down the country, troupes of black entertainers traveled from town to town gathering audiences where they could. Josephine was soon on the road with the Dixie Steppers. She traveled all over the southern states and, eventually, north, to the liveliest black community in the world—Harlem.

Accompanying this sequence in rapid succession are shots of the 1917 race riots, a Ku Klux Klan rally, cotton picking, plantation dancing, a childhood photograph of Tumpy, rare found footage of the Dixie Steppers, and a longshot pan of a turn-of-the-century Harlem street scene. Using this rapid montage strategy, combined with the narrative historical overview, the filmmakers simplify Josephine's life decisions into B-roll cutaways interwoven by scenes of the ambiance of the era. The New York section continues with shots of the Cotton Club narrated by the music-hall star Adelaide Hall, who was both Josephine's colleague and her competitor. Once again, Josephine's point of view is woven into the historical context when Todd narrates, "Clubs and music halls were opening all over town. Whenever she could, Josephine found a way of getting in to absorb the artistry of performers like the great Bojangles Robinson." The film cuts to Robinson tap dancing. This segment is followed by vitaphone footage of Eubie Blake at the piano and Noble Sissle singing. The narrator explains that Sissle and Blake launched Baker's musical career in *Shuffle Along,* and Adelaide Hall continues with a description of Baker's "delightful" comedic performance of "the monkey."

The scene rapidly shifts to Paris, where the social historian Alain Weill, speaking in heavily accented English, describes the early performances of *La Revue nègre:* "And soon, everybody saw that there was no director and that it was a complete mess. All these crazy black entertainers messing around with no real idea of what the show was going to be. So the people from the Théâtre des Champs-Elysées called upon Jacques-Charles to direct the show, Paul Colin to design the decor, and that's how it was built." Note that Jacques-Charles was a producer at the Moulin Rouge music hall, and André Daven requested that he rework the show because it lacked continuity and professionalism.

Weill's comment is corroborated by Baker's longtime friend Jacqueline Cartier, a journalist, who describes the opening night of *La Revue nègre.* A montage of classic photographs and images of Baker accompanies these commentaries. It include shots of Paul Colin's famous 1925 poster for *La Revue nègre,* an image of Baker in ostrich feathers from the 1926–27 production of *La Folie du jour,* and Madame d'Ora's 1928 photograph of a seminude Josephine as a lioness. Although they are neither identified by captions nor contextualized on the screen, these photographs appear in chronological order and constitute a rapidly progressing visual history of Baker's early career.

Baker's 1926 and 1928–29 trips to Germany are combined into a single montage with no distinction between the two. Shots of street scenes and cabarets in Berlin during the 1920s are accompanied by Todd's narration concerning the rise of fascism. Baker's presence on the scene is subordinated to political history. Todd describes the social world and atmosphere of political tension that Baker encountered.

The streets were bustling, the lights were bright, but Berliners' mask of gaiety was paper thin. In a city where democratic politics had never really taken root, there were times in the early twenties when orderly daily life looked as if it might break down all together. Hitler's brown shirts were beginning to flourish like rats in a sewer. To them, this dusky visitor was not exactly a fair and blue-eyed symbol of their purity. They began to denounce Josephine in their literature. But she had little interest in such things. She had come to immerse herself in that other side of life for which the city was notorious.

If the hallmark of Paris night life was infectious gaiety, Berlin preferred to take its pleasures rather differently. The emphasis was often on the morbid and the perverse. To Josephine, it hardly mattered. She wanted to experience everything, no matter how bizarre. And she was more than willing to contribute to the fun. When a newspaper reporter asked her to describe her ideal world, she replied, "One in which we can all go naked, as in Paradise."

Gérard Genette describes metalepsis as "the transition from one narrative level to another."[39] By combining an impersonal description of war-ravaged Berlin with a fabrication of Josephine's intentionality ("she wanted to experience everything"), the narrator engulfs the story of a character within the metanarrative of reportage. The history of fascism remains unresolved in the film, as does that of racism. Yet, these narratives are used as motivations for Josephine's actions, which are described alternately as rational, irrational, or confusing. These nested narratives allow the filmmaker to reinforce the contrasts between frontstage and backstage, or Josephine the legend versus Josephine the quixotic, emotional, and "real" person.

The narrator takes an interesting turn when he reviews Baker's performances, including her own films, of which the first three are described and intercut along with film clips from the opera La Créole. Every story has its heroes and villains. Pepito Abatino is treated as a self-serving opportunist who masterminded Baker's floundering film career rather than as a clever and supportive partner. In his introduction to Sirène des tropiques, Todd remarks that "in case anyone has missed the obvious comparison, Pepito himself plays her film escort. No doubt he drew three salaries as her manager, producer, and leading man." Todd describes Princesse Tam-Tam as "the most ambitious film Josephine ever made." Ironically, the music-hall and conga scenes, which are the most filmically complex, are not shown and, instead, we see a closing shot of Aouina and her donkey that reaffirms Baker's return to primal simplicity.

Zouzou is handled in a cursory manner, and Fausse alerte (1940) is not mentioned among the films at all. Todd concludes the narration of the films within a film with a sobering assessment of Josephine's cinematic career: "The truth was, she might be the biggest star in Europe, but American distributors remained stony faced. It would be many years before a major colored star would be seen on the cinema screens of America. Josephine might sing of her two loves, but one of them still rejected her completely. Her film career was over, but her faithful public in France were not to know it." This statement returns to the issue of Josephine's national identity, which the filmmakers view as troublesome. Rather than addressing her assimilation into France, they emphasize her nostalgic and uneasy attachment to the United States.

Once again, the filmmakers turn their attention to the war years. Describing music-hall life during the German occupation, Todd offers a qualification: "In cafés and cabarets, it was almost business as usual, even if the clients who could afford to pay were often the occupying Germans. [*Shot to a music-hall floor show during the German Occupation.*] But Josephine Baker was nowhere to be seen."

Narrative suspense is created by shrouding Josephine's wartime activities in mystery. Jacques Abtey's 1948 book *La Guerre secrète de Joséphine Baker* describes in detail her work for the Bureau of Counterespionage. Although this bureau worked with the Maquis, the local cells of the French Resistance, it was technically an autonomous unit. Todd states:

> Special agents were already gathering intelligence about German units pinned down by the activities of the Maquis. Josephine could carry this written on her sheet music in invisible ink to the neutral city of Lisbon. [*Street sounds and explosions*]
> For a time, she even appeared in uniform. It was all most confusing.
> Josephine, herself, had no need for fawning explanations. First, she was awarded the most highly coveted of decorations, the Medal of the Resistance. Then, some years later, she was made a member of the Legion of Honor, one of France's highest awards—not generally given to ex-nude dancers from the Folies-Bergère. [*Sounds of cheering*] . . .
> But what exactly had she done during the war? Was it really so secret? "That," she said, "is something I'm not at liberty to talk about."

The ambivalence with which Josephine's honors are treated sustains the opposition of legend versus real person that is so central to the film's argument. This attitude is maintained in the discussion of Baker's utopian Rainbow Tribe. In order to preserve its narrative consistency, the film does not explore the ideology behind Baker's humanitarian project but, instead, presents it as irrational and extravagant. Jo Bouillon is depicted as the source of stability and rational management at Les Milandes, and Josephine as egotistical and idealistic. Concerning the demise of Les Milandes, Todd remarks:

> Nevertheless, when yet another baby arrived, this time from Venezuela, Jo decided he would stand no more. Ten years of marriage, at times happy ones for both of them, ended in mutual recriminations. For the first time, Josephine had to face the double burden of supporting both the château and the Rainbow Tribe alone. Worse still, she'd brought over several members of her own family from St. Louis, and they, too, had to be paid for. Grand ideas and extravagant gestures were no substitute for sound management. . . . To make matters worse, Les Milandes was beginning to have its detractors. Why was it necessary for the children to have their own castle? There were those who said it was nothing more than a gigantic publicity stunt, and that twelve young lives were being exploited for the greater glory of one.

Footage of Brigitte Bardot's 1964 televised defense of Les Milandes could easily have been included for a contrasting perspective. Instead, various narrative voices are introduced in support of and in counterpoint to the criticism of Les Milandes, including that of the pro-Baker journalist Jacqueline Cartier, the Rainbow children Marianne and Brian, and Josephine's fellow Rainbow traveler Jean-Claude Baker. All of them comment on the positive and negative aspects of the Rainbow experiment as they perceived it.[40] But the narrator's criticism of Baker's irrational extravagance dominates all other points of view. A more detailed analysis of Baker's universal brotherhood project in relationship to similar utopian movements is necessary to contextualize this portion of the film. Nonetheless, the image of Baker presented here has become part of an enduring legend reiterated in various permutations in written and filmic biographies.

Baker's stance on civil rights is documented in two sequences of Ralling's film. The first deals with her performances at the Liberty Clubs in Morocco during the war. This section of the film is narrated by Sidney Williams, an African American lieutenant in the U.S. Army. Williams had sociological training in small-group behavior and organized the Liberty Club canteens in North Africa. He provides a retrospective eyewitness report reinforcing the factual character of the documentary. The second sequence relates the Stork Club incident, as narrated by the journalist Jack O'Brian. The interview with O'Brian is circumspect. As with the depiction of the Rainbow project,

Josephine's political ideology is not explored in depth. O'Brian describes the repercussions of the incident in an ambivalent manner:

> The whole thing turned into a vendetta, which Walter [Winchell] then declared a counter-vendetta. And as I've always said about Walter, and to his face, he only knew one way to fight, and that was unfair. Because I told him his motto was "never above the belt." He was able to dig up facts, or at least information, from France about Josephine Baker as a hyper-left liberal. Well, she was a liberal, of course. And, uh, he . . . he either felt sure that he was right in accusing her of either Communism or pro-Communism, I didn't know, so I never . . . and I didn't get into this, simply because I wasn't that important.

Although Baker's political views make sense in terms of her passionate commitment to human rights on the one hand and her obsession with showmanship on the other, these two approaches often clash, creating the illusion of confusion or, from Oliver Todd's perspective, political naïveté.

The film begins to move toward a conclusion with an interview montage of the Rainbow children. The camera cuts to one of Baker's many performances of "Dans mon village":

> In my village
> I tenderly raised
> Eleven children
> Orphans from here and there
> Who were so sad and alone.[41]

Baker's move to Paris with the children, their expulsion from Les Milandes, and their rescue in Roquebrune-Cap-Martin by Princess Grace of Monaco are dealt with in rapid succession. The film continues with a commentary from André Levasseur, the costume and set designer for Baker's last show, which was performed at the Monte Carlo Sporting Club and later at the Théâtre Bobino in Paris just before her death. Todd concludes the film with a description of Baker's final moments of celebration, as Baker sings "Me Revoilà Paris": "At the gala after the show, dozens of celebrities, Princess Grace herself, Sophia Loren, Alain Delon and Mireille d'Arc among them, gathered to do her honor. The following night there was another party—this time, for members of the cast. Was Josephine tired? Certainly not. She went to bed later than any of them . . . and never woke up. Doctors diagnosed the cause of death as a cerebral hemorrhage. But a friend said, 'I think she died of joy.'"

As the credits roll, a 1920s image of Baker flashes on the screen, showing her in the short leotard in which she originally posed on the rooftop of the Théâtre des Champs-Elysées. We have come full circle from the primal image to death and back again. And, after all, the primal image marks a certain death of the soul and of the person behind the performative persona.

Chasing a Rainbow employs a linear filmic narrative to describe Baker's life course. Its strengths lie in its assembly and presentation of rare footage and photographs of Baker. Yet, Baker's own voice is seldom heard. The recorded public interviews with her are short and sketchy. Her ideological motivations are not explored in depth, and her own writings, personal correspondence, and speeches are absent from the script. The documentary is a complex metaleptic story composed of photographs and films within films. The conventional narrative and story lines situate Baker in her life and times and silence her active participation in the shaping and review of her extraordinary career.

Final Reprieve

During the 1960s and early 1970s, Baker's live television performances consisted of variety shows and fund-raising pleas to save Les Milandes. She treated television as a publicity vehicle and did not develop a televisual persona that equaled in popularity her images in the theater and on film. Baker's televisual persona was, instead, constructed posthumously via the documentary and docudrama productions made about her. Brian Gibson's 1991 television special *The Josephine Baker Story,* produced by John Kemeny for HBO Pictures with RHI Entertainment, Inc., and Anglia Television, Ltd., is an American-style cinematic homage that touches in interesting ways on issues of race, gender, and politics. It is an important and skillfully produced film that presents Baker's image for the contemporary period. The film reflects comprehensive factual details with the artistic license necessary to produce a piece with broad audience appeal. Gibson uses the technique of the epistolary narrative to frame the life story recounted by Baker to her adopted Rainbow children. Although shots of Lynn Whitfield as Baker performing the danse sauvage appear with the opening credits, the film's narrative begins with the intertitle "May 10, 1969," accompanied by the following voiceover:

> NEWSCASTER: News reached Paris this morning that Josephine Baker is on the verge of bankruptcy. Adored in Paris, but banned in her native America,

she was once the richest black woman who ever lived. Her years of fortune began in the 1920s with her scandalous banana dance. But now her château in southern France is in danger of being taken away from her. It's been the home of her twelve adopted children of all races, her Rainbow Tribe.

VOICES OF THE CHILDREN: Janot, Akio from Japan, Jary from Finland, Luis from Colombia, Möshe from Israel, Marianne . . . Marianne.

The anonymous narrator continues with an account of Baker's last stand at Les Milandes: "Yesterday, Josephine said good-bye to her children, sending them to friends in Paris. Vowing to keep her dream alive, Josephine is threatening to lock herself in her medieval castle and take on all comers."

The loss of Les Milandes frames the letter through which Josephine explains her actions to her children and lays the foundation for the story of her life. Although the children are Baker's epistolary and diegetic audience, the television viewing audience is symbolically adopted into the family. The viewers become both voyeurs witnessing the inside story of Josephine's life (the real Baker) and adopted children incorporated into a simulated media family. To her children and the audience, Baker explains, "My dearest children . . . I want you all to know that I love you and that I've been forced to send you away. By now, you're in Paris, hearing stories about my scandalous past and crazy ideas, and I must set the record straight. I've got slave and Indian blood, which I always claimed made me more American than most people who called themselves that. So, what am I doing here, so far from where I began?" This strategy breaks down the barriers of spectatorship by challenging the audience of television viewers to become participants in her struggle and witnesses of her legacy.[42]

Through this strategy, Gibson is able to incorporate the linear narrative of Baker's life into a discourse directed toward her children. This approach allows Baker's character to use two narrative voices: first person, to experience the events in past and present, and third person, to editorialize about the events and provide a moralistic and interpretive commentary on what has taken place. Interlaced in the dialogue are quotes from Marcel Sauvage's 1927 biography *Les Mémoires de Joséphine Baker,* lending a feeling of verisimilitude to the film's narration. Since the children generally remain silent, apart from introducing themselves by name on two occasions, viewers can easily slip into the role of anonymous adopted children. By deploying these narrative techniques, the filmmakers are able to recycle nested narratives on contrasting discursive and visual planes that allow for the creative use of flashbacks to and juxtapositions of Baker at different stages of her career. All of these flashbacks and moral commentaries are "double framed" within the linear structure of Baker's life from childhood to adulthood as recounted to her children. This imbricated linear narrative closely follows the formula established by Christopher Ralling in *Chasing a Rainbow* and by the Cinderella narrative reiterated in the written biographies of Baker. Interestingly, Baker's own films are not used or alluded to in the narrative, perhaps because they would invoke a cinematic legacy that is still alive in the made-for-TV movie.

At key transitional moments, the letter to Baker's children is reintroduced to bridge time lapses and to create continuity in the story. The letter is bolstered by aphorisms and quotes from Josephine's mother, Carrie McDonald, referred to throughout the film as "Mama." McDonald, played by Vivian Bonnell, is presented as both a stern matriarch and a stereotypical "mammy" whose understanding of Baker's new life as a performer in France is limited and distorted. After her first disappointment with love in France, the Baker character comments, "I thought more and more of Mama's words. A colored woman's life is from 'can't do' to 'can't don't.'" Carrie's voice is also introduced as the voice of reason counterbalancing Baker's extravagances; she remarks to Jo Bouillon (David Dukes), "Nobody's never been able to tell her nothin'. Least of all me."

Throughout the film, Baker's character is consistently presented as quixotic, irrational, petulant, headstrong, and childlike. The opening letter alludes to Baker's "scandalous past and crazy ideas." Les Milandes is treated as an extravagant and irrational dream, and, at one point, the film even suggests that Baker suffered from manic-depressive mood swings after her battle with Walter Winchell.

> BAKER [*sobbing*]: Jo! Jo!
> BOUILLON: Hmm?
> BAKER: It's here again. That feeling.
> BOUILLON: Oh. Let's go back [to France]. It's fine to go back.

The philosophical motives for Baker's humanitarian work in later life are not examined, and her course of action at Les Milandes is treated as an extension of her emotionalism and her early primal image. In the establishing scene between Paul Colin and Baker, Colin describes her primal image as he sketches her: "érotique, cruelle, sauvage, infantine, dangereuse" (erotic, cruel, savage, childlike, dangerous). This dialogue is followed by a scene in which a half-nude Baker examines her reflection in a mirror and comments, "There she was. She'd been there all the time. I'd been too busy making faces so folks would like me. I'd never seen her. There she was. [*Savage dance drumming begins. Cut to danse sauvage.*] . . . One dance had made me the most talked-about woman in the world."

Male figures are repeatedly used to introduce balance, planning, and the voice of calculated reason to Baker, whose initial reactions are portrayed as impetuous and emotional. Sidney Bechet, played by Kene Holliday, convinces a reluctant Baker to perform the danse sauvage in feathers. He advises her that if she does not calm her emotions and overcome her scruples, she will be on the first ship back to the United States.

> BAKER: Yeah, they want my bare ass, but shit, they want my bare black ass. My "prim-a-teev," . . . my essential ass. If my mother found out, she'd knock me into next week, come Monday. I want respect, Bechet. I came here to be a dancer. Maybe I could be a singer too. I headlined on Broadway, I do comedy . . . I'm good at it.
>
> BECHET: Well, they want somethin' else. You gonna be outta here on the first thing smokin', if you don't deliver. Now, I'm your friend. I tell 'em what you want. You want to go back to five shows a day on the chitlin' circuit? Lookin' for lodging in places that don't say "No dogs, no Jews, no niggers"? Look Josie, you and your sweet ass have got 'em right here. Now don't it feel good? Ain't you a long way from East St. Louis?

This passage introduces Carrie's moralistic superego as a basis for Josephine's hesitation. Baker quickly transcends these problems and goes on to perform the danse sauvage and to pose for Paul Colin.

The sage advice that Baker receives from men is framed by an assessment of her emotional character used to advance the narrative. In two scenes with Pepito Abatino (Rubén Blades), Baker makes key, life-changing decisions based on opinions delivered by an intervening male voice. At their first meeting in the film, Pepito counsels Baker to take a more calculated view of her life options and to adopt him as her manager.

> ABATINO: Learn this— No Frenchman will sacrifice his respectability to make you his wife.

BAKER: [*Gasp!*]

ABATINO: Josephine . . . Mistress, yes. Lover, yes. Wife . . . no. And not because of your color, but because you have no family, no history. Adio sine ricore. Give your farewells without bitterness and enjoy Paris while it lasts for you. Remember, everything is possible here. Back home, I was a stone mason who liked to dance. I come here to Paris, give myself a title, and the next thing I know, rich women are paying to dance with me . . . with Count Giuseppe Pepito Abatino, at your service.

BAKER: Stateside, we call it being a no-account count.

ABATINO: Hah ha! What are your going to do when they get tired of you? When they get used to you. When they begin to look for the next spectacle . . . the next Josephine?

BAKER: Read the American papers, Count. I'm the most famous colored woman in the world, and I plan on being the richest.

ABATINO: As long as you're the latest novelty, the freshest scandal. It won't last. Dancers don't last. Next week, they'll want something different, and if you can't give it to them, then it's good-bye Josephine. Ciao. Josephine, are your ready to go home, to America? Are good things waiting for you there? I see a young, lonely girl who would have gone back home a long time ago, if only to visit. But something is keeping her here. She's still looking for something. Make me your manager.

Later in the same scene, Pepito urges Josephine to reflect deeply on her life goals as a way of reinforcing his request.

BAKER: Make you my manager? Look at you, are you crazy? Well, you're half a century older than me to start with . . .

ABATINO: Josephine . . . please. Inside of you, what do you want?

BAKER: To dance and be left alone by people like you who just want a piece of me, to use. All I want is . . . just to dance and be left alone.

ABATINO: Josephine. You think I'm trying to rob you? I'm not a thief! I am *not* a thief. I work for my money. What do you want? Inside, in the secret place?

BAKER: When I walk down the street and everybody's staring at me, I want one day to be able to know, really *know*, that they're doing it 'cause they see me. They're not starin' at my color; they're starin' at me. At Josephine, for who I am and what I'm worth.

ABATINO: I am a black Italian. I'm from Sicily. I'm also from the south. I know this feeling. I promise you this, dancers don't last, but Pepito and La Baker will. I promise you.

This scene diminishes Baker's agency in her decision to collaborate with Abatino and reintroduces the theme of racial discrimination, which is a leitmotif of the film. Much like Coton in *Princesse Tam-Tam,* in responding to Baker, Pepito refers to himself as a "black Italian" from "the south" who shares her concerns about pride and self-esteem. As Pepito begins to sculpt his Galatea, he provides the second assessment of Baker as a result of their European tour.[43] Backstage in Berlin, Pepito comments, "First they want to kill you, now they adore you. I love you! I love you because when I ask you to learn this, to try something more, you not only learn and try, but you become it. I love you because when something is put in your way, you fly over it, and it does not happen very often. I love you. [*As a sign of his adoration, he drinks a glass of water left by Josephine.*] I still love you, my Josephine."

While they are on tour in the United States in 1936, Pepito and Josephine argue, and he returns to France alone and dejected. Unknown to her, he is dying of cancer. Pepito's death sparks another male-advice sequence, once again with Sidney Bechet. Josephine has opened a nightclub in Harlem, and Bechet shows up unexpectedly. They commiserate over Pepito's death.

BECHET: Hey, there.

BAKER: Hi, Sidney baby.

BECHET: Thank you. [*Josephine sits down at a table with Bechet.*] Josephine, I guess we're a long way from Paris, girl. I'm sorry.

BAKER: He's dead.

BECHET: I know. Come on. Let's get outta here. [*Camera pans to closeup on Josephine.*]

BAKER: I sent him back and he died. He didn't tell me how ill he was. I sent him back, and he died by himself.

BECHET: And someday, maybe you'll get a chance to pay him back. Someday, maybe, you'll come to this bend in the road, and you can turn around and make it all right. Maybe.

BAKER: I'm tired. I'm through. I'm all used up. I can't do it anymore.

BECHET: And now you just goin' to turn your back on the music, Josie? You just goin' to hand in your crown?

BAKER: He made me.

BECHET: And you took. And now it's time for you to give back. What I know is, ain't no one ever been punished for givin' back. Go on and wear your crown, Josie.

The theme of "giving back," which is so central to Baker's Marian motif and her humanitarian efforts, is presented as driven and reinforced by male advice. In introducing Baker's 1943 performances for the American soldiers at a Liberty Club in North Africa, Lieutenant Sidney Williams, played by Lou Gossett Jr., interprets Baker's war efforts as "giving something back." Williams says to the other soldiers:

> Most of you boys were drafted, but there's somebody here who volunteered. Who was in France when Hitler invaded. . . . But she didn't cut and run, she stayed. She was one of the first to join the Resistance. She helped smuggle people and information across the border to safety. Her house was searched by the Gestapo. When things got too hot for her, she was ordered to North Africa. She's here for the same reason she stayed in France. She wants to give somethin' back. She's Josephine Baker.
> [*Crowd cheers. Jo Bouillon strikes up the band.*]

We are now presented with a new and mature Baker, dedicated to larger social and political causes, but the motivation is traced back to Pepito's death as the male figure that inspired her work. Although Josephine is presented as genuinely committed to humanitarian causes, an aura of irrationality surrounds her obsessions. In her obstinacy and dedication, she is depicted in the stereotypical guise of "Sapphire," or a shrew, a role also played by her mother, Carrie, both as an actual character and as a mnemonic device recurring in the film's narrative. On the occasion of Baker's marriage to Jo Bouillon in 1947 at Les Milandes (which the film erroneously describes as taking place in May, rather than June), Jo Bouillon offers a toast that provides a rapid assessment of his relationship to Josephine. This entire interaction is framed as part of Josephine's letter to her children, even though the remaining events that transpire at Les Milandes are not presented exclusively from her point of view.

> [*Noise of people celebrating and background of accordion music*]
> BAKER: Children, if you're going to get married, get married in France. Get married in May [sic] like your father and I did. [*Voices of children at play*]
> BOUILLON: I have to make a speech about the Josephine Baker I already know. I could make a dozen. There is a Josephine that I shared a foxhole with, more than once. When we were playing for the troops in North Africa, I don't know who I was more scared of . . . the enemy, or Josephine's temper if I didn't get the music just right.

BAKER: Oh, don't believe him. . . .

BOUILLON: There's also the Josephine who went, by herself, to Buchenwald and sang for the survivors. To the Josephine you are, to the Josephine you will become. [*Pause for toast*] I love you.

Bolstering the interpretation of Josephine's passions and emotionalism is a glimpse at her unorthodox religiosity. While this scene perpetuates the Marian motif, it is also used as the source of another analeptic reference to the deep scars of racism that may lead to rage and madness. Josephine stands before a statue of the Virgin Mary.

BAKER: Father, I saw her once. I was in St. Louis, and I was running from something terrible. [*Flashback to shots of a young Josephine in the 1917 St. Louis riot*] In the midst of all the smoke and noises and hate and hurts, she told me it would be all right. I was going to be okay. And something else . . . she had work for me. I had a job to do.

PRIEST: So you are a believer, Madame.

BAKER: Oh yes, I am a believer. But I don't think he's in only one place. I think he's as likely to be in a synagogue, or a mosque, or in a warehouse.

The Marian motif recurs during the staging of Baker's 1951 return trip to the United States with Jo Bouillon. Even Baker's commitment to racial desegregation, which was crucial to her crusade during this trip, is presented as influenced by male advice. Sidney Williams enters the picture again to update Baker on the racial climate of the United States and solicit her help to improve the situation.

WILLIAMS: Speak up now and they call you a Red. And they open up your mail. They bug your phone . . . look at Paul Robeson.

BAKER: Oh, Paul.

WILLIAMS: He's branded a Commie. They took away his passport. Since the war ended, fifty-four black men have been lynched in the south. A lot of them still wearing their goddamn uniforms. Fifty-four.

BAKER: But isn't anybody fightin' back?

WILLIAMS: Our colored leaders? . . . They split.

BAKER: And you? . . . What do you think, college boy?

WILLIAMS: Josie, we have come back to see the big ol' toad still sittin,' honkin' on his lily pad . . . honkin' louder than ever. We need all the help we can get.

This incident triggers Baker's U.S. civil rights campaign culminating in Josephine Baker Day in Harlem and the famous Stork Club affair. The Stork Club episode allows Winchell's critical commentary on Baker's activities to be introduced. In addition to providing important documentary facts on Baker's life, this sequence challenges the saintly image of Baker by humanizing her choices and bringing her struggles down to earth. Once again, the commentary and assessments come from a male, this time, Walter Winchell. This scene problematizes racial issues for an American public, and it places Baker's actions in perspective, although there is a lingering subtext that those actions are obsessive and extreme. Winchell says:

> Turning to someone right at the top of my drop-dead list. Josephony Baker . . . self-proclaimed Joan of Arc of the colored races and communist sympathizer. Don't you think that she's just about had all the free chicken that she's due here? She carries a French passport since she chose to renounce her American one when she married husband six, seven, or eight a few years back. Don't we have any say in who can get into the States to stir up trouble between the races? You know what would do us all a favor? For somebody to send this French citizen a list of the S.S. *Normandy*'s sailing times back to France . . . and maybe they could stamp her passport "No Admittance."

Returning from the U.S. trip emotionally bruised and battered, with less material success than expected, Baker turns her attention to Les Milandes and the building of the Rainbow Tribe. It is at this point that the filmmakers take another interesting ideological stand that departs from recorded facts on Baker's life. The film presents Jo Bouillon as the voice of reason, backed by Carrie McDonald's ongoing superegoic commentaries. The concluding sequence at Les Milandes supports a vision of Baker not only as overwhelmed by her financial difficulties, but also as an irrational actor. An alternate perspective might have portrayed her hunger strike at Les Milandes as a noble fight for her château and her dreams of universal brotherhood. At the close of the U.S. tour, Bouillon first asserts the sage voice of reason.

> BAKER: Are you mad at me too, Jo?
> BOUILLON: You told me this was the real reason you came back to America. So what can I say? That I only want to make a million dollars? That it's the only way that we can pay for the château, the way we live? No. I've learned my lesson. Don't stand in front of a moving train, and don't argue with Josephine.

BAKER: Jo, how could I come back here and not fight?

BOUILLON: I did not think it would be this hard.

Back at Les Milandes, after committing to build the Rainbow dream, Jo balks at the adoption of Noël, which, in the film, prompts his departure from Les Milandes on amicable terms without divorce.[44]

BAKER: Jo! He was found nearly frozen in the snow, sweetheart.

BOUILLON: But why should it be us who take him in. You cannot save the entire world, Josephine. You cannot adopt every abandoned child.

BAKER: Who will do it? Who will do it, if we don't?

BOUILLON: Josephine.

BAKER [*speaking to one of the children*]: Marianne, you're not to be around that tree until tomorrow morning. Upstairs now.

BOUILLON: You gave me your word. You promised. You have your family now.

BAKER: I want to give a home to every child whose parents don't want it. Why is Josephine wrong for that? Why is she bad? Don't I love the ones I have?

BOUILLON: Nobody could love them more than you. But that's why you have to listen when I tell you. We cannot afford to live here. You do this, and we lose this house and everything. Believe me.

BAKER: Noël. I shall call him Noël.

BOUILLON: Josephine. You do this, and I will leave.

At this point, Josephine's film dialogue switches to reflections in which she refers to herself in the third person, a technique used when she is obstinate about her obsessions and passions, and which increases the irrational tone of her discourse by reinforcing the imagery of a dominatrix. She repeatedly asserts that she *is* Josephine, the matriarch and the celebrity.

BAKER: I'm Josephine. I can't stop at four. Four and some boring little house with no fields or trees to play in, no farm, no animals, no rivers to swim in. I don't want any child to hurt anywhere. Because I am Josephine, I cannot stop at four, or six, or eight, or ten. I won't do it. I can't. Don't ask me, Jo. I won't.

BOUILLON: Then you will lose me! I will not divorce you. I will give the children what help I can, but I cannot stay!

This scene concludes with dialogue that paraphrases an interview in *Chas-*

ing a Rainbow with Jean-Claude Baker, who characterizes Josephine as the sun, a figure who burns everyone close to her but doesn't touch the theater audience distanced from her by the orchestra pit.[45] This metaphor is used to humanize Baker and to convert her from a mythic heroine into a vulnerable antiheroine.

BAKER: Jo. Jo. The first week I was in Paris, I saw a box of candy. About this big. It cost two weeks' wages, and all the other girls thought I was crazy to buy it, but Jo, I know . . . I know . . . I was born knowing, you have to want that big box.

BOUILLON: I have heard this too many times, about wanting so much. This time, no. No, Josephine. Let someone else.

BAKER: But Jo, you won't leave. You won't leave. What about the children?

BOUILLON: Do you think it's good for them to see their father destroyed? 'Cause anyone who gets too close to you, you burn. Oh yes. When it's up there on the stage, it's fine. But down here, you burn anyone who gets too close to you.

BAKER: Love me here. Now. That's all I'm asking, Jo. Just love me. Do what I say.

BOUILLON: Do you hear? You're not asking for love. Just for everything to be done your way. You just said it.

BAKER: Just one more. Please. How could you say no, Jo? Please.

BOUILLON: You cannot trust anyone. You never listen. Never, never, never have you listened to me. You respect *me*, now. Let someone else!

It is at this point that Carrie's superegoic voice reenters the scene in a private conversation with Jo Bouillon.

BOUILLON: I kept my part of the bargain. I gave up my band, my life. I sold the house my parents left me. I put all the money into the château . . . every penny I ever had.

CARRIE: Nobody's never been able to tell her nothin'. Least of all me.

Jo promises Baker that he will not divorce her, and Carrie warns Josephine not to divorce Jo.

CARRIE: I can't change. I'm too old to change.

BAKER: Well, I can't either. I couldn't do what he wanted me to do to keep him. I couldn't. I have to do it my way, Mama. I have to. There's no other way.

If I wasn't like that, we'd still be hauling those wet sheets back in that boxcar in St. Louis.

   CARRIE: But no divorcin'. You promise me. And no badmouthin'. They love him, Josie, and he went as far as any man's ever goin' to go with you.

   BAKER: I'm going back on the road. I'm going to keep this place.

Shortly after this exchange, Carrie dies while preparing to pass out lemonade to the Rainbow children. Josephine is dejected and alone as she defends her château. The film presents the last moments at the château in a poignant manner, ending with Josephine in her nightgown of misery. The closing sequence then cuts to her farewell performance at the Théâtre Bobino in Paris in April 1975. The epistolary technique is reinserted for the last time in the form of a backstage telephone call to the Rainbow children.

   [*Baker sings "Me Revoilà Paris."*]

   BAKER [*On the telephone to her children backstage*]: I just wanted to tell you that you're wonderful children, every one of you, and I'm so proud and happy that you let me be your mother. And perhaps, perhaps, your mother isn't as old-fashioned and out of touch as you think, no? Especially you, Jean-Claude. Mick Jagger is in the audience this evening, so there! Mmm-wa [*kissing sound*].

   [*To the Bobino audience*] Thank you sooo much. It has been such a marvelous, marvelous evening. You know, it's not often that an old girl like me gets to look back over her life—over all the bends in the road—and be here with such a giving audience, like you. I have learned. I have learned that the one thing you never, ever get punished for is giving.

   [*Chord plays. Baker sings "The Times, They Are A-changin'."*]

It is appropriate and consistent that the film ends with Baker's rendition of Bob Dylan's composition "The Times They Are A-changin'." This song signifies that we have just witnessed a compilation of Baker's images for a new era, for changing times in which her dreams, aspirations, and obsessions still have an important contribution to make to politics and popular culture as Josephine Baker "gives back" her talent to the world.

Familiar Closings

Films by and about Josephine Baker reflect consistency in their narrative formats and messages. Each film uses a variation of the Cinderella or the

Pygmalion-and-Galatea motif. Baker's primal image as the savage dancer frames her rise to fame in each film and in certain cases (*Sirène des tropiques* and *Princesse Tam-Tam*) results in her downfall. Although the primal imagery used in *Sirène* and *Princesse Tam-Tam* builds upon colonial stereotypes, the deployment and interpretation of these images differs in the two films. *Sirène* uses the colonialist image of the primitive at a zero-degree level, playing into the audience's expectations about an exotic other, while *Princesse Tam-Tam* parodies nativistic images through crisp dialogue, clever camerawork, and a verbal and visual critique of discontent with "civilization." *Zouzou* marks a crucial turning point by introducing both working-class and glamourous images that challenge and counterbalance the primal stereotype of the caged bird. Although *Zouzou* ends with the heroine's sacrifice, the character remains autonomous and successful in the world of the Parisian music hall. Thus, *Zouzou* is a pivotal film in Baker's career. Interestingly, it receives little attention in the documentaries about her and is not even alluded to in Brian Gibson's HBO docudrama.[46]

The documentary film and the docudrama may be reviewed intertextually. *Chasing a Rainbow* serves as a model for *The Josephine Baker Story* released five years later. The HBO special follows the same chronological timeline as the earlier documentary. Both of these films play to a limited range of audience expectations. While *Chasing a Rainbow* situates Baker with respect to large world events (the Depression, war, and the civil rights movement), *The Josephine Baker Story* emphasizes Baker's struggle against racism for a contemporary American audience. Both pieces attempt to develop narrative motivations for Baker's actions, but Ralling's documentary is the more cautious and conservative. When Baker's actions do not fit into the mold set by the film, they are described as "confusing" or "secret." Hence, her activities during the war years are glossed over and supplanted by newsreel footage of the victory of the allied forces. Brian Gibson's docudrama is equally wary of this period and, instead, introduces a narrative focus on Baker's work with Sidney Williams and the Liberty Clubs in North Africa. This sequence is used as a narrative buildup to Baker's political activities in the United States in 1951, where Williams is reintroduced as a sage counselor and supporter.

In both documentaries, the Rainbow Tribe is treated as an irrational obsession leading to Baker's demise. Little attempt is made to explore in depth the philosophy behind her experiment. Links between Baker's universalistic, humanitarian vision and her activism in the United States are minimized, precluding an overview of the consistency of her actions and her dedication to performing politics. Baker's political activism makes more sense when her philsophy of universalism is framed in terms of her increasing involvement with French politics and her humanitarian commitments to a battle against racism worldwide. Omission of the French framework in order to appeal to the Anglo-American audiences of the two documentaries results in proleptic gaps in the narratives, as well as in the undertone of "confusion" to which Oliver Todd refers.[47]

As with her performances and the photographs of her, the films by and about Baker highlight her body as a symbol as she moves from the role of savage dancer to mature sophisticate and humanitarian. It is the contradiction between the primal bodily image and the changing messages that it was used to communicate during Baker's life that creates the genuine "confusion" attributed to her by some filmmakers and biographers. By associating the primal body as a medium with the larger messages that Baker ultimately used her body to convey and promote, the filmmakers permit us to understand the sense of rupture that is so critical to Baker's enigmatic persona. The filmic image of the body also carries with it deep personal and psychological messages that open the door to interpreting how Baker developed the public persona she used to change the worlds of art, entertainment, and politics.

Baker's films are semiotically revealing as much for what they do not show as for what appears on the screen. Her incessant battles to alter the unidimensional and stereotypical characters of her heroines and to change the disappointing endings of her films constitute the unseen and unstated subtexts of Baker's celluloid projections.[48] The films leave viewers with the legacy of Baker's body in motion; frame her images in extended, entangled narratives; and raise haunting questions about the limitations of colonialist representations of assimilation and change. Reviewing the nested narratives of these films provides a rich and enduring resource for the interpretation of Josephine Baker's cultural influence as an icon and an image.

Part Two

Living the Dream

4 Dress Rehearsals

Art Deco; the blues—St. Louis, Memphis, New Orleans; George
Gershwin; Josephine Baker at the Casino de Paris; dance teams
. . . turbaned Indian maharajas doing the Charleston . . ; red
lipstick, rouge, and red varnished nails.
—Diana Vreeland, 1977

Josephine Baker's persona provides a means for viewing the coalescence of art, style, and fashion during the Jazz Age. Baker's
early image construction occurred against the backdrop of the Parisian environment and its art world. Paris was the site of the birth and blending of
vibrant artistic movements—cubism, surrealism, dada, and art deco—and
dramatic changes in fashion. Modernism's mechanical domination gave way
to a nostalgic quest for primal purity in art. The Paris that Baker encountered
in 1925 contained a series of small villages cross-cut by the grand boulevards
designed by Georges Haussmann in the 1860s to create order and erect barriers between the social classes.[1] This landscape that separated official Paris
from the popular city, the territory of administration from the worlds of labor
and leisure, was the public domain of the *flâneur* who freely explored the
city.[2] Hidden from public view, the music hall was associated with the wild
and free demimonde, while the Opéra de Paris and official theaters occupied
public spaces on the grand boulevards. Therefore, it is particularly interesting

that the Théâtre des Champs-Elysées, located on avenue Montaigne in the fashion district of official Paris, housed Josephine Baker's first performance in *La Revue nègre*. Revitalization of the theater through the revue took place in the context of colonial exoticism. The premiere of *La Revue nègre* coincided with the opening of the International Art Deco Exposition of 1925, which featured new forms of art, architecture, and fashion. These innovations in art and performance set the stage for debates about the future of modernism.

Disrobing Primitivism

When she exploded onto the Parisian scene, Baker constructed and was associated with multiple images: the savage dancer, the Black Venus, the exotic Jazz Age star, the liberated new woman, and the gender-bending cross-dresser. Focusing on Baker's primal and glamour images as captured through art, photography, fashion, and architecture brings her into view from the perspectives of expert observers, that is, artists and their audiences, who possessed the agency to transform and adapt what they saw. Baker began to dress the part and live her life in accord with the images that she projected to these audiences. The primal Baker and the glamorous image are dichotomous elements united by the overcoding of a Cinderella narrative through which Baker used theatrical and film performances to display her transformation and its fragility. Overlapping narratives building on these images are nested one within the other, weaving a pattern of subtle seduction that ranges from Circe in Baker's Temple of Love to Cinderella in her autobiographies and films. These nested narratives were constructed through Baker's live performances and her excursions into the art world. The image of the primal and exotic seductress, Fatou, which became affixed to Baker when she arrived in Paris with the Revue nègre troupe, haunted her for the rest of her life and remained part of the essential Baker signature. As it is reworked through art, photography, and architecture, this signature image creates a powerful story with a modernist twist that masks many contradictions.

Images of the black woman as a "sexualized savage" have a long history dating from antiquity. In the nineteenth-century French artistic worlds, literary works by Balzac, Baudelaire, de Pons, Loti, and Zola, among others, drew on the symbolism of atavistic black desire and the European fascination with primitivism.[3] The tragic case of the naturalist Georges Cuvier's anthropological and biological experiments with Sartjee Baartman, known as the Khoikhoi (Hottentot) Venus, reinforce the power of the primitive stereotype. In 1810, the twenty-two-year-old Baartman was transported from Cape Colony to London, where she was placed on display. Four years later, Baartman was taken to Paris where scientists and entrepreneurs exhibited her as a curiosity (the Hottentot Venus) and also examined her as a laboratory specimen.[4] As an object of what Bernth Lindfors has termed "ethnological show business," Baartman was displayed at expositions and in private salons.[5] Cuvier measured her, recorded her reflexes, and arranged to have her painted and diagrammed. In this pre-photographic era, paintings and drawings exaggerated the features of cultural stereotypes. After her untimely death, Baartman was dissected, and her genitals were placed on display. Plays and stories were written about Baartman, who provided a dramatic link between show business and science in the early nineteenth century. Along with literary fantasies and artistic caricatures, Baartman's presence casts an ominous shadow over images of the black female body in France. Baker's primal image in the 1920s and 1930s combined Baartman's legend and Pierre Loti's fantasy of Fatou, both of which challenged French notions of order and civilization.

Although Baker's primal image partook of a long cultural legacy over which she had little control, she eventually manipulated aspects of the stereotype to her advantage. Baker, who had been called "the monkey" as early as her American debut in the cast of Sissle and Blake's *Shuffle Along*, "monkeyed around" a great deal to capitalize on her primal image. When Baker arrived on the Parisian scene, the lingering totalizing image of the sexualized savage was already in transition and signified not only primitivism to be feared by the West, but also a symbol of freedom and experimentation for the French artistic avant-garde. Thus, an analysis of Baker's roles and personas must also take into account the ways in which primitivist imagery provoked cultural protest in a mechanized, modernist society where she performed the savage dance in front of a stage set of skyscrapers.

Baker's Parisian story begins with the creation of an exotic image through theatrical and nightclub performances. The artist Paul Colin was responsible for molding the visual images, and the music-hall producer Jacques-Charles for choreographing the danse sauvage. But the success of the exotic image results from Baker's ingenuity at improvisation and from the reception of the disrobed primal image by an audience eager to incorporate Baker into escapist colonialist and modernist fantasies.

Orientalist and exotic images have a long history in French culture. By the seventeenth century, elements of Persian design were firmly ensconced in the décor and dress of the French court. In the nineteenth century, figures of Orientalist escape, from Cleopatra to Salomé, were central to French literature.[6] The world of the music hall, with its ties to commercial art and fashion, fed off of and intensified these popular images.

First published in a limited edition in 1927, and inspired by Baker, Paul Colin's portfolio of lithographs entitled *Le Tumulte noir* depicts the fervor and excitement of the music hall as it spilled over into the art worlds of Paris and beyond. Baker appropriated Colin's exotic caricatures as part of her performative persona. She used this imagery as a central device in developing her new identity in collaboration with Parisian artists and impresarios.[7] Fernand Léger, the cubist painter who had designed the sets for Stravinsky's African-inspired ballet *La Création du monde,* which debuted in Paris on October 1923, was a close friend of André Daven, director of the Théâtre des Champs-Elysées. Léger encouraged Daven to hire the cast of *La Revue nègre* and remained one of Josephine's staunch supporters during her early career.

Paul Colin, a graduate of the École des Beaux-Arts in Nancy, was hired to make the publicity posters for the show, and the Mexican artist Miguel Covarrubias designed the sets.[8] As an *affichiste,* or commercial artist, Colin was influenced by sources as diverse as Toulouse-Lautrec's circus paintings and the works of surrealists. Colin was an ambitious artist and a quick study with an eye for women and a rapidly expanding social network in Paris. He learned a great deal from his collaboration with Covarrubias, who began his work as a caricaturist and was known as the Picasso of the boulevards. Traveling around the world with his flamboyant wife, Rose, Covarrubias spent several years in New York, was involved with black vaudeville, and became a regular illustrator for *Vanity Fair.* In 1927, he published a collection of his works in New York under the title *Negro Drawings.* Covarrubias, who was also a performance artist, took with him to Paris the traditions of minstrelsy and caricature and introduced his jazzy images to the music-hall scene. In particular, his 1924 caricature entitled *Jazz Baby* had a great influence on Colin, who adapted the image from the set designs of Covarrubias to represent Baker in his 1925 poster for *La Revue nègre*[9] (figs. 27 and 28).

The appearance of Colin's first lithographs and posters of Baker overlapped with the 1925 Exposition Internationale des Arts Décoratifs et Industriels Modernes (International Exposition of Modern Decoration and Industrial Art), which had opened on July 18. While art deco constituted the theme of the exposition, the Pavillon de l'Esprit Nouveau featured the work of a new young Swiss-born architect, later to become one of Baker's friends,

Figure 27. Miguel Covar-
rubias's "Jazz Baby," *Vanity
Fair,* December 1924.
© 1924, Condé Nast Publi-
cations, Inc.

Le Corbusier (Charles-Edouard Jeanneret), whose minimalist functionalism
contrasted with the decorative emphasis of the exposition. Colin made sure
that posters for *La Revue nègre* reached all corners of the Parisian art world,
including the exposition at Pont Alexandre III.

In his sketches, Colin experimented in bold ways with color, contour, and
form. His *Tumulte noir* series consists of forty-five lithographs circulated in a
limited edition. In their introduction to the 1998 republication of *Le Tumulte
noir,* Henry Louis Gates and Karen Dalton note, "Each page measures 18$\frac{1}{2}$ x
12$\frac{1}{2}$ inches. Henri Chachoin, a printer Colin often used until the mid-1930s,
ran an edition of five hundred unnumbered copies, on wove paper, and twenty
numbered copies, ten on Japan paper and ten on Madagascar paper. Paul
Colin drew the images onto lithographic stones, and J. Saudé stenciled in
the color. The complete edition sold out from one day to the next."[10]

Figure 28. Paul Colin's poster for *La Revue nègre*, 1925. © 2005 Artists Rights Society (ARS), New York / ADAGP, Paris.

Le Tumulte noir opens with a preface by the art and music critic Georges Thenon, known as "Rip" in the collection, and a handwritten introduction by Baker in which she describes the Charleston as a black dance craze and recounts the dramatic changes that it portends for Paris. In contrast, Thenon's preface to the volume ironically warns against the new dance invasion, cautioning people to calm down while the contorted convulsions of dances like the Charleston and the black bottom make their way across the city. Colin picked up on the irony in his sketch of Rip (plate 19 in the portfolio) in which he depicts a bronze-skinned Thenon in an open tunic contemplating three monkeys dancing on a limb. Colin repeatedly used monkey imagery to represent savage rhythms and combined images of monkeys with caricatures of blacks.

It is not possible to pinpoint exactly why Colin chose to use anthropometric monkey imagery or how much ironic distance he established from it. Strong arguments may be made about the continued scientific domination of the anthropometric vision in 1920s France and its links to colonial ideologies, museum culture, and the music hall. Haney points out that Josephine, who was unaware of these theories, was hurt and embarrassed when the French cartoonist Georges Goursat drew a caricature of her in which "the top half of her torso is elegant and theatrical, bedecked with jewels, but a monkey tail swings from her derrière with a fly buzzing around the tip."[11] The iconography of savagery was just below the surface in the popular French imaginary, and Colin's work echoed these exotic racialized images.

Although he was an innovator in his domain, Colin incorporated Baker's images into the existing aesthetic styles and discourses of an era (cubism, poster art, lithography, and caricature). Some of the drawings in *Le Tumulte*, such as the portrait of dancer and choreographer Jean Borlin, used cubist stylization. Other pieces depicting Josephine and the cast of *La Revue nègre*, including the now famous publicity poster for the opening, influenced by Covarrubias, used minstrel-like caricatures with large red lips, dark skin, and black-and-white clothing (see fig. 28). Colin deployed color to signify an artistic code, using red, white, and black on many of the most obvious racial caricatures. His plate 43 in *Tumulte*, entitled *Goodnight*, ostensibly presents the image of a black doorman dressed in a tuxedo bidding the musical-hall audience farewell. Only a few years later, in 1932, would Josephine herself appear on stage as a tuxedo-clad band leader. *Goodnight* presages this cross-dressed image by representing the doorman with an hourglass figure, a small, rather feminine head, and shapely legs. Just as Josephine "doubled" her own images of race and gender, Colin played upon doubling and irony in his representations.

Mistinguett (Jeanne Bourgeois) was one of Baker's music-hall arch rivals. Fearing that the younger, exotic Baker would eclipse her popularity, Mistinguett—a close associate of Maurice Chevalier—took every opportunity to block Josephine's solo appearances. Mistinguett's 1954 autobiography *Toute ma vie* demonstrates that she used many of the image-construction strategies, such as extravagant costumes, moralistic ballads, and the Cinderella story, that were appropriated by Baker. Colin's sketches of Mistinguett and Chevalier in *Tumulte* (plates 18 and 4, respectively) are interesting inversions of style. Chevalier is copper-toned in color and drawn with an hourglass figure. He appears cavalier and graceful. Were his name left unidentified, however, he could easily be confused with a member of the cast of *La Revue nègre*. Mistinguett is depicted in copper tones with bare feet and bangles. Only a swatch of blonde hair and one blue eye appearing beneath her top hat suggest Mistinguett's identity. Actually a brunette, she often wore blonde wigs. Her bared teeth and vicious stare illustrate Colin's attitude toward her and the resentment toward her that he seems to have shared with Josephine.

Inspired by both African sculpture and cubism, Colin repeatedly sketched the "S" shape and the hourglass in his figures. West African fertility figures, for example, those of the Lobi and the Senufo, use the "S"-shaped bodily curves with enlarged or elongated hips as signs of feminine beauty and fertility. In order to reflect the energy and exoticism of tumultuous black dance, Colin transferred this type of iconography into his images of Josephine and the other *Revue nègre* players. Gates and Dalton suggest a refinement and evolution in Colin's artistry from crude, minstrel-like figures to sculpted dancers in motion based on his artistic sessions with Josephine. They write, "To say that Josephine 'posed' for those drawings seems to be a contradiction, for each explodes with movement. They have more in common with stop-action frames than with traditional studio sketches."[12] Each frame of the dancers, musicians, and audience, in fact, freezes a jaunty movement in the air, creating a sense of motion, visual tension, and suspense that convey the effervescence of the Jazz Age. Paul Colin's lithographs of Josephine raise profound questions about art as a reflection of social context and as a cotextual commentary on relations of race and gender.

By Baker's own admission, Colin's images of her reshaped how she saw herself. Initially, she felt uncomfortable about posing in the nude for Colin (who typically seduced his music-hall models), but she quickly changed her mind and took charge of her new image. In her autobiography with Jo Bouillon, Josephine describes her responses to the first session with Colin: "The next day several people drew me aside to explain that I would never be anything without the poster, that I would not be the first person or the last to undress in front of Paul Colin, that artists had certain rights and I as a mere beginner had certain *duties*. Just think—my likeness would be plastered all over Paris! Yes, but *naked!* What would they say in St. Louis? That night I removed all my clothes."[13] Other artists also contributed to the primal mystique, including Alexander Calder, whose 1927 and 1929 wire sculptures of Baker are well-known templates for her early image (fig. 29).

James Clifford contends that Baker's body, as represented in Fatou's danse sauvage, inspired by André Daven and Jacques-Charles, and represented in Colin's lithography, was itself an "ideologically loaded" form that evoked the vitality and magic of primitivism.[14] Yet, this form was also a social construction and an elaboration of exotic fantasies, plunging its makers into an emotional abyss of nostalgia and neoprimitivism. Hammond and O'Connor write, "For the Parisians Joséphine seemed to create an art formed by influences from the jungle, from African sculpture, filtered through New Orleans: she was the 'Douanier' Rousseau of the music-hall, a living Gauguin, the 'Black Venus' of Baudelaire."[15]

The iconography of Baker's primal image was based on stereotypes and objectifications, that is, on her transformation into an object for the audience's gaze. A detailed deconstruction of Baker's public and private images, however, cautions against reducing her to an essentialist projection without reviewing the historical and cultural contexts of image production. Baker's own actions suggest that she was less concerned with the constraints placed on her image by racial stereotypes than she was with the freedom achieved by appearing on the French stage as a rising star.

Montmartre was the center of black expatriate Paris during the late 1920s and early 1930s. Often referred to as Harlem on the Seine, it became not only the home of black American musicians, but also the locus of a network of small clubs that became after-hours meeting places for musicians and artists and places where African American music, food, and hospitality were packaged and sold to an audience of Parisians and tourists. On December 14, 1926, Baker realized one of her early dreams when she opened the nightclub Chez

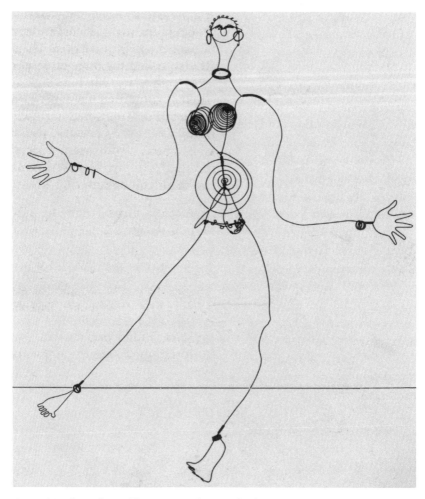

Figure 29. Alexander Calder's wire sculpture of Baker, 1927. © 2006 Estate of Alexander Calder / Artists Rights Society (ARS), New York / ADAGP, Paris.

Joséphine on rue Fontaine in Montmartre. With the backing of Dr. Gaston Prieur (later staunchly defended by Josephine when he encountered troubles with the law) and Pepito, the club was a tremendous success. The high point of each night was Josephine's grand entrance at about midnight after her music-hall performance. Clad in an extravagant gown and jewels, she would parade through the club, then change costume, and perform a few songs. Following a pattern developed by her friend Bricktop, Josephine attempted to establish the appearance of an intimate personal relationship with her customers, converting the nightclub from a public into a quasi-private space. This personalistic approach to the audience became the hallmark of black cabaret style in Paris. Josephine gave Charleston lessons; set the menu, which combined soul food and cordon bleu cuisine; and organized the roster of performers. In these activities, she engaged in a friendly competition with her colleagues Bricktop and Florence Jones of Chez Florence.

The club gave Baker a chance to experiment with images that went beyond her music-hall persona and allowed her to work on new song-and-dance routines. She used the club as a point of departure for an image transformation that allowed her to perform with more freedom than she had with *La Revue nègre* and the Folies-Bergère. Although still under Pepito's protection and management, at the club Baker was on her own as the main attraction. Throughout her career, Baker would use this early experience to move in and out of the nightclub circuit as a source of revenue and artistic experimentation. Janet Lyon claims that Chez Joséphine became a "modernist salon" for the Parisian avant-garde.[16] Interestingly, it is in the club that Josephine composed large portions of her first memoirs with Marcel Sauvage. This nightclub phase established Josephine's ties to the Montmartre jazz community and laid the foundation for her eventual break from it with her new image as a rising music-hall star.

Poses of African Art

Picasso's use of a Fang mask from Gabon as a model for *Les Desmoiselles d'Avignon* launched a movement that would redefine perspective, line, and form in European art. Despite denials of some of the cubists that they ever saw or appropriated aspects of African art, the historical record indicates that they were influenced by the increasing interaction between France and its colonies. The *Exposition Universelle* (World Fair) of 1900 brought African art and artifacts to the forefront. Cubism challenged classical norms of human representation by drawing on exotic images and objects as inspirations for experiments with perspective, line, form, and color. Its spare lines were an attempt to penetrate the visual essence of an object.[17] By the time of cubism's decline in France in 1914 and after, this visual paring down became a standard device used by many popular artists. Underlying this artistic coalescence was a critique of Enlightenment rationality and a search for the primitive sources of creativity in the "savage mind." Baker, too, learned about African sculpture and used it to model poses for her photographs and dances (fig. 30).

At the same time, André Breton, Georges Bataille, and other surrealists saw the Dionysian element of civilization as purifying and liberating.[18] French anthropologists were not immune to this romantic search for the primitive elements of art, culture, and the human psyche. Bataille had worked with Georges-Henri Rivière to organize France's first exhibition of pre-Columbian art. Bataille viewed pre-Columbian art and African art as the sources of dark and violent forces that engender all creativity.[19] Rivière, who was hired permanently by the Musée de Trocadéro in part on the basis of the popularity of this exhibit, was a jazz buff and a fervent supporter of Josephine Baker. For him, Baker's image and the power of her early performances evoked mystery, magic, and eroticism.

Continued links between the French museum and show business were neither fortuitous nor abstract. In 1925, the year in which Baker arrived in Paris with the Revue nègre ensemble, three young anthropologists, Marcel Mauss, Lucien Lévy-Bruhl, and Paul Rivet, established the Institut d'Ethnologie. They developed a plan to reorganize the Musée de Trocadéro, which had been based on outmoded concepts of race and evolution promulgated by Armand de Quatrefage and Théodore Hamy, into a culturally rich environment that thrived on its allusions to exotic popular anthropology. To this end, they enlisted the skills of Rivière, who had built a reputation as a cultivated collector, innovative scholar, and entrepreneur. Rivière adored the music-hall and cabaret life and introduced wax dioramas resembling music-hall tableaux to the museum. Moved by Josephine's music-hall sketches, Rivière had even written a song for Baker to perform at the Casino de Paris in which he confessed to dreaming about her image (idées noires) day and night. He recalled, "I wrote an operetta for Jacques Fray and Tristan Bernard: 'Le Loulou florentin.' And a song for Baker that she performed at the Casino de Paris. I remember a fragment of one of the couplets, 'On va fonder, on en jase. Une usine à jazz.' (We're going to create, we're bubbling over about it. A veritable jazz factory.)"[20]

Figure 30. Baker and a piece of African sculpture, 1928. Photo from Madame d'Ora's photographic series, courtesy of Getty Images, New York.

Studio d'Ora

Rivière and his colleague Marcel Griaule enlisted Baker's help, along with that of the black Panamanian boxer Alfonso Teofilo Brown, to raise funds for the 1931 Dakar-Djibouti anthropological expedition, a trans-African mission that would collect and document artifacts and languages. A protégé and lover of Jean Cocteau, Brown also frequented the jazz club circuit and performed briefly as a singer and dancer in a circus when he retired from boxing.[21] Josephine was photographed by the press in 1931 in an improvised exhibition boxing match with Brown refereed by Roland Toutin. In 1933, Baker returned to visit the Musée de l'Homme and examine the objects collected by the expedition. Boris Lipnitzki photographed her there with Rivière (fig. 31).[22] By the time the new Musée de l'Homme opened in 1931, Josephine had already begun to marshal the emblems of her performative primitivism to the aid of avid collectors. Although her nomination was later revoked because she was not a French citizen or colonial subject, in 1930 Josephine had been selected as Queen of the Colonies for the Universal Colonial Exposition, which opened on May 29, 1931, and was used, in part, to inaugurate the new Musée de l'Homme at the Palais de Chaillot. In spite of the withdrawal of her title, Baker's spirit of colonial exoticism permeated the controversial exposition and intensified the rift between pro- and anti-colonial forces in the Parisian avant-garde art world.

Another version of African art eventually emerged through the voices of African and Antillian students, writers, and artists in search of their cultural roots and legacies. Léopold Senghor explored the rhythms and sonority of African art in his vision of négritude, while the Martinican poet Aimé Césaire conjoined his surrealist verse with sketches by Picasso, in their collaborative book *Corps Perdu,* published in 1950. Alioune Diop, founder of the journal *Présence Africaine* and the publishing house of the same name, edited several volumes on *art nègre* with the aim of fostering a new pride in African traditions. In his preface to *L'Art nègre,* published in volumes 10 and 11 of *Présence Africaine,* Diop argued for the necessity of establishing an artistic language that endows the work of African artists with a "universal resonance."[23] Twenty-five

Figure 31. Josephine Baker and Georges-Henri Rivière, 1933. Photo by Haim (Boris) Lipnitzki, photothèque of the Musée de l'Homme, file D.84.1072, from the collection of Lipnitski-Viollet, courtesy of Documentation Photographique Roger-Viollet, Paris.

years after her original appearance in *La Revue nègre,* Baker lent her support to *Présence Africaine* as a member of the patronage committee and, for a time, vice president of its cultural arm, the Société Africaine de Culture.[24] Although Baker's early performances appeared to be light-years away from Senghorian négritude, the two approaches were linked as pathways to assimilation and alternative expressions of black autonomy in French culture. Diop, Senghor, and Césaire wrote about cultural universalism with the inflections of négritude, but Baker performed her version of négritude by fashioning an exotic public persona based on a combination of racialized stereotypes that evolved into more nuanced and sophisticated images.

From Neoprimitivism to Haute Couture

Fashion allows its wearers to assume and discard virtual identities.[25] Viewed in this way, fashion emerges as a discourse, or expressive form, independent of the codes of style, yet constantly referencing them. The links of fashion to the theatrical world further reinforce the identity-transforming power of costuming. Baker became a master manipulator of fashion and both used and served the fashion world in developing her public image. When Baker arrived in Paris in 1925, she wore brightly colored, homemade outfits from Harlem. In her memoirs recounted to Marcel Sauvage, Baker described these outfits: "My attire made everyone laugh. Now I'll tell you why everyone laughed, and I laugh about it more than anyone else. I wore a checkered dress with pockets held up by two checkered suspenders over my checkered blouse. I wore a hat with feathers on the top of my head, and I carried a camera on my left hip, and a large pair of binoculars on my right hip."[26]

Remarking on her ensembles with dismay, Paul Colin decided to take her to Paul Poiret, although some accounts say that she first went there with Caroline Dudley Regan.[27] Baker described her first visit to Poiret's fashion atelier as an astonishing experience: "I was quickly stripped of my clothes by two young women who instinctively sensed their master's wishes. Here I was, nude again. At least I was getting used to it. A third flunky now appeared, carrying a bolt of the most beautiful silvery material I had ever seen. It looked like a flowing river. Monsieur Poiret poured the gleaming torrent over me, rolled me up in it, draped it about my body, pulled it tight, ordered me to walk, then loosened it around my legs. I felt like a sea goddess emerging from the foam."[28]

From 1904 until the end of the 1920s, Paul Poiret was one of the leading couturiers in Paris. Corpulent, bearded, and turbaned, Poiret resembled a white sheik. Inspired by the popular interest in Orientalism, he adapted ethnic designs to the world of Parisian high fashion. He used Indian, Turkish, and Persian styles to fashion loose-fitting tunics, flowing robes, and flared trousers, and he often dressed in these styles himself. He advocated abandoning corsets and constricting clothing for women in favor of loose, brightly colored garments.[29] He was also one of the early proponents of short and simple hairstyles, making a revolutionary statement by cutting the hair of all the models for his 1908 fashion collection. He influenced Baker's short, slick hairstyle, which eventually became part of the Bakerfix publicity campaign but was at first the hallmark of the Poiret style.[30] In many ways, Poiret inspired the "flapper" look, but he went far beyond that in his appropriation of exotic designs. Intrigued by flamboyant costumes, Poiret designed for the theater as well as high fashion. His work included several revues organized by the impresario Charles B. Cochran, whose extravaganzas transformed the aesthetics of the Parisian music hall.[31] Baker became a cause célèbre for Poiret, and he provided her with garments, occasionally without receiving full payment. In 1926 alone, Baker received 285,000 francs worth of dresses and furs from Poiret, who ultimately asked her for a partial repayment.[32] In her public persona, Baker quickly moved away from homemade dresses to her own unique and contested relationship with Parisian haute couture.

Poiret's fashions were frequently featured as sketches in the *Gazette du Bon Ton*, a fashion magazine established in 1908 by Lucien Vogel.[33] Every issue of *Bon Ton* presented several pages of illustrations, including both design sketches and fashion caricatures. These designs and the accompanying texts included what Valerie Steele describes as "imaginary clothing" designed by *Bon Ton*'s illustrators.[34] These fabricated designs were the beginning of modern image-driven clothing in which the media promoted a certain look and the codes of fashion dictated what was actually worn. Although *Bon Ton* ceased to be published on a regular basis after 1914, the influence of its editors and contributors was still pervasive when Baker arrived in Paris, and it was the precursor of the French edition of *Vogue* magazine. The works of Poiret and other former *Bon Ton* contributors were displayed in the Pavillon d'Élégance of the 1925 International Art Deco Exposition and became the talk of all Paris. The *Bon Ton* and *Vogue* crowds were the fashion arbiters of the 1920s, and they found Baker's exotic image to be both intriguing and useful. In a practice that has become popular with designers, celebrities, and socialites today, other couturiers of the time, such as the celebrated Madame Vionnet, also offered Josephine gowns as advertisements for their work.

In 1925, *Vogue* magazine described Baker as the "most astounding of mulatto dancers, in her necklets, bracelets, and flouncing feathered loincloths."[35] Two years later when John McMullin interviewed Baker for *Vogue* after she made an entrance at her nightclub in Montmartre, he described her as graceful, "swathed in a full blue tulle frock with a bodice of blue snakeskin," wearing an "enormous diamond ring with a very impressive diamond bracelet."[36] It was in this period that George Hoyningen-Huene created the new, svelte fashion image of Baker in a nude pose of the Black Venus, draped with a diaphanous veil (see fig. 4). Meanwhile, a total transformation of Baker's public persona from the exotic savage to the sophisticated, liberated woman was in progress, and fashion magazines chronicled every moment of the change. Baker had left Paris for her European tour in 1927 with 15 steamer trunks, 137 dresses and costumes, 196 pairs of shoes, and 64 kilos of stage powder.[37] But the banana skirt from the Folies-Bergère—already a relic—would continue to overshadow Baker's essential image for years to come and to mark the thin line between the flapper and the feline.

Changes in European fashion were deeply connected to modernist ideologies in art, architecture, and social life. Baker's second European tour started in Vienna in February 1928 amid great controversy, as riots broke out over both her primal eroticism and her race. Count Adelbert Sternberg's impassioned defense of Baker's morality before the Austrian parliament in the wake of complaints by the Clerical Party was inspired by Secessionism and the local nudist movement, which advocated a return to nature as a moral response to modernity. The Secessionist architect Josef Hoffmann, a founder of the Viennese reform fashion movement, had influenced the local art scene.[38] This was also the Vienna where Freud and Wittgenstein explored the primal energy and purity of emotions, thought, and language. Reform fashion emphasized liberation through clothing, comfort, a return to nature, and bold designs. Clothing became an extension of the environment, a house for the body, apparel that was intended to be both flexible and functional. Several of the dresses and costumes depicted in photographs of Josephine's Vienna tour reflect the continued influence of reform fashion. The languages of reform dress and Secessionist architecture focused on purity and simple elegance—in other words, a return to the primal and the primitive.

One of the fellow travelers of the Secessionist movement, Adolf Loos, also became involved in the fashion revolution. Loos was fascinated by tailored, functional, and understated clothing for men and women.[39] He detested overdone, constraining outfits that challenged the aesthetics of purity, and he believed that modern clothing should be simple and stark.[40] From 1922 to 1928, Loos lived in Paris where he saw Baker perform and took dance lessons from her.[41] He was mesmerized by what he saw as the exotic purity of her primal stage persona, and he eventually designed a house that would allow Baker to be on display from all angles.[42] This ingenious house plan drew on geometrical African and Mediterranean structures and featured an impressive glass-encased swimming pool on the second and third floors. Although Loos's design for Baker's house never materialized as a dwelling, it remains a testament to the influence of her exotic image on modern architecture.

In turn, Baker became the architect and sculptor of her own body. From the lessons learned in her early touring days with the Dixie Steppers, *Shuffle Along,* and *Chocolate Dandies,* Baker brought the cosmetic processes of masking and blackening up, minstrel-style. Once in France, she became obsessed with both natural (lemon juice, milk, and flour) and artificial skin-lightening products. Skin, hair, costume, and cosmetic changes were critical to the Baker mystique. In this carefully chosen makeup and dress, Baker posed for photographs and theatrical scenes.

Counterbalancing Josephine's frenetic dancing and Paul Colin's portraits-in-motion was the music-hall tableau, which resembled a posed, single-frame photographic image. The revue *Paris qui remue* (Swinging Paris), which opened in October 1930, was one of Baker's most impressive early successes using the tableau format.[43] Produced by Henri Varna and Léo Lelièvre, with music by Vincent Scotto, sets and costumes by Georges Barbier and André Bay, and choreography supervised by Earl Leslie, the revue ran for over a year with more than 550 performances at the Casino de Paris. The cast included the Eight Jackson Boys (not to be confused with the Jackson Five) and the Sixteen Jackson Girls, with music by Edmond Mahieux and the Melodic-Jazz Band of the Casino de Paris.

An article published in the Parisian newspaper *Ami du Peuple* on October 22, 1930, referred to *Paris qui remue* as "incontestably the most beautiful revue presented in Paris since the war."[44] It consisted of forty-five tableaux, or sketches, in two acts. Each sketch was five to fifteen minutes long, featuring poses, songs, and dances, including one of Josephine's first appearances in a ballet, entitled "L'Oiseau des forêts" (Forest Bird), choreographed by Josephine's dance partner Joe Alex, and the famous number "Vénus noire," immortalized in posters, cards, and photographs. The interplay of the stage sets, the costumes, and the performances created a total ambiance. One tableau, "L'Orage sur l'océan" (Ocean Storm), even simulated a hurricane blowing off the performer's costumes on stage under pink and blue flashing lights. "Le Point de Venise" presented a Venetian ballroom scene complete with live pigeons released from the back of the theater. "Noblesse d'auto" was a tribute to the automotive world with designs of a Mercedes, Voisin, and Rolls reproduced by Paul Colin. In the concluding tableau, "Amour et électricité" (Love and Electricity), Josephine appeared as an electrically illuminated firefly with huge wings (fig. 32). The firefly was an important transitional image that was both primal and elegant. It also emphasized the power of modern technology. In addition to introducing Josephine's signature song "J'ai deux amours," by Henri Varna and Vincent Scotto, *Paris qui remue* contained other memorable numbers that were recorded in a 1930 album, such as "Voulez-vous de la canne à sucre?" and "La Petite Tonkinoise." Josephine appeared as Antillian, Vietnamese, and African in these sketches, with over fifty costume changes per show.

Paris qui remue marked a critical step in developing Baker's artistry and changing her fashion image. The revue was lavish and extravagant. Although critics of the show still referred to her as a "strange and savage animal,"[45] Baker had abandoned, although not forgotten, her banana skirt and solidified the sophisticated high-fashion image that she had begun to create during the late 1920s.[46] While Baker's early performances at the Théâtre des Champs-Elysées and the Folies-Bergère relied primarily on dance, *Paris qui remue* included complex vocal scores with Baker clothed as a diva. Baker had recorded six of the songs for the show, including "J'ai deux amours," for release with Columbia Records in Paris on October 23, 1930. No longer promoted exclusively using a silent film or photographic image, Baker had acquired the ability to express herself in French and describe her position in Paris. As the quintessential new woman of the late 1920s and early 30s, her libertine image was used to advertise hair pomade, skin lotion, culinary recipes, cigarette cards, and summer

Figure 32. Josephine Baker as a firefly in *Paris qui remue*, 1930. Photo by Haim (Boris) Lipnitzki from the collection of Lipnitzki-Viollet, courtesy of Documentation Photographique Roger-Viollet, Paris.

vacations. Baker returned to the Parisian stage after her European tour as a cultural commodity and an icon whose new style spoke for itself. She began to live her dream of the high life with Pepito as her consort and guide.

Scholars of Baker's fashion image often remark on her first campaign to advertise body cream, in 1926, because it involved marketing a superficially nonracial cosmetic ideal to a large French audience, although Valaze cream, with its resultant Bakerskin, could, in certain ways, be compared with suntan lotion.[47] A sign mounted near Place de l'Opéra read, "You can have a body like Josephine Baker if you use Valaze cream." A large Josephine Baker doll was displayed in an adjacent boutique.[48] Small dolls in banana skirts and the doll-faced maquette, which are now collector's items, were marketed as children's toys and souvenirs. Pepito and Josephine posed with the original small doll, complete with Josephine's hair curl, in an early photograph, dated around the mid-1930s (fig. 33). Baker copied the hair pomade developed by the African American entrepreneur Madam C. J. Walker. Abatino arranged for her to market her own version, Bakerfix, a type of brilliantine cream invented by an Argentine chemist. Bakerfix billboards were plastered across Paris. Baker also posed for the best fashion and art photographers of her day, and her image was emulated by people of all ages and backgrounds. According to Baker, Le Corbusier even donned a Baker costume complete with blackface on a cruise that he made with her to South America.[49] As a result of makeup and photographic retouching, images of Baker from within any given period often appear completely different from one another as she crisscrossed racial and gender lines. Upon close scrutiny, one has the impression that the photographs do not even depict the same person; eyes, nose, and lips appear smaller or larger, and there are radical variations in skin tone. These photographic images contrast with the images of the essential early Baker (1925), who could be identified by a racialized sexual stereotype conveyed by the stroke of a pen on a cartoon postcard.

As a poster icon, Baker titillated men and freed women to dream of lives far removed from domestic drudgery. Baker also challenged her own unidimensional primal image as she moved into the worlds of cabarets and high fashion. She was given a Voisin touring car by its manufacturer and learned to drive with the public watching every shift of gears. She had the car painted in a copper tone, its seats upholstered in brown snakeskin, and used it to parade around town and participate in automobile rallies. On her travels around Paris, she was often accompanied by her pet snake, Kiki, and her leopard,

Figure 33. Josephine Baker displays an engagement ring and Giuseppe "Pepito" Abatino poses with a doll made in Josephine's image, mid-1930s. Photograph by Albert Harlingue from the collection of H. Roger-Viollet, courtesy of Documentation Photographique Roger-Viollet, Paris.

Chiquita (actually a male), the latter given to her by the theater producer and songwriter Henri Varna to celebrate the opening of *Paris qui remue*. In 1933, she learned to fly an airplane, and this feat was also documented by the press.[50] During 1934–35, she made two feature films promoting new fashion looks. Baker moved away from the wild, savage image to become a symbol for the chic and independent twentieth-century woman. She was the visible *flâneuse*. While Baker wore cotton housedresses and simple sandals at home, she adopted increasingly elaborate stage and film costumes to challenge her primal image, and her well-documented public fashions reflected the changing styles of each season.

Architectural Fantasies of the Body

Born in 1870, thirty-six years before Baker, Adolf Loos became one of the most important architects of the modern era. For Loos, a house, like a contemporary dress, had to be simple, pure, and austere. His architecture was characterized by a simplicity of form in which he juxtaposed pure cylindrical shapes and austere, angular lines. In addition to residing in Vienna, where he was a moving force in architectural and artistic circles, Loos had spent the period 1893–97 in the United States and also lived for six years in France during 1922–27.[51] Loos outlined his aesthetic philosophy in his 1908 treatise "Ornament and Crime," in which he criticized decorative excess.

Both Loos and Baker played on the contrast between forbidding exteriors and sensual interior spaces. In spite of his dedication to aesthetic purity, Loos was fascinated by cabaret culture and the extravagance of the music hall. Just under the surface of placid purity lay Loos's attraction to the primal forces of the exotic and the erotic. Two of the women Loos married were stage performers.[52] He adored modern and jazz dance and considered himself to be an excellent amateur dancer. In the winter of 1927, Loos met Baker at Chez Joséphine, where he took Charleston lessons from her. A year later, they reconnected in Vienna, where she complained to him about the poor architectural designs of a house she was planning to build. Loos explained, "It was in Paris. She came up to me, and had a bad temper. Imagine Loos, she was sulking, I want to make a big, big rebuilding of my house and I don't like the plans of the architects. I could not contain myself. . . . Don't you know I can make the best design in the world for you? Astonished Josephine looks at me . . . and asks slowly: Are you an architect then?—She had no idea who I was."[53]

Adolf Loos's model for Baker's house was a dress rehearsal for modern architecture. Though unbuilt, it was destined to become one of his most famous works by virtue of its innovative juxtaposition of exterior and interior elements. In 1926, Loos had completed the plans for a house that was built in Montmartre for the surrealist poet Tristan Tzara, who collected African masks and statues and Oriental rugs. Loos's design used pure rectangular forms in energetic contrast with outdoor cylindrical shapes and patio gardens to create an exotic atmosphere. The architect introduced similar ideas into his model for Baker's house (fig. 34).

The 1928 model for Baker's house shows the house was to be anchored by a cylindrical turret, although the rest of the design was rectangular in form. The walls were pierced by very small portal windows. The three-story house was to be built in alternating courses of black and white granite and marble, producing a striped effect. On the bottom floor were servants' quarters; the

Figure 34. Adolf Loos's 1928 striped granite-and-marble palace for Josephine Baker. Photo based on the axonometric reconstruction drawing of Loos's model by Paul Groenendijk and Piet Vollaard, courtesy of Groenendijk and Vollaard.

second and third floors were devoted to reception rooms and living quarters. A small corridor separated the dining room from the two bedrooms and the living room. The centerpiece of the house on the second and third floors was a large swimming pool, measuring $4 \times 9 \times 2$ meters, with the capacity to hold two tons of water.[54] The pool was surrounded by large glass doors and had a glass ceiling, permitting visitors to watch their hostess swim from various angles in a panoptical sweep. Since Baker swam in the nude, Loos's idea was that she would provide a floor show for special guests within this seductive interior. Much has been made of the voyeuristic design of the pool and the rest of the interior.[55] The pool breaks through the walls of spectatorship and draws visitors into a shared erotic space. This experience is reinforced by the exotic North African design of the small, square windows cutting off vision from the outside and by the Mediterranean look and feel of the exterior stonework. This would be the perfect home for Aouina, the exotic Princesse Tam-Tam.

The house design combined two aspects of Viennese modernism—primal purity masking erotic extravagance, and the sensible versus the sensual. Both the primitive purity and the sense of erotic excess were grafted onto Baker's image as an exotic other who simultaneously symbolized and subverted bourgeois aesthetic canons. It might be argued that Loos's design for Baker's house contrasted greatly with the design of her home of many years, the Château des Milandes. However, close analysis of this thesis shows that it is flawed. Both during Baker's lifetime and later, Les Milandes was a tourist destination for curiosity seekers. Her adopted children complained of living in a fish bowl. Baker designed the château as a resort. Although the J-shaped marble swimming pool that she installed was outside, it was as extravagant as Loos's indoor atrium. The two bedrooms in the tower of the château also resembled in placement and design the second-floor bedrooms in Loos's granite-and-marble palace. While Baker brought her own sense of eclectic style and domesticity to the castle, it too combined the spectacular and the mundane in the voyeuristic spirit of the modernist palace that Adolf Loos designed for her in 1928.

Modernism's Mystique and Baker's Dream

As the embodiment of an image and as an actor, Josephine Baker was situated at the intersection of several strands of modernism. She entered France at the height of the colonial period and at a point of rapid social and economic change between two world wars. Paris was a metropolis transformed by war, industrialization, migration, overcrowding, and urban redesign. In this atmosphere, colonial discourse and the new political and social ideologies of the early twentieth century crossed paths, creating an idyllic quest for simplicity, peace, and purity in an era of decadence.[56]

In this complex setting, Baker did not exercise complete control over her own image, nor was she merely the pawn of external social and economic conditions, unscrupulous impresarios, and scheming fashion cartels. Instead, the dialectics of modernism and its mystique were at play, giving Baker a unique opportunity to experiment with fashioning a public image by commodifying evocative stereotypes and exploiting avant-garde trends.

According to Homi Bhabha, colonial discourse asserts its power through "the recognition and disavowal of racial/cultural/historical differences."[57] This discourse dominates the colonial subject through "stereotypes of savagery, cannibalism, lust and anarchy" that are both feared and desired.[58] Baker's *danse sauvage* and banana-skirt images are part of a colonial discourse and syndrome in which the subject is at once derided and desired. This discourse reflected the type of pure passion that both the Parisian surrealists and the Viennese intellectuals were trying to tap. Initially, Baker learned to enjoy the banana dance and internalized its frenzy and ecstasy. Even when she had outgrown the dance, Baker was unable to abandon the cultural baggage of the banana skirt's problematic image. This image became a part of her being and an emblem of her persona. The gaze of the spectator also became part of the image, and Baker internalized her theatrical mask as a cultural sign. Frantz Fanon reflected on the ambivalence of primal images of négritude and the feelings of self-doubt and aggression that they triggered in him: "Black Magic, primitive mentality, animism, animal eroticism, it all floods over me. All of it is typical of peoples that have not kept pace with the evolution of the human race. Or, if one prefers, this is humanity at its lowest. Having reached this point, I was long reluctant to commit myself. Aggression was in the stars. I had to choose. What do I mean? I had no choice."[59] While Fanon detested primitivism and the demeaning implications of its distortions, Baker manipulated primal imagery under a public gaze as a way of appealing to the fantasies and expectations of her audiences.

This exotic imagery is part of modernity's double-pronged mystique in which primitivism is also a subversive sign of liberation. The cubists and surrealists used primitivism to challenge the artistic establishment while modernist architects deployed the lines of primal purism to transform domestic and public spaces. Baker used the subversive spaces of primitivism to transform herself and live her dream, moving from bananas to fashions by Bertaux, Chanel, Dior, and Balenciaga. But there were other sides to Baker too—the gender bender, the mother, the social activist. In performing these roles as part of her public persona, she exposed the contradictions of modernism and pushed their limits.

5 Baker's Scripts

You don't know what it is: to write, oh là là! Me, I dance, I like
to dance, I like only that, I'll dance all my life.
—Josephine Baker, 1927

Josephine Baker is conventionally viewed as a performer, not as
an author. Her literary productions, however, open a window
onto her art and life. Baker was a masterful storyteller in everyday life and in
literature. She wrote and collaborated on autobiographies, screenplays, literary pieces, and songs. Each piece builds upon and reiterates her biography
in allegorical terms. Through autobiography, the "self" is transformed into
the "other," a strategy that Baker also employed in her stage performances.
Erving Goffman describes this tenuous relationship between art and life as a
"laminated adumbration" in which the social actor models courses of action
on morality tales, fictional characters, and myths.[1] This modeling process
involves the scripting of accounts that project and justify courses of action.
In Baker's case, much of this scripting was a matter of public record intended
for the consumption of specific audiences. Through her memoirs, books, and
copious letters, Baker fashioned a public image that reinforced her performative persona. She incorporated everyday scripts and literary self-writing into
her performances, which in turn, influenced her behavior.

Self-writing is the conscious framing of a life through scripts, discourses,
biographies, and performances. It provides the core data for semiography,

or the symbolic study of a life. Achille Mbembe defines self-writing as the integration of "symbolic elements" into the "collective imaginary."[2] These elements include philosophies, ideologies, and ways of thinking that shape a collective worldview. Styles of self-writing reflect audience responses as well as the author's creative goals. Baker's self-writing encompasses literary pieces, performances, and song lyrics that express her personal beliefs and cultural ideologies (fig. 35).

From 1927 to 1935, Baker collaborated on three memoirs produced by journalists aspiring to capitalize on her fame: *Les Mémoires de Joséphine Baker* (1927), by Marcel Sauvage; *Voyages et aventures de Joséphine Baker* (1931), also by Sauvage; and *Une Vie de toutes les couleurs* (1935), by André Rivollet.

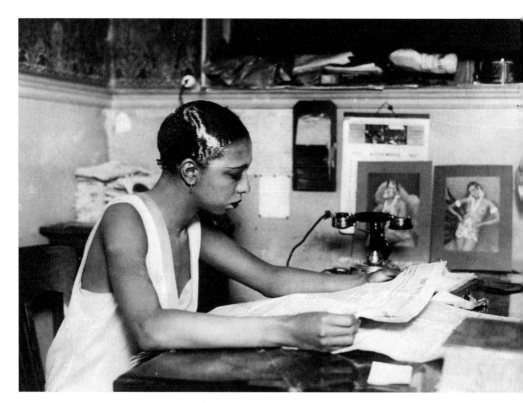

Figure 35. Josephine Baker at her office desk in Montmartre, early 1928. Photo courtesy of Corbis, Inc., New York.

Excerpted as newspaper articles and publicity releases, these biographies helped to popularize Baker's primal image. They were followed by two collaborative fiction pieces, a third biography with Sauvage in 1947, and Baker's posthumous biography with Jo Bouillon and the journalist Jacqueline Cartier, first published in French in 1976. Although it is not always possible to determine the exact extent of Baker's participation in her early projects, her voice was evident in every piece. Therefore, the fact that much of the early writing was collaborative does not mean that Baker was without agency in its production. Her early pieces consisted of accounts told to and embellished by men—Marcel Sauvage, Paul Colin, Pepito Abatino, Félix de la Camara, and André Rivollet. Much of this writing was used for publicity purposes and riddled with racial and gender stereotypes, as well as statements that Baker would later regret or retract.

Baker's flowery and hyperbolic writing style grew out of her collaborations with Marcel Sauvage and Pepito Abatino. She later adopted that style as her own. As she became more sophisticated in her use of language (both French and English), Baker's self-authored stories grew more elaborate and the narratives more complex. The literary progression of Baker's narratives foregrounded the Cinderella and Marian motifs that were the mainstays of her biographical repertoire. She also deployed these narratives in song lyrics performed, improvised, and modified for diverse audiences. In her role as an author and a dancing troubadour, Baker continually rewrote and refashioned herself.[3]

Savage Journey

In 1927, Paul Colin published the lithographs of Baker, accompanied by her short handwritten introduction, in *Le Tumulte noir,* and in the same year he illustrated her first memoirs as told to Marcel Sauvage, a young journalist for the newspaper *L'Intransigeant.* These memoirs read like an extended press release. Although Baker allegedly told Sauvage that it was too soon to write her memoirs because she could not even remember the last night's performance, she became a willing biographical subject whose image in print paralleled Colin's visual caricatures. Sauvage was an eager but timid writer who often brought his wife, Paulette, to sessions with Josephine. Egged on by Colin and a coterie of friends, Sauvage became Baker's first official biographer and collaborator. In her work with Sauvage, Baker initially followed a pattern of allowing male voices to shape her words and images, just as she had done with her early impresarios, theater directors, artists, and photographers. Baker arrived in France with sporadic schooling and without formal literary training or a conventional family history. A credible life history needed to be produced through her performances and in her own words. Although she began as a malleable subject in this process, she quickly learned to manipulate the image construction process to her own advantage. She transformed herself from a passive to an active narrative subject and narrator.

Sauvage opens his memoirs with a third-person account of Baker's importance as an artist and of the circumstances surrounding the writing of the book. He writes, "Joséphine personified for us this strange poetry that comes to us from the adventure stories that we have read for more than twenty years."[4] Every afternoon between four and five o'clock when Baker awoke to prepare for her night's performances, Sauvage would arrive at her apartment for his interview session. Later interviews took place at Josephine's cabaret, Chez Joséphine. Although she was often preoccupied, talking on the telephone and playing with her pets, she would begin to tell the fragments of a story, at first in English with an interpreter, and then in halting French. Sauvage places Baker's accounts in the first person, using simple language that reflects the experiences of a naïve and uninhibited young woman amazed by the sights and delights of Paris.

Just as she did with her primal dance image, Baker later exploited aspects of these accounts as scripts when she became a seasoned performer. In certain respects, Sauvage's first book with Baker resembles the biographical sketches that Guillaume Apollinaire crafted to establish the artistic history and credibility of the cubists for a new Parisian audience in 1913.[5] This hybrid biographical genre places the artist in the public eye by combining personal accounts and publicity with popular art criticism. For his part, Sauvage writes that *Mémoires* constitutes "a collection of notes, impressions, and images" intended to represent the exotic star who captured the imagination of European audiences.[6]

Following Sauvage's preamble, the book is divided into a preface and eight chapters describing Josephine's childhood, her early days as a performer, her arrival in Europe, her favorite recipes, beauty tips, songs, reflections on the future, and letters from her fans and admirers. The first-person descriptions of Josephine's childhood are written in a light tone with several narrative distortions used to reinforce her rags-to-riches image for a new European audience. After briefly discussing St. Louis, Josephine introduces her parents: "My mother and father met at school and afterward no one wanted them to get married. Then they were married, and they were poor because no one helped them. They were even abandoned. My mother and my father then separated, so that they could work and live on their own."[7]

Some accounts claim that Carrie McDonald met Eddie Carson, Josephine's putative father, while working on vaudeville routines in which Carrie was a dancer and Eddie the drummer at a St. Louis theater.[8] Other accounts agree with Sauvage that Carrie and Eddie met at school and married when Carrie was twenty-one. Baker and Chase, however, doubt Carson's paternity.[9] According to Jean-Claude Baker, the identity of Josephine's biological father remained a mystery: "The secret died with Carrie, who refused till the end to talk about it."[10] As with the rest of the Baker myth, what actually happened is less significant than what Baker made of it in her multilayered life stories, which always involved the unfulfilled search for a father figure. For the European public, she was born into a modest show-business family and managed to survive amid great adversity. Baker reminisced, "When I was young, we were awfully poor."[11] In Sauvage's account, Baker asserted that her father was Spanish: "I don't resemble my mother, and not my father either. My father was Spanish."[12] Whether the term "Spanish" is a euphemism for Creole or a total fabrication is unclear. Nevertheless, the intended appeal of this description to a European audience is clear.

There are noticeable gaps and reinventions in Baker's early biographies. Later biographers use interviews, oral histories, and press clippings to fill in the gaps, but they also continue to mine Sauvage's account, which contains the earliest idyllic narrative. In Sauvage's biography, Josephine describes herself as obstinate, headstrong, and independent. She says, "I don't like anyone to tell me to do this or that. I always preferred my freedom." Josephine cut school, embarrassed Carrie with friends and neighbors, and remained a loner in her growing family with her siblings Richard, Willie Mae, and Margaret. Josephine used music as an escape: "Every Sunday, I went to see dances for 15 cents at the Bascher [sic] Washington Theater, a very small theater with a very small stage. There were only two boxes there, two small boxes with panels of light flooding the heads of people. I watched different sorts of dances, but I never liked the ballets."[13]

It was at the Booker T. Washington Theater in St. Louis that Josephine first sought work as a performer. She ran errands, danced at the end of the chorus line, and pulled comic faces. At about the same time (around 1916), she also began to frequent the home of the Jones family, who comprised the Jones Family Band. Josephine lived with the family for a while, and Mrs. Dyer Jones taught her to play the trombone, the ukelele, and other instruments. With these limited skills, she began to tour with Bob Russell's vaudeville troupe. Sauvage does not mention that the entire Jones family came along too. He states that Josephine was barely eleven years old but told everyone that she was fifteen—a cleverly crafted fib that reflects the social obstacles that she encountered. Josephine performed on the black vaudeville circuit for several years before arriving in Philadelphia and New York. In recounting those early years to Sauvage, Josephine stated, "In reality, I made nothing at all because I was almost never paid, and I was always hungry. I was famished, empty to the point of breaking in two. My teeth pushed out of my mouth. I dreamed of New York, of an enormous amount of money, and of a load of treasures."[14]

Sauvage briefly describes Josephine's first break in New York in *Shuffle Along,* by Sissle and Blake, and her starring role in their production *Chocolate Dandies.* These sketchy descriptions are merely intended to move along the narrative, which culminates in Josephine's discovery at the Plantation Club and her departure for Paris. It is as if her previous life were merely a foggy dream and a preamble for future fame in Paris.

Sauvage is at his best when he constructs the narrative of Baker's arrival in France and her first impressions of Europe. These impressions crystallize in the often quoted Sauvage/Baker phrase, "Paris is the dance, and I am the dancer."[15] Sauvage's descriptions of Paris are lyrical and expansive. Inspired by Baker's enthusiasm, he places his impressions in the first person, making it impossible to determine where Sauvage's imagery ends and Baker's impressions begin. "Beautiful women, beautiful dresses . . . I love Paris, its movements, its sounds, its mystery, all of its mysteries, I try to understand them. . . . I imagine."[16]

The juxtaposition of an idyllic Paris with Baker's primal energy creates the magnetic appeal of her early image. All of her performances are seen through this lens as Baker moves from the Paris music-hall stage to the cabarets of Berlin. In this book, Sauvage pays scant attention to the content of her performances, the daily conditions under which she worked, or the immediate responses of her audiences. He even admits having missed the opening performance of *La Revue nègre* at the Théâtre des Champs-Elysées in 1925.[17]

The goal of his narrative is to express the power of Baker's primal image and the success of her unbridled and energetic performances. Later, in his 1931 piece on her travels, he tempers his hyperbolic enthusiasm with a description of the obstacles that Baker encountered on stage in prewar Europe and South America. But the objective of all of these descriptions is to make Baker a star and a heroine in the face of adversity.[18] In the 1927 biography, brief accounts of performances are punctuated with Paul Colin's drawings caricaturing the primal Baker, reinforcing her image as an emblem of libidinal freedom.

Descriptions of Baker's performances are capped by two chapters containing her tips on cuisine and beauty. Having established that she is a star, Sauvage now takes us backstage to see how she lives, eats, and sleeps. Rather than presenting exotic fare, Baker describes her favorite midnight supper as spaghetti with red pepper sauce and gives out recipes for hotcakes with syrup and corned beef hash (spelled "hached" by Sauvage). These recipes were widely published in newspapers and ladies' journals with a copyright by Baker's publisher, Éditions Kra.[19] The African American recipes and the natural beauty tips establish the link between the exotic primal Baker and the sophisticated, urbane star entertaining audiences at her after-hours supper club where the entrées publicized by Sauvage were on the menu.

Treatment of Baker's life as a performer ends with a medley of her American songs, entitled "chansons nègres." The songs include selections by Gus Kahn and Irving Berlin translated into French. It is possible that Sauvage intended these song lyrics to advertise Baker's 1926 releases with Odéon, which included tunes by George Gershwin, Irving Berlin, and Spencer Williams along with several ukulele songs composed by Baker herself. The era of Baker's new and specially crafted music-hall songs was yet to come, but the established performer, counting her gifts and fan mail, was waiting in the wings to sing them.

Sauvage's concluding chapter ends with Baker's reflections on her future. With uncanny precision, she predicts that she will live in the south of France: "I'll retire to live in Italy or the south of France. I'll buy a property on the Riviera. I'll marry simply. I'll have children and lots of animals. I love them; I want to live in peace among children and animals."[20]

To complete the portrait of Baker as a star, Sauvage adds an epilogue of fan mail from politicians, engineers, sailors, soldiers, animal lovers, and a host of male and female admirers. It is as if he wants to include canned applause at the end of each performance. If the reader is not already celebrating

Baker's successes, the book gives a few more reasons to start. Nevertheless, not all responses to Sauvage's biography turned out as planned. The limpid and innocent first-person narrative masked impressions that some people found offensive. World War I veterans were offended by a remark presented at the opening of chapter 2, on Europe: "I have heard about the war. What a strange story. I admit that I don't understand anything about it, but that it disgusts me. I am so afraid of men who have only one arm, one leg, or one eye. I pity them with all my heart, but I am physically repulsed by anyone who is crippled."[21]

This infelicitous remark resulted in a letter of complaint from a delegation of disabled war veterans, who also staged a protest in front of Josephine's Montmartre cabaret. She retracted the statement and demanded that it be removed from any further editions of her book. When Sauvage, who was a pacifist, did not respond immediately to removal of the passage, she threatened him with a lawsuit. Ironically, at the end of the same chapter, Sauvage had defended Baker's established practice of suing managers and collaborators as the whimsical prerogative of a star. He quotes her as saying, "I'll have other lawsuits. It happens like that from time to time, you understand?"[22] Little did Sauvage expect that he would become the subject of Josephine's ire. "Why this trial?" he responded elsewhere. "My proofs were submitted to censors and corrected and modified several times. So why?"[23]

Nevertheless, Sauvage continued with a second book, written in even looser and more lyrical prose. In February 1928, Baker and Pepito left on their two-year world tour that included twenty-five European and South American countries. Sauvage's 1931 book *Voyages et aventures de Joséphine Baker* provides a first-person, embellished account of Josephine's travels. From Berlin to Santiago, Baker recounts to Sauvage the cities, music halls, and theaters she visited, offering impressions of the audiences and atmosphere of each country. The political climate was heating up, and Sauvage could not ignore the animosity that Baker encountered in Germany, Austria, Hungary, Romania, Scandinavia, and even South America. Although Baker's tour was scheduled to start in Vienna, Sauvage opens his account with the Scandinavian countries, where Baker surprised and dazzled the audiences. Donning the Swedish national costume and singing in several languages, Baker triumphed against all odds in Stockholm. Sauvage uses this success to set the tone for the book.

In Vienna, the serious problems began. Catholic priests joined with politicians to ban Baker as an immoral demon and a threat to public morality.[24] As Baker entered the city, church bells warned residents to clear the streets, and people crossed themselves to ward off evil spirits. Baker was accompanied by an armed police guard, and her performances at the Ronacher Theater were canceled. Pamphlets circulated condemning not only her, but anyone who dared to perform the Charleston or play jazz music in public. Finally, Baker succeeded in opening her show at the Johann Strauss Theater, a small building directly across from the Saint Paul Cathedral, whose clergy, led by Father Frey, had condemned her performance. Baker described the event: "They were waiting for an appearance of the devil. I entered the stage very simply. There was an instant of great silence and surprise. Then I sang with all my heart, with a fearful and beating heart: 'Sleep My Poor Little Baby,' an old slave song. . . . Excuse me, but it seemed to me that the entire audience melted. . . . When the applause and the cries calmed down, I danced as I've always danced, as I always will dance, without thinking of good or bad, but about my dance."[25]

Although the audiences responded enthusiastically, the conservative opposition petitioned the Austrian parliament to ban Baker's performances. The city of Vienna taxed Baker fifteen thousand dollars a month if she wished to perform.[26] The trip to Vienna was also marred by a young Yugoslavian singer named Gabor, who, acting out of passion, committed suicide at Josephine's feet in a local cabaret.[27] Mysteriously, Count Adelbert Sternberg, a Viennese aristocrat, returned from a vacation in the Alps just in time to defend Baker in parliament. He made an impassioned speech about the positive attributes of jazz as a source of liberation, African art and dance as primal art forms, and nudity as an expression of freedom, arguing that the female nude represented the highest and most natural artistic ideal.[28] In spite of Sternberg's plea and the applause of her audiences, Baker left Vienna wiser and more wary of the forces of political and religious opposition.

In Romania, Baker was once again greeted by religious opposition and followed from city to city by protesters. Religion was an important factor in Romanian political life in Baker's time, much as it is today. The Orthodox Church was dominant in Romania in the 1920s and 1930s. Its hierarchy was very close to the political right and the emerging fascist movement. Baker, however, had no idea of the extent of the opposition that she confronted. She viewed the situation in terms of the immediate response that her arrival and her performances in Romania evoked when she remarked, "It was necessary to mobilize hundreds, even thousands of police and soldiers."[29]

Protests continued in Hungary and Czechoslovakia. When Baker reached Berlin, the overt protests had subsided, but the show in which she participated at the Weston Theater was under-rehearsed and poorly organized. Josephine did her best, but she could not salvage the show. She explained that "a star, whoever she is, cannot save a show that is otherwise ugly, stupid, and pretentious."[30] Baker denied responsibility for the failure of the show and insisted that her own numbers were always well received. She left Berlin before the end of her engagement and wrote a public letter of apology in halting German to the local press. Munich closed its doors to her, but she ended her German tour in Hamburg without incident.[31]

From Buenos Aires to Rio, Baker's travels to South America were equally riddled with religious and political protests. The opposition in Buenos Aires was so intense that she wrote several letters to the government and almost stopped the tour. Nevertheless, at each venue, there were always loyal fans to counter the opposition. Sauvage attempts to soften the account of public dissent by describing the landscapes, flora and fauna, and positive experiences that Josephine encountered while on tour. Left out of these idyllic accounts, however, is any mention of the specter of war or the impending economic crisis that would end the freedom and decadence of the Jazz Age.

The travelogue closes with an epilogue on cinema. At each port that she visited, Baker claimed to have seen advertisements for her film *La Sirène des tropiques*. Another apology was warranted. Baker praised the qualities of cinema as an international art form, but criticized *La Sirène,* asking, "Should a director worthy of this name sacrifice the artistic side [of film] in favor of the commercial?"[32] She blamed the director for her lack of preparation, the visual shortcomings of the film, and the fact that she had to play scenes in the tropics wearing a fur coat. The book concludes with her announcement of two future film projects, an advertisement that seemingly was intended to erase all past mistakes.

When they returned from their two-part world tour, Baker and Pepito moved to Le Vésinet, and Baker began yet another autobiographical collaboration with a new author, André Rivollet, a journalist. Rivollet's 1935 book *Une Vie de toutes les couleurs* (A Many-Colored Life) covers much of the same ground as Sauvage's first biography, but it is written in a more sophisticated language with a new image in mind. Photographs in the book depict Baker in a glamorous gown and in a modern suit standing in front of an airplane. The latter publicity photograph was one from the series made in 1933 with M. Demay, her flight instructor. Although the narrative outline was almost identical to that of Sauvage's 1927 *Mémoires*, the caricatures, primal images, recipes, and beauty tips were eliminated. Baker was already an established star in need of image repair and boosting rather than primal image construction. Rivollet achieved this repair by making scant mention of the two-year world tour and including chapters on Baker's new shows at the Folies-Bergère and the Casino de Paris. A discussion of the making of Baker's recently completed film *Zouzou* (1934) counterbalanced the earlier criticisms of *Sirène* (1927). The book closes on an optimistic note, with Baker thanking France for making the dreams of a forlorn St. Louis urchin come true. The biographies by Sauvage and Rivollet use Baker's Cinderella narrative as an overcoding to create a fictive audience for a rising star.

On March 21, 1935, André Rivollet organized a lecture and gala evening of music at Neuilly to celebrate the publication of his new book, *Une Vie de toutes les couleurs*, and to commemorate Baker's success in the lead role in a revival of Jacques Offenbach's operetta *La Créole*. He introduced the gala evening of music with a rousing speech reviewing the highlights of Baker's career and the history of jazz in France. He described "hot jazz" as the source of inspiration for all popular music, from Ravel to Debussy, and identified Baker as the "exteriorization" of this musical inspiration.[33] His introduction received a standing ovation, and the new image of a more worldly and sophisticated Baker from *Paris qui remue* and *La Créole* was reconfirmed for the Parisian public.

Written in Blood

While on their international tour, Josephine and Pepito had begun to concoct plans for the novella *Mon sang dans tes veines*, which I have already discussed as a key element in Baker's Marian motif. During their long train trips, they wove together the story of Joan, the daughter of a black maid, and her true but inaccessible love interest, Fred Barclay, son of a Massachusetts chewing-gum tycoon. *Mon sang* was far more than a fictional recreation of Baker's new residence at Beautiful Oak transposed to an American setting. The book was controversial and sold poorly, not so much because of its melodramatic plot, but rather as a result of its avant-garde message. It represented Josephine's response to the deeply felt discrimination that she experienced in Austria, Germany, and Eastern Europe. When she was on tour, Baker had encountered the prewar fascist literature about the tainted blood of foreigners and blacks. Protests against her in the streets and the closing of her shows had reinforced her feelings of marginality and fear. Joan was a saint-like figure capable of transcending racism and challenging issues of contamination from blood mixing. Baker's identification with her heroine is asserted in her preface to the book:

> While tasting the fruits gathered from here and there in large baskets, Joan and I have a thousand plans to escape, in following the great river, and to flee an unjust continent . . . We will reach a country where we'll be treated like Fairy Tale princesses. . . . We will dance, we will sing, covered with diamonds, pearls, and feathers, under lights brighter than the suns of Africa. But Joan said that she would have preferred the beautiful land of Devotion!

> [Tout en mordant aux fruits chipés par ci par là dans des grosses corbeilles, nous faisions, Joan et moi, mille projets pour nous évader, en suivant le grand fleuve et pour fuir un continent injuste . . . Nous gagnerions un pays où l'on nous traiterait comme les princesses des *Fairy tales* . . . Nous danserions, nous chanterions, couvertes de diamants, de perles et de plumes, sous les lumières plus brillantes que les soleils d'Afrique. Mais Joan disait qu'elle aurait préféré le beau pays du Dévouement!][34]

Fred, the hero of the story, is labeled as a "nègre blanc."[35] This is the same term that Father Frey of Vienna used to describe Austrians who learned to dance the Charleston.[36]

Baker's presence in Germany and Austria had threatened ideals of racial purity by summoning memories of the Sénégalese occupation of the Rhine and suggesting that colonial populations were too close to Europe for comfort. The symbolic threat posed by Baker's performances, however, did not issue so much from her presence among Europeans as it did from the desire of Europeans to imitate her. The specter of hybridity emerged from an audience that wished to cross racial lines (at least in the domain of popular culture) as well as from Baker's own primal image in the danse sauvage. Baker handled this issue with clever strategies of image construction. On the one hand, she assumed an assimilated posture of glamour and sophistication. On the other, she transcended assimilation by taking on the role of a saint. This psychological strategy was already evident in her remark to Sauvage concerning Father Frey's attack on her morality in Vienna: "Say this, Monsieur Sauvage, and repeat it well, that the black demon, the little negress, no matter how tired she is, says her prayers every night when she returns from dancing."[37]

Baker's expression of religious devotion was also an assertion of her essential humanity. In her self-writing she moved from the decadence and frivolity of the dance hall to a realization of the contradictory and emotionally charged impact of her image. *Mon sang* gave Baker an opportunity to reflect on the political atmosphere of the times and the social role of her performances. At this point, she began to manipulate and modify her primal image based on her political values. She did not make an effort to discard the image but instead modulated it and bolstered it with a series of moral justifications (Sternberg's plea) and examples of self-sacrifice (Joan's saint-like image). As Baker transformed herself from Fatou to a ballerina on point, from a showgirl to a saint, her newly embodied image was virtually written in blood.[38]

Once having achieved stardom, however, Baker continued to recycle both the Cinderella and the sacrifice motifs in tandem. She never tired of retelling and reinventing her rags-to-riches story, adding more embellishments and signs of devotion with each reiteration. The same story was repeated, reworked, and reappropriated through fictive characters such as Joan, Zouzou, and Aouina. Yet, subtly and at each moment, Baker struggled to break out of the mold and make a new statement.

Rainbow Motif

The motifs of marginalization and rescue continued in Baker's next fiction project. In 1957, with Opéra Mundi, she published *La Tribu arc-en-ciel* (The Rainbow Tribe) in collaboration with Jo Bouillon and the illustrator Piet Worm (fig. 36).[39] Bonini states that *La Tribu arc-en-ciel* was produced in an effort to cover a nearly four-million-franc ($100,000) debt incurred in making repairs on Les Milandes.[40] Although the book was financially successful, and she also sold her apartment on avenue Bugeaud, she was not able to raise sufficient funds. *La Tribu,* however, did serve as a persuasive advertisement for the utopian multicultural goals of Les Milandes. This children's book is the tale of Kott-Kott, a one-eyed black hen who is shunned by all of the other chickens on the farm. The book is written in the past-perfect tense, using prose that was fairly sophisticated for a children's tale. Even though some of the writing and editorial work was completed by Bouillon, the story is clearly Josephine's. Its encrypted messages of multiculturalism recall Josephine's sheet music inscribed with invisible ink to convey secret messages of liberation to the Allies during the war. Kott-Kott the hen is a metonymical symbol of marginalization and freedom.

One day, Kott-Kott impulsively decides to leave the safe confines of her chicken coop and venture out into the world in search of her lost eye. She wears a scarf over her empty eye socket, a signifier of her infirmity that increases her unsightly appearance. On the road, Kott-Kott meets two young girls who befriend her and guide her toward a town where an eye doctor resides. Aided by a series of local residents, colorfully illustrated by Piet Worm,

Figure 36. Cover of *La Tribu arc-en-ciel* by Piet Worm (Paris: Opéra Mundi, 1957). Photo courtesy of Piet Worm.

Kott-Kott eventually finds the eye doctor's home. Although he is welcoming and gracious, he informs her that it is impossible to restore her eye and that she will never find her lost eye in the vast world outside.

Dejected, Kott-Kott leaves the village for the forest, where she meets many animals who are sympathetic to her cause. The birds, the rabbit, the fox, and the deer all offer their help to no avail. A mole suggests that she look underground and, after a frightening thunderstorm, she finds herself at the entrance to the caves of Lascaux. Led by glow-worms through the dark caves, she encounters a statue of Cro-Magnon man. Standing in stony silence, he is unable to guide her to her eye. Awed by the prehistoric cave paintings, she tries to talk to the animals depicted there. Finally, she reaches the mouth of a cave, where the sunlight initially nearly blinds her remaining eye. She is able to make a small paper boat and escape to the comfort of daylight.

Emerging from the cave, Kott-Kott finds herself in front of the Château des Milandes. Symbolically, she has made a descent into the prehistoric netherworld and has resurfaced in paradise. Les Milandes, her final stop, is a miraculous safe haven. Kott-Kott is amazed by the lush landscape of Les Milandes. She arrives at the Place Joséphine Baker, where she sees a statue of the Virgin Mary with Josephine's face. The statue is surrounded by carvings of little children. This inspirational moment spurs Kott-Kott to continue her journey past the sign reading "Deux Amours" into a large park. There she witnesses a procession of seven little boys, the Rainbow children, on their way to bury a dead bird, a symbol of Kott-Kott's impending transformation. She is fascinated by their diverse appearances. At the end of the ceremony, she timidly introduces herself: "Hum, Hum, Hum! . . . Dear little children, please tell me if you've seen my eye."[41]

At first, the boys are so astonished that they can barely speak. Then they question her about her loss. Each child offers to help her in his own way by telling a myth or legend from his country of origin. These myths fulfill Baker's goal of multiculturalism with its roots in tradition. Akio offers the assistance of Buddha, assuring Kott-Kott that the deity will give her a beautiful jade eye. Jary (also spelled as "Jari" in the text) recounts the myth of the Scandinavian giant Alvader and says that the giant will blow a large wind that will unearth her eye wherever it may be in the world.[42] Luis promises the help of South American birds of paradise to search for the eye. And Jean-Claude offers the assistance of his ancestor, the Knight Templar Godefroy de Bouillon, to find the eye as part of his holy pilgrimage. Moïse promises the moral support of the biblical Moses to locate the lost eye. All of the animals of Les Milandes cheer. But when nothing actually happens, Kott-Kott cries out that she has been deceived.

At one of the lowest points in her journey, Kott-Kott experiences another miracle. Marianne, then the only girl in the Rainbow family, arrives dressed in regal garb and distributing good-luck flowers to everyone. Crowned with flowers and followed by birds and butterflies, Princess Marianne puts an end to Kott-Kott's misery. She caresses Kott-Kott and questions her about her problems. Then Marianne proposes that Kott-Kott remain at Les Milandes with the children and the other animals who already adore her. After some hesitation, Kott-Kott agrees to stay and experiences a moment of revelation. The sun shines brightly on her as she exclaims, in an oddly punctuated passage, "Ah! . . . , if all people could just understand that they must look for happiness in their own hearts. . . . . . . The world would be a better place and . . . . would become . . . . paradise!" (Ah! . . . , si tous les hommes voulaient comprendre que c'est dans leur propre coeur qu'il faut chercher le bonheur. . . . . . . Le monde serait meilleur et . . . . deviendrait le paradis!)[43] Not surprisingly, a dove descends to carry this message of love around the world. The message of universal love is also spread by boat, train, telephone, and telegraph. Kott-Kott has witnessed the worldwide victory of the philosophy of Les Milandes.

Kott-Kott decides to make her home permanently at Les Milandes, where she lives in a miniature castle modeled on the big château. She gives birth to eight baby chicks of all colors and finds true happiness with her rainbow family, the real Rainbow children, and their animals. Content with herself and in love with the world, Kott-Kott abandons her search for the eye and discards her scarf, which she places in the safety of an old jewelry box. Although Baker herself never appears as a character in the narrative, the parallel between her retired banana skirt and Kott-Kott's old scarf is evident.

This allegorical tale is much more than a children's fairy story. Using the standard elements of a fairy tale, with all of its Proppian protagonists and narrative twists, Baker has once again rewritten her life story with Les Milandes as the fairy castle that will protect her and her family from the injustices of the outside world and change the world itself into a paradise. Although both *Mon sang* and *La Tribu* are allegories in which Baker identifies herself with the protagonists, the narratives end differently. Joan flees into the woods in search of escape in the "empire of nature," while Kott-Kott finds acceptance and happiness in an idyllic paradise built as a fortress against prejudice. Kott-Kott's character is fashioned not only as a reflection of Josephine, but also of her sister Willie Mae. Reportedly, Willie Mae lost one eye as a child. According to Baker's biographers Baker and Chase, Josephine's brother Richard Martin explained that when the family lived on Gratiot Street in St. Louis, Willie Mae lost her eye as a result of a splinter that her father maladroitly tried to remove.[44] Other accounts report that Willie Mae's eye was lost by an attack of the ferocious family dog.[45] In any case, the infirmity seems to have served as a narrative resource for Baker's book and was used as a powerful symbol of loss and exclusion.

The subtext of Baker's fairy tale is her rise from poverty and marginalization to riches and fame through her symbolic construction of a sense of community with the Rainbow Tribe at Les Milandes. Metonymically, Josephine is the château and the mother to a far-flung human family. She is also the lost hen, who, after a search in vain for the objects of success, finds peace and redemption in her own family. In contrast to her coproductions with journalists and even the novella with de la Camara and Abatino, the children's book is motivated by Josephine's own intellectual work, and she is supported by Bouillon and Worm, much in the same way that a lead singer is backed by a band. Baker has come full circle from having others tell a story in which she is constructed as a fairy-tale heroine to writing her own narrative based on a metaphorical image. The happy ending proleptically projects a new voyage of search and self-discovery.

Literary Duet

With the assistance of the journalist Jacqueline Cartier, and drawing on Baker's papers, letters, and memorabilia, Jo Bouillon published the collaborative biography *Joséphine* in 1976. He used Opéra Mundi, the same publishing house that had produced *La Tribu arc-en-ciel* nearly twenty years earlier. In his introduction, Bouillon states that he wrote the book to assure the future of the members of the Rainbow Tribe and preserve the memory of their mother.[46] Describing the origins of the project, he explains:

> And so I set to work, sorting through those overflowing folders, turning up mementos, outlines, anonymous letters, correspondence with celebrities. . . . Josephine scribbled on everything: stationery from the deluxe hotels she

visited on tour, scraps torn from bistro tablecloths, bits of newspaper, printed pages. Gradually everything fell into place, reconstructing an intriguing, unpredictable, sometimes disconcerting being whose fate was determined from childhood by a guiding light. Or was the quality of the guiding light determined by fate?

Wherever there was information lacking, I turned to Josephine's friends, her sister Margaret, our children and my own memory to fill the gap.

And that is how Josephine's book was posthumously born.[47]

The book contains twenty chapters spanning a period extending from Josephine's childhood in St. Louis to her death on April 12, 1975, just three days after her last performance at the Théâtre Bobino in Paris. The first seven chapters, covering the early years, resemble the works of Sauvage and Rivollet, but they are distinguished by excerpts of interviews with family members, fellow performers, impresarios, and friends. The text alternates between Jo Bouillon's first-person revelations, which provide a sense of intimacy and an insider's voice, and Baker's carefully quoted first-person descriptions and notes. Baker's voice is a well-crafted mnemonic device that dominates the narrative and conveys the feeling of an autobiography. The book opens with Baker's recollections of the 1917 St. Louis race riots presented in the first person. Interviews with family members are then interspersed with Josephine's and Jo's first-person statements in the format of a screenplay. This mélange of first- and third-person narrative voices draws the reader into the saga of Baker's early life in a convincing way. Baker emerges as a thoughtful, reflective intellectual aware of her images and evolution as a performer and, retrospectively, in control of her destiny.

As with the earlier biographies, it is difficult to determine how much invention and speculation are involved in the descriptions of the early years. Baker's volatility, energy, and appetite for performance are emphasized, along with behind-the-scenes descriptions of her shows. The intersection of the memory work of Jo and Josephine is compelling, and where there are gaps, Bouillon honestly admits them. For example, in discussing the 1934–35 period of Josephine's performances following La Créole, Bouillon writes, "Josephine left no further written account of this period of her life. Nor would she talk about it. This was typical of her wish to suppress anything that wasn't a personal victory. The past had no value except as a stepping stone in her fight for success."[48]

Bouillon describes the setbacks that Josephine faced as key events forging her character—her failure to achieve fame in the United States during the 1930s and her loss of Les Milandes near the end of her life. Between these two events, he sees the war years as strengthening her resolve. This scenario may also be interpreted as the emergence of Josephine as a humanitarian who is able to use her performances to support her dream. Happily, between the setbacks, there is a great deal of excitement in the life and art of the performer.

Chapter 12 begins the description of Jo and Josephine's life together at Les Milandes and on tour. Bouillon discusses the years at Les Milandes, the 1951–52 return trip that Baker made with him to the United States, and the building of the Rainbow Tribe. This part of the book inscribes memories of the early lives of the children and includes their reminiscences and short interviews with them. It is here that Bouillon describes Josephine as reading and writing constantly in an effort to both make and preserve her own life history.[49] A new, more mature, yet still idealistic and impetuous Josephine emerges from these pages. Although Bouillon does not mask the couple's conflicts over scheduling, children, and finances, he presents Josephine as a concerned parent and a complex intellectual, activist, and performer who remained resolute and dedicated to her ideals until the very end. This portrait of Baker builds upon previous narratives but creates a more serious multidimensional image of Baker, whose thoughts and actions are inflected by Bouillon's idealistic portrayal of her. At each point, Josephine, as depicted by Jo, questions her own image. "Was Josephine still Josephine?" she asks.[50] She speaks in the third person about the performer and public figure that she had created—a figure whose life was preserved in her ever-changing performances.

Dancing Troubadour

From the beginning of her performance career in France until her death, Baker recorded hundreds of songs. In 2004, the French government recognized her as a moving force in the development of French popular music as part of a retrospective exhibit at the Bibliothèque Nationale in Paris. Her complete discography lists over three hundred releases.[51] Her first 78 rpm recordings, made in English with piano and violin accompaniment, were produced by Odéon during the fall of 1926.[52] They included "I Love My Baby" (Warren/Green), "I Found a New Baby" (Jack Palmer/Spencer Williams), "Skeedle

Um," and "Always" (Irving Berlin). Jacques Fray, a well-known French jazz musician, is believed to be the pianist, although he is unidentified on the recordings. On a second set of recordings released during the same year, Josephine provided her own ukulele accompaniment to "You're the Only One for Me" (Monaco/Warren), "Feeling Kind of Blue" (Wohlman/Ruby/Cooper), and "Brown Eyes" (composer unidentified). In 1926, she also recorded "I Want to Yodel," a song specially written for her by Jack Palmer and the composer and music producer Spencer Williams, a longtime friend who was her accompanist with *La Revue nègre*. During 1927, she continued to record folk and Broadway tunes for Odéon. While she was on her two-part world tour in 1928 and 1929, there were no new releases.

Describing Baker's 1930 show at the Casino de Paris, Janet Flanner remarked on the evolution of her voice and the changes in her performance. "There is a rumor she wants to sing refined ballads; one is surprised that she doesn't want to play Othello. On that lovely visage lies now a sad look, not of captivity, but of dawning intelligence."[53] In October 1930, coinciding with the opening of her revue *Paris qui remue*, Baker made a recording of the songs included in the show with the Melodic Jazz Band of the Casino de Paris under the direction of Edmond Mahieux, who also conducted the orchestra for the stage performance. This Columbia Records release marked the beginning of her new musical and performative image. It included her first recording of the signature song "J'ai deux amours" by Géo Koger, Henri Varna, and Vincent Scotto. This version of the song was performed in duet with Adrien Lamy, whose voice Baker encircles and dominates with her refrain. The tune became an immediate bestseller and was released in the form of sheet music as well as sound recordings (fig. 37). "Deux amours" established Baker's Parisian roots and sophisticated image.

Also in French on the Columbia release were "La Petite Tonkinoise" (Koger, Varna, and Scotto), "Voulez-vous de la canne à sucre?" (Lelièvre, Varna, and Paddy), and "Dis-moi Joséphine" (Lelièvre, Varna, Cab, and Zerkowitz). Each song created a different persona for Josephine from Parisian to Vietnamese and Antillian. She was at once exotic and familiar, wild and tame in her new French vocalizations. Henri Varna was the principal lyricist and creative motor behind the new and more sophisticated melodic image and stage persona that Josephine adopted during the 1930s and used, to some extent, for the rest of her life. He also participated in composing two more French hits for Josephine, "Si j'étais blanche" (Varna, Lelièvre, and Falk), and "Les Mots

Figure 37. Sheet music for "J'ai deux amours," by Géo Koger, Henri Varna, and Vincent Scotto from the revue *Paris qui remue,* Casino de Paris, 1930. Courtesy of Éditions Salabert and BMG Music Publishing, Paris.

d'amour" (Varna, Fournier, and Ranzato), both of which appeared in the 1932 Casino de Paris revue *La Joie de Paris* and were released the same year by Columbia Records. On the same album was another hit, the torch song "Sans amour" (Farel/Borel-Clerc), which was very popular in Paris. Baker recorded all three songs with her own orchestra and later with professional studio accompaniment. Several of Baker's songs from the 1930s have been remastered and released on the centennial album *Homage à Joséphine Baker,* produced by Sepia records in 2006.

By the mid-1930s, Baker was established as a music-hall performer and a recognized recording artist. The new lyrics in French expanded her range and popular appeal locally and internationally. Her songs spoke of romantic and exotic landscapes, sex, love lost, love regained, children, and family. The resilience and versatility of her persona that had emerged through dance was refined in song. In fact, Baker's recordings and writings reflect her evolution and enormous talent as an international performer. In the United States, the black press, the National Association for the Advancement of Colored People (NAACP), and black colleges followed Baker's performances, carefully filtering out the more scandalous music-hall material in order to make her a successful role model.

With film added to her repertoire, Baker released "C'est lui" (Bernstein and Van Parys) and "Haïti" (Koger and Scotto), the two signature songs from *Zouzou,* in 1934 under the Columbia label. These songs helped to promote the film, and "C'est lui," the famous torch song, became a hit in its own right. In 1935, she released two more film tunes—this time from *Princesse Tam-Tam*—"Sous le ciel d'Afrique" (de Badet/Dallin), with Columbia, and "Le Chemin de bonheur" (Dreamship) (de Badet/Dallin), which was recorded for the radio in New York on October 21, 1935. During the late 1930s, she continued to make albums annually, mining her old French repertoire and adding new songs in French, English, Spanish, Portuguese, German, and Russian.

After a wartime hiatus, she resumed recording, this time with Jo Bouillon and his orchestra, releasing albums under the Pacific label with him in 1944, 1945, and 1949. Her recordings with Bouillon continued into the 1950s and included such hits as the calypso tune "Don't Touch My Tomatoes" (Lemarch-and/Bouillon, 1959). Many of the recordings from the late 1950s to the end of her life were compilations of older hits and live recordings of performances in New York, Havana, Berlin, and Paris. In her official discographies, some of these releases are listed as including previously recorded tunes.[54] During her numerous comeback performances and recordings in the late 1960s and the early 1970s, Baker nostalgically recycled her image and spiced up her perfor-mances with contemporary Broadway tunes and popular hit songs performed in several languages. With a lower pitch and an increased vocal range, she employed her strategies of improvisation and combination to create a blend of old and new pieces held together by the performative narrative of her life. Josephine embellished the diverse elements of her performance through blend-ing song, costume, and dance into a charismatic synthesis through which she reinvented herself for each performance. Much like a jazz musician improvis-ing on a melody, she brought new materials to life within old patterns.

In her recorded songs and live performances, Baker deployed a strategy of self-writing that resembled that of her journalistic biographers. First she created an image within a narrative, often spoken as a preamble or a verse in her songs in performances, and then she expanded, reworked, and repeated key images. As song writers such as Varna, Scotto, Lemarchand, Dallin, and, later, Bouillon began to compose and arrange especially for her, she developed a distinctive repertoire of jazz, swing, music-hall, and popular pieces on which she would improvise. The repertoire became a tapestry into which she would weave elements of her life story through patter, using herself as the ultimate signifier and source of narrative coherence. This process is particularly evident in her songs about the Parisian and Dordogne landscapes recorded during the 1960s—"Joséphine chante Paris" and "Dans mon village." Josephine Baker exited with a recording of her final performance, "Joséphine à Bobino 1975," intended to review her life and keep the memories alive. The songs, performed as medleys, were accompanied by a spectacular floor show that reinforced the often told stories and highlighted her multilayered performative image.

Innovations in Performance

Baker's early images were inscribed through performance, and she regarded dance as both the foundation and the pinnacle of her art. However, few remnants of Baker's early dance routines exist today. As noted earlier, Baker danced in Sissle and Blake's musical *Shuffle Along*, which debuted on Broadway and toured between 1921 and 1924. She then held a lead role in the duo's *Chocolate Dandies*, which ran for ninety-six performances starting in September 1924 at New York's Colonial Theater.[55] *Shuffle Along* marked a watershed in black Broadway theater. It introduced multilayered musical plots and complex dance routines driven by the storyline of the play. Dancers were encouraged to play comic roles and view their dancing as a supplement to the overall performance. In *Chocolate Dandies*, black vaudeville dance routines were integrated with synchronized tap and chorus-line dancing copied from the John Tiller Girls, a British touring troupe. Josephine Baker excelled at these routines, as did her colleague Florence Mills, and she continued to perform in the black Broadway-vaudeville style at the Plantation Club. Her dance routines were considered sophisticated and polished for the genre, and her comic timing was impeccable. Baker arrived in Paris with this repertoire of American stage skills, which she employed as the foundation for her exotic savage dance. Through dance improvisation, Baker was able to shed her inhibitions.

La Revue nègre was not the first black show to tour Europe. Numerous black American musicians, from World War I veterans to classically trained musicians such as Will Marion Cook and Sissle and Blake, had studied in Europe, toured, and even settled there. These shows were also linked in the popular imagination to the Ballets Russes performances staged during the early 1920s. In 1925, a German impresario joined forces with the New York producer Arthur Lyons to assemble the show *Chocolate Kiddies,* based on Sissle and Blake's *Chocolate Dandies. Kiddies* featured Lottie Gee as the lead and Adelaide Hall as the main vocalist.

From May through December 1925, *Chocolate Kiddies* was performed in Berlin, Stockholm, Copenhagen, Prague, Budapest, and Vienna with great success. In fact, it was the success of *Chocolate Kiddies* that inspired Caroline Dudley Regan to assemble the Revue nègre troupe. The *Kiddies* show featured music-hall and comic routines with a score written by several acclaimed young musicians, including Duke Ellington. According to Iain Cameron Williams, the "impact *Chocolate Kiddies* had on Europe opened the floodgates for American black performers."[56]

Kiddies and *La Revue nègre* were followed by the European tour of *The Blackbirds of 1926,* featuring Florence Mills in similar Broadway-vaudeville routines. While Baker's theatrical roots lay squarely within the genre of the all-black revue, in Paris she experimented with new techniques as she adapted herself to the French music hall and developed a unique stage persona that could no longer be limited to the vaudeville circuit and its routines.

In 1927 and 1928, two of Baker's Folies-Bergère performances were recorded on film. *La Folie du jour* appeared in *La Revue des revues,* produced in 1927 by Joé Francis and Alex Nalpas. The following year, the Folies-Bergère produced *Le Pompier des Folies-Bergère* as a trailer for *Un Vent de folie.* As noted earlier, this film was digitally remastered by Kino International in 2005.[57] In *La Revue des revues,* Baker performed the famous danse sauvage as Fatou in her banana belt. This dance consisted primarily of Charleston steps, high kicks, splits, and improvised shimmying with erotic stomach and hip contortions. In *Le Pompier,* Baker danced with a broom in Charleston-like moves at the entrance of a subway station. She then paused to adjust the knobs on a painted radio poster. This enigmatic performance combined servile and erotic imagery as part of Baker's primal appeal.

During her early performances of the savage dance, Baker creatively combined elements from American popular dances—the Charleston, the quadrille strut of the cakewalk (which became Baker's chicken dance), and the black bottom—with improvised acrobatics and her own inspired high kicks and contortions. She viewed each performance as an athletic endurance test that had to be completed perfectly for the audience. Recalling her opening performance in Prague during the 1928 world tour, Baker stated that the orchestra played too fast, and she had difficulty keeping up with the rhythm. She pushed herself so hard that she collapsed of exhaustion. "I was burning like a torch. The spectators applauded and wanted to call me back on stage. They didn't raise the curtain. . . . I had fainted. I was bleeding gently onto the carpet, my arms crossed."[58]

While Paul Derval, director of the Folies-Bergère, had organized extravagant music-hall tableaux featuring Josephine as a star in the 1920s, her principal role was still that of the savage dancer.[59] She transformed American folk and popular dances into neoprimitive displays with jungle scenes as backdrops.[60] After returning from her first world tour in 1929, Baker expanded her repertoire through voice and dance coaching. International musicians such as George Gershwin and some of France's early jazz headliners, including Fred Mélé, Alain Romans, and Romeo Silva, were associated with her productions.[61] With voice lessons from the renowned coach Madame Paravicini and dance lessons from George Balanchine, among others, Baker's new performative persona emerged.

In *Paris qui remue* (1930), Baker continued some of the neoprimitive numbers in the tableaux "La Beauté coloniale" and "Les Idoles exotiques," but she also introduced new elements. Her signature song ("Deux Amours") and a series of glamorous costumes and stage sets helped to transform Baker from a music-hall feline into a superstar. This pattern continued with the 1932 production of *La Joie de Paris* and the films and recordings that Baker made during the 1930s. She assembled her own band, the Sixteen Baker Boys, with whom she toured and recorded, and she assumed increasing artistic control over her repertoire. These changes coincided with Pepito Abatino's extensive photographic and publicity campaigns during the heyday of Baker's short film career.

Baker's most significant break with the old music-hall genre occurred with her 1934 appearance as the lead in a revival of Offenbach's operetta *La Créole*. To play this role, she expanded her vocal range and modified her dance styles. Hammond and O'Connor call the production "Josephine's greatest artistic triumph in Paris in the 1930s."[62] Baker played Dora, a Creole Jamaican who falls in love with a French sailor and travels to France in pursuit of him. This comic operatic role firmly placed her in the "Boulevard tradition" of legitimate musical theater and moved her beyond the tableaux, erotic displays, and medleys of the music hall. Two recorded arias and a brief film clip of her acrobatic dance survive from the operetta, documenting her transformation as a comic-opera star.

The films *Zouzou* and *Princesse Tam-Tam* contain musical numbers that feature the new Baker. Already discussed in terms of their narrative content and music, these films also contain significant innovations in dance and choreography. Baker's glamorous image in the performance of the torch song "C'est lui," while somewhat out of character for Zouzou, enhances the film's plot about unrequited love and showcases the transformed star. *Princesse Tam-Tam* features a medley of musical numbers that display Baker's new musical self-writing. The first musical scene takes place at the ruins of Dougga, where the protagonist, Aouina, performs her famous chicken dance. Although this sequence invokes the primal image, it also includes authentic elements of indigenous North African folk dances that Baker formally studied as part of her expanded repertoire. The second dance sequence is set at a sailors' bar in Paris. It contains Baker's more typical rubbery jazz dance, but it also demonstrates her expanded range, with new combinations of high kicking, shimmy sequences, a simple tap time-step, a strutting sequence, and acrobatics. The entire interlude is preceded by the performance of the sentimental tune "Sous le ciel d'Afrique" (Neath the Tropic Blue Skies), which contrasts in tone and mood with the raunchy dancing. Odette, a scheming socialite slumming at the bar, sums up the entire performance as "a savage dance in a sailor's bar." The message of this scene is that the savage remains uncivilized wherever she is. This performance iconically reconnects Baker with her earlier primal image, although the new choreographed performance is quite complex.

The concluding dance sequence in *Princesse Tam-Tam* takes place at the Parisian palace of the Maharajah of Daetane. The mise-en-scène combines art deco with exoticism and is an extravagant spectacle that draws inspiration from both upscale music-hall style and 1930s Hollywood musical comedies in the Busby Berkeley tradition. The palace dance sequence includes synchronized chorus-line dancing, intercut with special effects and shots of an "Indian" gong player and an African drummer resembling Joe Alex, creating a pulsating tom-tom effect. During this sequence, Odette plies Aouina with drinks and encourages her to dance. The sequence ends with Aouina ripping off her glamorous gown to perform the conga. She is carried offstage by adoring male fans amid applause from the men and jealous hisses from several of the women. By using the diegetic audience responses as signifiers, this sequence represents the range of public reactions, from pleasure to shock and outrage, actually surrounding Baker's early performances of the savage dance.

Princesse Tam-Tam contains the most comprehensive and among the longest sequences preserved from Baker's dance performances. It extends from the primal dance to the glamorous music-hall images. Classic vaudeville dance routines based on the Charleston, the strut, the chicken, and acrobatic moves are integrated with balletically inspired synchronized choreography and Hollywood-style flamboyant cinematography. *Princesse* also gives Baker the opportunity to display her newly honed vocal and acting skills. In spite of its limited plot, which remains consistent with the rags-to-riches and lost-love motifs in the form of the Galatea myth, *Princesse* is a vehicle through which Baker is able to exhibit her performative innovations as an actress, singer, and dancer. Many of Baker's later musical performances were elaborations on the genres and styles presented in her 1934 and 1935 films. In 1948, Baker watched the African American performer and anthropologist Katherine Dunham and her dance troupe perform at the Théâtre des Champs-Elysées. Baker incorporated elements of Dunham's choreography along with classical ballet into her 1949 show *Féeries et folies* (Fairies and Follies) at the Folies-Bergères. Throughout her career, Baker continued to absorb and rework new performance routines as she perfected and polished her stage images.

An Inscribed Life

Self-writing consists of a philosophy, a personal ideology, and a worldview.[63] Baker's self-writing builds upon iterative narratives that allow her to develop and deconstruct stereotypical roles. The early narratives recounted to Sauvage and Rivollet emphasize Baker's primal image, her humble beginnings, and her rise to stardom. While fashioning Baker's new image, Sauvage had agendas of his own: his political pacifism, his criticism of puritanical mores, and his liberal defense of Baker's idiosyncrasies. In *Voyages et aventures,* published in 1931, Baker becomes the champion of a free and open society and combats the forces of racism and hypocrisy. These forces are described in dual narrative voices by Baker and Sauvage. Baker chronicles the process of winning over hostile audiences on her tour, while Sauvage provides the social and historical contexts of each setting. Sauvage also furnishes the ideal spectator's viewpoint as he molds Baker into a naïve, erotic, and exotic figure. These biographies are the building blocks for much of the later biographical work on and by Baker. The stories that she tells Sauvage are reiterated as Cinderella and Galatea narratives not only in later writing about her, but also in her self-descriptions and public performances. Although it is slightly more sophisticated, Rivollet's work essentially repeats Sauvage's motifs.

A crucial break, as already discussed, occurs with *Mon sang*. Race is foregrounded as a narrative motor, and the cure for a racist society is formulated as blood mixing and self-sacrifice. Baker's dream of a rainbow world of blended races begins to emerge, along with the Marian motif of sacrifice and selfless love. This motif counterbalances the primal erotic image and provides a vehicle for Baker's evolution. Yet, even Joan, Baker's alter ego in the narrative, seeks approval through the male gaze and the vain hope for Fred's love and gratitude. The novella is also an allegory for the very act of literary creation through which Baker tells her story to Pepito and allows him to remold her image-ideal.

The collaborations with Bouillon are of a different order. Here we see Baker transferring the intensity of her dedication to the Rainbow children and to humanity as a whole. Although portions of *La Tribu arc-en-ciel* were written and edited by Bouillon, that book is thoroughly Baker's story. Even the illustrations by Piet Worm were inspired by Baker's ideas—her love for animals, children, the helpless, and Les Milandes. The female ego-ideal is the mother, but the source of magical transformation is Princess Marianne, who lives an idyllic life in a fairy castle. Les Milandes is a public space, a private retreat, and an imaginary utopian environment that Baker endows with the power to change the world around it. Self-writing about race continues in *La Tribu* by collapsing the walls of prejudice and difference.

Baker's performances establish a counterpoint to her literary self-writing. She uses the performances to mold her public image and, in turn, draws on the inscribed images in writing and photography to structure new performances. This dialectic of writing and performance creates "La Bakaire" as an image-ideal and a cultural commodity. The diegetic and real audience responses generate symbolic contradictions that are beyond Baker's control, extending from the moralistic reactions to her early performances in Europe to the critical press coverage of Les Milandes. Although Baker is baffled and even shocked by some of these reactions, she manages to incorporate them into her performances with twists of humor, irony, and pathos. She learned these strategies during her early days as a minstrel-vaudeville performer, blacking up in order to transform a negative image into a spectacle larger than life. This introversion of racial self-hatred is sublimated in the Marian sacrifice for humanity.[64] Baker's protean capacity to slip from one image to another in the flash of a costume change makes her fascinating and unpredictable. The recurrence of the nested narratives around which the performances are structured, however, creates the indelible and enduring continuity of her character.[65]

Several studies of Baker's life as a performer end with the peak of her early career in 1935.[66] These studies are misleading because they do not connect the early erotic images and rise to fame to the evolving narrative of moral transcendence. A litany of loss overshadows Baker's later life at Les Milandes. This loss, however, was merely part of the unfolding of a larger-than-life, utopian ideal and a reflection of the hues of the rainbow in a global village. Baker's self-writing coalesced to create the ultimate script and totalizing narrative that she would use to build her utopian dream of the composite universal family.

6 Hues of the Rainbow in a Global Village

If my village

Could serve one day

As a witness

And a symbol of love

If all people from here and there

If all people here below

Without concern for color

Had one heart

All villages

Then would be happy. . . .

    —"Dans mon village"

On April 3, 1968, Josephine Baker, who had been in and out of retirement since 1956, appeared before a full house at the Olympia Theater in Paris in one of her many comeback performances.[1] Her number was preceded by the performance of a baby elephant named Tanya, who lumbered through a mechanical dance to the tune of "Roll Out the Barrel." Josephine presented a medley of songs in French, English, and

Spanish; did the Charleston; and brought the house down with her finale of "J'ai deux amours." At age sixty-one, then known as the "comeback queen," Baker pushed herself to the limit to save her château at Les Milandes and her dream of interracial harmony with the Rainbow Tribe. Through her performances for international audiences, Baker developed a way of transcending barriers of race and culture that went beyond words. Baker's dream of universal harmony was constructed around her role as a nurturing mother and the Rainbow Tribe as a domestic and political image-ideal.

In certain respects, however, the Rainbow Tribe was not a family at all, but a social and quasi-religious utopian movement in which the concept of the primal family was used as a metaphor. Purveyors of utopian visions walk a fine line between their dreams of perfection and lived realities. Sir Thomas More's original Utopia was a fictive island in which laws, governance, and social conditions assured peaceful bliss and equality. Baker acted as the charismatic leader of her own utopian movement with its sacred text, *La Tribu arc-en-ciel,* the children's book that she published in 1957. The communitarian ethos of experiments such as Baker's Rainbow Tribe is a response to the creative cultural spaces left open by the state—spaces in which the collective emotions and the sense of belonging characteristic of "neotribalism" can develop.[2] Baker's utopian community may be viewed as a neotribe that became a short-lived movement of social reform.

The image of a color-blind France of liberty and equality intrigued African American artists and expatriates who settled in France between the 1920s and the 1950s. Ignoring the plight of the Sénégalese soldiers and the rising North African and Antillian populations during the interwar years, African Americans sought new freedom in a society that was not, in their terms, overtly segregated.[3] In the Paris that Baker encountered in 1925, the rosy possibilities seemed endless, but her experiences in Germany, Austria, Hungary, and Romania before World War II had opened her eyes to bleaker alternatives. Baker's Rainbow Tribe was a manifestation of the dream of equality. Behind this dream lurked a variety of negative tensions ranging from colonial exoticism to extreme nationalism and xenophobia. As the charismatic leader of a utopian movement in a larger French social environment that she conceived of as genuinely supportive, Baker attempted to bypass these racial and cultural barriers. Her adopted children became the honorary acolytes of her interracial movement and the symbols of her universalistic dream.

One might ask whether the Rainbow Tribe and its dream stood in a positive or an antithetical relationship to official France. Although the tribe incarnated the French values of equality and fraternity, the family also represented an alternative lifestyle that deviated from conventional social norms. The family's ideal was based on "the spiritualization of politics" described by Karl Mannheim and a politics of representation as the foundation of all utopian communities.[4] In liberal democracies when such utopian challenges occur, the groups may coexist peacefully with other institutions until a point of legal and socioeconomic infraction or a publicly acknowledged weakness is found. In the case of the Rainbow Tribe, these weaknesses were epitomized by the departure of the group's cofounder, Jo Bouillon; the vulnerability of the children; and the financial fragility of the enterprise. By 1969, Josephine Baker's charisma as a performer, a mother, and a group leader was not sufficient to offset these obstacles. Nevertheless, the ideal of world unity and cultural diversity lives on in the legacy of her universalistic discourse and the revival of Les Milandes as a site of tourism and pilgrimage.

The moral and ethical objectives of the Rainbow project involved the creation of a perfect community with appreciation for all forms of cultural difference. Similar propositions have a long history among utopian and communal movements. Isolation of the community to avoid contamination from outsiders' beliefs and practices is also a common feature of utopian communities. Les Milandes is no exception in this regard, as seen by Baker's reluctance to allow the Rainbow children to attend schools outside of her domain and her preference for what is now known as "home schooling." Baker wished to shield her community from negative external influences and, at the same time, to receive praise and public acclaim for her accomplishments. It was her hope that once the utopian multicultural community came to fruition, it would serve as a model for other communities, states, nations, and the world at large. In a conversation with me on June 2, 2006, Akio Bouillon confirmed my thesis when he stated, "Yes, the Rainbow family was a utopia, but that doesn't mean that it was any less real." Josephine Baker believed that this imagined community would become a global reality.

Numerous antecedents and contemporary parallels come to mind when one views Les Milandes as a utopian community. Stephen Papich visited Les Milandes on several occasions and was impressed with the experiment. He compared it to New Harmony, a utopian community established in upstate New York in the 1820s.[5] But the conditions of that experiment differed from Baker's in terms of both financial support and the political tolerance for pioneer communities during that era in the United States. Utopian visions often emerge when older social forms are questioned or become outmoded. Seventeenth-century Puritans in England and the colonies hoped that their perfect community of saints would replace what they perceived as a corrupt social order of the monarchy.[6] From the utopian communes following the French Revolution to late twentieth-century religious utopianism, charismatic leaders have encouraged their followers to dream of idyllic lives that transcend the struggles and temptations of the outside world. In recent times, some of these dreams, such as Jim Jones's Peoples Temple and Agricultural Project, have ended in tragedy, while others, such as Michael Jackson's Neverland, remain suspended creations of childlike fantasies with ambiguous and controversial social outcomes. In contrast to these cult-like closed utopias, Baker attempted to create an open multicultural community as a model for the future. The theodicy of this utopia involved the return to a world in perfect harmony with nature and the creation of a social universe in which all prejudice and social conflict would be absent.

The Primal Family

The French family was historically based on a patriarchal model. As James Corbett explains, "Under the absolute monarchy it mirrored the organization of the state—the pater familias ruled over his household just as the king ruled over his subjects. The Napoleonic code consecrated fatherhood—the famous *puissance paternelle,* tempered by the revolutionary idea of equity husbands were supposed to be endowed with."[7]

Josephine Baker's upbringing in the slums of St. Louis had little in common with this patriarchal model. As noted earlier, Eddie Carson, Josephine's mysterious putative father, disappeared before her birth and made no visible contribution to the family. Josephine was brought up under her mother's strict hand, with siblings Richard, Margaret, and Willie Mae Martin. Carrie McDonald, Josephine's mother, had been an amateur dancer but worked as a laundress to support her family during Baker's youth. The children were also forced to work. Reared in a culture of austere poverty in what has come to be interpreted as a stereotypical black matrifocal family, Josephine had a fragmented family life that contrasted starkly with the Napoleonic patriarchal ideal characterized by authoritarian protection and financial stability.

Baker's early years as a performer were based on appropriating and manipulating racialized gender stereotypes. As she entered middle age, Baker chose, and was perhaps forced, to use the family as the symbolic locus for building her new image and dreams of brotherhood. As both the savage dancer Fatou and the glamorous fashion icon, Baker had existed in a world without children, although, as noted earlier, the self-sacrificing Madonna image was foreshadowed as early as 1931 in *Mon sang dans tes veines*. All of Baker's films involved unrequited love resulting from crossing racial barriers without children, and, to a certain extent, her life followed a similar script. For Baker, the Rainbow Tribe became an ideologically charged vehicle for confronting these social obstacles while simultaneously rewriting her life and attempting to change the world. Jan Relf argues that women's utopias often involve a "retreat into fantastic pastoral enclosures, or walled spaces in which they guard and protect a cluster of values perceived as characteristically feminine."[8] The Rainbow experiment displayed some of these characteristics with Baker as the ultimate mother figure who dominated the children, her natal family, and a small community within the enclosure of Les Milandes.

Elements of the Rainbow project exhibited continuity with the root paradigm of the primal, savage image. The master narrative of return to an idyllic paradise—a lush garden of Eden—might be applied to the Rainbow Tribe living on the vast and isolated property of Les Milandes in the rural Dordogne. On June 3, 1947, Baker's birthday, Josephine and Jo Bouillon married at the Château des Milandes in a civil ceremony presided over by André Lahillonne, prefect of Dordogne, immediately followed by a religious ceremony in the château's Gothic chapel and a festive reception. Bouillon stated that in marrying Josephine, he was also marrying her dream. In this idyllic landscape, Baker hoped that the prejudices and social barriers of the outside world would vanish, to be replaced by a life of harmony and cooperation. The famous photograph, now a postcard, of Baker and Bouillon with eight of their Rainbow children in front of a Christmas tree at Les Milandes, in 1956, reflects this harmonious ideal, replicated in other poses (fig. 38).

In 1948, after Josephine's brief visit in the United States, Carrie joined her daughter at Les Milandes along with Josephine's sister Margaret and her husband, Elmo. Carrie left her husband in the United States to follow her daughter. Everyone was put to work. Carrie helped with the household duties and later the children. Margaret worked on the farm and, for a short time, ran a bakery where she sold American-style pastries. Elmo was in charge of the paddle boats on the Dordogne River abutting Les Milandes. Josephine's

Figure 38. Jo Bouillon, Josephine Baker, and the Rainbow children at the park of Château des Milandes, circa 1959. The family's pose is reminiscent of the one in the 1956 Christmas photo. Copyright © CAP/Roger-Viollet.

brother Richard joined the group in 1952. Leaving behind a trucking business and a family in St. Louis, he became a chauffeur at Les Milandes and later ran a gas station that Josephine had purchased for him near the estate. Yet, in spite of the presence of Baker's natal family, the Rainbow Tribe was not a natural family. It was what Goffman describes as a "fabrication" intended to convey a specific impression and message to the public.[9] MacCannell elaborates on this notion of the simulated family when he describes some modern families as conscious self-representations: "There are some families here on earth that are modeled as closely as is humanly possible on the Holy Family. In these cases, the symbolic form of social organization is the original, and the 'real-life' families are mere copies. . . . The commodity has become an integral part of everyday life in modern society because its original form is a symbolic representation (advertisement) of itself which both promises and guides experience in advance of actual consumption."[10]

Josephine began the Rainbow family project when she was well into her forties, informally adopting the children at the rate of two a year between

1954 and 1956. Formal adoption proceedings were conducted for eight of the children as a unit at the administrative prefecture of Sarlat, in Dordogne, on June 21, 1957, making the commemoration of their joint adoption just three weeks after Baker's own birthday. The eight children formally adopted in 1957 were Akio (of Korean origin, from Japan); Luis (from Colombia); Janot (also Korean, from Japan); Jean-Claude (from France); Moïse (French, of Jewish background); Brahim, now called Brian (Berber, from Algeria); Marianne (French, from Algeria); and Jary, or Jari (from Finland).

Subsequently, four more children were added to the family: Mara (a boy from Venezuela); Koffi (from Côte d'Ivoire); Noël (from France); and Stellina (Moroccan, born in France). For some reason, perhaps appearance, Bonnal lists Mara as a girl born on April 19, 1958, and, therefore, initially not adopted with the original group.[11] All children received the surname Bouillon, which also became Baker's legal married name.[12] As adults, some of the children have retained the name Bouillon, while others use Baker. The group represented nationalities from four continents, and they were of diverse cultural and religious backgrounds of which none of them was fully aware. Baker's desire to have children of her own as part of the legend is confirmed by Jo Bouillon, who claimed that she miscarried during the early years of their marriage, an assertion that appears to have been embellished, given that she is reputed to have had a hysterectomy in Morocco during the war.[13] Phyllis Rose points out, "To have had that many children so close in age, had they been biologically hers, she would have had to bear three sets of twins in three years."[14]

Initially, there were to have been four male children of different races and nationalities, but Josephine's plan expanded to include eight more children, two of them girls, Marianne and Stellina.[15] The classic French pattern of patriarchy was overturned by Baker's domineering matriarchal control of her mostly male brood in their sheltered castle environment. The primal family was matriarchal, matrifocal, experimental, iconoclastic, and legendary. Josephine was the boss. Just as she had with her primal exotic image, Baker used existing stereotypes to break the rules and challenge bourgeois norms and expectations about family life and education. She created a composite community based on the ideals of ethnic and cultural blending in a simulated touristic space. The acquisition of each child was surrounded by a nested narrative that paralleled Josephine's own Cinderella story. There was a sense in which the Rainbow Tribe reflected Baker's performative persona by representing the multiple national and cultural identities that she had assumed on stage, on film, and in song. The children's public stories were subtly woven together to duplicate Baker's foundling myth in a new narrative program, and they cleverly excluded some of the financial and interpersonal negotiations surrounding the adoptions. The family was converted into a spectacle in which Josephine and the children were the stars.

Life with the Rainbow Tribe

In interviews with the press, Josephine repeatedly stated that the Rainbow Tribe "represented" for her the ideal of universal brotherhood. Her use of the term "representation" in connection with the family is interesting. It points to the complex and contradictory symbolic status of the Rainbow Tribe as a narrative fabrication. Families are the locus of tradition, heritage, and a sense of belonging. Baker consciously built an international family in which she wished to instill this sense of belonging symbolically and even mythologically. Yet, modern families are also situated in territories, nations, and neighborhoods. Les Milandes would become not only the home but also the territory of Baker's family in the ideal world that she wished to construct beyond the French nation-state.

Les Milandes was an island that magnified Josephine's escape from her two loves, the United States and France. As with other utopian communities, its success would depend on its internal harmony and its relationship to the external forces of territory and state.[16] The territory of Les Milandes had its own rules, regulations, and sense of order. It was the *village du monde* (world village), *le domaine* (territory), and the international capital of brotherhood. This world of brotherhood was, nevertheless, located in the Dordogne in France and, therefore, subject to the governance and norms of the French state. The children would be prepared to be citizens of the world. They were also French, went to local schools on and off, and interacted with their neighbors. The rainbow dream left open the question of socialization and the interface between the ideals of brotherhood and the realities of social life in a remote rural community in southwestern France. The world village at Les Milandes evolved into a utopia with a unique structure.

Aspects of colonial discourse evident in Baker's primal image were also at play in the conceptualization of Les Milandes as an autonomous territory. It was a neofeudal fiefdom ruled by Baker, a property in the French Département de Dordogne, and a family home. Although the plan did not entirely work for a variety of practical reasons, the award-winning experimental farm at Les Milandes was intended to feed both the tribe and part of the surrounding community and to make Les Milandes a self-sufficient enclave year round. Josephine had finally become the real Queen of the Colonies. In her military uniform, she would represent the domain as its head of state (fig. 39). As a colony, Les Milandes would ultimately return to the control of the state when the debts were recalled and its multicultural vision was challenged. The taxes owed to the French state were symbolic of Les Milandes's political, economic, and cultural dependency.

Given the territorial and ideological organization of Les Milandes, it was inevitable that the split identity of the colonial subject would be reflected in the socialization of the Rainbow children. In everyday life, issues of identity conflict emerged as disciplinary problems and internal family disputes. The onus was placed on Baker for being inconsistent in her childrearing practices, frequently absent on tour, unrealistic in her expectations of the children, and, in the end, overwhelmed by the organizational and financial responsi-

Figure 39. Josephine Baker receiving the Legion of Honor medal at Château des Milandes, August 18, 1961. Photo courtesy of Getty Images, New York.

bilities of her vast global project. Jean-Claude Baker (Rouzaud), Josephine's protégé, quotes her friend Marie Spiers as commenting that "everything was overdone, the punishment was overdone, the love was overdone, the makeup was overdone."[17] Others have described the uneven discipline in the family and Josephine's practice as Maman Cadeau (Gift Mother) of showering the children with lavish gifts on holidays and upon returning from each of her tours.[18] A larger issue concerns the objectives of these indulgent practices and how they shaped the children's lives in the composite community. The children were trained to be tolerant of racial and cultural differences, and their strong bonds to each other were evident and genuine. They were, however, pampered and sheltered from a world in which these differences were objective facts. The contradictory childrearing practices were not simply an inadvertent byproduct of Baker's personality and whims. They were rooted in a deep-seated ideological conflict between the family as a utopian composite community suspended in space and time—a "representation," in Baker's own terms—and the larger social world in which the experiment existed.

During a tour of Japan in 1954, Josephine visited an orphanage where she found Akio (meaning "autumn," in honor of the season of his discovery by the orphanage), whose mother was Korean and whose unknown father was believed to be an American serviceman.[19] At the same orphanage, she found another child of similar parentage, Teruya, and made plans to adopt him, re-naming him Janot. Both of these children were castoffs in their society—marginalized in Japan as Korean war orphans. Their Asian background fulfilled the first step in Baker's quest for an international composite community.

A year later, while on tour in Colombia, Baker searched for another child. She made arrangements with a family near Bogota to adopt one of its many children, Gustavio Valencia, and changed his name to Luis. She also wanted to adopt a Native American child from either South America or the United States and ultimately found Mara in Venezuela and engaged in complex negotiations to adopt him. While on tour in Scandinavia in 1955, she visited an orphanage in Helsinki, where she discovered two-year-old Jary, and brought him to Les Milandes. Her project was now gaining more momentum and publicity. People would send her press clippings and leads about abandoned children and would even help her to locate them. She also attempted to assist many of the orphans that she did not adopt.

In an orphanage in Paris, she found Jean-Claude (Bouillon), who was French. While on tour in the Middle East, she looked for a Jewish son in

Israel, but was turned down due to strict Israeli government regulations on international adoptions. Returning to France, she located Moïse in an orphanage in Paris to fulfill that part of her dream. Moïse was the sixth child to be brought to Les Milandes, and Josephine had now exceeded the limit of four set in her original plan with Jo Bouillon. Governesses shouldered some of the childcare, with which Baker's mother, sister, brother-in-law, and brother also helped. Juliette Pallas Jaton, one of the children's governesses that I interviewed in 2004, described the scrupulous organization of every minute of the children's activities from dawn to dusk.[20] Baker gave her personnel detailed, typed daily schedules for the children, including their meal times, dietary preferences, toilet training, play periods, nap hours, and bedtimes. Any deviation from the schedule was to be reported directly to Baker. Governesses were required to wear starched white uniforms for all formal occasions and to dress the children in the appropriate matching outfits.

In spite of the tight organization of the children's activities, Bouillon worried about running the large estate with so many children and employees. Family photographs and his own statements demonstrate that he was a caring father, very close to the children, and he served as their major parental figure during Josephine's long absences on tour. His family was also involved in overseeing the purchase and touristic renovation of Les Milandes, which was beginning to take on the allure of a resort and mini-state.

The myth continued in 1956. On tour in North Africa, Baker found two children who were refugees from the Algerian war, allegedly hidden under a bush after a skirmish. She brought Brahim, of Berber descent, and Marianne, a French colonial, back from North Africa, filling out her tribe with displaced war victims. The following year, while in Africa, she adopted Koffi, an orphaned child from an Ivoirian hospital. Although it would have been three years before Félix Houphouët-Boigny became president of Côte d'Ivoire, the future statesman is said to have facilitated the transaction, acted as the child's godfather, and also helped out later with a donation to Les Milandes.[21] On June 21, 1957, with the formal adoption of the first eight children at the Tribunal of Sarlat, Les Milandes regularized its relationship to the state, making the Rainbow children not only citizens of the world, but also French, with two French parents. During this period, the couple's conflicts escalated.

In 1959, after adopting Mara from Venezuela, Josephine impulsively responded to news from Paris that an abandoned child had been found in a trash dump. It was near Christmas when she rushed to claim him at a Parisian hospital, naming him Noël because of the season. Three years later, she received distressing news about a Moroccan baby born to an indigent mother in Paris. Baker took in Stellina in 1962 even though her resources were quickly dwindling. Stellina completed the Rainbow Tribe and, by this time, Les Milandes was already in serious financial difficulty.

Based on her philosophy of universalism, Baker decided to educate the children in their cultures of origin. Moïse had Hebrew lessons. Brian learned about Islam and Qu'ranic liturgy. Akio and Janot were instructed in Buddhism and Shintoism and eventually given an opportunity to visit Japan. The children had tutors in French and basic subjects. For a time, they attended local schools and were later sent to boarding schools. Josephine's educational philosophy was visionary and far ahead of her time. Had she been exposed to contemporary approaches to multiculturalism, she could certainly have instructed the children more explicitly about what she conceived to be the family's mission. Nevertheless, they all came to understand her version of the battle against racism. They considered her ideals to be rooted in the experiences of exclusion and prejudice that she had endured while growing up in the United States and witnessing war-torn Europe. Josephine was pleased when she saw evidence of tolerance, bonding, and solidarity among the children as they joined forces in confronting outsiders who exhibited curiosity and, occasionally, hostility toward them. External skepticism merely drove Josephine to pursue her dream with more determination.

The children, nonetheless, lacked a full grasp of Baker's daily decisions and strategies, viewing her courses of action as capricious. When Moïse was given Hebrew lessons, he schemed to run away from the tutor, and, fearing ridicule and exclusion by his classmates, he refused to wear a yarmulke to school, a decision that would now be in complete accord with French laws on secularization. Stephen Papich described an incident that he witnessed at Les Milandes:

> Little Moïse had three times run away from his Hebrew lessons; each time he was found alone, playing about the pool. The Israeli tutor wanted to discipline him but felt that a confrontation involving himself, Moïse and Josephine would be good.
>
> When the child saw his mother in bed, he began crying and ran to her. She put him under the covers with her.

"Now, what is the matter here, Monsieur? Tell me all about this."

The tutor, I felt, told his story very well. It was really only a matter of a little discipline.

"But, sir," she responded, "you obviously don't understand children. Don't you see, there is something down by the pool that is more important to him than his Hebrew lesson. So you must go to the pool with him and discover what that is. Then, as his tutor, you will see that that desire is fulfilled first, then the Hebrew lesson will come easily for him."[22]

Without further notice, the tutor resigned and left Les Milandes the next day. Josephine then sent Moïse to a Jewish couple of Polish descent, André and Jacqueline Barasche, who resided nearby. Moïse also resisted their instruction, and Josephine's plan for the transmission of cultural traditions was thwarted. Brian experienced similar frustrations with his Islamic tutor and his childhood trip to North Africa with his mother. Josephine sent Akio and Janot to Japan for a year to learn Japanese and explore the possibility of continuing their education in Tokyo. This plan also backfired, as the two had difficulty adjusting to the Japanese language and culture and became homesick for French food and the comforts of life in a château.

Papich observes, "The children of Josephine Baker were the most pampered, looked after, educated, played with, and cared for children of any in the entire world."[23] Relatives and governesses found them difficult to control and discipline when they were young. Margaret Wallace, Josephine's sister, considered her child-care duties in Josephine's absence to be very trying. Marie Spiers, Josephine's close friend and supporter from Paris (and the wife of her pianist and orchestra leader, Pierre Spiers), was equally frustrated when she had the children on her hands. Although the dormitory-like structure of Les Milandes resembled a boarding school, the pedagogical philosophy was diffuse, and there was no central source of structure apart from Josephine's charismatic authority and Jo Bouillon's displays of ludic paternal warmth. As the couple's relationship began to deteriorate, the family ideal disintegrated as well. The children found tutors and outside schools to be too strict and, as they grew up, they resented Josephine's domineering master plans for their lives and careers.

Living a utopian dream in the fish bowl of Les Milandes was challenging. According to Baker's biographers, some of the children were vociferous in expressing their complaints about Josephine's absences and the constraints of their unusual upbringing as celebrity children.[24] But each child had his or her own multifaceted experience that was both positive and negative. For the children, the struggle to the hilltop was long and hard, and the path of multicultural redemption for a new era was not one that they had freely chosen.[25] As with offspring of other celebrities, the Rainbow children were caught in a maelstrom of grandiose dreams and incessant, confusing publicity. Rainbow Tribe member Brahim (Brian) B. Baker explained, "The main problem was that for the best part of our school days, we had all the disadvantages. . . . We were orphans *and* then we were children of a broken home. Over and above that, coming from different origins, we had nothing to compare our lives with."[26] In retrospect, the children have come to terms with their special roles and Baker's legacy.

Resource mobilization for Les Milandes as a family home, a social movement, and an enterprise was ad hoc and inconsistent. Sustaining the domain involved Baker and Bouillon in a large touristic and agricultural enterprise with complex and mixed economic agendas and an immense financial overhead. Multiple social pressures, mixed goals, and increasing debts led the couple into conflict. In May 1957, while Josephine and Jo Bouillon were completing the final adoption papers for eight of the Rainbow children, Josephine contacted Maître Bardon-Damarzid, her lawyer in Dordogne, to initiate divorce proceedings against Bouillon.[27] Although the finances of the château and Josephine's obsession with adoption were the underlying issues motivating the rupture from Bouillon's perspective, the couple's interpersonal tensions had also escalated. Jo's family fortune had been invested in the château, and Jo's brother, Gabriel Bouillon, representing the family, had signed the purchase papers in proxy at his Paris apartment on behalf of the couple during their absence on tour.[28] Jo's sister Maryse occasionally helped out with the children and the management of the château. At the peak of its functioning, Les Milandes had one hundred eighteen employees. Bouillon argued that Les Milandes should be more efficiently managed, and that he should play a greater and more autonomous role in the control of its business, agricultural, and domestic affairs. In their interview with me, Albert and Juliette Jaton speculated that Josephine's decisions about changes in the agricultural management of the model farm were the source of many of her economic problems at Les Milandes while they worked there. Bouillon had suggested converting Les Milandes into a large corporation by consolidating the income from agriculture, the hotel, and the theme park, but Josephine resisted. Contrary to popular accounts of the story in documentary films, docudramas, and some of the press coverage of the day, it was Josephine, rather than Jo, who formally initiated the divorce proceedings on personal and business grounds and refused to reconcile. She sued Bouillon in the Sarlat tribunal for alienation of affection and refusal to perform his marital duties, although she ultimately never divorced him.

As was his right as a co-owner of the château and the property, Bouillon drew a salary from Les Milandes, much as the employees did. According to Haney, Bouillon and a friend, who he had hired to manage the charter house, may have augmented their incomes with the profits from the hotel and night-club.[29] In Bouillon's view these sums may justifiably have belonged to him because he was in charge of much of the accounting for Les Milandes, but some of these activities were carefully hidden from Josephine. One Baker biographer, Ean Wood, argues that Bouillon engaged in these activities in order to provide a nest egg for the Rainbow children.[30] Although Bouillon's actions may have been altruistic, they further depleted the fragile financial resources of Les Milandes. Baker, in turn, had remortgaged the property without consulting Bouillon. Some of the workers at the château were also involved in secret financial schemes and overcharging that depleted the resources of the farm and the tourist attraction.

The prevailing narrative surrounding Bouillon, which has become part of his mythical persona, portrays him as the anchor of reason and stability in Baker's life at Les Milandes, in keeping with the Pygmalion and rescue motifs. In spite of his good efforts, there are bound to be a few cracks in the shining armor of this chivalrous knight. Bouillon, like Baker, was a bon vivant as well as a loving parent. In an interview for the 1986 documentary *Chasing a Rainbow,* by Christopher Ralling, Jean-Claude Baker states that the marriage between Baker and Bouillon was an unlikely match because of the differences in their backgrounds. Bouillon continued to work throughout the war, but he subsequently wished to avoid the stigma of having performed on stage during the German occupation. His marriage to Baker helped to reestablish his credentials as a performer in postwar France where he occasionally made public appearances under a new alias of Jo Duval and his orchestra (see the discography). He was a mainstay of the utopian family, a musical partner, and a tremendous source of support for Baker and Les Milandes in spite of the couple's disagreements. A preliminary divorce hearing with a possibility of reconciliation was set in Sarlat for July 5, 1957. At this time, the newspaper *L'Aurore* claimed to have received a personal letter sent by Bouillon from La

Chartreuse des Milandes expressing hope for total reconciliation and blaming the rupture on Josephine's "nervous depression" and "extreme fatigue."[31]

Bouillon continued to be present at Les Milandes on and off for the next two years, living in a separate house near the château. He took charge of the funeral arrangements for Josephine's mother, Carrie McDonald, who died at Les Milandes on January 12, 1959, while Baker was away on tour in Istanbul. He left for Paris in 1960 and later settled in Buenos Aires, where he opened a restaurant modeled on La Chartreuse with financial backing from his friends. Although he was absent, the last two children adopted after Baker's separation from Bouillon, Noël and Stellina, were registered in his name along with Baker's. Many people, including celebrities such as Brigitte Bardot and Zsa Zsa Gabor, tried to come to the moral and financial assistance of Les Milandes, but to no avail. Villagers referred to Les Milandes as the Rolls Royce without gas. Although Baker was able to hold on to the château for another decade, its days of prosperity and glory had passed, and Baker's utopian dream was rapidly fading away.

Family Photographs

The 1956 Christmas photograph of Baker and Bouillon with eight of the Rainbow children, discussed earlier in this chapter (see fig. 38), represents a moment of harmony and celebration. Seated beneath an ornately decorated Christmas tree, Josephine holds Brahim, and Jo clutches Marianne, with the six other children between them. Dressed in matching white outfits, the children appear angelic. The tribe of cherubs was nearly complete and ready to face the public. Although this photograph is part of a family album, it is also well crafted as a publicity tool and is now a postcard. Marianne Hirsch points out that photographs "perpetuate family myths while seeming merely to record actual moments in family history."[32] Posed photographs and studio shots unite the public and private images of a family. In the case of the Rainbow Tribe, the public images also accentuated the myth and message of blissful interracial harmony.

Most of the publicly available photographs of the Rainbow Tribe date from 1956 and early 1957, when Jo Bouillon was present and the family still appeared to be happy and unified. Group photographs were also used as publicity shots and templates for posters well into the 1960s, after Bouillon's departure. In later press photographs from the mid-1960s, Josephine is often pictured on tour with the children. Taken collectively, the photographs fall into three categories: group poses of the entire tribe, candid shots of the children at play among themselves, and action shots of a parent with one or more of the children. While group poses such as the one in the 1956 Christmas postcard and a 1959 publicity shot in front of the château reflect the ideal family, the candid shots are intended to show that the children had a normal upbringing full of spontaneous moments of love, happiness, and good humor. These photographs reproduce the family by iconizing moments of togetherness as familial narratives.[33]

A group photograph from the Departmental Archives of Dordogne, Collection Diaz, shows eleven of the children (Stellina is absent) posed in front of the château wall, in 1961, with the caption "All eleven children reunited in happiness!" (fig. 40).[34] In the front row, left to right, are Luis, Janot, Jary, Akio, Jean-Claude, and Moïse (the latter sitting). In the second row are Koffi, Marianne, Noël, Brahim (Brian), and Mara. The older boys in the front row are all in suits, which are similar but not identical, with shiny leather shoes and string bow ties. The suits have a uniform-like quality. Brian also sports a suit and tie, and Marianne wears a fancy dress. Koffi and Mara wear matching checkered jumpsuits, and Noël has on a white tunic top with a large collar. The children posed for this photograph with varying degrees of interest, but they all look as though they cannot wait to have the session end. The formality and near-uniformity of the clothing suggests that the family is on display. On special occasions, Josephine insisted on this type of uniform dress and even encouraged her mother and her sister as well as the governesses to dress in matching white outfits. Unlike the Christmas shot, however, this picture of the smiling children does not include the parents (Bouillon having left by this time), and the occasion is ambiguous. The message projected by this photograph is one of staged solidarity. It also resembles the type of photograph made for school yearbooks and class reunions.

On July 1, 1955, Jo Bouillon organized a photographic press session at Les Milandes. Bonnal's caption reads, "Papa Jo wanted this press coverage to make known the humanitarian and universalistic goals of his wife Josephine Baker: already six Children of the World in the Bouillon family from three different countries: Japan, Colombia, and Finland."[35] In a variation on the group photo, Jo poses behind the six oldest children (Moïse, Luis, Jary, Janot, Akio, and Jean-Claude) who are seated on a porch swing (fig. 41). The children appear distracted. Only the oldest, Akio, smiles at the camera.

Figure 40. Eleven members of the Rainbow Tribe in front of the Château des Milandes. Photo from Collection Diaz, Departmental Archives of Dordogne, in Jean-Claude Bonnal, *Joséphine Baker et le village des enfants du monde en Périgord* (La Bugue, France: PLB Éditeur, 1992), 56, reproduced courtesy of the author.

Figure 41. Jo Bouillon and six of the Rainbow children at play at Les Milandes, circa 1956. Photo from Collection Diaz, Departmental Archives of Dordogne, in Jean-Claude Bonnal, *Joséphine Baker et le village des enfants du monde en Périgord* (La Bugue, France: PLB Éditeur, 1992), 62, reproduced courtesy of the author.

Candid shots of the parents and the Rainbow children at play or engaged in daily routines are also photographs with a purpose. In one sequence of the July 1955 photographs, Jo frolics on the grass with Janot, Moïse, Jary, and Luis.[36] All of the children except the black child, Luis, are dressed in identical sunsuits with straw hats. Luis wears a flared sunsuit with a cotton cap. It is not possible to determine whether the uniformity in costumes has to do with the children's color, size, and age or with individual preferences. The governesses were given daily instructions on how to dress the children for special events. In these candid photos, the children are mixed and matched. Luis and Jary are seated together on a lawn chair in a perfect picture of black and white brotherhood.[37] Akio and Janot are photographed on an adjacent chair, balancing out the hues of the rainbow. Janot is also photographed playing with a beach ball, both alone and with Jo. Throughout this series of photos, Jo emerges as a loving and playful father who gives the children both individual and collective attention during the course of a normal day at Les Milandes. Jo is also photographed with his pals and band members, with the caption "Jo Bouillon et sa bande de copains."[38] This photograph continues the ludic spirit of Jo's play with the children as he poses on the steps of the nightclub stage, bonding with his male colleagues.

Parallel to Jo's 1955 photo shoot is a series of photographs of Josephine and her mother, Carrie, alone with the children. In a 1957 photograph, Josephine, wearing a white cocktail dress, is seated in the garden holding three of the youngest children while six others surround her.[39] Akio is facing his mother, with his hand on her shoulder while the others face the camera. The children appear to be unhappy. They are crying and scowling. This image is certainly not material for a positive publicity photo, but it is a posed shot. Other family photographs show Josephine changing diapers, feeding the children, and putting them to bed, with Carrie rocking them to sleep. Although Josephine plays a nurturing maternal role, some of the photographed embraces seem contrived rather than spontaneous. Bouillon's whimsical playfulness is absent in Josephine's serious and single-minded approach to the tasks of motherhood. Even the candid shots demonstrate a performative display of affection, which, while it is genuine, also plays to the camera. The photographs exhibit a subtle reversal of gender roles. Although Josephine is maternal, she also introduces the children to the public while Jo occupies the playful domestic spaces at home.

In a series of candid action shots, the children accompany Josephine to special events and on forays into the community.[40] One photograph from the departmental archives of Dordogne, Collection Diaz, shows Josephine standing with the children as they examine posters for her 1957 antiracism conference. Jo appears with her in some of the photographs from this sequence, which look spontaneous but have the purpose of advertising the conference and exhibiting the children as an example of the rainbow ideal. The children are also photographed with Carrie at a long table in the conference hall. Other special-event photographs show the children attending concerts, family weddings, and baptisms with Josephine and going to school in Castelnaud on their own. All of these photographs present images of the children in a wider society as they play out their roles as French citizens and representatives of multiculturalism. In December 1990, Jo Bouillon brought the family together again for a commemorative performance honoring Josephine Baker at the Folies-Bergère. In a photograph of the occasion, their pose on the steps of the theater's stage resembles the poses they struck during their youth at Les Milandes, although they had not lived together as a family for many years (fig. 42).

Domestic photographs convey an ideological message that emphasizes the family's cohesion in the context of its larger social mission. Hirsch states that "the family photograph . . . can reduce the strains of family life by sustaining an imaginary cohesion, even as it exacerbates them by creating images that real families cannot uphold."[41] Photographs of the Rainbow Tribe reflect the dual processes of family cohesion and rupture transferred into the public sphere of media representation. Examining these tensions via photography provides insight into the challenges and contradictions surrounding the Rainbow Tribe's universalistic mission both inside and outside of the picture's frame. The symbolic importance and unity of the family as a legacy is also expressed in Chouski's 2006 commemorative statue of Josephine and Akio (fig. 43).

Figure 42. Ten of Josephine Baker's children on stage at a 1990 homage to her at the Folies-Bergère. Photo © Micheline Pelletier/Corbis Sygma.

Figure 43. Centennial commemorative statue of Josephine Baker holding her son Akio, by Chouski. Photo by Alain Bogaert, courtesy of Château des Milandes, Dordogne, France, 2006.

The Ideal of Universal Brotherhood

When independence struggles raged across the African continent, and the civil rights movement began to gain momentum in the United States, Baker started to adopt her Rainbow children and develop the utopian space of her *village du monde*.[42] The ideology of the Rainbow Tribe surfaced in the shadow of négritude's domination as a universalistic philosophy and identity discourse in France. At the conclusion of his discussion of Richard Wright in *The Black Atlantic*, Paul Gilroy asks, "What would it mean to read Wright intertextually with Genet, Beauvoir, Sartre, and the other Parisians with whom he was in dialogue?"[43] Baker also needs to be "read" intertextually with respect to the French intellectual and ideological environment that she adopted, with its concepts of universalism, ideals of assimilation, and utopian visions of liberty, equality, and fraternity.

Baker's concept of universal brotherhood treats the ideal of fraternity literally. It also closely follows Sartre's dialectic of négritude, in which white supremacy is the thesis; négritude, as an affirmation of blackness and a riposte, is the antithesis, and a society without races is the synthesis.[44] In their various versions of négritude, Césaire, Senghor, Damas, and their colleagues emphasized the antithetical moment in the dialectic as an essentialist affirmation of cultural pride that provides a basis for black participation in universal civilization. Although it was performative rather than literary and philosophical, Baker's primal image shared much in common with négritude's essentialism, and the Rainbow Tribe paralleled Sartre's synthesis of a society without races. Sartre viewed négritude's ultimate goal as self-destructive for it would erase and transcend the antithetical moment of racial affirmation in favor of the universal ideal. Sartre argued that négritude is like a "woman who is born to die and who senses her own death even in the most rewarding moments of her life."[45]

In certain respects, Baker's dream of universal brotherhood was an implementation of the communitarian Sartrian ideal. She believed that racial antagonism was destined to disappear. In a 1970 interview with John Vincour of the *International Herald Tribune*, Baker supported her view of interracial marriage and stated, "Mixing blood is marvelous. It makes strong and intelligent men. It takes away tired spirits." Born of racism, poverty, alienation, and neglect, like Baker herself, the orphaned Rainbow children would transcend their suffering in a new harmonious environment. As seen through the photographic documentation of their lives, the children were reared in an environment of comfort, luxury, and protection in which social and racial boundaries were removed, leaving only the inflection of cultural traditions transmitted to them through tutors. Baker's plan for maintaining this utopian ideal as the children grew older, however, was not fully developed, and they experienced frustration as role models on display for an ideal community that could be described to them only in vague and general terms. They were no longer disadvantaged orphans; nor were they adults reclaiming civil rights and equal job opportunities. Instead, they were members of the *village du monde* being groomed as good citizens of the world.

The family experiment was successful in that it did create a genuine atmosphere of solidarity, harmony, and mutual tolerance of difference among the children. It also equipped them for diverse and successful lives in business, performing arts, and public service. In a nine-page letter to Stephen Papich, excerpted here, Baker outlined her goals for the world village and concluded that her multicultural ideal and her children were her reason for living:

> I wanted the Milandes to be known and respected as a world village.
>
> Destiny wanted me to find this little hamlet which is, without a doubt, a little earthly paradise for those in search of peace for their soul.
>
> I didn't look for it specially.
>
> I found it naturally, and I held on to it fiercely, for it is my resting place.
>
> It is here that my children can pursue their brotherly education in peace, without being influenced by bad spirits, for this is very important for the ideal which they represent.
>
> It must not be thought that I am trying to make little gods of them, but only normal beings—just, honest toward themselves and toward others, guided by purity and the conscience of sensible men.
>
> I know that we are ahead of our time.
>
> That is why there has been so much confusion about me and about others who think as we do.[46]

Beyond the Rainbow Tribe, Baker hoped to create the College of Universal Brotherhood at Les Milandes, where students of all backgrounds would devote their attention to problems of racial discrimination, human rights issues, and the religions and cultures of the world. Education would be based on new experimental methods that would take into account the diverse backgrounds of all of the students. Josephine wrote numerous letters and proposals to promote her college and had several offers to help support it, but the plans never materialized. Although the demise of Les Milandes was, in large part, material, the confrontation between a utopian dream and the practices of the surrounding society came into play as a crucial determinant of the end of the experiment. In the eleventh hour, when Bruno Coquatrix arrived in Sarlat from the Olympia in Paris with resources necessary to save Les Milandes, the creditors had already made their decision.[47] The absence of one of the creditors from the tribunal officially invalidated the possibility of accepting Coquatrix's offer. Ultimately, the uneasy relationship of this composite community to the surrounding countryside and the French state made the dream impossible to sustain as a lived reality.

A Dream Deferred

During her last years at Les Milandes with the Rainbow Tribe, Baker's every move was covered by the press. She wanted the media there to witness her situation down to the last hunger strike in her nightgown of misery in 1969 (fig. 44). Journalists found her to be good copy. Debates escalated in the press and on television about whether the family deserved help from the state, whether the children were to be considered privileged or pitied, and whether they constituted a true family. On Monday, June 4, 1964, immediately following the ten o'clock news, Brigitte Bardot launched a televised appeal for support of Josephine and the Rainbow Tribe in response to the threat of the château's impending sale.[48] While some people responded sympathetically, there was a tremendous negative backlash. In an article entitled "La Télévision au secours des orphelins de luxe" (Television to the Aid of the Orphans of Luxury), the journalist Raymond de Becker wrote, "Not everyone is Josephine Baker or Brigitte Bardot. This is a sham [le comble de l'imposture]."[49] De Becker also argued that television, which was an arm of the French state in 1964, before privatization, should under no circumstances be used to support the private interests of Baker and her family. Articles debating the pros and cons of the problem appeared in *Le Monde, Le Figaro, France-Soir,* and *Paris-Jour* during the summer of 1964. Some journalists, like Jacqueline Cartier, were favorable toward Baker, noting the plight of her children, the promises of support, and the successes of her various comeback concerts across Europe, while others were more cynical about the fund-raising efforts for Les Milandes. Bardot's campaign resulted in the formation of a French committee to aid Baker and promote her cause, consisting of, among others, François Mauriac, Jean-Paul Belmondo, and Bruno Coquatrix.[50]

As the situation deteriorated, the children were sought out for interviews. At the time of the final sale of Les Milandes, Akio gave an often quoted interview to Jacqueline Cartier in which she described the creditors: "I had the impression of seeing ferocious beasts. But the important thing is that we are all together, and we can pursue our ideal elsewhere."[51] Cartier adopted a sympathetic attitude toward the situation, and part of Akio's statement appeared as a subtitle when her article was headlined in *France-Soir.* In a 1999 filmed interview, Akio, by then an adult, still expressed bitterness about the legal proceedings. One of the most poignant short pieces at the time of the sale was an interview with Baker in the *International Herald Tribune* on

Figure 44. Josephine Baker at the time of her eviction from the Château des Milandes, 1969. Photo courtesy of AFP Getty Images, New York.

September 30, 1968. The article concluded with Baker's lamenting, "I have nowhere to go and I do not know who is going to look after us."[52] Josephine was transformed from an independent matriarch to a dependent child looking for support from the state and private investors.

It seems fitting that Princess Grace came to the rescue, not only on personal grounds, but also because Monaco, as an isolated principality, in many ways represented the benevolent monarchical utopia in a Cinderella narrative.[53] Josephine and her Rainbow children were housed at the Villa Maryvonne in Roquebrune-Cap-Martin, on the French side of the Monaco border, under the care of the state of Monaco and the Red Cross, for which Baker performed fund-raising benefits. Josephine and, later, Jo Bouillon (who died on July 9, 1984) were interred in the same plot in Monaco. The state of Monaco, via Princess Grace, had miraculously intervened to restore the fragile balance between ideology and utopia, and the dream of the multicultural world village was, once again, deferred.

Part Three

Changing the World

7 Legendary Legionnaire

My life, like that of so many others, is a constant struggle. I've
placed my worldwide reputation as an artist on one side of the
scale and human justice on the other. The choice is easy for me
because I've always placed human justice above materialism.
—Baker and Bouillon, 1977

One of the first stories that Josephine Baker learned to tell in
French was "The Emperor's New Clothes." At press conferences and interviews, she would recount this tale as if she were in the presence
of eager schoolchildren. The story's moral about the egotistical and disrobed
leader was not lost on Josephine. Baker adored the trappings of politics and
used them to convey her message of interracial harmony. She spent much of
her life promoting the political causes of social justice, racial equality, and
human rights. Her political opinions, however, were not without contradictions, exaggerations, and glaring errors of fact. As with her collaborative biographical writings, she would later retract or simply ignore some of her first
impressions and responses. Baker was a political "reactionary." That is, her
political causes were often reactions to positive or negative personal experiences and emotionally charged incidents. Nevertheless, as she matured, her
overriding political commitment was to her Rainbow Tribe and the utopian
ideal of a multicultural society. Baker held this dream long before multicul-

turalism became a popular and contested slogan. She molded her image of multiculturalism in a French environment, while drawing on memories of her American past.

Although her outspoken political goals were often intertwined with diverse personal, national, and international agendas, Baker remained forthright about her humanitarian commitment to a society in which racial difference would become a rainbow of cultural enrichment rather than degenerate into a scar of shame. While Baker retrospectively constructed her political education as a linear narrative, she actually "backed into" her role as a political figure and then began to clarify her ideas and consolidate her image, much as she had done in other arenas of her performance career. She moved from being a counterintelligence spy during World War II to a charismatic leader placed under international surveillance after the war.

Framing a Political Image

As Josephine Baker began to rise to public prominence in France, she found herself in the political limelight. Her 1928–29 world tour politicized her primal image. This period marked the first stage of her political education and activism. From Vienna to Buenos Aires, the moral content and the racial inflections of her performances were called into question. The collaborative biographies with Marcel Sauvage in 1931 and André Rivollet in 1935 addressed these racial stereotypes and Josephine's responses to them. She became an ambassador for racial and moral tolerance and made political statements on stage and in the press. These responses framed her political persona and awakened her awareness that a song or dance was not merely a performance but also a political statement. Yet, the staging of politics in Baker's performances remained implicit.

The war years brought her activism to fruition and repositioned her political commitment as an adjuvant to her performances.[1] Baker's body, in itself, became a political challenge in the late 1920s. The fact that her danse sauvage and erotic displays left the music hall and entered public discourse in France, Germany, Austria, and Argentina opened up racial and gender images that had previously been confined within the bounds of demimonde performances. By inscribing her experiences in the press and in biographies, Baker broke through the boundaries of the music hall into a broader public space, which, years later, she would exploit to her advantage. In France, celebrity biographies such as Baker's were used not only to publicize the works of performers but also to express political opinions and establish genres and schools of thought and art.[2]

Baker assumed four significant political roles during her lifetime: (1) the spokeswoman; (2) the warrior and spy; (3) the militant and martyr; and (4) the head of family and state. These roles were interconnected across four stages of her political career, and each built on the other, creating her total political persona. Each role also involved a costume change to accompany the new political image. She first became a spokesperson as her political consciousness was raised through international travels in 1928 and 1929 and her brief return to the United States to perform in the Ziegfeld Follies in 1936. In part, she was forced into this early role by the circumstances of her notoriety and public visibility as a performer. The war years brought on her role as a soldier and spy for French counterintelligence and Resistance forces, a role that, ironically, was reversed when she became the object of international surveillance during the 1950s. At this time, she transformed the role of the warrior into that of a militant for justice in her battles against racism and desegregation. The similarities between the warrior-spy and militant roles led to public confusion and accusations, fueled by Walter Winchell's 1951 attack, that she was an international spy and propagandist for a variety of contradictory radical causes. The martyr image overlapped with and drew on her role as a warrior and spy but also had deep roots in her political awakening during the late 1920s. As a head of family and state, she continued in the martyr role until the end of her life, a role that was sustained by the Marian narrative motif at Les Milandes and Villa Maryvonne. At Les Milandes in military garb, she ran the domain like a small empire and received dignitaries. The domain had its own post office, educational system, theme park, and farm for experimentation and sustenance. It was a total environment in which she hoped to realize her utopian political dreams. As a charismatic leader and performer, Baker was among the pioneers in combining art, performance, and politics locally and in the international arena. Her pattern of image creation and public role playing was later to become a mainstay of twentieth-century "image politics."

Secret Agent

World War II marked a political turning point for Baker and the second stage of her activism. *La Guerre secrète de Joséphine Baker,* published in 1948 by Commander Jacques Abtey of the French Information and Counterespionage

Services, offers an insider's account of Baker's activities during the war years, about which she was often reluctant to speak.[3] The war years crystallized Baker's dedication to France and her campaign against racism. Daniel Marouani, an impresario connected with the Casino de Paris and a secret agent for the Counterespionage Services, organized Abtey's introduction to Baker in 1939. Abtey initially had serious reservations about approaching Baker because of the difficulties that the French intelligence bureau had experienced with the music-hall star and double-agent Mata Hari, whose unreliability eventually led to her execution. Nevertheless, in September 1939, shortly after France entered the war, Abtey met with Baker at her Beau-Chêne mansion and was pleasantly surprised by her frankness and her enthusiasm for the wartime cause.[4] When Abtey arrived with Daniel Marouani, Baker had been collecting snails in her garden. Abtey described the scene: "Smiling broadly, she stood there, one hand in the pocket of her old pair of pants, and the other holding an old tin can full of snails. 'Pleased to meet you, Mr. Fox. Hello, Marouani.'"[5]

As a secret agent, Abtey donned as many costumes as a stage performer, while Baker, during the war, eventually shed her costumes in favor of somber clothes and military garb. When Abtey first met Baker, he was masquerading as a British officer, Mr. Fox. He subsequently changed his identity to Jack Sanders, a neutral American, and later to Jacques-François Hébert, a French performer and press secretary to Baker. Mr. Fox, or Foxy, as Baker came to call him, and Marouani spent the afternoon and evening with Baker, seated in front of the fire at Beau-Chêne while working out a game plan over several glasses of champagne. Abtey was quickly convinced of Baker's sincerity as she promised to repay France, her adopted country, for all of the good fortune that it had bestowed on her. Baker later reminisced, "When I gazed deep into my own inner self, I realized I would be incapable of functioning as a real spy. But intelligence work was different. It seemed the perfect way to fight *my* war."[6] It is important to note the distinction between the Maquis and the Free France underground espionage units that operated under de Gaulle's leadership. There were tensions in strategies and goals between the two groups, as indicated by Baker's decision to join the Free France intelligence efforts in order to fight her war.[7]

At the end of 1939 and into 1940, Baker continued to work at the Casino de Paris. In early 1940, Henri Varna decided to open the theater's season with a show entitled *Paris-Londres*, proposed as a wartime public morale booster.[8] It involved performances by Baker and Maurice Chevalier. Baker performed in the evening and did humanitarian and social service work during the day while awaiting Abtey's instructions. During the show's run, she also released her last feature film, *Fausse alerte,* directed by Jacques de Baroncelli. Finally in 1940, after what the French called the *drôle de guerre* (phony war), the Maginot Line fell and German forces crossed over into France. By May, Varna was forced to close the show, and many of the entertainers, producers, and impresarios either fled or went into hiding. Abtey departed for the Loire Valley, and Josephine, along with her personal assistant Paulette and a refugee couple that she was harboring, escaped to Les Milandes. The period of playing both sides of the footlights in Parisian performances was over, and Baker began to assume her wartime roles of spy and morale booster.

Abtey joined Baker at Les Milandes under his assumed American identity, Jack Sanders. They listened to Charles de Gaulle's radio broadcasts from London about Free France and tried to develop a plan of survival, support, and escape. Colonel Paillole, who was one of de Gaulle's liaisons, approved Baker's official participation in the espionage activities of Free France. Although Baker and Abtey wanted to join de Gaulle in London, the Free France secretariat decided that they would be more effective on French territory. Baker would carry military secrets written on her sheet music in invisible ink for transmission to Lisbon and then to London. Abtey would accompany her on any journeys disguised as her press secretary and assistant. As the Nazi threat approached Les Milandes (nearby Bordeaux had been an occupied provisional capital before Vichy), Baker and Jacques-François Hébert (Abtey) prepared to leave for Lisbon. Using the leverage of her celebrity status, Baker was able to obtain travel passes for herself and Hébert under the pretext that they were traveling from Lisbon to Brazil for a performance.

After a brief waiting period in Lisbon, Colonel Paillole and the Free France secretariat ordered the couple to Marseille, where they ran out of money. Pushed once again to balance stage performance against wartime activity, Baker managed to obtain the lead role in *La Créole,* which was being revived in Marseille. *La Créole* opened at the Théâtre de l'Opéra in Marseille on December 24, 1940. Baker rehearsed diligently and managed to remember her old part. Her former dancing partner from Paris, Frédéric Rey, then stranded in Marseille, helped Josephine to recreate the Parisian décor and costumes.[9] On opening night, Daniel Marouani, Abtey, and a small coterie of Baker's friends were present in the audience to witness the success of the performance. For her part, Baker was biding her time waiting for the next orders from Free

France. They came sooner than expected, and Baker was called to leave for North Africa by mid-January 1941. Because Baker was suffering from pneumonia and fatigue, Abtey negotiated a legitimate medical termination of her contract with the theater after a brief run of the show in Nice. Baker then departed for North Africa, carrying her secretly inscribed musical sheets with her, first to Algiers, then to Casablanca and Marrakech. These movements were largely clandestine, and Abtey's account is the most reliable source currently available for reconstructing them.[10] The Marian narrative of sacrifice and rescue was in full force with Baker's wartime mission.

In Morocco, through a series of contacts, Baker met Si Thami el Glaoui, the powerful Pasha of Marrakech. Even though the Marseille theater did not believe her, Josephine genuinely had pneumonia and was able to prove it through her x-rays. El Glaoui offered her hospitality and support in his lavish palace during her recovery. He staged an elaborate dinner for her, and thereafter they became close friends. According to two of Baker's biographers, Haney and Rose, El Glaoui may even have fathered Baker's stillborn child in Marrakech.[11] Haney reports, "At the time when Josephine's friendship with El Glaoui was still fresh, she became pregnant. It has never been clear who the father was. Regardless of paternity, El Glaoui took an active interest in the sad events that followed. Late in her pregnancy Josephine gave birth to a stillborn baby, delivered at the Comte clinic in Casablanca. Labor was followed by a high fever and incipient infection."[12]

During 1942, Josephine recovered from her acute infection at El Glaoui's palace. Maurice Chevalier, who was visiting Casablanca, came to see her at the Comte clinic, although accounts differ about whether he actually received access.[13] In any event, Chevalier issued a statement to the French press that he had seen Josephine, and that she was impoverished and at death's door. The rumor of Josephine's near death began to circulate worldwide, and many believed that she had already passed away. Baker, however, recovered at El Glaoui's residence with Commander Abtey constantly at her bedside. It was shortly thereafter that she began to assist Sidney Williams in setting up Liberty Club canteens sponsored by the Red Cross.[14] With Williams's support and Jo Bouillon's band backing her, Josephine performed for American, French, and British soldiers across North Africa. Williams described her role in glowing terms: "She is one of the most remarkable women alive. She was a balance between French and British and Americans, on the one hand, and the Arabs and Negro GI's on the other. She was always doing something for somebody."[15]

From 1942 to 1944, Baker crisscrossed North Africa for the U.S. Liberty Clubs and the Free French forces. She performed in Morocco and made a transcontinental trip to Cairo and Lebanon. Her performances also took place in Corsica for the French and in Sardinia and on the Italian mainland. In total, she raised 3,143,000 francs for Free France during these tours.[16] Baker performed in spite of ailing health, with open wounds from her operations, and, after the liberation on August 25, 1944, she returned to Paris, where she was immediately hospitalized in a weak condition. On October 14, 1946, she was awarded the Medal of Resistance by de Gaulle while hospitalized in Paris for yet another operation resulting from her wartime illnesses. De Gaulle, who was not present for the ceremony, sent a letter delivered by his daughter stating, "It is with all my heart and knowledge that I send you my sincere congratulations for high distinction of the French Resistance which you have received."[17]

Now in her forties and seasoned by the war years, Baker returned to a new and more visible public role in France. She had been decorated as a war hero and had witnessed the emergence of both positive and extremely negative political regimes. A rational accounting might argue that she had been an eyewitness to the rise of democracy, fascism, and dictatorship, and that her political choices and allegiances were crystal clear. Returning to the narrative programs that inspired Baker, however, illuminates the contradictions in her political choices, statements, and allegiances. Before the war, she had been mesmerized by the glamour, pomp, and appeal of Mussolini. Her early statements supporting him against Emperor Haile Selassie of Ethiopia had created much bad press for her but gave her inroads into Italian intelligence sources during the war. After the war, she had been impressed not only by de Gaulle's cause, and the war that she thought he had waged against racism, but also by the pomp and circumstance that de Gaulle brought to postwar France. In North Africa, Baker apprenticed herself in a politics of liberation and authoritarian control. Although he had been educated in France and supported the liberation forces, El Glaoui was a despot among his people. Baker's later attraction for Juan Péron was to follow a similar pattern. While she advocated the support for the helpless and the homeless that was used to publicize Péron's regime, she also dreamed of a fairy-tale kingdom in which a benevolent leader would dispense largesse and mercy to the people. Baker's actual politics and her fairy-tale dream collided and coalesced. She believed in supreme authority, benevolently meted out on an egalitarian basis to the subjects of a realm, who would become its protected children. These contradictions in her political vision, though perhaps not conscious, were the seeds of its unraveling.

Desegregating Performance and Public Spaces

In spite of the genuine emotions involved, Baker's marriage to Jo Bouillon on June 3, 1947, was based on a number of pragmatic considerations. Among them were the clearing of his war record, the possibility of their ongoing creative and economic collaboration as performers, and, most significantly, the future building of an estate and a utopian political dream together. It took a decade for Baker's dream of the Rainbow Tribe to materialize, and in the interim, she fought many postwar battles with Bouillon at her side.

Baker's personal political vision was clear and focused. During the war years, it involved ridding the world of the threats of racism, fascism, and xenophobia. After the war, her vision of a multicultural utopia and a "family of man" crystallized at a moment when anticolonial and civil rights struggles were being waged around the world. Baker's own political agenda was emotionally charged and emerged from her personal experiences. These personal traumas and challenges entailed both actual biographical events and the constructed myths and narratives developed through her self-writing. One Baker biographer, Alan Schroeder, points out that "Baker was not a Communist or anything else, for that matter. Her beliefs concerning brotherhood were simply too naive to make her an effective member of any political organization."[18] In contrast, when questioned about his mother's political allegiances, Jean-Claude Bouillon asserted, "Mother was not a Communist. She was a Gaullist! It didn't make any difference to her. The important thing was to be with people who could get things done. If they were capitalists, marxists, communists, that was not the important thing."[19]

Both Schroeder and Bouillon are partially correct in their assessments. Baker performed politics much as she would stage an appearance at the Casino de Paris. Role playing and numerous costume changes, often forgotten or obliterated, were marshaled toward the larger goals of intercultural cooperation and equality. Baker used the glamour of media events for her own purposes. Although Baker's methods for achieving these ends tended to be indirect in her performances, they could be assertive and confrontational in everyday life. She engaged in ironclad negotiations, face-to-face confrontations, citizen's arrests, and legal actions to achieve her goals. Although some of these activities may seem self-centered and irrational to outsiders, for Baker they were driven by the ultimate goal of fostering a harmonious society in which racial and cultural differences would not be impediments to the recognition of human dignity.

In 1948, when they were still in the process of finalizing the purchase of Les Milandes, Baker and Bouillon made a brief concert tour to the United States. They were refused reservations at thirty-six New York hotels and experienced the growing racial tensions of the postwar years in the United States. Alarmed by what she perceived as a stagnant and reactionary political environment, it was then that Baker made arrangements to bring her family from St. Louis to Les Milandes. By the end of 1952, her mother, sister, brother-in-law, and brother had all joined Baker and Bouillon at Les Milandes.

After some hesitation, because of the 1948 debacle, Baker decided in 1950 that another U.S. tour would be useful. This decision was triggered by a telegram she received that summer from her New York agent, Willard Alexander, proposing a lucrative contract at the Copa City Club in Miami.[20] Following several days of negotiating with Baker, Copa City's co-owner, Ned Schuyler, offered Baker a contract of ten thousand dollars a week, plus costumes and expenses, for three months in 1951, starting with a two-week run at the Copa City in Miami, to be followed by a two-and-a-half-month U.S. tour, including San Francisco, Los Angeles, Las Vegas, Chicago, and New York. Baker believed that she would be able to save a good deal of the money from the tour to cover expenses at Les Milandes. She made public announcements, however, to the effect that the main reason for the tour was political. She informed the Olympia Theater manager, Bruno Coquatrix, from whom she was taking a leave, that her music-hall career would now take a back seat to her political dedication to help her people in the United States.[21] Whether by design or circumstance, her statement turned out to be true. This trip marked the third period of Baker's political education and activism.

From the outset of the tour, Baker demanded that she perform only for integrated audiences at every venue. If curfew and segregation ordinances were still in place, she requested that they be lifted for the duration of her performances in the hope that they would change permanently. She also required integrated stage crews. This meant that Baker refused to perform at all-black as well as all-white venues—a technicality that would cause trouble for her later in the tour. Because of all of the constraints she placed on her performances,

Baker acquired a reputation of being politically dangerous, demanding, and difficult to handle. Nonetheless, her overbooked Miami performances were a resounding success, and the first leg of her tour exceeded all personal and public expectations. On the first part of the tour, she netted more than one hundred thousand dollars and, hoping to make four times that amount, she turned down some lucrative engagements where club owners refused to comply with her demands for desegregation and fair work conditions.

Baker's political activities extended beyond the symbolic act of desegregating performance venues. She supported the cause of Willie McGee, a young black man who was convicted of raping a white woman in Mississippi. Before McGee's execution in May 1951, Baker paid for his wife, Rosalee, to travel from Detroit to Mississippi to visit him, and she supported and subsidized rallies to publicize McGee's plight.[22] The American Labor Party also adopted McGee's case as a cause. Baker championed McGee on an emotional basis without fully realizing how his case fit into a larger political picture. She also defended the integration of housing in Cicero, Illinois, amid a violent riot and supported the Trenton Six, African American men that she believed were being unjustly accused of the murder of a white shopkeeper in New Jersey. In Oakland, California, she met with the mayor of the city and members of the transit authority to demand integrated hiring of bus drivers and municipal employees. She also wrote to the National Association of Radio and Television Broadcasters to protest its hiring practices and the use of racial stereotypes in the media.[23]

The segregated vaudeville traditions in which she had her roots now became the object of her relentless criticism. One of her more unusual moves was to place a disruptive nightclub patron under citizen's arrest after he made a racist remark. Her action resulted in his paying a hundred-dollar fine. Although Baker was frequently in contact with NAACP officials about this and other incidents, she embarked on most of these activities on her own without the advice or support of any social or political group. Her ambitious and idealistic campaign garnered her recognition and resulted in some incremental and temporary changes. She was, however, operating essentially alone in a tense and volatile racial climate, the contour of which she was not fully aware. In this atmosphere, she was no longer a French war hero but instead a foreign visitor in the United States on a temporary performance visa.

Celebration of Josephine Baker Day, organized by the NAACP in Harlem on May 20, 1951, lifted Josephine's spirits. Baker Day included parades, performances, a banquet, parties, and tributes to Baker for her role in de-segregating performances and public spaces. Members of social clubs, the Girl Scouts and Boy Scouts, and the American Legion, along with a host of diplomats and celebrities, attended and supported the event. Baker, who had received the NAACP's Outstanding Woman of the Year Award earlier in 1951, felt rewarded for her struggles and included in a community that she had temporarily adopted as her own (fig. 45). But the euphoria of the day, where Baker was the star of the show performing politics for an eager and receptive audience, was not to last. On October 16, 1951, the repercussions of Baker's activism came to a turning point with the famous Stork Club incident.

Jo Bouillon had returned to Les Milandes to work on repairs while Baker stayed on alone in New York to perform at the Roxy Theater.[24] After her evening performance at the Roxy, Baker arrived at the Stork Club with Roger Rico, the French star of *South Pacific*; his wife; and Bessie Buchanan, a black

Figure 45. Josephine Baker receiving an NAACP award from Dr. Ralph Bunche, New York, 1951. Photo © Bettmann/Corbis.

performer turned local New York politician. Although Rico was a regular at the club and had a reservation for the evening, his arrival with Baker and Buchanan raised the eyebrows of some conservative Stork Club members, the owner, and the staff. The group ordered drinks, and Baker asked for a crab salad and a steak dinner. When the meal had not been served after an hour, and the waiters were unresponsive, Baker suspected discrimination on the part of the Stork Club's owner, Sherman Billingsley, who had an unstated policy against admitting blacks. Coaxed by Bessie Buchanan, Baker left the table and telephoned her lawyer and a New York City police commissioner to report the incident. When going to the lobby to telephone, she passed the *Daily Mirror* columnist Walter Winchell and his friend Jack O'Brian, also a journalist, at a nearby table. Baker considered Winchell to have been a witness of the incident and wanted his support, but by the time she had returned to his table, he had disappeared.

The next day, Baker went to see Walter White, an NAACP official, to tell him what happened. Based on his assessment of the incident, White organized a picket line to be placed in front of the Stork Club one week later.[25] Baker continued to challenge Winchell concerning his silence. Meanwhile, Winchell began to attack Baker on the radio and in his syndicated columns and refused to come to her support against his old friend Sherman Billingsley. Winchell also wrote to J. Edgar Hoover requesting an FBI investigation of Baker's political activities. The investigation was opened on October 25, 1951. The battle between Winchell's *Daily Mirror* and the *Daily Worker* began. The negative press and government surveillance instigated by Winchell's accusations eventually resulted in the cancellation of Baker's U.S. performance contracts and of Rico's contract with *South Pacific*. Baker and many of her friends suffered greatly from Winchell's attacks. Due to her escalating political and financial difficulties, Baker felt compelled to leave the country to continue her tour in South America in January 1952.

The FBI files on Baker have been publicly available since 1982, although they contain some ellipses within censored and classified materials.[26] They span a seventeen-year period and are copious (over five hundred pages) and highly repetitive. The files are divided into two parts. Much of part 1 consists of letters from Winchell to J. Edgar Hoover and other FBI officials. Part 2 contains newspaper articles, excerpts from biographies, and surveillance reports of Baker's activities. Winchell sent the FBI summaries of his columns; background materials on Baker, including Sauvage's 1947 biography, *Les Mémoires de Joséphine Baker;* and letters of support from his fans, among whom was a black student from Springfield, Massachusetts, and a black doctor who argued that Baker's conduct was erratic, arrogant, and damaging to the black community. Winchell accused Baker of pro-Communist, pro-fascist, and anti-Semitic leanings in spite of her wartime activities and preparation for conversion to Judaism. Baker responded to Winchell by filing a $400,000 libel suit, which was eventually dropped in 1955. Winchell used Baker's trips to the Soviet Union and her frequent interviews with reporters from the *Daily Worker* as evidence against her. In addition to instigating FBI surveillance, Winchell's feud with Baker resulted in restrictions of her opportunities to work freely in the United States as well as internationally, and there was close scrutiny of her by U.S. immigration officials for over a decade. Winchell himself also suffered negative publicity, and Sherman Billingsley was forced to close the Stork Club several years later.

Baker aggravated the situation during her trip to Argentina. Originally scheduled for a little over a month in 1952, Baker's trip to Argentina ended up lasting over six months.[27] As a special guest of the government, Josephine was initially sheltered from, or chose to ignore, the unsavory aspects of the Péron regime. Baker had admired Eva Péron as a performer and popular figure, calling her "my sister." Juan Péron intended to use Baker as a figurehead and goodwill ambassador after Eva's death, continuing in the role that his wife had assumed of the "national Samaritan" pacifying the masses. In turn, Baker hoped that Péron would promote and fund her ideas of universal brotherhood at Les Milandes. She spoke at a memorial rally for Eva in which she denounced racism in the United States and misguidedly praised Péron and the Argentine government for humanitarian compassion. Her statements were widely covered by the local press, and excerpts of her remarks, along with press clippings in Spanish, were transmitted to the FBI.

When Adam Clayton Powell Jr., an African American congressman, learned of Baker's vocal criticisms of U.S. race relations, he requested that the State Department cross-check the sources and then called a special press conference at his New York office. Feeling compromised and betrayed, Powell denounced Baker as a self-styled anti-American crusader ("a manufactured Joan of Arc") and criticized her talents as a performer. Powell, the State Department, and the FBI all wished to silence Baker and keep her from further criticizing the United States abroad. An American embassy report included in the FBI files stated that Baker was dangerous because she kept "running off at the mouth."[28] Baker wrote that she found Powell's statements to be "grim" and his attitude to be deceptive, especially because she considered Powell and his first wife, the pianist and performer Hazel Scott, to be among her close friends.[29] Meanwhile, under the misapprehension that Péron would support her antiracist cause at Les Milandes, Baker continued to visit hospitals, hostels, and orphanages as his goodwill ambassador until she had finally seen enough. She eventually became disillusioned with Argentina and planned to leave for a tour of Peru and Colombia.

Officials at the State Department and the local American embassy managed to have these trips canceled through internal memoranda, which are recorded in the FBI files, and Baker stayed on in Argentina. She claimed that her speeches, originally given in English, had been mistranslated by the press into Spanish and then back into English for international consumption, and that she had been unjustly maligned because of these distorted messages. She found herself caught in a web of cold-war intrigue and politics that overwhelmed her. Any remark that she made about her negative experiences of racism in the United States placed her in jeopardy. Baker conceived of herself as an activist in the battle to improve race relations in the United States, as well as abroad, and perhaps, in Phyllis Rose's terms, as a "martyr."[30] This image, which is part of Baker's Marian motif and rescue narrative, was exactly what the State Department wanted to avoid exporting during the volatile postwar years.

After leaving Buenos Aires, Baker performed briefly in Rio and then went on to Havana, where her reception was lukewarm. Her purported pro-Communist leanings were not welcome in Batista's Cuba. She performed for one week there and was forced to cancel the rest of her Caribbean tour, which was to continue in Haiti. In Cuba, she was detained, fingerprinted, labeled as a Communist Party spy, and pressured to sign a document stating that she was a paid propagandist hired by Moscow. She refused to sign and left Cuba for France with the impression that her life was unraveling before her eyes.

Returning to Paris again by the end of December 1953, she spoke at a rally for the International League Against Racism and Anti-Semitism and then returned to Les Milandes to pursue a new phase of her dream of multiculturalism on more familiar ground.[31] This return marked the beginning of the fourth stage of Baker's political career and activism.

Mary Dudziak, a law professor at the University of Iowa, contends that

Baker was a victim of cold-war politics along with other activist performers and leaders of the period, such as Paul Robeson and W. E. B. Du Bois.[32] Baker's case differs significantly from those of Robeson and other U.S. civil rights activists, however, because she was not a member or official representative of a particular group or party, and she did not use her performances exclusively as political platforms. Her political actions were ideologically inconsistent from the perspective of any formal organization. Instead, the messages of her political ideals and demands were encoded through her performative persona and based on her personal vision of an ideal world. Even her political speeches tended to be autobiographical accounts of her racial and economic struggles projected onto the lives of others. She saw the larger political picture through the lens of her own life rather than in terms of the historical and structural forces that shaped social conditions. This personal perspective allowed her to hold seemingly contradictory political positions such as simultaneously supporting human rights and the Péronist regime. Politics for Baker was a removable costume worn on a stage of appearances against the backdrop of her conception of fundamental human rights.

Baker's unique multicultural vision masked all other political contradictions. Although supporting the causes of organized groups, Baker shied away from strong affiliations with such groups in favor of individually meaningful action. She responded spontaneously to new political situations. Her ideal of political order vacillated between an idyllic vision of a benevolent monarchical realm (the Cinderella narrative) and an egalitarian family of man in which everyone lives together in natural harmony (the rainbow motif). Neither of these ideals, however, included a clear blueprint for long-term action, and both depended on the charismatic leadership of Baker as a political performer. Dudziak argues that Baker retreated to "domesticity as the locus of her politics" because her resources dried up when international venues were closed to her.[33] This argument assumes that Les Milandes was a "domestic" rather than a utopian communal solution to a political problem. If, in contrast, we view Les Milandes as a political domain in which Baker saw herself as sovereign, this enlarged "domestic" arena becomes yet another legitimate realm for Baker's individual performance of international politics. Even the FBI investigations eventually concluded that Baker's activities were individual and identity-based ("pro-Negro") rather than group-oriented ("pro-Communist"). Left out of the equation, however, was an understanding of the active role that Les Milandes, as an institution, a political model, a domain, and a dream, played in Baker's conception of multiculturalism and human rights.

Baker's Multiculturalism

With the end of World War II, old systems began to crumble, and a new political and economic order emerged. Anticolonial liberation movements stirred around the world as Europe lost its economic control of African and Asian colonies. The Afro-Asiatic Conference, held during April 18–24, 1955, in Bandoeng, Indonesia, convened to address possibilities for decolonization across Asia and specifically in Indochina, was the first of many opportunities for dialogues intended to break down the restrictions of the old colonial order. In 1947, the Sénégalese politician, author, and publisher Alioune Diop founded the journal *Présence Africaine* to showcase the works of African and Antillian authors and to address human rights issues affecting the black world. Diop surrounded himself with African and Antillian intellectuals and students in Paris, including Aimé Césaire, Jacques Stéphan Alexis, Léopold Senghor, Léon Gontrand Damas, and Jacques Rabemananjara, as well as French supporters such as Jean-Paul Sartre, Michel Leiris, and Georges Balandier, who formed a patronage committee for Présence Africaine, the publishing house. In 1956, Diop added a social and cultural arm, the Société Africaine de Culture (SAC), to the journal's editorial board. He then appointed an umbrella executive committee to promote SAC's activities, which included seminars, conferences, lectures, and weekly discussion sessions. Alioune Diop served as the secretary general of the association, and honorary officers included Josephine Baker, Louis Armstrong, James Ivy of the NAACP, De Graft Johnson, Émile Saint-Lot, and Peter Abrams.[34] While some committee members held only formal titles, others were active in the organization of Diop's events for well over a decade.[35]

Although members of the Présence Africaine cartel and its fellow travelers actually held a broad spectrum of political beliefs, they were unified on the political and cultural significance of decolonization. One of Diop's first, and probably most famous, conferences was the First Congress of Black Writers and Artists, held September 19–22, 1956, at the Sorbonne. This conference brought together writers, artists, and political activists from Africa, Europe, and the United States to discuss black heritage, literature, and politics in the first of an endless round of encounters held in Europe and Africa. SAC's conferences became a model for subsequent conferences, festivals, and art biennials, displaying and debating the works of African and African diasporic scholars and artists. The conference-festival format became the hallmark of black cultural politics in France and francophone Africa during the 1960s and 1970s and continues to function as an important point of access and a locus of cultural criticism for African and diasporic artists on the international scene. Although Baker's organizational role in these conferences was minimal, she did participate in the SAC-sponsored 1966 World Festival of Black Arts in Dakar and in similar conferences held in Havana to commemorate the Cuban Revolution, and in Rio. With her reputation, image, and considerable experience as a politically active performer, Baker made important contributions to these conferences through her very presence as a public figure on the scene.[36] Combined with political rallies and marches, conferences were major venues through which Baker shared her multicultural vision with the world, often giving speeches recapitulating her biography in the context of an antiracist struggle. Conference agendas fit neatly into Baker's model of performing politics by giving her a chance to play a public role and to stage presentations of her political views for a receptive live audience.

A State Department entry in Baker's FBI files for May 18, 1956, lists her participation in the organization of the 1956 Congress of Black Writers and Artists and mentions invitations extended to Louis Armstrong, who did not participate, and to Richard Wright, who was an active contributor. The conference was covered by both FBI and Central Intelligence Agency (CIA) surveillance.[37] The FBI files describe the journal *Présence Africaine* as a publication skewed toward the left. American embassy officials warned that the conference should be monitored and every effort made to steer its participants to the West and control their leftist tendencies. The anticolonial emphasis of the journal was considered potentially destabilizing in the context of the dominant French and American political climate of the day. Baker's association with Présence Africaine and SAC was much the same as it had been with other political organizations. Baker willingly endorsed causes, occasionally without realizing their full implications, and she participated in activities as a performer and figurehead.

In 1956, when Alioune Diop and his colleagues at Présence Africaine organized the first congress, Baker was busy preparing for a concert tour of North Africa, followed by an extravagant music-hall revue at the Olympia

Theater in Paris. While in North Africa, she began to plan more adoptions for her Rainbow Tribe. She also organized political conferences. She had her own personal and political agendas that interfaced ideologically with other organizations but did not connect with their agendas in practical terms. Nonetheless, her performative participation in the larger political arena was visible enough to implicate her as a planner and promoter of many events. Her diverse commitments raised the larger question of the social responsibility of the artist in the political arena, a question to which she often replied with ambivalent, contradictory, and multivalent actions, masked by a reiterative personal narrative.

While the form of Josephine Baker's political involvement was one of performance, its content of antiracism and multiculturalism consisted of complex and textured messages. Conceptually, Baker blends the French notions of fraternity and republicanism with American ideals of equality and redressive justice that came to fruition in the civil rights movement. Baker traces the rhetoric about race back to her childhood experiences in St. Louis. This discourse is reinforced and embellished by her wartime experiences of fighting Nazism and is further transformed by her desegregation crusade in the United States in 1951. It is not clear what role, if any, her visits to the Soviet Union and Eastern Europe played in her political education. The emergent civil rights movement in the United States reinforced her beliefs about social equality, but it did not transform her political strategies. As an independent spokesperson, she incorporated available resources (the NAACP and the civil rights movement) into her preexisting rhetorical model, while continuing to maintain the image of herself as a wartime militant in uniform. She also marshaled to her own ends the forum of the political conference as a platform—literally a stage—for purveying her ideas.

On Sunday, January 13, 1957, Baker convened the Conférence Anti-Raciste (Antiracist Conference) at the Château des Milandes. Appearing on stage in a somber black-beaded suit, Baker opened the conference with an audience of local officials from the Dordogne and visitors from Paris. Her entire family, including Carrie and eight of the Rainbow children, was seated at the head table. Photographs from the conference show few Africans in attendance, although one table appears to seat a North African contingent. The faces of the audience expressed everything from tolerance to disinterest and even somnolence (fig. 46).[38] Baker's opening speech was yet another version of her standard autobiographical narrative about racial discrimination during

Figure 46. Attendees at the Conférence Anti-Raciste, Les Milandes, 1957. Photo from the Collection Diaz, Departmental Archives of Dordogne, in Jean-Claude Bonnal, *Joséphine Baker et le village des enfants du monde en Périgord* (La Bugue, France: PLB Éditeur, 1992), 130, reproduced courtesy of the author.

her youth in the United States, concluding with a plea for cooperation and "understanding among people of diverse nationalities and colors."[39] Although the complete text of Baker's speech is not available, Bonnal summarizes it as relating "very sad personal anecdotes" about racism.[40] It was another rendition of the Marian motif about the hardships of her youth and the necessity to rise above the obstacles of racism. The speech was vigorously applauded. The conference did not include academic panels. Members of the *Présence Africaine* editorial board and the SAC committee, who had planned the elaborate Paris Congress just one year earlier, are significantly absent from the photographs.

During the 1940s and 1950s, new politically active African American expatriate communities emerged in France, but Baker remained relatively distant from them.[41] Paris of the late 1950s and early 1960s lost its luster as a mecca for many black American artists because they were able to pursue more lucrative opportunities at home. In any event, Baker's conference activities did not build a bridge across African, Antillian, and African American communities in France, although her image resonated in different ways with each community.

Baker appears to have aimed the Antiracist Conference toward the local French population. The people of Dordogne were as impressed by the conference as they had been by some of Baker's extravagant stage performances at La Chartreuse. Although Baker appropriated the idea of a cultural and political conference from SAC, her antiracism event was a one-woman show used to launch the multicultural ideology of Les Milandes. She later summarized her ideas when she developed plans for a College of Brotherhood (Collège Universitaire de Fraternité Universelle): "How is it possible for people of different continents to respect each other if education remains centered around differences between the races, things like skull configurations and skin color? Think of the effect this has on innocent young minds!"[42] Baker's multicultural vision was not simply one of mixing races as it had been in *Mon sang*. She promoted a complex project of cultural sharing based on a revolutionary, if somewhat sketchy and idealistic, model of resocialization and formal education, in which diverse traditions would be preserved, communicated, and learned across cultural groups. This was not merely the Sartrian society without races or the extension of an essentialist négritude but, instead, a rainbow culture of diversity beginning with the family and the school and reaching out to the entire world. Baker did not know exactly how rainbow multiculturalism would spread, but she was certain that, incrementally, it would create a more harmonious world. Although she employed a host of tutors at Les Milandes, there is no evidence that she drew on the help of trained scholars and educators to design her plans for multiculturalism or even on the assistance of her intellectual colleagues at Présence Africaine, with whom she shared the goals of cultural pride and human dignity. As her plans evolved, Baker believed that buildings and a physical plant were essential for her fraternal college, and these plans often overshadowed the pedagogical dimension of her program. Overall, the impact and appeal of Baker's Antiracist Conference appear to have been local and limited. She would be forced to move outside of the confines of Les Milandes to find a larger audience for promoting her ideas.

Baker attained another peak of her political performance when General Martin Valin awarded her the Légion d'Honneur and the Croix de Guerre with Palm at Les Milandes on August 18, 1961 (see fig. 39). While such awards would normally be conferred in Paris, Baker insisted that she receive hers at Les Milandes, where she functioned as a head of state over her small realm. General Valin arrived from Paris to conduct the ceremony. President de Gaulle was not present but sent a letter of congratulations, signed with his wife, that was read publicly when Josephine received the honor. Bonnal presents a fascinating photographic documentary of the ceremony based on images from the Dordogne archives.[43] The photographs cover onstage and backstage activities and show Baker in both the official ceremony and her role as a mother. Much of the backstage activity involved organizing the Rainbow children's participation in the event. The Rainbow boys were dressed in their best matching suits, and Marianne wore a frilly white dress with a bow in her hair (fig. 47).

Josephine hovered over the children as the ceremony was set to begin. In addition to Valin, one French air force colonel, a commander, two captains,

Figure 47. Rainbow children at Legion of Honor ceremony, August 18, 1961. Photo from Collection Diaz, Departmental Archives of Dordogne, in Jean-Claude Bonnal, *Joséphine Baker et le village des enfants du monde en Périgord* (La Bugue, France: PLB Éditeur, 1992), 174, reproduced courtesy of the author.

and a former government minister attended the event. Also present were the diplomatic consuls from the United States, Spain, Italy, and Finland, all of whom had traveled from their regional offices in Bordeaux to Les Milandes to witness the ceremony. The mayor of Castelnaud, an assistant from the mayor's office in St. Cyprien, the captain of the local gendarmerie in Castelnaud, and Josephine's close friend and confidant Abbé Tounebise, the curate of Castelnaud, filled out the audience. Baker had managed to bring together local, national, and international political figures to observe the conferral of one of the most important honors bestowed by the French state. She wanted the Rainbow children to partake of her history and that of France by witnessing and participating in this event. She was also adamant that the event be held at Les Milandes to reinforce the significance of her experiment conceived in the French spirit of freedom and brotherhood.

Even more than the Antiracism Conference of 1957, the 1961 ceremony epitomized Baker's combined martyr, militant, and domestic images in full force. It also firmly positioned Baker as a revered heroine and figurehead of the French state in the 1960s. At de Gaulle's behest, she would perform at several honorific occasions over the next decade, presenting inspirational lectures and songs, and would march with him down the Champs-Elysées in May 1968 to preserve what she conceived to be the order and stability of a free France.[44] No matter that at an earlier time she might have been on another side of the divide, supporting students and workers. So too would many of the other ex-militants who saw France changing as their grip on national identity and historical continuity slipped away.

The Légion d'Honneur celebration, which had been postponed by the French government for several years, came at a financially troubled time for Baker at Les Milandes. But in terms of Baker's narrative program of promoting Les Milandes and her utopian dream, the public ceremony was not only an honor, but also a timely opportunity to garner publicity and support for her Rainbow experiment. Using techniques that she had learned well under Pepito's mentorship during the 1930s, Baker took every opportunity to raise funds through concerts in France and abroad, publicity posters, magazine ads, and tourist attractions at Les Milandes. Not least among these projects was a trip to the United States proposed to her by an African American performer turned producer and impresario, Jack Jordan, in 1963. Jordan was aware that a coalition of civil rights groups was planning a march on

Washington as a strategy to encourage the passing of the Civil Rights Bill that was before Congress. The coalition groups (the NAACP, Congress of Racial Equality [CORE], Southern Christian Leadership Conference [SCLC], Student Nonviolent Coordinating Committee [SNCC], and the Urban League) had not invited Baker, and some civil rights leaders were skeptical about her after her 1951 solo desegregation crusade followed by a dubious association with Péron. If Adam Clayton Powell's earlier criticism were still a measure of the climate of the day, Baker might even be considered to have obstructed the cause. But Jordan was convinced that times had changed and that Baker would be one of the most prominent celebrity supporters of the march. Robert Kennedy, who admired Baker, arranged for all visa restrictions to be lifted.[45] The plan for Baker to return to the United States to perform politics for one of her largest captive audiences ever was now in full swing.

After much difficulty resulting from Baker's political reputation and her volatility with managers in the United States, Jordan hired a young African American manager, Henri Ghent, a classically trained vocalist who had performed in France and worked for Columbia Records, to book Baker's 1963 appearances. Ghent organized several press conferences for her in which she spoke in French using an interpreter. She was scheduled to give a series of concerts at Carnegie Hall starting in mid-October 1963. Meanwhile, she had summer's end free to follow her political pursuits. Through Jordan's influence and with the approval of Martin Luther King Jr., Baker was placed on the roster of speakers for the 1963 March on Washington, an event that she hoped would not only support the desegregation and civil rights causes, but would also promote her multicultural experiment at Les Milandes.

On August 28, 1963, a scorching day, over two hundred thousand people participated in the historic March on Washington. Then a high school student, I was among them.[46] The pavement of Pennsylvania Avenue leading toward the Lincoln Memorial was so hot that it burned through the marchers' shoes. Many marchers passed out from heat exhaustion. Organizing committees had met for weeks to work out the logistics for the march and to line up places to house the participants. The city was paralyzed. The marchers moved along the avenue almost ten abreast. Celebrities had been flown in, but it was difficult to see the politicians and leaders on the platform across the sea of marchers. I glimpsed Baker at a distance in her French air force uniform, unaware of the importance that her presence at this monumental event would hold for me in the future—a personal and symbolic significance parallel in many ways to the importance of the event itself. As a result of this event, I traveled to France for the first time one year later.

Martin Luther King Jr. gave his groundbreaking discourse on the dream of equality and human dignity at the end of the day. He was preceded by others, including Josephine Baker, whose very popular speech, according to her account, lasted twenty minutes.[47] Although I do not remember how long her speech was, I recall the resounding applause. Apparently, Baker had not prepared a formal discourse, but instead, spontaneously launched into her standard personal narrative. Her speech was not widely disseminated, and its complete text is difficult to locate. She stepped forward amid a resounding round of cheers and applause and told her familiar story:

> Friends and family . . . you know I have lived a long time and I have come a long way. And you must know now that what I did, I did originally for myself. Then later, as these things began happening to me, I wondered if they were happening to you, and then I knew they must be. And I knew that you had no way to defend yourselves, as I had. . . .
>
> And as I continued to do the things I did, and to say the things I said, they began to beat me. Not beat me, mind you, with a club—but you know, I have seen that done too—but they beat me with their pens, with their writings. And friends, that is much worse. . . .
>
> When I was a child and they burned me out of my home, I was frightened and I ran away. Eventually I ran far away. It was to a place called France. Many of you have been there, and many have not. But I must tell you, ladies and gentlemen, in that country I never feared. It was like a fairyland place. . . .
>
> And I need not tell you that wonderful things happened to me there. . . .
>
> You know, friends, that I do not lie to you when I tell you I have walked into the palaces of kings and queens and into the houses of presidents. And much more. But I could not walk into a hotel in America and get a cup of coffee, and that made me mad. And when I get mad, you know that I open my big mouth. And then look out, 'cause when Josephine opens her mouth, they hear it all over the world.
>
> So I did open my mouth, and you know I did scream, and when I demanded what I was supposed to have and what I was entitled to, they still would not give it to me. . . .
>
> Now, I am not going to stand in front of all of you today and take credit for what is happening now. I cannot do that. But I want to take credit for telling

you how to do the same thing, and when you scream, friends, I know you will be heard. And you will be heard now. . . .

I am not a young woman now, friends. My life is behind me. There is not too much fire burning inside me. And before it goes out, I want you to use what is left to light that fire in you. So that you can carry on, and so that you can do those things that I have done. Then, when my fires have burned out, and I go where we all go someday, I can be happy.

You know, I have always taken the rocky path. I never took the easy one, but as I grew older, and as I knew I had the power and the strength, I took that rocky path, and I tried to smooth it out a little. I wanted to make it easier for you. I want you to have a chance at what I had. But I do not want you to have to run away to get it. And mothers and fathers, if it is too late for you, think of your children. Make it safe here so they do not have to run away, for I want for you and your children what I had. . . .

I thank you, and may God bless you. And may He continue to bless you long after I am gone.[48]

Baker's 1963 March on Washington speech contains the habitual Cinderella story of her life framed in terms of racial injustice and miraculous success. France plays the role of the rescuer, the adjuvant, in the narrative. The heroine's role is to protest, to scream as loudly as possible until unjust conditions around the world change for posterity. This dream is not one of collective action, but one of individual agency against enormous obstacles. As a political actor, Baker used her example to inspire collective action in the form of coordinated individual acts of protest and resistance. Baker's speech recapitulated the terms of her own idiosyncratic battle against racism, which, while it was encouraging and uplifting, was also somewhat marginal to the discourse of the collective civil rights struggle emerging in the United States during the 1960s. In a letter to Martin Luther King Jr. after the March on Washington, Baker commended him and signed her correspondence "Your great admirer and sister in battle."[49] Her goals differed from his in their personalistic framing and their literal definition of multiculturalism in terms of interracial familial and communal life. Baker's quest, however, cannot be dismissed as limited to the domestic sphere and multicultural blending. Her strategies may be interpreted more productively as part of a complex utopian dream based on changing the world through example. The sources of the example were her own persona and her educational experiment. The virtuality and challenges of her vision did not prevent her from attempting to actualize her multicultural ideals in order to make her dreams become a social reality.

The College of Universal Brotherhood

The College of Universal Brotherhood (Collège Universitaire de Fraternité Universelle) began to take concrete form with the adoption of the first Rainbow children in 1956 and 1957. Baker's early experiences with the children made it clear that a more structured educational plan was necessary. Combining tutors with instruction in public and private schools did not work well enough with the Rainbow Tribe and would be an inadequate design for resocializing a larger community into a truly multicultural world. Therefore, Baker planned to develop an autonomous educational institution encompassing secondary school and university training.[50] To this end, she established the Josephine Baker Foundation, with its own Swiss bank account, to which she contributed her performance royalties and other funds deposited under the pseudonym of Mrs. Kaiser, which was ironically the name of one of the strictest employers in her St. Louis youth. Through the foundation, she hoped to acquire the resources to build the college on the grounds of Les Milandes, hire professors and an administrative staff, and provide subsidized tuition and room and board for the students. Haney quotes from an interview in which Baker described her plans for the college to a reporter: "We'll have a series of professors from different countries, of all colors and religions and all standards of life to teach the essentials of brotherhood. . . . The students must be able to have board and education without having to worry about the cost. . . . The future of the village will depend on the world's heartbeats."[51]

Baker's lofty designs for the curriculum and planning of her college were not different from many contemporary university curriculum plans in their early stages of development. She had a model in mind, and she planned to bring in some experts to execute it. She called on the Italian architect Bruno Fedrigolli, who had designed a college in Brescia, to draw up the blueprints for the buildings. He designed a series of ten pods resembling flowers with radiating petals linked by pathways to a central college square. Each pod contained dormitories, staff housing, classrooms, and administrative offices. There were also a central auditorium and assembly rooms. All of these structures would be located at some distance from the château and La Chartreuse so as not to interfere with the normal functioning of Les Milandes as an experimental farm and tourist attraction. One could even imagine that students eventually might have served as interns on the farm and at the tourist attractions had Les Milandes survived as Josephine wished. Her plans for multicultural education foreshadowed programs that would not come into existence in the United States until twenty years later and still do not exist in France. Baker's idea of preserving and sharing cultural traditions was far in advance of her times, especially in France, where the notion of multicultural education as a formal part of secondary school and university courses of study continues to meet with resistance.

Although Baker had started to draw up a charter for the college in 1965, the plans never came to fruition. Her fund-raising for the project was erratic, and maintaining Les Milandes, with its leaky roofs and expansive grounds, in operating condition was a difficult task. As her financial burdens increased, the dream of an international learning center began to recede, but her hopes for its realization never disappeared. She approached King Hassan of Morocco to help fund Les Milandes. He was willing to offer her land in Marrakech for a large residence to house the Rainbow Tribe and build a restaurant and nightclub.[52] But there was no room for the college. After a brief trip to Morocco, she concluded that the college would have to be located in France in order to serve as a model for democratic education. She continued to try to build up the Josephine Baker Foundation, traveling across Europe and to California and Mexico to raise funds. The college was mentioned in every plea to save Les Milandes. Even after the sale of Les Milandes, Baker persisted with the dream of the college. She began negotiations with Marshal Tito of Yugoslavia, who favored her plan. Tito proposed to give her the Adriatic island of Brioni on which to build the college, and the proposal was unanimously approved by the government and the local town council of Sibenik. Part of the island, which contained a medieval fortress and an abandoned prison previously used for hardened criminals, would be converted into the school. But the island—rocky, desolate, and forlorn—was a disappointment, and the project proved to be too great a challenge for Baker.[53] The plans never materialized.

Baker's multiculturalism was based on her adopted family and her educational ideals. From 1951 forward, these ideals fueled her social and political activism and motivated her performances, which had been transformed from hedonistic spectacles into fund-raising extravaganzas. By the 1960s, most of her performances were retrospectives of her life peppered with pleas to aid

Les Milandes and her children. After her move to Roquebrune on the Riviera under the sponsorship of Princess Grace, Monaco's Red Cross, and other charities, her activism was foregrounded, and she became a professional fund-raiser and philanthropist. Even at her new Villa Maryvonne, Baker kept her dream of multicultural education alive and, had it not been for the constraints imposed by her sponsors, she would have renewed her plans for the college once again before her death.

Had she survived her 1975 comeback at the Théâtre Bobino, her educational dream may eventually have come true. Tyler Stovall argues that Baker's death signaled the end of utopian dreams about a color-blind France among many black American expatriates.[54] However, Baker left an important and powerful legacy that combined French ideals of *fraternité* with a quest for equality linked to the American civil rights struggle. With the rise of debates over multicultural politics during the 1980s, Baker's political image and ideals assumed new relevance for another generation. In France, during the 1980s and 1990s, debates over multiculturalism emerged in the context of issues of citizenship and the rights of individuals of different national, cultural, and ethnic backgrounds to express, and even impose, their identities in public spaces.[55] These debates were aired not only in the media and public forums, but also in films, music, and art. A host of new biographies, films, and commentaries about Baker's life began to appear on the international scene at this time.[56] Her brand of multiculturalism, coupled with image-based political performance, was suited to the new era. Yet, uneasy questions lingered about exactly what went wrong. Just as Baker had criticized the unhappy endings of her early films, the new biographers and filmmakers searched for ways to rewrite the script of Baker's multiculturalism and her political performances to be in tune with the times.

Performing Politics

Performance and politics may be analyzed productively from the vantage point of three major axes: (1) images of the performer in idealized narratives and everyday life; (2) activities of public performers in the political arena; and (3) audience responses to both images and political action. Each approach implies a distinctive method. In the first case, an interpretive sociological, or sociosemiotic, approach may be used to identify narratives and performance styles and strategies. In the second instance, an analysis of the techniques used by performers to mobilize opinions and resources highlights the collective dimensions and impact of political performances. In the third case, audience responses to the content and credibility of the performer's ideals and actions are critical. Through her self-writing, Baker developed images to be used in her stage performances and then transferred them to the political arena, where she acted as a charismatic political leader promoting her causes to an ever-widening audience. The responses to her performances ranged from enthusiastic support to skepticism, surveillance, and severe criticism. Baker's reactions to criticism involved shifting performative claims, characters, and venues in order to support her causes. Although these shifts appeared to produce political and ideological inconsistencies, they were also strategic moves intended to broaden her audience appeal. The model of stage performance, with Baker at the center, is crucial to understanding all of the strategies of performance that she employed.

Erving Goffman's dramaturgical analysis of performance in theater and in everyday life sheds light on Baker's strategies. Goffman states that although the term "role" may be used to describe onstage and offstage performances, observers "apparently find no difficulty in understanding whether a real role is in question or the mere stage presentation of one."[57] Baker, however, manipulated the cultural space between "real roles" and stage presentations by moving from one stage (the artistic) to another (the political), and then into the arena of domestic and everyday life, while retaining a fabricated stage persona. Goffman emphasizes that a stage persona derives from a "part" or a "character" that is grounded in biography and narrative. He explains, "Interestingly, in everyday affairs, one is not always aware of a particular individual's part in life, . . . awareness often focusing more on the role he plays in some particular connection—political, domestic, or whatever."[58] The public performer's biography is available to the audience, however, in terms of constructed images, the history of previous parts played, and a personal biography created for public consumption. When Baker stated that she was placing her political activism first and her art second during the 1950s desegregation crusade, she invoked her theatrical character as a resource for her political activities. Baker used stage performances, ads, conferences, and television campaigns to communicate her political ideas. In other words, she performed politics. The public success of these types of performances relies on the willingness of the audience to accept and act on them. Too many infelicities, or contradictions, in the performances frustrate spectators who merely want to be entertained by familiar, unthreatening, or stereotypical acts and who question the sincerity of the performer.[59]

A narrative performance is based on a story in which all participants share some knowledge of the expected outcome. In everyday life, this knowledge is not always available, even to the performer. Baker dealt with this problem by reiterating her life story and inscribing herself in the narrative with every political speech. Thus, whether she was at the Antiracism Conference in Dordogne or the March on Washington, she framed her public narratives with her childhood experiences of racism in St. Louis and her rise to fame in France. From this standpoint, she developed a discourse for political action. Since her narrative program was idiosyncratic, she often found it difficult to obtain public support for her recommendations and courses of action beyond a single performance, and she elicited criticism from some quarters.

During the 1950s and 1960s, colonial struggles in Africa took place both on the battlefield and through conferences, festivals, and cultural manifestations in which celebrities played an increasingly important role. In turn, the United States sent African American performers and politicians around the world as cultural ambassadors to support cold-war political agendas. The March on Washington involved a large contingent of musicians, actors, and performers who lent their names and support to the civil rights cause. This pattern was to continue with an overlapping cast of characters, such as Harry Belafonte and Sidney Poitier, who contributed their efforts to the promotion of causes and oppositional discourses, such as the antiapartheid struggle in South Africa, by forming Artists and Athletes Against Apartheid in 1983.[60] Although Baker participated in conferences and festivals during the 1960s and early 1970s and used the media to promote her causes, she did so with her own agenda and remained an isolated political actor. Baker's unique style of performing politics was based on her idealistic and unfulfilled vision of a multicultural society in a racially harmonious world.

8 Echoes and Influences

We set to work in high spirits, but as the days passed, I felt a
subtle change, a creeping doubt, fear, hesitation. Was Josephine
still Josephine? . . . A performer is like a country cousin: when
he bids us good-bye, we feel overcome with love and memories
and shed a sentimental tear. But should he return we say, "So
soon?"

—Baker and Bouillon, 1977

Echoes of Josephine Baker's life and images reverberate across
the successive generations that come into contact with her.
Although each image originates within a specific narrative frame and worldview, Baker's multifaceted persona transcends historical epochs. Her appeal
derives from her self-representation and self-writing as a "culturalized, symbolic sign."[1] Baker's legacy may be seen not only in terms of her direct influence on artists, performers, and audiences, but also with respect to the
structures of communication that she engendered.[2] These structures involve
combinations of visual images and discourses that create new frameworks
of representation in literature, film, video, and the art world. In this context,
the term "images" refers to visual and verbal symbols, and the concept of
"representation" encompasses a collection of images. Through its strategies

of juxtaposition and appropriation, postmodernism returns us to Baker's primal image. While Baker separated the primal and the Marian images during her lifetime, postmodernism relies on their kaleidoscopic combination and juxtaposition.

From Madonna and Grace Jones to Michael Jackson and his sister La Toya, many contemporary performers have drawn on Baker's primal image and her identity-doubling persona. These performers use Baker and her legacy as an inspiration and are not merely her clones. To varying degrees, they are concerned with both image construction and changing the world. When Baker gave three taxi-loads of her designer gowns to the female impersonator Lynne Carter in 1970, she repositioned her own image in a new cultural frame.[3] Baker's gift helped to launch Carter's career at the Jewel Box Revue. In addition to promoting Josephine's camp and retro images, Carter also impersonated Marilyn Monroe, Bette Davis, Marlene Dietrich, and Pearl Bailey, taking his show as far as Carnegie Hall. The Parisian transsexual cabaret performer Michou also used Baker's image. Films, posters, postcards, and book covers inaugurated further representations that incorporated Baker's primal and her glamour images as a "referential illusion."[4] Baker was fascinated by her own reflection and by performers who were her copies and clones. Each of Baker's images spawned a new one, resulting in an echo effect within shifting narrative frames. In the simulation of Baker's images—whether primal, glamour, or Marian—the signifier is reproduced in a cycle of expression, display, commodification, and exchange. Nevertheless, the core primal image constitutes the backdrop and foundation for each new simulacrum.

Primal imagery was based on a racialized colonial fantasy that mitigated the guilt of European domination through ecstasy. Although elements of the primal image sprang from eighteenth- and nineteenth-century Orientalism and can even be traced to antiquity, Baker's manipulation of the image was new. Her danse sauvage addressed a Jazz Age public hungry for the spirit of liberation that reflected the ethos of the avant-garde. This image was inscribed in her 1927 and 1931 biographies with Marcel Sauvage, in numerous art works, and in repeated performances on stage and in films. During the 1930s, her Marian image emerged first in a novel and then in her wartime activities. Each image was folded into nested narratives with variations and multiple points of reference for new historical periods. The switching of actantial roles between the dominator and the dominated in colonial discourse discussed in the context of Bhabha's doubling theory is also relevant to the role changes performed by Baker's followers. Just as Baker reworked her own narratives, those who followed, admired, or wrote about her incorporated her image into narratives that suited their times and purposes.

Baker as an Image-Ideal

The essentialist négritude of Baker's primal image challenges rationality with passion and pleasure. It is based not only on the Senghorian blending of rhythm and sensibility but also on pure sensuality.[5] Baker's primal image is contextually framed. Edmund Husserl describes how the meaning of a cultural object shifts through framing and memory work.[6] A painting, for example, is an artistic representation, a memory, and a commercial commodity. This process of meaning modification applies to Baker's image as it changed over time. The image creator and the audience both endow the object with its significance. As the meaning of the image shifts from artistic fantasy to commercial commodity, the cultural framing of the image also changes. Baker's primal image is particularly suited to the meaning modifications of postmodern representation and resurfaces in the flashing frames of music videos and animated hypertext.[7] Her image is a floating signifier for erotic abandon. The characters that Baker portrayed on stage derived their power from the historical salience of her scripts and from her ability to perform them for enthusiastic audiences.

Early in her career, Baker combined advertising with stage performances, cinema, and self-writing as an image-construction technique. Music-hall tableaux consisted of quick and turbulent sketches intended to arouse emotions. These sketches were the forerunners of cinematic and video montages in which a rapid juxtaposition of shots conveys a condensed and aesthetically powerful message. Baudrillard argues that cinema was one of the first media forms to collapse historical events into a series of imbricated images that could be manipulated by ellipsis, flashback, and omniscient narration to create fluid new stories with a strong reality effect.[8] The novel, the wax museum, the panorama, and early twentieth-century advertising performed similar image-creating functions. In discussing the evolution of postmodern representation, Kaplan traces its roots to "advertising and the department-store window."[9] At issue is the development of new strategies of display that commodify objects by converting them into images and symbols. Using the media available to her at each stage of her career, Baker cleverly crafted her images, exploiting a split between the signified and the signifier, the everyday actor and the performer.

Postmodern Paradigms

Whether we contend that postmodernity is primarily a cultural extension of social and economic processes of mass production arising in late nineteenth-century modern society, or if we view it as a phenomenon in its own right, rapid economic, technological, and social structural changes have resulted in the transformation of cultural images and their modes of dissemination. Fragmentary postmodern images are held together by archetypal narratives that are reframed for new audiences, purposes, and media. Throughout my discussion of Baker, I have emphasized the ways in which her image construction was tied to external social and cultural structures of the modern era. Her approach was what Baudrillard has referred to as an "objective strategy," that is, the conversion of herself into an object of performance and consumption.[10] Her legacy, as well as the images and master tropes that linger, have been reworked and transformed by postmodern forces of cultural reproduction. In his essay on the postcolonial and the postmodern, Kwame Appiah sheds light on the resistance of the content of Baker's primal image to change.[11] Baker's primal image becomes postcolonial not in its content but by virtue of being reappropriated by the postmodern media. Although the styles of representing the image change with postmodern media, the primal fantasies evoked by the image have underlying sexual and racial associations that do not disappear.

Baudrillard argues that the postmodern image has three characteristics: (1) its staging; (2) the relationship of its staging to a challenge to ("destructuration of") the social order; and (3) the collapsing of both the medium and the message in the image.[12] Elaborating on Marshall McLuhan's famous dictum that "the medium is the message," Baudrillard asserts that both medium and message are attenuated as meaning is "imploded," or collapses, in the dispersion of its multivocality.[13] The implosion of meaning is a compelling notion that actually masks several processes of communication involved in media such as television, video, and the Internet. The first process consists of the manipulation of real and mediated time, which was already at work in the cinema. The second is the distortion of the image through its cutting, pasting, and manipulation, which is intensified by digital media and hypertext. The third process is the opening up of new mass audiences whose access to the medium is not solely determined by education, social class, or ticket sales. The postmodern media image is ever present in advertising, sound bytes, and popular discourse. It is like a lingering disease, a flu caught by everyone regardless of the precautions they take. The postmodern media do not implode meaning in the social order, but they do reconfigure it. They transmogrify the historical terrain into a web of referential signs. At the center of this web are stereotypical images that seem to elude erasure—for example, the primal Baker and the bawdy body.

During the 1980s, a rereading of black cultural politics influenced film, literature, the art museum, and conceptions of identity. The notion that racial and cultural identities are constructed, and therefore could be reconfigured, provided a new screen onto which Baker's images could be projected. Fredric Jameson describes this new arena of projection as postmodern pastiche, in which the past is recreated without irony as an allegorical collage of mnemonic fragments and nostalgia.[14] Jameson laments the hiatus between the fragmentary montage of virtual postmodern images and the conventional linearity of documentary history. Nevertheless, the postmodern pastiche represents a genre unto itself, a form that is not devoid of narrativity but instead creates its own synthetic, collisional narratives by combining old and new texts into a metatext of mimetic montage, exemplified by music videos, Web sites, and Internet digital clips.[15] Old master tropes still inform the postmodern pastiche, which relies on the past, as well as on fantasy, for its execution.

The Dionysian myth of the idyllic return to nature and guilt-free self-indulgence serves effectively as a means of assembling the fragments of Baker's postmodern pastiche into a coherent narrative.[16] Baker's erotic Black Venus image had roots not only in European Orientalism but also in the racialized performances of American minstrelsy. In both cases, a dialectic of desire exists between the dominant culture that appropriates the savage imagery of its subjects and the stereotyped, or dominated, culture onto which the image is projected. The dominant figures and the dominated subjects collude to create a new discourse by exchanging actantial and moral positions through the performance and reproduction of the myth.[17] Although Baker added parody to her primal image by donning Cocteau's concocted banana skirt, the image of primitive eroticism remained at the core of her performance as the savage Fatou and offered a unifying ideological and visual foundation perfect for the postmodern media.

The anthropometric vision inspiring the primal image lingers as a definition of racial difference.[18] In the postmodern context, strategies for "universalizing difference" through excerpting, fragmenting, colorizing, and manipulating images still maintain the foundational phenotype and its racialized message.[19] The major difference between old and new deployments of racialized erotic images lies not in their content but in audience responses to them and in the persistence of the stereotypes. Nineteenth- and early twentieth-century versions of the primal image incarnate a dominant social reality. Postmodern versions of the primal image resurrect a historical reality in a fragmentary pastiche. In his discussion of primal imagery in modern art, Hal Foster further argues that the "inscription of the primitive onto woman as other threatens male subjectivity."[20] One way to escape this threat, along with its racial challenge, is through taming the imagery in art and performance.

In his review of the Museum of Modern Art's 1984 exhibit Primitivism in Twentieth-Century Art: Affinity of the Tribal and the Modern, James Clifford addresses what he conceives to be the flawed premise of the show by criticizing its historical character.[21] He argues that the definition of the black body that links African art to modernism should be seen in terms of historical responses to images of primitivism in Paris of the 1910s and 1920s. More than historicism is involved. Clifford juxtaposes an image of Baker in the pointed banana skirt of La Folie du jour (1926–27) to a Chokwe carving and to Fernand Léger's cubist rendering of an African costume design for Stravinsky's 1923 ballet La Création du monde. Josephine Baker's figure totalizes primal atavism. Interestingly, in spite of his plea for historical precision, Clifford neither dates nor contextualizes Baker's photographic image, but instead uses it evocatively in juxtaposition to the African carving and the cubist piece. He implicitly argues that Baker's iconography is the unstated subject of the sentence for which the Chokwe rendition and the Léger sketch are the predicates, and he states that displaying her body among the images in the exhibit "would suggest a different account of modernist primitivism, a different analysis of the category nègre in l'art nègre, and an exploration of the 'taste' that was something more than just a backdrop for the discovery of tribal art in the opening decades of this century."[22]

On the surface, Clifford's argument calls for a more explicit exploration of the cultural roots and aesthetic goals of modernism. His "sampling" of Baker's powerful primal image, however, is itself a postmodern pastiche. The reader's eye moves directly to Baker's image at the upper left-hand side of the page, as she dominates, and nearly effaces, the presence of the Chokwe carving and the Léger costume.[23] The images do not appear in historical sequence but are, instead, positioned in terms of their visual impact. Baker's image is only superficially similar to the others, and the parody, in Jameson's sense, that Baker associated with her spiked banana skirt is overlooked. By intertextually referencing Baker, Clifford has created a space for her in the postmodern reinterpretation of *l'art nègre* as a cultural construction.

The Black Female Body, a photographic history of black women's images by Deborah Willis and Carla Williams, uses one of Baker's images from the Folies-Bergère in 1925 and a pose from Madame d'Ora's 1928 photographic shoot in Germany to illustrate the bawdy black body.[24] Although their argument and photographic selection emphasize black female sensuality within a primitivist motif, the authors also discuss black women performers as public personalities and the limited expressive roles available to them. Included in Willis and Williams's selection of photographs is a reproduction of Paul Poiret's carousel figures of black women. The authors explain, "At the same time that Baker became the toast of café society wearing a Poiret design, Poiret's carousel figures offered a black woman's back to sit on. In both instances, the black female body was reduced to its exaggerated parts."[25]

Willis and Williams state that they wish to demonstrate how racist stereotypes degraded the black female body and how, at the same time, black women have appropriated those stereotypes for their personal, social, and economic advantage. They, too, have created a postmodern pastiche of image bytes. Willis and Williams close their photographic essay with the rhetorical question, "How does one map a self-image out of this history?"[26] They conclude that this mapping should be completed by a collective of concerned women scholars who would interpret the social meanings of the images that they have assembled and similar documents for posterity. But the real issue goes beyond the interpretation of the provocative, and occasionally unsettling, images that Willis and Williams have collected. It extends to an analysis of the processes of cultural reproduction that ground and motivate the dissemination of these images regardless of whether the subjects photographed are complicit in their production.

One of the most important sociological questions arising around Baker's career concerns the socially controlled complicity of the performer in reproducing primal imagery. Baker both benefited and suffered from this complicity. The longevity and tenacity of primal images and their reproduction via postmodern media point to the cultural processes that sustain them.[27] Postmodern images of primitivism are not merely random signifiers but are, instead, symbols inserted with specific intent into the cultural production of new narratives of domination and panoptic control. In this respect, négritude, in particular Baker's version of it, cannot, in Trinh Minh-ha's terms, "be belittled" because it forces the confrontation of hegemonic value systems through the very presentation of primal imagery.[28] Another site for this confrontation is located in global popular culture.

Cosmopolitan Homegirls and Global Popular Culture

The cultural critic Manthia Diawara's discussion of the homeboy cosmopolitan depicts globalizing youth culture as an image-based and male-inflected phenomenon.[29] Homeboys roam the street, compose rap lyrics, create hip-hop culture and consume its products, and threaten the establishment with their brazen attitudes. Diawara convincingly demonstrates the global linkages of homeboy images and cultures, tracing them to Hollywood stereotypes of young black males during the 1970s, rhythm-and-blues lyrics and recordings, and popular literature. The reworking of these images abroad, particularly in Africa and the African diaspora, emphasizes the ways in which American cultural products of late twentieth-century capitalism have been deployed to represent and resolve generational conflicts across cultures. The homeboy cosmopolitan is equally at home and equally marginal on the streets of Lagos, London, Paris, Rio, New York, Washington, and Los Angeles. Although the cultural processes that Diawara discusses are market driven and gender neutral—such as the packaging and consumption of hip-hop music, hood movies, fashion, and paraphernalia—the products that he describes are created and used primarily by young men. Certainly at its inception, music video, like hip-hop, was also a predominantly male terrain, but market studies show that women were its main consumers.[30]

By adding the modifier "cosmopolitan" to "homeboy," Diawara refers not only to the consumption and globalization of the homeboy image in popular culture, but also to the trappings of sophistication assumed by homeboys from blaxploitation films of the 1970s to hip-hop music and culture of the 1990s.[31] The homeboy cosmopolitan is, thus, a composite concept, an image linking the streetwise rude boy and the worldly homegrown philosopher. The homegirls to whom Diawara refers are diegetic responses to the homeboy, whose discourses they reaffirm and critique within the circumscribed limits of a male-dominated narrative.[32]

When one explores the shadows and echoes of Josephine Baker's image, however, it is critical to make not only a shift in the gender coding of the analysis, but also a perspectival shift that sheds another light on the production and globalization of popular culture. The homegirl cosmopolitan is not a simple binary opposite of the homeboy. Instead, the contradictory metaterms of local versus global and male versus female complicate the semiotic paradigm in which the "homegirl" complements the "homeboy." Diawara's homegirls are endowed with agency through male-oriented perspectives (those of filmmakers, song writers, and homeboy fashion cartels). The diegetic homegirl makes the homeboy's discourse possible by providing an audience and an arena for his symbolic displays. Although the homegirl with agency is constructed in and through male narratives, distantiation from and manipulation of these narratives foregrounds another type of symbolic statement. In contrast, Baker's version of the homegirl cosmopolitan dominates the scene and is able to change social positions within popular discourse. Her identity transformations provide for a powerful recoding of male-centered images and narratives.

Brian Gibson's 1991 HBO special, *The Josephine Baker Story*, opens with the introduction, "Before Madonna, before Marilyn, there was Josephine, who dreamed of a fairy-tale life and found it." Popular icons in film, music, and literature have appropriated different aspects of Baker's "homegirl cosmopolitan" image, doing so both by consciously using her as a role model and through indirect influences. They do not simply reproduce Baker's images; they recreate and transform her for a new generation. Among others, four key figures clearly emerge as homegirl cosmopolitan icons in the Baker tradition—Grace Jones, Madonna, La Toya Jackson, and Calixthe Beyala. Whether or not they refer to Baker's influence directly, these four figures deploy narratives and performative strategies that she popularized, including the Cinderella narrative and the primal, femme fatale, and androgynous images. All four, but most notably Jones and Madonna, engage in repeated and frequent identity shifts.[33]

Each of these women comes from a working-class background and has made a spectacular rise to international stardom and fame amid considerable controversy. In different ways, all four figures have used Paris as a staging ground for building some aspect of their careers. Their images use sensuality and sexuality as a source of appeal while challenging what Kaplan terms the "patriarchal feminine," or traditional male-centered roles for women, by introducing androgyny and the image of the tough woman and single survivor into some features of their role representations.[34] Often the roles and images that they assume clash or contain multiple, opposing semiotic dimensions condensed within a single representation. This condensation is achieved by the surface presentation of a simulated role (i.e., Madonna's "virgin" or Jones's "vampire"), underneath which a contradictory role and set of messages appears through a process of continual unveiling that may be imitated and reproduced by others.[35] The allure of power and control, combining public success with materiality, is also critical to the appeal of these divas. Jackson and Beyala admit to patterning some of their strategies on Baker's images, while Jones and Madonna sample Baker in undeniable and obvious ways that have attracted the attention of cultural critics.[36]

Jones in Vogue

Carolyn Anderson's groundbreaking work on Grace Jones and Josephine Baker provides one point of reference for this discussion.[37] While Anderson foregrounds Jones in her analysis and considers Baker's influence on her to be indirect, I argue that Baker furnishes a direct model of communication and performance for Jones's postmodern primal image. Much of Jones's early life remains a public mystery. Jean-Paul Goude's *Jungle Fever* contains an imagined depiction of Jones at age seven in her birthplace in Spanish Town, Jamaica.[38] Born Grace Mendoza, an immigrant from Jamaica, Grace Jones grew up in Syracuse, New York, where she attended high school and, preparing for a major in theater, spent one year at the University of Syracuse during the 1970s.[39] Already a flamboyant figure and nonconformist as a young student, Jones consolidated her early image through her work in the fashion and music industries.[40] She combined fashion modeling with disco performances that used voguing and outrageous posing. Voguing was a choreographed dance form developed in gay discothèques and performance venues during the late 1970s and early 1980s. Cindy Patton describes voguing as the "choreography of the conjunction between body and space" involving "moves that simulate applying make-up and opening the jacket."[41] Men borrowed voguing styles of erotic posing, hyperfeminine seduction, and flamboyant displays from fashion modeling, striptease, and softcore pornography. Parallels may be drawn between voguing and its tamer successor, *sape,* or the public posing of young African men wearing European high fashions in Paris, Brussels, and on the streets of African cities such as Brazzaville and Kinshasa.[42] With her androgynous appearance as both a female dominatrix and a seductive male, Jones became a master manipulator of the voguing and *sapeur*-like styles. Voguing is both voiceless and appearance-driven. It relies on the illusion of gender-crossing to create its exaggerated and seductive appeal.

In addition to being a woman, Jones possessed another attribute that many amateur voguers did not. She was black and prepared to flaunt her blackness in a performance medium where both race and gender were blurred. When she arrived in France in the late 1970s, Jones placed herself under the control of the impresario, photographer, and designer Jean-Paul Goude with whom she lived and had one child. While Jones may have been unaware of Baker's legacy, Goude was more than ready to exploit a popular icon whose primal imagery had a long history in France. Goude first encountered Jones at the Paris discothèque Les Mouches, where he was impressed by her allure as "a demi-goddess, black, shiny, her face more than just pretty."[43] Viewing Jones as the intersection of the primitive and the postmodern, he created a romanticized version of Jones's blackness, which he said "is free of all social connotations because I am a European."[44] Goude drew on Baker's primal image to reconstruct a new persona for Jones as the soul of blackness and an idealized work of African art. He explained, "Grace's face is geometric in design, like an African sculpture. Her cheekbones are triangles, her mouth is an oval, her eyes are little slits. So it seemed a natural thing to move toward a design for her that was geometric—for the stage and her costumes, too."[45] This image had its roots in the savage Fatou, the Black Venus, and the archetypal negress. Sharpley-Whiting aptly captures the essence of this primal image in her analysis of Gaspard de Pons's 1825 novel *Ourika, l'Africaine*.[46] Sharpley-Whiting writes, "The lure of the négresse, then, was her adeptness at sexual arts. She epitomized Black Venus. Her lure was loathed also, for she represented danger, a sexual passion capable of satiation and consumption, the literal siphoning off of life through the draining of precious seminal liquor."[47]

Goude directed Jones in a series of tableaux, resembling in format Baker's music-hall performances. The tableaux were released in a video entitled *A One-Man Show*, in which Jones posed with a troupe of dancers who performed wearing masks of her face and moving to the tunes of 1930s French jazz, complete with trombone and accordion. In *A One-Man Show*, Jones wore a tailored black suit open to the waist with no shirt (fig. 48). The square shoulders of the suit, coupled with the masked Jones clones, created a sculptured appearance of androgyny and uniformity. Jones's glistening body, Amazonian stature, and sculpted face fit the image of the primal sophisticate that Goude wanted to project. He wrote at length about the magnetic appeal of this exotic image in *Jungle Fever,* a 142-page photo essay in which he discussed his black and Puerto Rican models, lovers, and creative inspirations.[48] The primal image continues in Jones's 1987 video *Slave to Rhythm,* produced by Goude, and in her appearances as Zula, the primitivistic sidekick of Arnold Schwarzenegger, in the *Conan the Destroyer* (1984), and May Day in the James Bond thriller *A View to a Kill* (1985). Her totalizing image is also featured in *Vamp,* a 1986 movie in which she poses and vogues in avant-garde fashions as a vampire stripper, recapitulating primal versions of the female destroyer. All of these roles rely on the racialized image of a devouring, androgynous

Figure 48. Grace Jones wearing a tailored black suit similar to her costume for *A One-Man Show.* Photo by Andy Warhol, 1984, © 2006 Andy Warhol Foundation for the Visual Arts / Artists Rights Society (ARS), New York / ADAGP, Paris.

female who intimidates and overpowers her audience (which is diegetically male) and who remains essentially voiceless. Similar to Baker in her 1927 tigress pose, Jones resembles a primitive animal, a flashback to her early 1978 Halloween appearance at the Roseland Club in New York as a naked, caged tigress, snarling as she eats a raw piece of meat behind a sign reading, "Do not feed the animal."[49] Jones carries primal imagery to an extreme as a simulation of libidinal artifice and animal passion in a carefully constructed narrative of neoprimitivism. While Baker's primal dance parodies primitivism, Jones and Goude transform primitivism into a postmodern pastiche of vogue and mode.

In her thesis on Baker, Jessica Peterson makes a similar argument about the Somali fashion model Iman.[50] Peter Beard, an impresario and photographer, brought Iman to international attention with his exotic images of her accompanied by a narrative that resembles the script of *Princesse Tam-Tam*. Iman is portrayed as a shepherdess, an exotic jungle queen, and a raw primal figure. At the time of her discovery in Kenya and her promotion as a media figure, however, Iman was a university student from a comfortable bourgeois background in Nairobi, and her real life contrasted sharply with her primal image as a black Amazon. Although the cultural encoding of this primal image predated Baker, Josephine was among the first and the most prominent figures to manipulate modern media for its dissemination. The primal image remains an active source of nested narratives reworked for new pop icons and postmodern divas.

Madonna's Prayer

Exaggerated artifice characterizes Madonna's performances and reinforces her affinities with Baker's primal and glamour images. This discussion does not address the full range of fascinating press coverage and scholarship on Madonna's popularity and influence, but instead focuses on her affinities with Baker.[51] By performing the roles of other women, Madonna creates an ambiguous and mutable space for gender construction. Although Madonna does not explicitly sample Baker with intertextual visual references, as she does Marilyn Monroe, Greta Garbo, and Marlene Dietrich, there are significant parallels to Baker in her manipulation of images and the roles that she plays. Both Baker and Madonna occupy controversial positions with respect to official religion. During her 1928–29 world tour, Baker's erotic primal image presented a direct challenge to the Catholic Church by triggering Father

Frey's protest in Vienna and religious censure in South America. Issuing from a working-class Catholic family, Madonna frames much of her erotic imagery as a symbolic protest against patriarchal authority and religious conventions. She drew the critical attention of the Catholic Church early in her career with the release of her 1984 album *Like a Virgin*. The video for the album's title track combined images based on virginal purity and seductive sexuality. The church's complaints continued with the 1986 release of "Papa Don't Preach," a track about teen pregnancy with a pro-life message. Pope John Paul II called for a boycott of Madonna's 1990 Blond Ambition World Tour due to its amalgamation of sex and religion through simulated masturbation and supplication in search of spiritual redemption.[52]

Described as a chameleon, a trend-setter, and a pop legend, Madonna uses her performances and total persona to make a statement. She made several recordings produced by Otto Von Wernherr in Paris as early as 1979, and these compilations introduced her to the trendy Euro-pop scene. In her 1989 music video release *Like a Prayer*, she appropriates the religious and racial motifs associated with Baker's Cinderella and Marian narratives. In *Like a Prayer*, Madonna uses the force of her passionate and eroticized prayers to attempt to rescue a black man falsely accused of raping and murdering a white woman. Entering a church, Madonna reclines on a pew and falls into a dream state. In her dream, the statue of a black saint comes to life with the face of the murderer. The statue hovers over Madonna and kisses her. An erotic sequence containing some intentionally ambiguous shots follows.[53] Madonna crusades to free the murderer as images of the Ku Klux Klan's burning crosses flash in the background.

One is reminded of Baker's description of the 1917 race riots in St. Louis. The mise-en-scène is similar, but the resolution is different as Madonna, rather than fleeing the scene, is single-handedly able to bring about a victorious resolution. She closes the video celebrating interracial harmony with a gospel choir. Musically, Madonna appropriates rhythm-and-blues and call-response formats in the tape. She becomes a musical heroine and a crossover artist, using the video to celebrate the benefits of cultural sharing. In a discussion of Madonna's early image, bell hooks compares her to the image of the Black Madonna that she witnessed in France, in terms of her evocation of a "sense of promise and possibility, a vision of freedom."[54] In the Live 8 concert on July 3, 2005, organized by Bob Geldof in London and nine other cities around the world to support African debt relief, Madonna, dressed in white, performed a medley of her spiritual tunes, including "Like a Prayer," "Ray of Light," and "Music" with the London Community Gospel Choir for a crowd of two hundred thousand people in Hyde Park. Madonna's racialized erotic scenarios echo Baker's image, and the narratives recapitulate Baker's Marian rescue motif. The elements of Baker's legacy have become so pervasive in popular culture and the parallels are so clear that it does not matter whether Madonna publicly acknowledges them or not.[55]

As with Grace Jones, Madonna includes posing, or voguing, as a key element of her performative image construction in her 1990 music video release entitled *Vogue*. She has sampled legendary hyperfeminine Hollywood screen idols such as Jean Harlow and Marilyn Monroe, as well as more controversial and mysterious figures such as Garbo and Dietrich, whose roots in the European music hall and avant-garde art resembled Baker's origins.[56] Baker claimed that Dietrich, the Blonde Venus, had copied some of her routines. In discussing Madonna's cultural politics, Kaplan argues that much of the inspiration for Madonna's work derives from the surrealists and expressionists.[57] In her 1985 video *Material Girl*, Madonna samples Marilyn Monroe's musical sequence "Diamonds Are a Girl's Best Friend" from the film *Gentlemen Prefer Blondes*. With blonde hair and dressed as a Marilyn clone, Madonna recreates the image of materiality, glitz, and glamour for a new era, with the subtextual message that women who use these seductive techniques to their advantage are really in control. Monroe's seductive persona bears close affinities to Baker's glamour image, which emerged in the 1930s with *Zouzou* and reappeared in a more pronounced way with her designer fashions of the 1950s.[58] Although Madonna's twist on the glamour girl was a parody, so too were Josephine's 1950s and 1960s music-hall performances in which she performed "herself" in elaborate gowns, in a seemingly endless series of retrospectives.

A final parallel in Madonna's and Josephine's glamour personas concerns their mutual fascination with Eva Perón, the archetypal glamorous figure living out a Cinderella narrative. Madonna fought hard to obtain the film role of Eva Perón and considered her lead in the 1996 musical *Evita* one of the peaks of her performance career. A final similarity concerns their publications and self-writing. In 2003 and 2004 Madonna wrote a set of books aimed at children between the ages of four and eight. The first book, *The English Roses*, sets the tone for a series of narratives and morality tales drawn from diverse cultures. This project parallels Baker's children's book *La Tribu arc-en-*

ciel and broadens Madonna's audience appeal.[59] Although Madonna's image is more technologically driven and synthetic than Josephine's, parallels in their object-oriented performance strategies and shifting narratives result in a similar style and phenomenon—the postmodern homegirl cosmopolitan.

La Toya's Mimesis

Less well recognized or acclaimed as an international artist than Madonna or Jones, La Toya Jackson nonetheless modeled one phase of her career directly on Baker's music-hall performances. The middle sister in a family of eight, La Toya had a career that was overshadowed by that of her five brothers, in particular Michael, and her younger sister, Janet. Her early childhood was spent under the strict religious oversight of Jehovah's Witness doctrines and under the stringent rules imposed by her father, Joseph Jackson, as he shepherded the children to stardom, occasionally using allegedly abusive tactics to achieve his ends. La Toya Jackson first appeared on stage to back up her brothers' group, the Jackson Five, in a song-and-dance routine. She later joined her brothers in their 1980 reunion album, *Triumph,* and a related tour and had a hit solo, "Night Time Lover," closely following the tour. Her solo career took off in the 1980s when she released four albums, including hit songs produced by Michael Jackson, and began to make international concert tours and professional appearances.[60] During this period, she married her manager, Jack Gordon (not to be confused with Jack Jordan, one of Baker's managers), and the two made plans to move to Paris, where Jackson had a contract to perform at the Moulin Rouge. The move followed on the heels of Jackson's 1987 *Playboy* centerfold spread, which sold millions of copies but caused a final rupture with her family. The *Playboy* spread relied on primal eroticism, which Jackson would tame and transfer into an act at the Moulin Rouge. During six months of performances at the Moulin Rouge, Jackson played to capacity audiences. She also began the process of assembling her diaries and family photographs for an autobiography with Patricia Romanowski that covers her childhood years and her career through 1990. The autobiography is an attempt to find her identity within an active and talented family and to settle scores with her parents, siblings, and husband-manager, whom she divorced in 1996. Although the autobiography does not contain a detailed account of her time in Paris, it does include a 1990 photograph of Jackson together with Grace Jones at a party for Ursula Andress at Maxim's in Paris with the caption: "Gay Paris . . . exciting . . . wild . . . fun. I love Paris every moment of the day" (fig. 49).[61]

Figure 49. La Toya Jackson and Grace Jones at a party for Ursula Andress held at Maxim's, Paris, 1990. Photo © Eric Robert/Corbis Sygma.

Jackson's calculated imitation of Baker drew on only a fragment of Baker's music-hall image in a new historical context. By the 1990s, the world of the music hall was in decline and had become primarily a tourist attraction for non-Parisians. Although these audiences were large, they did not help to catapult Jackson into public visibility in France. Jackson did not become an active part of the French art and pop scenes. Her esteem for Baker thinly disguised her own desire for international stardom. While her humanitarian work in antidrug and world hunger campaigns reflects aspects of Baker's philanthropy, she has not been the primary organizer of these programs. Jackson became a momentary simulation of Baker and a fleeting postmodern pastiche of primal eroticism. Through careful planning, she was able to model a successful part of her career abroad on the master tropes of a Baker-like image. Jackson exemplifies Baudrillard's notion that neither the message nor the content count as much as the referentiality of the signifier in postmodern performative discourse.

Beyala's Feminitude and Multiculturalism

Born in Douala, Cameroon, in 1961, Calixthe Beyala is a prolific author and a public figure. Her numerous novels include *C'est le soleil qui m'a brulée* (It Is the Sun That Has Burned Me) (1987), *Tu t'appeleras Tanga* (You Will Call Yourself Tanga) (1988), *Le Petit prince de Belleville* (The Little Prince of Belleville) (1992), and *Les Honneurs perdus* (Lost Honors) (1996), for which she won the Grand Prix Littéraire of the Académie Française.[62]

In 2000, Beyala published *Comment cuisiner son mari à l'africaine* (How to Cook [for] Your Husband African-Style), a novel recounting how an African woman schemes to seduce her neighbor using twenty-four African recipes. The account parallels Marcel Sauvage's biographical presentation of Baker's favorite recipes that were used to seduce the Parisian public.[63] Beyala's work problematizes race and nationality, gender identity, mother-daughter relations, sexuality, eroticism, and power. Her writing style is nonlinear and image-driven—in other words, performative. She continues to write approximately one novel per year and has become a vocal spokesperson for multicultural-ism in the French media through the Collectif Égalité, a coalition of activ-ists supporting the participation of more women and minorities in French television and cinema. In the French tradition of intellectual protest, Beyala composed a series of open letters, including her 1995 *Lettre d'une Africaine à ses soeurs Occidentales* (Letter by an African Woman to Her Western Sisters) followed by her *Lettre d'une Afro-française à ses compatriotes* (Letter by an Afro-French Woman to Her Compatriots) in 2000.[64] In these open letters, she addresses both feminism and racism in France and attempts to develop a public space for dialogues. On February 19, 2000, representing the Collectif Égalité, Beyala and the Guadeloupean actor Luc Saint-Eloi interrupted the César Ceremonies (a French version of the Emmy Awards) by pushing their way onto the stage to read a proclamation about the lack of representation of black actors in French films and television.[65] Then on May 20, 2000, Beyala led the rally and march of the Collectif Égalité, after which she held several press conferences and televised interviews on media equality.

Beyala consciously draws on Baker's images and narratives. In her public persona, Beyala uses feminine allure and seduction echoing the primal and glamour images. She appears in televised interviews wearing elaborate wigs or hair weaves, miniskirts, and seductive attire. Although her discourse is that of an intellectual and an activist, she often shifts registers by referencing her upbringing in the bidonvilles (shanty towns) of Douala and conflating her history with the plight of French working-class women and disadvantaged minorities. Her carefully crafted accounts resemble Baker's narratives about the poverty and racial injustice suffered during her childhood in St. Louis, and she portrays herself as a "homegirl intellectual." In a 1990 interview with me, Beyala explained, "I can't talk about the Africa of traditions, so-called beauty, lyricism, and pastoralism. I was born in a bidonville. That was my world. For me, that is Africa. For many, Africa is the world of air-conditioned cars, beautiful clothes, and *boubous*. Not for me. I saw those people at a distance. For me, Africa is also the Africa of tomorrow where cultures mix and blend."[66]

Beyala's childhood experiences have fueled both her commitment to multiculturalism and her brand of feminism, which she labels *feminitude*. Although some feminist critics consider feminitude to be a reactionary compromise, Beyala adopts its combination of aggressive achievement and essentialist emotionality.[67] She proclaims her desire to become the new woman with three sources of power: "career, motherhood, and emotional life."[68] The rest of her open letter on feminism argues for the psychological, economic, and cross-cultural salience of women's empowerment drawing on examples from the lives of African women. Beyala inscribes her feminism in a literary and polemical discourse that operates in counterpoint to her seductive public image. She shares with Baker a sense of the French marketplace for cultural politics in which style and polemics are woven into public debates. Her hyphenated national identities and her public visibility situate Beyala perfectly as an element of Baker's symbolic legacy.

Although Beyala works with a number of different agents, publicists, and publishers (most notably Éditions Stock, Albin Michel, and Spengler), she is the author of her narratives and not the synthetic creation of an impresario or a media machine. As a novelist, she has capitalized on and manipulated the codes and fantasies of the primal and glamour images through the erotic power of her sexually explicit writing and the seduction of her public persona. Beyala merges writing with performance and pushes the boundaries of each medium.

In a 1993 interview in *Figaro Madame* magazine, Beyala stated that she had adopted twenty-four orphans in Douala, Cameroon, in order to fight

for children's and women's rights.[69] The parallel with Baker is obvious, and
it is interesting that Beyala exactly doubled the number of Baker's Rainbow
children to twenty-four, as if to drive home her point by exaggerating the
image. She also wished to start a school for the orphans and initiated plans to
fund a youth foundation in Cameroon. Beyala simultaneously became more
involved in French politics, running for office in her quarter of Belleville in
1993. Thus, Beyala added the Marian and rescue motifs to her glamour image, combining aspects of Baker's performative and political roles for a new
age. Although she is a writer and not a performer, Beyala's model of melding
public life and performance is closer to Baker's ideal than the approaches of
the other three icons. Beyala maintains the type of creative control over her
image that Baker developed during the latter part of her life. She has also
been subjected to criticisms of her sincerity, her calculated manipulation of
images, and the originality of her work that resemble the attacks on Baker
during the years of her political surveillance.[70] Whether calculated or not,
as an artist, public figure, recipient of the Académie Française honor, and
political activist, Beyala has successfully mastered, incorporated, and built
on Baker's images and narratives.

Similarities among the four figures—Jones, Jackson, Madonna, and Beyala—and Baker range from superficial primal images to more profound ideals. All four celebrities have been influenced by the Parisian art and music
scenes. Jones and Jackson use performative mimesis, while Madonna and
Beyala combine artifice with more complex appropriations of Baker's images
and narratives. Of the four personalities, Jackson copies Baker's music-hall
career directly without the identity doubling mystique. Baker's legacy as a
chameleon, changing characters to suit her narratives and using simple props
to transform her identity, is readily adapted to the postmodern structures of
communication reflected by Jones and Madonna, whereas Beyala combines
early and late Baker motifs as a charismatic Franco-African public intellectual. The androgynous aspects of Baker's performances also have parallels in
the images constructed by male pop icons such as David Bowie and Michael
Jackson and in the works of cross-gender performers such as Lynne Carter and
Michou who have deliberately imitated or impersonated Baker. Baker's mantle
has now settled on male personalities and not exclusively on the women who
have used her as a role model. Through her own self-impersonations, Baker
created a template for these performances. The four postmodern personalities discussed above demonstrate how Baker's pattern of cultural coding has

influenced artists' entire careers, as well as public perceptions of their staged and everyday performances. In these performances, Baker's images have been sampled, simulated, and reworked for a new generation across cultures via film, video, and the Internet.

Feminist Echoes and Protocols

Feminist studies analyze the early Baker both as a beacon of liberation and a victim of the restrictive gender stereotypes prevalent during the 1920s and 1930s. This tension makes Baker a fascinating and ambivalent figure in feminist discourse. In her analysis of MTV, Kaplan discusses the ways in which music videos embed images of the "patriarchal feminine"—that is, images of women in male-dominated and defined roles of mother, glamour girl, and prostitute—in discourses of pleasure and resistance.[71] Baker's image both supports feminist views and frustrates them. She manipulates patriarchal feminine images as a source of power and lays bare the mechanisms through which primal images reproduce archetypal stereotypes. Part of her legacy lies in her ability to cross borders through identity doubling and ambivalent symbolic manipulation of patriarchal feminine signs used as sources of empowerment.

Videos such as Madonna's 1985 *Material Girl* exaggerate and perpetuate female stereotypes. In spite of the spaces of resistance opened by these videos, they continue to reinforce conventional images of primal and glamorous women similar to those deployed by Baker. Although Baker drew on her early images as a source of economic and cultural self-liberation, these images reflected and sustained colonialist fantasies. As ludic spaces, the music hall and the cinema framed these fantasies as projections of pleasure and as parodies. The scene in *Princesse Tam-Tam* in which women hiss at Aouina's nativistic performance in the musical finale frames a double-edged public criticism of Baker's primal image through the use of a diegetic audience. Aouina both transgressed norms of bourgeois decorum and emphasized the spirit of rebellion and release characteristic of avant-garde philosophies and art. The duality of this process of image creation and reception continues to plague feminist scholars who critique the disembodying and distorted effects of the male gaze on the female body while retaining their own gaze on the primal body for the purpose of its deconstruction. Even research on Baker entails its own set of contradictions as one leafs through dusty archival photographs of her erotic music-hall performances and watches her films. These types of images are not merely relics of a forgotten past. They survive in the collective representations of contemporary media. This survival is both troubling and sociologically interesting in an era in which discourses of gender-flattening neutrality cross-cut and overlay the attraction of the primal image.

Studies of spectatorship, especially in the cinema, deploy psychoanalytic theory from Freud to Lacan to explain the structure of the gaze as a mirror of primal shock.[72] Feminist film theorists rely on Lacan's theory of the mirror stage and the screen to develop an approach to spectatorship. At the mirror stage, the child is held up for reflection by the invisible presence of the mother. The mother's gaze shapes the child's ego-ideal, which is always out of reach.[73] The photographic and film screens substitute for the mirror on which this unobtainable ideal is projected. Applying this theory, Silverman argues that "what is determinative for each of us is not how we see or would like to see ourselves, but how we are perceived by the cultural gaze."[74] Frantz Fanon's notion that the cultural gaze is inherently gendered and racialized, condemning the stigmatized subject to a "crushing objecthood," points to the power of the gaze.[75] If we accept the analogy between the mirror and the screen, spectatorship involves an endless struggle to identify with an unobtainable image-ideal in the same way as the child grasps for its mother.[76] Kaplan states, "This ideal image is reproduced for the male spectator in the male heroes who dominate the landscape and control the narrative in the main male genres."[77] The ideal male figure is out of reach, and the female figure becomes a source of fear, pleasure, fantasy, and maternal control. Modifications in film theory have begun to examine various actantial positions occupied by male and female protagonists and spectators and to focus on the permeability of definitions of lack, desire, and pleasure in the cultural imaginary. These theoretical modifications allow us to position Baker in maternal, seductive, dominatrix, and male authoritarian roles simultaneously.

When applied to Baker's body, spectator theory emphasizes both fear and sensual fulfillment of the primal image. If the primal image stands alone as a photographic representation or a caricature, it can be classified along the semiotic axes of fear, or disapproval, and acceptance. The situation is complicated, however, by the fact that Baker's body was in constant motion and that she parodied her own image. In addition, she shifted sources of gender identification. The gender doubling, moving from the nubile primal image to the tuxedo-clad male role in a single stage performance, satisfied different audience desires. Studies of Baker's primal and Black Venus images seldom include the Marian motif because it modifies the object of the gaze and alters the process of spectator identification once again. Although both the primal and the Marian motifs are part of what Kaplan terms the "patriarchal feminine," they imply different forms of social action and empowerment.

The situation is further complicated when we examine Baker's legacy as exemplified in the four postmodern personalities. Each of these figures elaborates on Baker's image through performance and self-writing and reappropriates it in a postmodern pastiche. Postmodern pastiche is not pure mimesis. As a result, the primal image is exaggerated (as in the case of Grace Jones) and the Marian motif is suppressed or modified (as in the cases of Madonna, La Toya Jackson, and Calixthe Beyala). These images are further mediated through the sound and visual bytes of postmodern technologies, where they become even more evanescent and fragmentary. As a result, Baker's complex images cannot be reduced to a single motif and elude simplistic reproduction. They challenge spectator theorists to search for new ways to analyze the intervention of gender in the changing roles of performers and their audiences.

Audience response depends on preexisting cultural frames of reference for performances as well as on the spectators' psychological identification practices. In her analysis of contemporary rap music, Tricia Rose notes the reluctance of black women rappers to identify with feminist causes even when the messages of their songs are aggressive and confrontational.[78] Feminism carries with it a transracial and intercultural alliance that some of these performers are hesitant to make. By focusing on Baker's primal image, we limit her to the role of a black, or exotic, female, who plays out the colonialist fantasies of a white male audience. This image may be reversed as well to that of a black female controlling her audience by manipulating the primal image. In either case, Baker is stuck within a unidimensional role and narrative motif. Baker's fluidity and refusal to be limited to a single stereotype, however, is part of her appeal, and it challenges both theories of spectatorship and cultural analysis. Although her cinematic images remain limited in range, Baker's rainbow and Marian motifs, elaborated in her later recordings, stage performances, and political ideologies, break out of the cultural frames that shaped her early appeal.

Legacies and Landmarks

Part of Baker's legacy involves the reproduction of images through appropriation, mimesis, and cultural borrowing in videos, Web sites, and films as diverse as Woody Allen's *Zelig* and MTV videos. More than a conscious adaptation of the images is entailed.[79] Both parody and pastiche come into play. In fact, individuals who have consciously attempted to be "like Baker" through costuming and performance have often missed or ignored the complexity of her persona and its layers of meaning. When music videos attempt to condense the history of civilization into two-second sound-and-visual bytes, the results are inevitably hyperreal and distorting. These hyperreal strategies affect how Baker is represented in the postmodern media. Baker's image may also be analyzed in terms of her concrete social and political roles. Even this analysis, however, is influenced by the implosion of the medium and the message in contemporary image politics. Baker's use of the stage as a political forum and her conversion of the domestic sphere into a utopian political space resonate with new forms of cultural politics.

Baker's desegregation and multicultural crusades began during a period when modern political organizations were just starting to experiment with the use of performance and publicity to mobilize resources for their causes through celebrity figures. As a solo performer with her own causes, Baker used her concerts and notoriety as a source of political support. Although she did not create the image-politics model, she was among its earliest and most active international proponents. Using this model made her the target of official political organizations and government surveillance, based not only on the messages that she conveyed but also on her methods. Both established groups and oppositional movements have engaged in media politics, a process that, with changes in technology, has become commonplace and increasingly accessible to small groups and individuals. Baker recycled her primal image as a source of cultural capital for political causes. Through her performance of politics, she combined old images and new models to make a social statement. The debates emerging from the image-politics strategy raise questions about the authenticity and authority of artistic performers in the political domain.

As artists unite to support a variety of causes, and their cultural products (music, film, and fashion style) are used to promote still others, both the depth of the causes and the oppositional impact of the imagery are attenuated. Some of the most vocal public criticisms revolve around how sincere artists are about their causes, how much artists profit from them, and how they manipulate their images.[80] While local and national boundaries may be effaced in these global political ventures, local people and artists are often implicated in causes that go beyond or may do disservice to the target audiences. This uneasy collaboration of artists and their audiences in image construction is part of the transfiguration of postmodern politics in which causes are converted into slogans, and political identification into mimetic performances.[81]

By transforming herself into a touristic landmark during her lifetime, Baker attempted to conserve her memory in wax and stone. In these artifacts, she blended primal and Marian imagery and made sure that everything was displayed in lights. She even thought that the cows at Les Milandes would produce more milk with their names in neon lights, and she sang about the virtues of neon. These self-styled efforts at publicity were not, however, the source of the survival of Baker's image, which has outlived them and changed with future generations. What MacCannell says of Marilyn Monroe is also true of Baker, who was equally "a genius publicist who crafted her own unique persona in such a way as to secure for it a permanent place" in popular culture.[82] Baker was able to appropriate archetypal images (the primal dancer and the Black Venus) nested in a series of narratives that could be reworked over time, giving the impression of timelessness. But the meanings of colonialist primal imagery in the 1920s and the uses to which Baker put it as an artifact of memory in the 1970s were different. The reinvention of these images by postmodern pop divas decades later relied on yet another type of mediated memory work.[83] Across all of these processes of rediscovery and symbolic change, Baker's primal image has remained intact, and she is still a hard act to follow.

9   Eternal Comeback

I believe in redemption. I believe in resurrection.
I believe in miracles.

　　—Josephine Baker, 1970

At the close of her life, Josephine Baker wanted to let people know more than ever who she was, what she stood for, and why. She attempted to organize a series of biographies with new collaborators, to convert the story of her life into a Hollywood screenplay, and to revive her music-hall career while continuing to support her political vision of multicultural harmony. Langston Hughes, James Baldwin, and Gerold Frank were among the potential biographers that Baker contacted.[1] She also hired new agents and promoters, and she placed herself under a grueling performance schedule, traveling to Copenhagen, Stockholm, Tel Aviv, New York, San Francisco, Johannesburg, Cape Town, and Durban. During her South African tour in 1974, she even tried to integrate audiences as she had in the United States, but to no avail. Between performances, she returned to her new French home, Villa Maryvonne, a four-bedroom house located in Roquebrune-Cap-Martin in southern France, just a few miles from Monaco and the Italian border. From her front window she could see the bay and the Grimaldi palace. A new era had begun as the old Cinderella narrative recycled.

In March 1969, Baker began a run of fifty-seven shows at La Gouloue, a Parisian nightclub renamed Chez Joséphine for her performance season.

Although the shows attracted small audiences, many of those who attended were celebrities, including Princess Grace of Monaco. Impressed by Baker's performance and moved by her plight, Princess Grace invited Baker to star in the annual gala benefit held at the Monte Carlo Sporting Club in August of that year. The performance was a resounding success, and, with the help of Princess Grace, Baker made plans to stay on the Riviera. There was finally an answer to Josephine's plea for the Rainbow Tribe recorded in the *Herald Tribune* of September 30, 1968, that she had nowhere to go and no one to look after her tribe. Princess Grace worked with the Red Cross of Monaco to help with the down payment on Maryvonne, and Baker's former film producer, Arys Nissotti, handled the mortgage, refusing to let her resell the house or use it for other projects.[2] Although Baker had several remaining debts to settle from Les Milandes, she was off to a fresh start and began once more to dream of her College of Universal Brotherhood. The older Rainbow children were now teenagers with independent spirits. She also acquired new protégés, Jean-Claude Baker (Rouzaud), who helped her with her travels and bookings, and her nephew Richard Martin Jr., who pursued a career in dance and for a time joined his father in France. Josephine could begin to see the strengths and weaknesses of her domestic experiment and her life choices. But she still needed to perform in order to survive both psychologically and financially.

While she was preparing for a new series of tours in 1973, Josephine heard from an old friend, Robert Brady, a textile artist who lived in Cuernavaca, Mexico. She had met Brady in Mexico City in 1967 and continued to correspond with him. He proposed to her a spiritual and platonic marriage that would link both of them as eternal companions. Although the spiritual ceremony did take place in September 1973 in Acapulco, the relationship did not last. Many Baker fans are curious about her relationship with Brady, but there is little concrete documentation apart from rumors that currently exist about it.[3]

Meanwhile, André Levasseur, a veteran set designer from the Paris Opéra, concocted the idea of a spectacular retrospective entitled *Joséphine,* scheduled to debut in August 1974 in Monte Carlo. While waiting for the plans to materialize, Baker continued her usual routines of running the house in Maryvonne, shopping for the children on the Riviera, and touring. Among the tours was one to New York with a new Carnegie Hall show and an appearance at the Victoria Theater in Harlem, scheduled by the producer Jack Jordan and his colleague, Howard Saunders, for June 1973. In the Carnegie Hall concert, which debuted on June 5 and ran four days, Josephine recreated her own legend and played herself in yet another successful comeback performance that critics considered to be clever, camp, and amusing. Stimulated by the positive reviews of the Carnegie Hall performance and the live recording of the concert, Baker continued to book more tours in the United States and Europe and traveled until she reached a state of exhaustion.[4] She collapsed from a heart attack and a stroke during her tour of Copenhagen in July 1973, but miraculously bounced back by the end of the summer for yet another tour of the United States in September. According to Haney, "Josephine looked her best in years."[5] But she was suffering from ill health and had difficulty keeping pace with an already arduous schedule to which she added spur-of-the-moment transcontinental trips and extra engagements. She seemed driven to reach her goal of an ultimate comeback performance—a show through which she would leave her mark on the world in a special way.

In August 1974, André Levasseur presented the gala revue *Joséphine* at the Monte Carlo Sporting Club. Held as a fund-raiser for the Red Cross of Monaco, the revue commemorated nearly fifty years of Baker's performances on the French stage. The actor and director Jean-Claude Brialy served as the master of ceremonies for a spectacle that included a series of tableaux on subjects ranging from Josephine's childhood (described in the program as being in Louisiana), her debut with *La Revue nègre*, her 1926 banana-belt dance performance at the Folies-Bergère, her war years, highlights of her 1930s and 1940s performances, and the final days at Les Milandes. Baker had helped to script a performative narrative that made all of the successes and obstacles of her life fit together in a coherent piece. Although younger artists performed Baker's dances from the early years, she remained on stage for the entire show and made numerous costume changes as she reenacted her turbulent life. Not since her early days in *Paris qui remue* had Baker been involved in staging such an ambitious performance. The stakes for the comeback were much higher in 1974, for not only was she proving that she could still perform at the peak of her capacity, she was also recreating a half-century of theatrical history. While her 1973 Carnegie Hall performance had been geared toward a mixed audience eager to accept a camp retrospective of her music-hall career, the Monte Carlo audience knew Baker's French history and was much more demanding.[6] They were sophisticated bon vivants who had watched Baker rise and fall over the years, and they did not want to see an aging performer struggling to entertain them. The Monte Carlo audience was astonished by

Baker's energy, range of performance styles, stage sets, and costumes. As the final phase of her career was launched, she received a resounding ovation. Henri Astric, the theatrical director of the Monte Carlo Sporting Club, described her performance in a now famous and often repeated report: "*Elle dépasse la rampe.* She went over the footlights. Pow! You had the feeling she was singing for you and only you. For everyone in the audience, she was sitting in each one's lap."[7] Levasseur and Brialy decided that the show had the potential to travel to Paris, and they began to draw up the plans.

Although Baker was poised at the brink of her reconquest of the Parisian audience, several obstacles stood in her way. Her age and frail health after a series of heart attacks made large insurance companies such as Lloyd's reluctant to underwrite her performances. The Parisian music-hall scene had also changed. Old theater owners and directors such as Paul Derval had long since passed away. Now catering to a new and younger international crowd, the Folies-Bergère did not want to risk rehiring the aging Baker. Finally, Roland Petit, the new director of the Casino de Paris, agreed to host the revue on the condition that Lisette Malidor, a rising young black starlet, serve as Baker's understudy in the event that anything should go wrong.[8] Insulted and enraged by the idea, Baker replied, "Il n'ya qu'une seule Joséphine, c'est moi!" (There's only one Joséphine, me!), a comment that would prove to have its own ironic wrinkles. Baker's emotions were intensified by the fact that *Joséphine* was a show named for her in which she enacted the history of her life. Jean-Claude Dauzonne, director of the Théâtre Bobino, had been impressed by the Monte Carlo show and proposed a counteroffer. A music hall on rue de la Gaieté in Montparnasse, the Bobino did not have the broad theatrical and status appeal to which Baker had become accustomed. Carnegie Hall it was not. It was, instead, a modest theater surrounded by small restaurants, cafés, bars, and peep shows attracting a new Parisian demimonde in an area that was fast becoming the center of an emerging Parisian red-light district and a mini–Las Vegas strip in the middle of the Left Bank.

In spite of the fact that Baker considered the Bobino a backdoor entrance to the Parisian theatrical world, she was pleased with the terms proposed by Monsieur Bodson, the theater's head, and Dauzonne, the director, including a large weekly salary and a percentage of the ticket sales. Baker planned that half of this sum, along with a portion of the $120,000 that she had earned at Carnegie Hall in 1973, would be invested in her College of Universal Brotherhood, to which she remained dedicated until the very end. The musicians,

who insisted on being paid in cash from the show's receipts, were also accom-
modated. Bodson and Dauzonne had the theater remodeled by extending the
stage, recarpeting the building, transforming the orchestra pit, and adding
more space to house Baker's costumes, including two hundred pairs of dancing
shoes. Levasseur devoted himself to rewriting the script and redesigning the
show by adding new tableaux, costumes, and songs and hiring a large cast of
young performers and dancers.[9] He designed and made miniature models of
new sets on a worktable at the Bobino until he was satisfied that the ultimate
revue—*Joséphine*—had been created. Baker herself experienced a breath of
new life as she transformed from an aging star into a performance legend.
The Parisian show was nearly an hour longer than the Monte Carlo version
and required all of Baker's stamina. The revue *Joséphine* became a landscape
of memory and a signifier incarnating an exciting lifetime of performance.

Rehearsals started in January 1975 and lasted until mid-March. Baker
rented an apartment on avenue Paul Doumer in the sixteenth arrondissement
near Trocadéro and once again became a fixture of the Parisian landscape.[10]
She reconnected with old friends and walked through the city immortalized
by Marcel Sauvage as the dream of her youth. Old financial and political
tensions seemed to dissipate as Baker rose to new heights of stardom. She
performed with young dancers, coached them in her routines, polished the
choreography and music, and worked tirelessly to prepare this show of shows
as the pinnacle of her career. Much of the revue involved conscious memory
work, not only as a lifetime retrospective, but also as a performance reiterating Baker's well-worn narrative of miraculous success. Levasseur placed cue
cards around the stage so that Baker would not forget her lines. Invited friends
and onlookers who were able to sneak in through the stage door during the
rehearsals commented on Baker's remarkable rejuvenation.

On March 24, 1975, a special performance of *Joséphine* was held for the
press. Festival, a local recording company engaged by Dauzonne, audiotaped
the performance for release as an album entitled *Joséphine à Bobino 1975*, containing the thirty-three numbers that she performed.[11] After an instrumental
overture, Baker's medley opened with the show's signature song, "Me Revoilà
Paris," followed by a series of songs in French and English, including "I'm
Just Wild About Harry" from *Shuffle Along*, "Stormy Weather," "Voulez-vous
de la canne à sucre?" and, of course, "J'ai deux amours." A new song, "Paris
Paname," was written and arranged especially for the show. Improvising on
each tune, Baker presented original and moving renditions. Baker's longtime

friend and colleague Pierre Spiers directed the Bobino orchestra, while his wife, Marie, helped Josephine to organize her new life in Paris. Dress rehearsals and trial performances went well, and the press coverage was generally favorable. *L'Aurore, France-Soir,* and *Le Quotidien de Paris* enthusiastically endorsed Baker's performance as elegant and complimented Levasseur on his masterful direction of a show that was sentimental and nostalgic but avoided the pitfalls of becoming camp and "retro."[12] A reporter from the weekly magazine *L'Express* observed, "Ce n'est plus un comeback. C'est l'éternel retour" (It's no longer a comeback. It's the eternal return).[13] This description framed the performance for many spectators. André Viso K., a reporter for *Libération,* however, attacked the show as a reunion of old fossils brought together by a "gaulliste notoire, vestige du passé" (a notorious Gaullist, vestige of the past), a comment reflecting the political controversy that Baker was still capable of igniting.[14] But a positive flood of praise, excitement, and Baker nostalgia had already been released by the press as she had moved toward her opening night at the Bobino.

Insiders labeled Baker's official opening on April 8, 1975, "J-Day." As the day approached, Dauzonne papered Paris with large posters of Baker in one of her most elegant costumes from the show, a frilly white tulle 1890s gown (fig. 50). The public seemed to have an insatiable curiosity about the mysterious, charismatic, and politically controversial figure that Josephine Baker had become, and tickets were sold out weeks in advance. Opening the show after the overture with a rendition of "Me Revoilà Paris," dressed in the 1890s publicity gown and a large flowered hat, Baker then presided over reenactments of her childhood in St. Louis with a twelve-year-old as the young Josephine, her Folies-Bergère premiere, a Brazilian carnival number, a New York–Broadway–Chicago scene in which she arrived in a white sequined motorcycle outfit on a vintage Harley-Davidson (fig. 51), a wartime enactment performed from the hood of a 1940s jeep with Josephine in a stage version of her famous air force sublieutenant's uniform, and a concluding music-hall scene performed in a translucent, jeweled body stocking. Resembling Baker's Jorama wax museum in motion, the tableaux even included a musical reenactment of her eviction from Les Milandes, in which she wore black tights and was carried offstage as a jubilant survivor on a pink sofa. The comic and tragic episodes of Baker's life had been condensed into musical skits recreating narratives in which all of the emotional intensity had been transferred into frenetic song and dance. Even her gloomiest moment became material

Figure 50. Josephine Baker appeared in an 1890s gown for her opening scene at the Théâtre Bobino, 1975. Photo courtesy of Getty Images, New York.

for performance. Breathlessly and in her typical way, she ended the revue with a theatrical farewell to her audience: "Goodnight, ladies and gentlemen, buona sera, buenos noches, shalom, shalom, ciao, ciao."[15] It was fitting that Baker made her comeback in the city of light that had been so good to her. Baker was so enthusiastic that she wanted to take the show on a world tour, starting in London and New York. Then she would retire.

The story of Baker's last days has often been told. What is unique about this account is the interpretation of this story in terms of the larger narrative of Baker's self-writing. During the April 8 show, Jean-Claude Brialy read a telegram from President Valéry Giscard d'Estaing paying tribute to Baker's fiftieth anniversary as a performer, "in the name of a grateful France, whose heart has so often beaten with yours."[16] It was no matter that her heart had

Figure 51. Josephine Baker wore a white beaded motorcycle outfit for her New York–Broadway–Chicago scene at the Théâtre Bobino, 1975.

skipped a few beats, with Baker in ailing health and still living on the cusp of two nations and multiple identities. She celebrated her triumph at the Hôtel Bristol with two hundred fifty celebrity guests, including Princess Grace as the guest of honor; Prince Rainier; international film stars such as Jeanne Moreau, Sophia Loren, and Mireille d'Arc; as well as rock legend Mick Jagger and Madame Sukarno. Dauzonne presented her with a seven-layer wedding cake with rosettes and spun-sugar frosting. The cake symbolically marked Baker's marriage to her profession and recalled the Cinderella narrative once again. On the night of April 9, after an equally successful performance, Baker attended a smaller gathering at La Barate, a café across from the Théâtre Bobino. She danced, joked with guests, and recounted life stories until nearly 3:00 A.M. Weary guests refused to accompany her to Chez Michou, a popular cabaret where Bobby, an African American female impersonator, vigorously recreated the banana-skirt dance.[17] Returning home to her apartment at avenue Paul Doumer close to 3:00 A.M., Baker fell into a deep slumber and rose late. After completing a leisurely morning routine, she ate lunch, perused reviews of her show, and took a nap, from which she never awoke. Pepito's niece Lélia Scotto, who had been living with her, found her in bed that afternoon amid piles of press clippings. She was taken to La Salpêtière Hospital where attempts to revive her from a coma on April 10 and 11 were unsuccessful. She was pronounced dead of a cerebral hemorrhage at 5:00 A.M. on Saturday, April 12, 1975.[18] As news of her demise rippled around the world, she was surrounded by close friends, including Dauzonne from the theater and her sister Margaret Wallace, who had flown in from Roquebrune. Tyler Stovall comments, "Her death could not have been more perfectly arranged had it been scripted by Hollywood."[19]

Beginning at La Salpêtière Hospital in the thirteenth arrondissement, the funeral procession on April 15 moved past the Théâtre Bobino in the fourteenth arrondissement, where her name remained in lights, and wove through Paris to the church of La Madeleine in the first arrondissement (fig. 52). Onlookers lined the streets, and by the time that the cortège reached La Madeleine, approximately twenty thousand people were in front of the edifice (fig. 53). As a Chevalier de la Légion d'Honneur and a decorated war hero, Baker was given a twenty-one-gun salute with a display of twenty-four official flags in a full French military ceremony. Wreaths and flowers lined the pathway to the Madeleine. Some of the floral arrangements required several men to transport them.[20] In the style of one of her music-hall reviews, Baker

Figure 52. Josephine Baker's funeral cortège in front of the Théâtre Bobino, Paris, April 15, 1975. Photo © Bettmann/Corbis.

was surrounded by supportive players and a large and enthusiastic audience for her final curtain call. Although Princess Grace is alleged to have referred to the April 15 Paris funeral as a "circus," the event was a spectacular popular celebration for a media icon that would be the harbinger of similar ceremonies for other dignitaries and public figures of the late twentieth-century. Baker's ability to transfer her stage appeal into the public domain was a byproduct of the image politics to which she had devoted so much energy during her lifetime.

In a strange foreboding of her future, Baker had once said to Marcel Sauvage that she would end her life on the Riviera. Her final interment took place in Monaco. Princess Grace organized a private ceremony attended by the Rainbow Tribe, Jo Bouillon, close family, and selected friends. After being held for six months in a mausoleum awaiting a plot, Baker's body was

Figure 53. Princess Grace of Monaco and her friend Michel Guy were in the large crowd of dignitaries and fans at Josephine Baker's funeral service at La Madeleine, April 15, 1975. Photo © Bettmann/Corbis.

finally buried in the Monaco cemetery. Haney concludes her biography with the remark, "What could be more fitting for Josephine, who hopscotched from one perilous crisis to the next, than to finish her days in a gambler's paradise?"[21] Another reading of the ending relies less on fate and chance and more on Baker's agency. Monaco is not merely a "gambler's paradise," but also a democratic monarchy, the fitting place for a contemporary Cinderella narrative to come to a close, or at least a temporary hiatus. Baker used key events of the twentieth century to reinvent herself as a public persona, a model, and a motif. Her roles as a performer, militant, and philanthropist are briefly summarized in the plaque erected in her honor and commemorated by the mayor of the commune on February 2, 2001, at the Place Joséphine Baker in the fourteenth arrondissement of Paris (fig. 54).

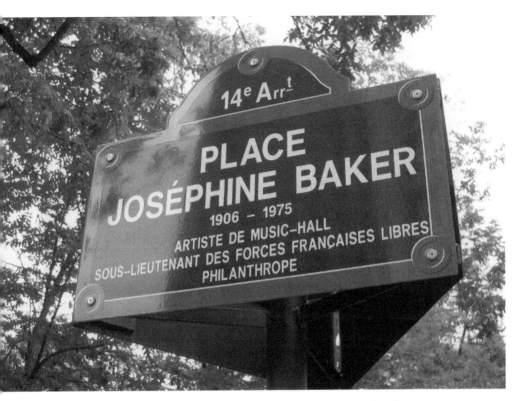

Figure 54. Place Joséphine Baker, fourteenth arrondissement, near the Théâtre Bobino, Paris. Photo by Franz Kennedy, October 2004, from the Black Paris Collection of Bennetta Jules-Rosette.

Unfolding Narratives, Models, and Motifs

The kernel of iterative narratives of Baker's life remains the same but is repeated over and over in different motifs.[22] Although this reiterative structure does not account for the popularity of Baker's narratives at any given moment, it does elucidate their staying power. As Baker's personal goals crystallized, her collaborative work with Colin, Sauvage, Abatino, and Rivollet brought to life the rags-to-riches narrative. Baker positioned herself as both subject and object in her unfolding narratives. The *zeitgeist* of the Black Venus (broadly read) provided the background from which Baker's primal image was drawn, both literally and figuratively. Although she may have been unaware of the deep roots of this and other images, she was able to take advantage of their surface manifestations through performance and self-writing. During the early phases of her career, theater directors and impresarios such as Derval and Jacques-Charles and artists and designers such as Colin, Calder, and Poiret emblemized the images. An archaeology of Baker's narratives reveals that some of the key symbols they generated were time-bound and audience specific. Hence, Baker was not able to transfer her European primal image to the American public in her 1936 Ziegfeld Follies appearance. Baker remarked, "Little did I know how things would turn out."[23] Numerous practical obstacles presented by contracts and staging interfered with the 1936 performance, yet the fundamental obstacle stemmed from the racial and national stereotypes of the era. While Baker had been able to exploit exotic imagery to her advantage in France, she was locked into the legacy of minstrelsy and the skepticism about the French music hall that influenced her New York public in the 1930s. Her primal image and the Cinderella myth had worked in France, but this message was clearly not universal. Nevertheless, the mechanisms of public image-building were rapidly becoming global.

From 1927 through 1940, Baker used feature films to bolster her image, but once again found herself cut off from the dominant American market evolving in Hollywood. Other European stars such as Dietrich and Garbo would make a transition to Hollywood that Baker could not because of the racial and institutional barriers that confronted her. Her autobiographies, novella, and children's book did not reach an international market during her lifetime. While the primal image had popular appeal, the impact of the narratives of her self-writing remained socially and culturally restricted. Baker became acutely aware of these restrictions as World War II blocked her ability to perform in Europe, and her desegregation crusade and political activism limited her ability to travel abroad in the 1950s and early 1960s.

During the war years, a new humanitarian image emerged, the seeds of which, I have argued, were already planted in *Mon sang dans tes veines*. The primal image became a relic with nostalgic staying power but also a negativity that could not be controverted. Whether she intended it or not, Baker's "négritude" now became rooted in a dialectic of race that she would be forced to evade and overturn. Baker emerged from the war as a public heroine in France and as a performer whose legend was still intact. But what was this legend and to whom did it speak? From the mid-1940s into the mid-50s, Baker expanded her repertoire, resumed touring, and made recordings that built on her music-hall career. She retained old images as nostalgic points of reference as she staged new performances in which she played "Joséphine," now an established stage persona whose Cinderella narrative was woven into the program.

Baker's 1951 return to the United States tested the waters and generated the new images once again. Vowing that she would place politics before performance when she sailed to Miami, Baker began her one-woman desegregation crusade. The time was certainly right for her efforts. The postwar promise of a better life for everyone fueled Baker's crusade as she traveled across the United States desegregating theaters and endorsing political causes. Baker did not anticipate the depth of lingering racial conflicts in the United States and the complexities of cold-war politics. As an international star, a French war hero, and a black American by birth, Baker was caught in a crossfire of suspicion and surveillance that surpassed her expectations. Whether one argues that she was forced into domestic exile or that she simply made a strategic personal retreat, it is clear that Baker was compelled to shift gears.[24] The power of her ideals and her master narrative, however, endured as she returned to France to build her own utopian community with the Rainbow Tribe at Les Milandes.

For some Baker biographers, the demise of the primal image in the 1930s is the end of the story. For others, the loss of Les Milandes in 1969 is the beginning of the end. Haney remarks of the loss, "She was licked."[25] Although Les Milandes was a totalizing symbol unifying Baker's Cinderella narrative and Marian motif, Baker was able to reconfigure its loss into a moment of music-hall history. It is not possible to overestimate the tragedy that losing Les Milandes represented for Baker personally. The realities of rearing the Rainbow Tribe alone stood in stark contrast to her utopian dreams of international unity. Yet, Baker maintained her utopian vision until the end and continued to invest resources into making her multicultural dream a reality. Her persistence, determination, and optimism are part of her legend and legacy. Baker's narratives were not free of contradictions. The tensions between a benevolent monarchical regime and an egalitarian society persisted in her utopian vision of a world without racism, poverty, and suffering—a world inscribed by the intersecting narratives of her life in art, performance, and social activism.

Baker and the African Diaspora

Recent scholarship, particularly in France and England, has begun to reconfigure notions of ethnicity and identity politics in the African diaspora.[26] In

French multiculturalism, the republican ideal of citizenship plays a central role in shaping processes of integration and assimilation that affect minority populations. Over the years, the French government has wrestled with redefinitions of the parameters of citizenship, swinging from liberal policies to more restrictive requirements based on birth, blood, and secularization.[27] Baker recognized the emergence of these tensions when she adopted French citizenship in 1937 as well as when she challenged the rules during the 1950s and 1960s by attempting to establish her utopian world village where races and cultures would blend.

This scholarship also reflects the spirit of Baker's visionary views. Stuart Hall argues for a reconfiguration of "the symbolic boundaries between racially constituted categories."[28] This reconfiguration relies on the conscious construction of symbolic categories that explore the negotiation of difference in terms of cognitively salient and subjectively meaningful categories with mutable boundaries. Baker's images play an important role in rethinking race and difference. The Rainbow Tribe may be viewed as a subjective projection of Baker's own identity. Through her children, she occupied diverse cultural spaces and changing social roles that she also developed in her stage personas, performances, and songs.

It is possible to pigeonhole Baker as a black performer, and certainly she took advantage of aspects of that image when she performed "blackness" as the actantial stance of one of her many personas. Nevertheless, Baker went beyond Fanon's notion of the riveting cultural gaze that fixes the subject's identity in terms of race and gender. Instead, she played upon the fixed core of stereotypical roles and perceptions by using an exaggeration of the stereotypes to criticize their very existence. Her identification was thus not limited to fixed selves and primal images, but consisted of the construction of new selves and positions from which to speak that exploded conventional narratives.[29] While the philosophy of classical négritude and its figurative representations restructured notions of race and manhood, Baker's négritude challenged reason with primal passion and introduced gender into the equation as more than a heuristic idealization.[30] Baker manipulated the male gaze and patriarchal fantasies as features of her performances. In classical négritudinist paradigms, the black male is the object of the riveting gaze of oppression. His anger must be shackled and his sexual threat must be harnessed. Baker represented the bawdy black female body as the flip side of this coin, but also sublimated female desire by occupying an androgynous and simultaneously acculturated space. Baker demonstrated that the links between theory and performance were palpable and concrete. She used her changing theatrical roles as a basis for forming alternative communities, performing politics, and setting new agendas of cultural possibility in the representation of self.

From the 1930s through the 1970s, France was a crossroads where Africans, Antillians, and African Americans met in various guises. Baker touched upon many of these encounters, from her early music-hall years, her role as the almost-elected Queen of the Colonies, her wartime service, and her participation in *Présence Africaine* and SAC. New diasporic research is currently reinterrogating the importance of anglophone and francophone encounters and the critical role played by Paris in the intersection of black arts, performance, and politics.[31] The themes and ambivalences of Baker's life, narratives, and commitments provide a window through which these encounters may be viewed and reassessed.

Eye on the Future

Research on Baker provides access to the study of transatlantic influences in diaspora studies. It also serves as a resource for analyzing late twentieth-century society and popular culture. The numerous and copious biographies of Baker complement primary archival sources; press coverage; private collections in Paris, New York, New Haven, Washington, London, and the Dordogne; and new Web sites and photo databanks. It is critical to centralize these archival sources and review them for accuracy so that they can become more accessible for scholars working on Baker's early period and the related performance genres and cultural products. Therefore, I have included in the present study detailed citations of many of the archival sources that I reviewed. The early Folies-Bergère film clips and written material on *Sirène des tropiques* have been difficult to obtain. If all of Baker's films were to be digitally remastered, they would become more accessible. More important, they would be preserved for future scholarship as emblems of an era of cultural and technological change. They hold the keys to understanding the development of postmodern media.

Public accessibility of certain aspects of Baker's biography at the expense of other valuable information results in the repetition of stock stories, clichés, images, and misrepresentations. The flurry of propaganda and florid press coverage about the Rainbow Tribe and the loss of Les Milandes demonstrates the ways in which the opinions of journalists and biographers have shaped a fictive and figurative Baker in an unnecessarily gloomy manner. Although I have argued that Baker was the first to mythologize herself, the semiotic layers of narratives and the stories told on her behalf need to be analyzed as autonomous constructions that reflect their eras and audiences. Penetrating research on these diverse audiences opens up another topic for future scholarly exploration.

Re-envisioning Baker as an intellectual and a performer encourages a closer review of her literary production. I have approached this project through a discussion of Baker's self-writing and an analysis of touring with Baker's image by examining how she began to scaffold images of herself on paper and in wax and stone for posterity. Rather than dismissing Baker's Jorama and theme park as extravagant and ego-driven projects of a flamboyant artist, I interpret them in the light of contemporary research on tourism and popular culture. The quest for exotic images and cultures characteristic of touristic narratives is a theme that extends from Baker's early performance career to her courageous utopian experiment at Les Milandes.

Baker was a symbol of hyphenated identities and new ethnicities. She was not merely an African American in exile. Instead, she recreated an international persona with national, racial, and gendered inflections. Honored as a French patriot at La Madeleine, she was paradoxically buried by another American expatriate in Monaco. Just when we think that we have fit the pieces of the puzzle together, something in Baker's life rearranges the pattern. And this constant reconfiguration of identity is precisely the model that Baker offers for cultural studies of performance in the postmodern era.

Coda

Throughout her life, Baker drew on her personal experiences to shape her performances. In turn, she transformed her everyday environments from Le Vésinet to Les Milandes into stage sets where exciting dramas unfurled.[32] In interaction with her audiences—both diegetic and real—Baker emerged as an "institution," reflecting the spirit of her times and pushing beyond ordinary and expected norms of performance. Part of Baker's distinctiveness resided in her boundary crossing and the audacity with which she experimented with new ideas. Baker's art was where she lived, and it manifested what her "real life" had been and was becoming. Real life notwithstanding, Baker lived her life as an echo, or reflection, of her art. These multiple resonating reflections enlarged her image again and again until it became more than she could ever have anticipated. It became an icon that represented an entire generation and a foretelling of the future. Absorbing new influences like a sponge, she appropriated others' images of her as her own and added to them new and unanticipated facets. Later in life, Baker used her own image and ironic sense of the camp, the cliché, and the retro to encode more new messages. This was part of what she called "doing Joséphine." Baker's life in review allows us to see how an individual epitomizes her era, and how life and the art of performance mirror each other in the production of new cultural forms.

Chronology

1906 • Birth of Freda Josephine McDonald on June 3 in St. Louis. Her mother is Carrie McDonald and her father is recorded as Eddie Carson.

1919 • Josephine marries foundry worker Willie Wells in St. Louis. She is thirteen years old but claims that she is fifteen.

1921 • Josephine marries railway porter William Howard Baker and assumes the name Josephine Baker.

1922 • Baker becomes part of the road cast of Sissle and Blake's *Shuffle Along* and begins touring. She learns vaudeville song-and-dance routines.

1924 • Baker assumes a leading role in Sissle and Blake's *Chocolate Dandies* on Broadway. She performs one number as a clown in blackface.

1925 • Baker works at New York's Plantation Club, where she is discovered by Caroline Dudley Regan.
       • Baker leaves for Paris on September 25 and opens in *La Revue nègre* at the Théâtre des Champs-Elysées on October 2. The image of savage dancer Fatou is born.
       • Paul Colin designs a famous poster for *La Revue nègre* depicting Baker as the "jazz baby."

1926 • Baker opens in *La Folie du jour* at the Folies-Bergère in Paris.
       • Paul Colin, with the inspiration of Jean Cocteau and Jacques-Charles, designs the banana skirt for Baker's 1926 performance at the Folies-Bergère. Baker's primal image is solidified.
       • Baker's first recordings in English, with Odéon, are issued in the fall.
       • Baker opens her nightclub, Chez Joséphine, in Montmartre, December 14.

1927 • Baker continues to perform at the Folies-Bergère. Her banana skirt undergoes several changes.
       • Marcel Sauvage and Paul Colin collaborate with Baker on her first biography. *Les Mémoires de Joséphine Baker* is published in Paris by Éditions Kra.
       • Paul Colin publishes his lithographs of Baker in a portfolio, *Le Tumulte noir.*
       • Baker begins work with Giuseppe (Pepito) Abatino. Campaigns for Bakerfix and Valaze Body Cream are launched. Baker develops her image as the "new woman."
       • Baker makes two short films produced by the Folies-Bergère.

• Baker records more releases in English with Odéon in January and February.

• Artist Alexander Calder makes wire sculptures of Baker.

• Baker stars as Papitou in her first feature-length film, *La Sirène des tropiques*, directed by Henri Etiévent and Mario Nalpas, with a script by Maurice Dekobra. The film premieres in Paris on December 30.

1928   • Two film clips of Baker's Folies-Bergère performances are released.

• Baker begins a tour of Europe and South America with Pepito Abatino.

• Baker is photographed as the Black Venus by Madame d'Ora.

• Architect Adolf Loos makes a blueprint for Baker's modernist house.

1929   • Baker is photographed as the Black Venus by George Hoyningen-Huene.

• Baker and Abatino return from their world tour. They purchase Beau-Chêne, a mansion in the Paris suburb of Le Vésinet.

• Baker begins serious vocal and dance training with Madame Paravicini and George Balanchine to change her image.

1930   • Baker is nominated as Queen of the Colonies for the 1931 Universal Colonial Exposition. The nomination is revoked because Baker was not a French citizen or subject.

• Baker debuts in *Paris qui remue* at the Casino de Paris in October. The successful revue includes Baker's first public performance of her signature song, "J'ai deux amours."

• Baker releases a recording of the songs from *Paris qui remue* with the orchestra Melodic-Jazz du Casino de Paris.

• Baker upgrades her fashion image with designer apparel.

1931   • The French government approves the Dakar-Djibouti Mission, an extensive anthropological expedition across Africa, headed by Marcel Griaule and sponsored by the Musée de l'Homme.

• Panamanian bantam-weight boxer Alfonso Teofilo Brown and Roger Simendé, from France, fight an exhibition boxing match on April 15 at the Cirque d'Hiver to fund the Dakar-Djibouti Mission. Baker helps to raise funds for the expedition by participating in an improvised boxing match with Brown.

• Universal Colonial Exposition opens on May 29.

• Marcel Sauvage publishes *Voyages et aventures de Joséphine Baker,* chronicling Baker's 1928–29 world tour.

• Baker releases several new recordings in French and English with Melodic-Jazz du Casino de Paris.

• Félix de la Camara and Pepito Abatino publish *Mon sang dans des veines,* a novella based on a story by Baker. The novella includes a preface by Baker in which she compares herself to its heroine, Joan. The Marian motif is launched in Baker's images and narratives.

1932 • Baker performs in Milan in February.

• Baker stars in the revue *La Joie de Paris,* opening at the Casino de Paris in December. Baker appears in cross-dress as a clown in blackface in an imitation of Johnny Hudgins and as a tuxedo-clad bandleader in this revue.

• Music from *La Joie de Paris,* including Baker's famous song "Si j'étais blanche!" is recorded with Baker's own orchestra, and the record is released in November by Columbia.

1933 • Baker releases a second studio recording of the tunes from *La Joie de Paris.*

1934 • Baker plays the lead role of Dora in a revival of Jacques Offenbach's comic opera *La Créole.* She alters her musical image by broadening her performative range and wins critical acclaim.

• Baker releases recordings, including "C'est lui" and "Haïti," from the film *Zouzou,* with Jazz du Poste Parisien, directed by Al Romans, in November.

• The film *Zouzou,* starring Baker and directed by Marc Allégret, premieres at the Moulin Rouge Cinema on December 14.

1935 • André Rivollet publishes his collaborative biography of Baker, *Une Vie de toutes les couleurs* (A Many-Colored Life), and presents a lecture and gala evening of music to launch the book in Neuilly on March 21.

• In September, Baker releases "Sous le ciel d'Afrique" (Neath the Tropic Blue Skies), from the score of *Princesse Tam-Tam,* with Columbia Records in Paris, with limited releases in the United States.

• Baker releases "Le Chemin de bonheur" (Dream Ship), from the score of *Princesse Tam-Tam,* as a radio recording in New York in October.

• Baker stars as Aouina in the film *Princesse Tam-Tam,* directed by Edmond T. Gréville. The film opens on November 8 at the Moulin Rouge Cinema.

1936 • Baker releases a recording of "La Congo blicoti" with the Lecuona Cuban Boys in November. The recording is derived from the conga number in *Princesse Tam-Tam.*

• Baker headlines on Broadway at the Ziegfeld Follies and receives mixed reviews from skeptical New York audiences. She is strongly affected by the racial content of the reviews.

• Pepito Abatino dies in Paris.

1937 • Baker marries French industrialist Jean Lion. She becomes a French citizen via marriage.

• Baker releases several recordings with Wal Berg and his orchestra.

1939 • France enters World War II in September after Germany's attack on Poland.

• Baker meets Commander Jacques Abtey and joins the French Counterespionage Services and Free France in September.

• Baker makes more recordings with Wal Berg and his orchestra.

1940 • Baker opens early in the year at the Casino de Paris with Maurice Chevalier in the revue *Paris-Londres*. The show closes in May. This is Baker's last public performance in Paris during the war years.

• Baker's last feature film, *Fausse alerte* (*The French Way* in its English-language release), premieres at the Théâtre Français on May 7 and the Impérial Pathé on May 27.

• Baker premieres in Marseille in the lead role of Jacques Offenbach's *La Créole* on December 24 while awaiting instructions on her wartime duties from General de Gaulle and Commander Jacques Abtey.

1941 • Baker leaves for North Africa in January as a counterespionage agent.

• Baker becomes ill and begins her recovery in Casablanca.

• Baker travels briefly to Spain to perform in Madrid, Valencia, and Barcelona.

• Baker returns to Casablanca, where she undergoes further medical treatment, including a hysterectomy, to deal with severe infections.

1942 • Baker spends most of this year in medical recovery in the Comte clinic as the guest of Si Thami el Glaoui, Pasha of Marrakech. She leaves the Marrakech medical clinic in December.

• Baker meets U.S. Army Lieutenant Sidney Williams and agrees to entertain the Allied troops in North Africa.

• Baker's divorce from Jean Lion becomes final.

1943 • Baker continues working for Free France and also entertains the Allied troops in North Africa. She travels to the Middle East (Cairo and Beirut) as part of her mission and raises funds for the cause of Free France through her performances. No recordings are made during this period.

1944 • After continuing her war efforts throughout most of the year, Baker returns to the Château des Milandes while retaining Beau-Chêne as a secondary residence. She continues to be plagued by bouts of ill health resulting from her experiences in North Africa.

• Baker releases an album with Jo Bouillon and his orchestra under the Columbia label on December 21.

1946 • Baker is awarded the Medal of Resistance with Rosette by the French government.

1947 • Josephine Baker marries Jo Bouillon on June 3, and together they purchase the Château des Milandes, with Baker as the registered owner.

• Baker sells Beau-Chêne and her apartment on rue Bugeaud in Paris to pay for the Château des Milandes.

• Baker makes plans to remodel the château with the proceeds of her real estate sales.

• Marcel Sauvage publishes a second edition of *Les Mémoires de Joséphine Baker* in Paris.

• Alioune Diop founds the journal *Présence Africaine* in Paris with international editorial and patronage committees consisting of French, African, Antillian, and African American intellectuals.

1948 • Baker and Bouillon tour the United States briefly and continue to make plans for remodeling Les Milandes. Baker visits her family members in St. Louis and brings some of them back to France. While she is on tour in New York, thirty-six hotels refuse reservations for Baker because she is black.

1949 • Baker returns to the Folies-Bergère, where she performs "Beauty and the Beast" and "Ave Maria" in the revue *Féeries et folies*.

• Baker releases three recordings with Bouillon in February, April, and June, respectively.

• Les Milandes opens to the public as a tourist attraction on September 4.

1951 • Baker and Bouillon record an album with Pacific, which is also released in the United States. Baker appears on the cover wearing an elaborate hairdo and a glamorous gown.

• Baker and Bouillon briefly tour Havana.

• Baker opens at Copa City in Miami in January, launching her famous U.S. tour and desegregation crusade that take her to New York, Philadelphia, Chicago, and San Francisco. She performs in glamorous gowns and sings in several languages. Baker grosses $100,000 during the first leg of her tour. She begins performing politics, and her militant image develops.

• Baker receives Outstanding Woman of the Year award in New York from the NAACP presented by U.N. Ambassador Ralph Bunche.

• Harlem celebrates Josephine Baker Day on May 20 with the support of the NAACP and other community organizations.

• Baker and other guests are refused service at the Stork Club on October 16. Baker enlists the aid of the NAACP and calls on Walter Winchell to be a witness.

• Walter Winchell begins vendetta after the Stork Club incident. FBI files are opened on Baker on October 25.

1952 • Baker leaves the United States for her tour of South America in January.

• Baker serves as Juan Péron's goodwill ambassador in Argentina for six months and leaves Argentina in disillusionment.

• Baker is criticized by U.S. officials and her South American tour is blocked.

• Baker performs in Rio and Havana. In Cuba, her movements are restricted, and she is placed under surveillance.

1953 • Baker speaks at a rally for the League against Racism and Anti-Semitism in December upon her return to Paris.

• Baker records "Dans mon village," by Henri Lemarchand and Francis Lopez, with Pierre Dreuder and his orchestra in Germany. The recording is released by Columbia during the same year. Baker launches the utopian, Marian image in music.

1954 • Baker begins informally adopting Rainbow children at the average rate of two per year. Her utopian plans for a world village crystallize.

• School segregation is officially ended in the United States on May 17 with the Supreme Court's ruling on the case of *Brown v. Board of Education*.

1955 • The Afro-Asiatic conference, held in Bandoeng, Indonesia, begins to establish the terms for decolonization in Africa and Asia.

• Jo Bouillon organizes a publicity photo session for the Rainbow children at Les Milandes on July 1.

1956 • Baker stages an elaborate retirement performance at the Olympia Theater on April 10. She presents the first of many retrospectives of her career.

• Baker performs on tour in North Africa.

• Alioune Diop and the Présence Africaine committee organize the First International Congress of Black Writers and Artists at the Sorbonne, held September 19–22. Josephine Baker is listed as a member of the patronage committee.

• Baker continues to build her Rainbow Tribe at Les Milandes and to work with the experimental farm.

1957 • Baker hosts the Conférence Anti-Raciste at Les Milandes on January 13.

• Baker and Bouillon publish the children's book *La Tribu arc-en-ciel*, with illustrations by Piet Worm.

• Baker regularizes the official adoption of eight of the Rainbow children at the prefecture of Sarlat, in Dordogne, on June 21.

• Baker files for divorce from Jo Bouillon, and the date for a reconciliation hearing is set at the Tribunal of Sarlat for July 5.

• Baker's former husband Jean Lion dies of the Russian flu.

1959 • Carrie McDonald dies at Les Milandes on January 12. Jo Bouillon handles the funeral arrangements while Baker is on tour in Rome and Istanbul.

• Baker performs in *Paris mes amours*, opening at the Olympia Theater in Paris in May and running for the rest of the year.

• Baker finds Noël, her last boy, in November and adopts him in December.

1960 • Jo Bouillon leaves Les Milandes for Paris and later moves permanently to Argentina.

1961 • Baker is decorated with the Légion d'Honneur and the Croix de Guerre with Palme at an official ceremony held at Les Milandes on August 18. The Rainbow children attend the ceremony.

1963 • Baker attends the March on Washington and gives a twenty-minute speech on August 28.
      • Baker tours the U.S. in concert.
1964 • Brigitte Bardot launches television campaign to save Les Milandes and help the Rainbow Tribe on June 4.
1966 • The album *Joséphine Baker en la Habana* with Tony Taño and his orchestra is released in January by Egrem. This compilation contains eleven tunes performed in Baker's 1951 Havana concert.
      • The First World Festival of Black Arts, sponsored by the Société Africaine de Culture (SAC), takes place in Dakar, Sénégal from April 1–24. Baker attends, along with Langston Hughes, Katherine Dunham, and other African American artists. Baker asks Hughes to write her biography at this time.
1968 • Baker tours Europe and opens to a full house at the Olympia Theater in Paris on April 3. Press coverage is mixed.
      • Proceedings begin for the sale of Les Milandes. Creditors seize the property in May.
      • Baker marches on the Champs-Elysées in support of President de Gaulle.
1969 • Baker is evicted from Les Milandes and removed from the premises in January, followed by her hospitalization.
      • Baker moves to Paris and performs for six months at La Gouloue, renamed Chez Joséphine for the spring and summer.
      • Baker settles in Roquebrune-Cap-Martin with the support of Princess Grace of Monaco in August.
1973 • Baker performs at Carnegie Hall for four days starting on June 5 and at the Victoria Theater in Harlem.
      • Baker tours the United States, Scandinavia, and South Africa during the year.
1974 • Baker makes a fresh start with a new image in a retrospective performance entitled *Joséphine* at the Sporting Club of Monte Carlo.
1975 • Designer André Levasseur and actor and director Jean-Claude Brialy schedule *Joséphine* for the Théâtre Bobino in Paris. The show opens on April 8 to a full house.
      • Baker falls into a coma on April 10 and is pronounced dead on April 12.
      • Baker is given a state military funeral with a twenty-one-gun salute at La Madeleine in Paris on April 15.
      • Baker's body is transported to Monaco for a private ceremony. She is placed in a mausoleum for six months, then buried in the Monaco cemetery.
1976 • Jo Bouillon publishes the posthumous collaborative biography *Joséphine* with Opéra Mundi in Paris.
1981 • Lynn Haney publishes Baker's life story in *Naked at the Feast*. Popular interest in Baker is renewed.

• Grace Jones performs her *One-Man Show* in which director Jean-Paul Goude draws on Baker's primal images.

1984 • Joseph Jean Étienne Bouillon (Jo Bouillon) dies in Buenos Aires on July 9.

1986 • Documentary film *Chasing a Rainbow: The Josephine Baker Story*, produced by Mick Csáky and directed by Christopher Ralling, is released in London.

1987 • Documentary film *Olympia Story*, directed by François Reichenbach and containing Baker's performances at the Olympia Theater, is released in Paris.

1988 • Bryan Hammond and Patrick O'Connor publish the biographical compilation *Josephine* in London.

1989 • Phyllis Rose publishes *Jazz Cleopatra*, a biography of Baker for the multicultural era.
• Madonna performs in the video *Like a Prayer*, using a pastiche of Baker-style images.

1990 • A commemorative performance is organized with the Rainbow Tribe to honor Josephine Baker at the Folies-Bergère in December.

1991 • Brian Gibson's docudrama *The Josephine Baker Story* is released by Home Box Office and Anglia Television.

1993 • La Toya Jackson performs at the Moulin Rouge, reviving Baker imagery.
• Franco-Cameroonian author Calixthe Beyala announces plans to adopt twenty-four international orphans, following Baker's example.
• Jean-Claude Baker and Chris Chase publish the biography *Josephine: The Hungry Heart* and introduce new and controversial images of Baker.

1998 • Henry Louis Gates Jr. and Karen C. C. Dalton write an analytical introduction for a new edition of Paul Colin's lithographs from his 1927 portfolio *Le Tumulte noir* and resuscitate Baker's Jazz Age image for a new era.

1999 • Maïté Jardin and the Association Joséphine Baker, in France, release the sixty-minute video *Dans mon village* on Les Milandes and the Rainbow Tribe.

2000 • Inspired by Baker, Calixthe Beyala leads the Collectif Égalité march for equal representation in the French media in Paris on May 20.
• Two new Baker biographies appear: *La Véritable Joséphine*, by Emmanuel Bonini, published in Paris, and *The Josephine Baker Story*, by Ean Wood, published in London.

2001 • Place Joséphine Baker in the fourteenth arrondissement is commemorated on February 2 by the mayor of the commune. It becomes the third site dedicated to an African American expatriate in Paris.
• A traveling exhibit of Baker's art and artifacts is organized in New York and Paris and at the chapel of the Château des Milandes.

2004 • Galeries Lafayette presents Baker Style, an exhibit displaying Baker's press books and costumes, with the collaboration of Alber Elbaz of Lanvin, in October.

2006 • Brian B. Baker publishes *Joséphine Baker: Le Regard d'un fils*, recounting his life with Josephine and the Rainbow Tribe.

• Charles Onana publishes *Joséphine Baker contre Hitler*, describing Baker's work during World War II and the international surveillance of her political activities during the 1950s.

• Olivia Lahs-Gonzales publishes the art catalog *Josephine Baker: Image and Icon*, accompanying exhibits at the Sheldon Art Galleries in St. Louis and the National Portrait Gallery in Washington, D.C.

• Celebration of the one hundredth anniversary of Josephine Baker's birth with events held at the Château des Milandes and in Paris, St. Louis, and New York.

Notes

Prologue

1. Sharpley-Whiting (*Black Venus*, 91–94) contrasts Fatou-gaye, the primal African woman, and Cora, the sophisticated mulatto, portrayed as female protagonists in Pierre Loti's *Le Roman d'un spahi*. Fatou's unbridled sensuality was a stereotype when Baker first performed her danse sauvage.

2. Genette (*Narrative Discourse,* 173) describes the hierarchical structure of entangled, or nested, narratives.

3. Haney, *Naked at the Feast,* 156.

4. Barshak, "Modern 'Primitive' Images"; Nenno, "Masquerade"; Peterson, "Bizarre Charm"; T. Francis, "Under a Paris Moon."

5. Fanon, *Black Skin, White Masks,* 109–12.

6. Geertz, *Interpretation of Cultures,* 26–28.

7. P. Rose, *Jazz Cleopatra,* xii; Baker and Chase, *Josephine,* 470–71.

8. Mannheim, *Essays,* 54–58.

Chapter 1: Touring with Baker's Image

1. This diorama is reproduced in an undated brochure entitled "Château des Milandes: Ancienne demeure de Joséphine Baker" (p. 14). The brochure contains photographs from the H. Roger-Viollet collection and the Studio Harcourt, along with selected photographs of the wax exhibit at the château.

2. P. Rose, *Jazz Cleopatra,* 266.

3. Lemarchand and Lopez, "Dans mon village."

4. Turner and Turner, *Image and Pilgrimage,* 38. Victor and Edith Turner point out that pilgrimages have assumed a new allure with the advent of tourism: "In the scientific and technological age, pilgrimage is becoming what Geertz has described as a 'metasocial commentary' on the troubles of this epoch of wars and revolutions with its increasing signs of industrial damage to the natural environment" (ibid.). The return to nature is also a theme that emerges in the primal images of Baker and the master narratives of touring her life.

5. MacCannell, *The Tourist,* 123. Note that MacCannell uses the term "sight" (as in "sightseeing") to demarcate the combination of the physical site with its symbolic meaning. I will refer to touristic "sights" in the same manner.

6. Gombrich, *Art and Illusion,* 356–58.

7. MacCannell, *The Tourist,* 192.

8. Hansen, *Expatriate Paris,* 260.

9. Jonas, "Sacred Tourism," 102.

10. Fiennes, *Time Out Paris Guide,* 186; Hansen, *Expatriate Paris,* 260.

11. Vanessa Schwartz (*Spectacular Realities,* 89–148 and 195–96) provides a comprehensive history of the Musée Grévin and situates it in the context of late nineteenth-century Parisian popular culture. She explains that the Grévin's light shows were forerunners of popular cinema and movie newsreels. The inclusion of peep-hole boxes increased the perspectives from which spectators could view the scenes and the verisimilitude of each diorama.

12. Schwartz, "Museums and Mass Spectacle," 13–15.

13. Kirshenblatt-Gimblett, *Destination Culture,* 34–40.

14. Howard, *Writers and Pilgrims,* 14.

15. Turner and Turner, *Image and Pilgrimage,* 197.

16. "La Foire à la brocante."

17. Marianne Hirsch (*Family Frames,* 106–8) argues that the interpretation of photographic images, including family photos and postcards, shifts with an ever-widening circle of social relations and the narrative frameworks that are part of each collectivity.

18. Kirshenblatt-Gimblett, *Destination Culture,* 53–54.

19. A postcard with the design conceived by J.-L. Chedal, labeled "Joséphine Baker (Scène Musée Grévin)," appears both as a card and a reproduction in a flyer advertising the château. The wax figure stares at a nonexistent audience while a young boy photographs it. This double-mirrored image reflexively references its own touristic construction.

20. See also Barshak, "Modern 'Primitive' Images," 38–39. Barshak analyzes the cropped photo and dates it from 1926, which contradicts the photographic information from the H. Roger-Viollet collection, which dates the photo as 1930 (Barshak, "Modern 'Primitive' Images," 69), and the fact that the photograph was taken backstage at the Casino de Paris in October 1930.

21. Hammond and O'Connor, *Josephine Baker,* 113; P. Rose, *Jazz Cleopatra,* 114; Barshak, "Modern 'Primitive' Images," 64.

22. Hammond and O'Connor, *Josephine Baker,* 75.

23. Haney, *Naked at the Feast,* 86.

24. Barshak, "Modern 'Primitive' Images," 25.

25. Camard, *Joséphine Baker et Paul Colin,* plates 75–94. Lucien Bertaux's sketches of Josephine Baker's fashions are reproduced in this catalog.

26. Bonnal, *Josephine Baker et le village,* 151–54.

27. Baker and Bouillon, *Josephine,* 206–7.

28. Ibid., 206.

29. This photograph reflects the image that many contemporary French fans still hold of Josephine. It combines her maternal and glamorous sides. The full-color version of Baker's costume in this photo appears in the 1987 film *Olympia Story*, directed by François Reichenbach. The film also shows the rainbow tailfeathers on the costume.

30. P. Rose, *Jazz Cleopatra*, 242.

31. Cultural productions combine a spectacle or a sight with a larger narrative that has popular appeal (MacCannell, *The Tourist*, 29–33). Baker treated her edifices as cultural productions and mnemonic relics that externalized the narratives of her life and exemplified her philosophies. See also Gabriel, "Ruin and the Other," on cultural ruins.

32. Baker's biographers include extensive discussions of her homes, although they do not treat them as tourist sights. See Haney, *Naked at the Feast;* Hammond and O'Connor, *Josephine Baker;* and P. Rose, *Jazz Cleopatra.*

33. Haney, *Naked at the Feast,* 172.

34. Ibid., 171.

35. De la Camara and Abatino (*Mon sang,* 14) describe Barclay's estate as "Oaks," using the English word. The fictional estate is located forty-five minutes west of Boston, just as Le Vésinet is forty-five minutes west of Paris.

36. De la Camara and Abatino, *Mon sang,* 23.

37. This translation from *Mon sang dans tes veines* is my own, as are the others in this chapter. No published English translation of the novella currently exists.

38. De la Camara and Abatino, *Mon sang,* 144.

39. Ibid., 171–72.

40. Ibid., 175.

41. P. Rose, *Jazz Cleopatra*, 135.

42. Haney (*Naked at the Feast,* 271–72) lists 500,000 visitors per summer at Les Milandes between 1954 and 1959; Bonnal (*Josephine Baker et le village,* 49) cites 140,000 visitors for 1950. If both authors are correct, the number of visitors substantially increased from the early 1950s to the middle of that decade.

43. Farcaros and Pauls, *Dordogne,* 181.

44. Ibid.

45. Baker and Bouillon, *Josephine,* 204.

46. Colomina, "Split Wall," 88.

47. Schwartz, *Spectacular Realities,* 179–81.

48. Papich, *Remembering Josephine,* 146.

49. A touristic simulation unites the expectations and stereotypes of visitors about a particular touristic landmark (Baudrillard, *Simulacres,* 24–28; Jules-Rosette, "Black Paris: Touristic Simulations," 680–82). Baker used Les Milandes in multiple ways as a touristic simulation of her images and life narrative. The refurbished château

reconstructs one version of this narrative for a new audience. Note that I refer to "the château" primarily when the building is discussed and to "Les Milandes" generically to describe the property. A summary of the new changes at the Château des Milandes appears in de Labarre, *Le Château des Milandes,* 21–31.

50. MacCannell, *Tourist,* xxi.

51. Baudrillard, *Simulacres,* 43–47.

52. Biographies provide a useful and comprehensive vision of life narratives, but biographies are also cultural productions, constructed and edited within the framework of their social circumstances. Hoskins, *Biographical Objects,* 4–7.

53. Vogel, *Art/Artifact,* 12.

54. Goffman, *Frame Analysis,* 226.

55. Ibid.

56. Propp, *Morphology of the Folktale,* 26–46.

57. Greimas, *Sémantique structurale,* 228, and Greimas, *Du Sens,* 172–76.

58. Propp, *Morphology of the Folktale,* 37.

59. Genette, *Narrative Discourse,* 127.

60. Ibid.

61. In his discussion of the semiotics of tourism, Jean-Didier Urbain ("Tourist Adventure," 112–14) describes the "going-away program" as a critical feature of the touristic narrative. The structure of the "escapade" in travel transforms the touristic subject in ways similar to the transformation of the departing hero in Propp's description of the narrative structure of Russian folktales (Propp, *Morphology,* 36–38).

Chapter 2: Opening Nights

1. Baker and Bouillon, *Josephine,* 51–52.

2. Portions of the present discussion were first published in my article entitled "Two Loves: Josephine Baker as Icon and Image" and have been reprinted with the permission of the *Emergences* journal and the Carfax Publishing Group.

3. Kirshenblatt-Gimblett, *Destination Culture,* 74–78.

4. Following Lacan and Derrida, Homi Bhabha (*Location of Culture,* 52–57) uses doubling as a lens for viewing the ways in which marginalized individuals and groups interact with the cultural mappings of a dominant society.

5. Bhabha, *Location of Culture,* 49–50.

6. In his literary criticism of the works of the Cameroonian poet Paul Dakeyo, Yves Dakou ("La Quête identitaire," 41–42) develops a theory of virtual identity discourses based on the poet's affirmations of belonging to France as well as Africa and his wish for a more egalitarian society.

7. See, for example, Sauvage, *Les Mémoires* (1927); Sauvage, *Voyages et aventures;* Baker and Bouillon, *Josephine.*

8. See Kühn, *Josephine;* Papich, *Remembering Josephine;* Haney, *Naked at the Feast;*

Hammond and O'Connor, *Josephine Baker;* P. Rose, *Jazz Cleopatra;* Baker and Chase, *Josephine;* and Bonini, *La Véritable Josephine;* B. Baker, with Trichard, *Joséphine Baker: Le Regard;* and Onana, *Joséphine Baker contre Hitler.*

9. Greimas (*Structural Semantics,* 241) discusses the redundancy of text, discourse, and narrative.

10. Genette, *Narrative Discourse,* 248–50.

11. Lipsitz, *Sidewalks,* 75.

12. Ibid.

13. Baker and Bouillon, *Josephine,* 2.

14. Haney, *Naked at the Feast,* 213.

15. Hammond and O'Connor, *Josephine Baker,* 7.

16. Baker and Bouillon, *Josephine,* 27.

17. Caroline Dudley Regan, referred to as Caroline Dudley in some accounts (P. Rose, *Jazz Cleopatra,* 3–4), was a socialite who frequented Harlem's jazz clubs and theaters. She hired La Revue nègre at a time when American jazz performers of all kinds were very popular in Europe (Tournès, *New Orleans,* 26–29).

18. Martin, "Du jazz band," 2; Moret, "Images de Paris," 97. There is some debate about how the cakewalk first entered France, but Williams and Walker definitely played an important role in popularizing it.

19. Bricktop, with Haskins, *Bricktop,* 85–90.

20. Baker and Bouillon, *Josephine,* 51.

21. Ibid., 51–52.

22. P. Rose, *Jazz Cleopatra,* 108–10.

23. Stovall, *Paris Noir,* 92.

24. Ibid. See also Baker and Bouillon, *Josephine,* 68–69.

25. Haney, *Naked at the Feast,* 78; Tournès, *New Orleans,* 26.

26. P. Rose, *Jazz Cleopatra,* 147. According to Hammond and O'Connor (*Josephine Baker,* 89), Baker began to improvise new words for this song as early as its original performance in 1930.

27. Goffman, *Presentation of Self,* 65.

28. Haney, *Naked at the Feast,* 159; Hammond and O'Connor, *Josephine Baker,* 91; Borshuk, "'Queen of the Colonial Exposition,'" 59.

29. See Hammond and O'Connor, *Josephine Baker,* 91, for an excerpt of the lyrics from "Si j'étais blanche!" taken from the 1932 Columbia recording of *La Joie de Paris.*

30. Hammond and O'Connor, *Josephine Baker,* 91.

31. De Pawlowski, "*Paris qui remue,*" 5–6.

32. Fanon, *Black Skin, White Masks,* 109. Fanon describes the overwhelming power of stereotypes in the construction of identity. In Josephine's case, a choice of sorts was made by doubling racial stereotypes in order to create her performative image.

33. Benstock, *Women of the Left Bank*, 59.

34. Baker and Chase, *Josephine*, 248.

35. Baker played upon a wide range of contrasting identities from the clown to the nubile siren. Both her theatrical personas and her music embodied these contrasts. Although Baker invoked mutable and multiple sexual identities, her work recalls the feminist critic Trinh Minh-ha's remark that "[i]n any case, 'woman' here is not interchangeable with 'man.'" Minh-ha, *Woman, Native, Other*, 104.

36. Baker and Bouillon, *Josephine*, 224.

37. Abtey, *La Guerre secrète*, 18–22.

38. Hammond and O'Connor, *Josephine Baker*, 150–51.

39. Haney, *Naked at the Feast*, 263.

Chapter 3: Celluloid Projections

1. The press coverage of the making of *Sirène des tropiques* enthusiastically chronicled the audience participation in the filming of Josephine Baker's first feature (Jorgefélice, "*La Sirène*"). The film had an international audience across Europe and launched Baker's cinematic career.

2. This description of the crowd scene from *La Sirène des tropiques* is contained in Huet, "Josephine."

3. Abel, *French Cinema*, 216.

4. Sauvage, *Voyages et aventures*, 135–36.

5. Louis Lumière's invention was publicly inaugurated in 1895 with a short film of workers leaving his factory in Paris. Within the next decade, film began to change both reporting and entertainment. Barnouw, *Documentary*, 6–8.

6. The balloon trip around the world, or Maréorama, lasted over one hour and simulated a sense of movement for viewers, who "traveled" from Paris to Istanbul. Schwartz, *Spectacular Realities*, 171.

7. Bloom, "Networks of Empire," 28–29.

8. Abel, *Ciné Goes to Town*, 7–8. Cinema's popularity in Paris soon necessitated the construction of large movie palaces. Between 1911 and 1914, both a collaboration of and a competition between cinema and the music hall emerged.

9. Most press reviews were positive. See the 1927 clippings in file Rf 56254, Bibliothèque de l'Arsenal, Paris.

10. Cripps, *Black Film as Genre*, 38.

11. Phyllis Rose (*Jazz Cleopatra*, 120) describes Pierre Batcheff as a dashing leading man and compares him with the 1930s film star Leslie Howard.

12. P. Rose, *Jazz Cleopatra*, 119–20; Baker and Chase, *Josephine*, 150.

13. Haney, *Naked at the Feast*, 192.

14. George, "Joséphine Baker revient à l'écran."

15. "Joséphine-Zouzou."

16. *Zouzou* eventually became a cult classic outside of France. The film demanded of Baker her most complex range of performances. See P. Rose, *Jazz Cleopatra,* 162–63.

17. This opening spiel sets the tone for the film *Zouzou.* Unless otherwise indicated, all English translations quoted in this text from Baker's film scripts are my own and are not drawn from the English subtitles by Helen Eisenman. Note that dialogue changes and updates were made in the 2005 release of *Princesse Tam-Tam.* Some of these changes bring the subtitles more in line with my translations.

18. Ezra, *Colonial Unconscious,* 112. Later, before her starring appearance, Zouzou dabs white powder on her legs, recalling her youth when she experimented with white powder in the circus.

19. Ibid., 101.

20. Ibid., 110.

21. Baker and Bouillon, *Josephine,* 94.

22. P. Rose, *Jazz Cleopatra,* 162.

23. Classic Hollywood musicals use song-and-dance interludes to advance the main plot or provide comic relief (Kaplan, *Rocking around the Clock,* 125). In contrast, Baker's films employ these interludes as a source of character development and a strategy for injecting moral commentary and reflection into the film.

24. Ezra, *Colonial Unconscious,* 107–8.

25. The translations of songs from Baker's films provided here are my own. Helen Eisenman's subtitles for *Zouzou* and *Princesse Tam-Tam* provide alternative song lyric summaries.

26. George, "Joséphine Baker revient à l'écran."

27. In this film, the narrator, Oliver Todd, criticizes the editing and pacing of *Princesse Tam-Tam* as an "overly commercial" imitation of Hollywood musicals. (Subsequent quotations from Todd in this chapter are from this film.) The musical sequences using special effects and rhythmic cross-cutting might, however, be viewed as the strongest and most innovative features of this film, placing it technologically ahead of its time.

28. This tapestry of images is based on an "entangled narrative" (Genette, *Narrative Discourse,* 137) in which Max de Mirecourt and Aouina's fantasies intersect and function as counterpoints in an elaborate dream sequence.

29. Sharpley-Whiting (*Black Venus,* 112) refers to the literal definition of *nègre* as a slave in describing Coton when she states that "he slaves away to help de Mirecourt's like a nègre plowing cotton/*coton* on a southern plantation for his master." She neglects to mention, however, the translation of *nègre* as "ghostwriter" and the implications of Coton's coauthorship of the narrative and the fantasy.

30. Kalinak, "Disciplining Josephine Baker," 328–29.

31. P. Rose, *Jazz Cleopatra,* 164.

32. Ezra (*Colonial Unconscious*, 116–18) also makes this argument.

33. Hammond and O'Connor, *Josephine Baker*, 102.

34. Sharpley-Whiting, *Black Venus*, 113.

35. Aouina's complaints about apartment life reflect the growing social and literary attention to the apartment as a unique environment in late nineteenth- and early twentieth-century France (Marcus, *Apartment Stories*, 32–34). The confining space of the apartment contrasted with the open boulevards of Paris and in Aouina's case, with the freedom offered by the natural environment of North Africa.

36. Baker and Bouillon, *Josephine*, 100–101.

37. Silverman (*Threshold*, 33) argues that the "exceptional woman" dazzles others with her beauty yet transcends sexuality and desire. In *Chasing a Rainbow*, even erotic images of Baker are displayed to demonstrate how she transcended eroticism to achieve fame.

38. This dual tracking of music and narration creates a sense of documentary authenticity while simultaneously building up Baker's role as an icon. The method of dual tracking is a powerful tool in documentary filmmaking. Jules-Rosette, McVey, and Arbitrario, "Performance Ethnography," 123–47.

39. Genette, *Figures of Literary Discourse*, 234.

40. *Dans mon village* (1999), a sixty-minute video documentary by Maïté Jardin, president of the Association Joséphine Baker, contains lengthy interviews with Akio, Jean-Claude, and Brahim (Brian), members of the Rainbow Tribe, as they revisit Les Milandes in the late 1990s. These interviews provide a well-rounded view of the idealism of Baker and Bouillon's experiment and offer a contrasting filmic framework for examining Baker's later years.

41. The song "Dans mon village" was composed by Henri Lemarchand and Francis Lopez in 1953. Baker often performed this song to new audiences with additional improvised verses to raise funds for the Rainbow Tribe.

42. By creating a maternal discourse and subjectivity, the film lures spectators to accept the reality of what they see and hear in the role of eavesdropping children.

43. The film collapses into a single tour several trips that Baker made between 1926 and 1929. P. Rose, *Jazz Cleopatra*, 138–40.

44. Josephine Baker actually initiated divorce proceedings against Jo Bouillon in Sarlat on July 5, 1957 (Bonnal, *Joséphine Baker et le village*, 135). The couple never officially finalized the divorce. See chapter 6 for a more detailed discussion of Baker and Bouillon.

45. The film script paraphrases Jean-Claude Baker's quote as a line for Bouillon, thereby preserving the authenticity of a genuine personal reaction to her.

46. Brian Gibson's 1991 HBO docudrama deals selectively with Baker's music-hall performances and omits a portrayal of her successful film career. Charles Whitaker,

a journalist for *Ebony* magazine, argues that the HBO docudrama does not do justice to Baker's early years as a performer in black vaudeville and the French music hall. Whitaker, "Real-Life Josephine Baker," 25–30.

47. Through time lapses, proleptic gaps (Genette, *Narrative Discourse,* 52), and partial contextualization, the documentaries omit the relationship between Baker's political agendas in France and her return to the United States in 1957 and 1963.

48. While filming *Zouzou,* Baker asked: "Why can't the story end differently?" (Baker and Bouillon, *Josephine,* 94). She wanted Zouzou to marry Jean, an ending that would have been taboo in the French culture and cinema of the day. The actual ending mirrored that of *Sirène des tropiques,* which was made seven years earlier.

Chapter 4: Dress Rehearsals

1. Des Cars and Pinon, *Paris-Haussmann,* 15–18.

2. Benjamin, "Paris, Capital of the Nineteenth Century," 150; Wolff, "Invisible *Flâneuse,*" 46.

3. Djikstra, *Evil Sisters,* 158–60; Sharpley-Whiting, *Black Venus,* 12–15.

4. Strother, "Display of the Body Hottentot," 32–33.

5. Lindfors, *Africans on Stage,* vii–ix.

6. Said, *Orientalism,* 180–90.

7. Ibid., 170–80. Baker's exotic stage persona was an extension of Orientalist discourses already well entrenched in France. These discourses also shaped colonial models of the savage, primitive, and primal African subject. Baker's image melded these two approaches with the eroticism of the music hall. See also Borshuk, "Intelligence of the Body," 46–48.

8. Colin's posters for *La Revue nègre* transformed his life and launched his Parisian artistic career. Gates and Dalton, *Josephine Baker and La Revue Nègre,* 8–10.

9. *Jazz Baby,* by Miguel Covarrubias, is also reprinted and discussed in Gates and Dalton's introduction to *Joséphine Baker and La Revue Nègre,* 6.

10. Gates and Dalton, *Josephine Baker and La Revue Nègre,* 10. Several of Colin's lithographs were also used to illustrate the controversial *Les Mémoires de Joséphine Baker* (1927) compiled by Marcel Sauvage.

11. Haney, *Naked at the Feast,* 105.

12. Gates and Dalton, *Josephine Baker and La Revue Nègre,* 10.

13. Baker and Bouillon, *Josephine,* 50.

14. Clifford, *Predicament of Culture,* 198.

15. Hammond and O'Connor, *Josephine Baker,* 119.

16. For a detailed discussion of Baker's performances and nightclub experiment, see Lyon, "Josephine Baker's Hothouse," 29–47. See also Shack, *Harlem in Montmartre,* 37–38, and Stovall, "Freedom, Community, and the Paris Jazz Age."

17. Fry, *Cubism*, 13. Through its experiments in space, shape, contour, and perspective, cubism allowed "the complete freedom to re-order the human image" (ibid.). A similar image reconstruction was also part of Baker's performance persona.

18. As with Orientalism, this Dionysian aspect of expression has strong roots in French philosophy's reactions against the tradition of enlightenment reason. Maffesoli, *L'Ombre de Dionysos*, 181–87.

19. Clifford, *Predicament of Culture*, 126; Price, *Primitive Art*, 39.

20. Schlumberger, "Georges-Henri Rivière," 101.

21. For the photograph of Josephine Baker and Alfonso Teofilo Brown at the improvised exhibition boxing match, see file #4° ICO-PER 1326, 1931, Bibliothèque de l'Arsenal, Paris. The anthropologist Jean Jamin also discusses Josephine Baker and Brown in Jamin, "Objets trouvés," 77–78.

22. As a young man, Rivière enjoyed nocturnal visits to the music halls and cabarets of Paris. Starting at the club Boeuf Sur le Toit on the Champs-Elysées, he would move to Moïse, the Grand Écart, and the Enfants Terribles. Rivière explained, "We followed the exterior boulevards to the rotunda of La Villette," moving from the sixteenth to the eighteenth and then the twentieth arrondissement (Schlumberger, "Georges-Henri Rivière," 19). He used ideas drawn from the rhythms and ambiance of the music hall to revitalize the concept of the public museum.

23. Diop, "L'Artiste n'est pas seul," 6–7.

24. Frédéric Grah Mel (*Alioune Diop*, 170–72) describes Baker's inclusion in the planning and patronage committees of the Société Africaine de Culture (SAC), organized by Alioune Diop and chaired by Jean Price-Mars.

25. See the discussion in Barthes, *Fashion System*, 252–53; Davis, *Fashion, Culture, and Identity*, 27.

26. Sauvage, *Les Mémoires* (1927), 84.

27. Hammond and O'Connor, *Josephine Baker*, 20; Baker and Chase, *Josephine*, 120.

28. Baker and Bouillon, *Josephine*, 52.

29. Vreeland, *Inventive Paris Clothes*, 14.

30. Zdatny, *Hairstyles and Fashion*, 25. The history of French hairstyles shows that it is not likely that Baker's flapper hairstyle was a forerunner of the "conk," as claimed by Borshuk in "'Queen of the Colonial Exposition,'" 60. Instead, it was a look that Baker promoted as her version of the flapper style. The hair stylist Jean Clement later developed several innovations on the flapper look for Baker as part of the publicity for one of her Bakerfix campaigns.

31. Battersby, *Art Deco Fashion*, 7.

32. "Danseuse et couturier."

33. Lynam, *Paris Fashion*, 65.

34. Steele, *Paris Fashion*, 220.

35. Howell, *In Vogue*, 51.

36. Ibid.

37. Hammond and O'Connor (*Josephine Baker*, 79) list the contents of Baker's luggage upon her departure for Vienna in 1928. Nenno ("Masquerade," 124–25) describes the images created by her apparel when she arrived in Germany during the same year.

38. Houze, "Fashionable Reform," 29–31.

39. Ibid., 35–36.

40. Colomina, "Split Wall," 93–94.

41. Hines, "Historic Architecture," 108.

42. Groenendijk and Vollaard, *Adolf Loos*, 30–36.

43. With costumes designed by Paul Colin, *Paris qui remue* expanded the repertoire of roles in which Baker appeared. Phyllis Rose (*Jazz Cleopatra*, 143) has translated the revue's title as "Swinging Paris," but it could also be translated as "Tumultuous Paris." In her translation of Josephine's autobiography, Mariana Fitzpatrick entitles the revue "Bustling Paris" (Baker and Bouillon, *Josephine*, 83). The show also included a Baker clone, Lulu Gould, whose hair, makeup, and appearance imitated those of Baker and indicated the popularity and pervasiveness of the Baker image among French women. *Paris qui remue* was so popular that a similar show, *Paris qui brille* (Glittering Paris), was organized for Mistinguett.

44. "*Paris qui remue*," *Ami du Peuple*.

45. De Pawlowski, "*Paris qui remue*," 5–6.

46. An extensive collection of 234 sketches of Josephine Baker's gowns and costumes was assembled by Jean-Pierre Camard (*Josephine Baker et Paul Colin*). This collection contains sketches by Paul Colin, Hugo Lederer, Jacques Armand-Prevost, and Lucien Bertaux, among others. The sketches range in subject from Josephine's exotic primal image to the fashions of the 1950s.

47. Haney, *Naked at the Feast*, 102–3; P. Rose, *Jazz Cleopatra*, 100; Barshak, "Modern 'Primitive' Images," 36.

48. Haney (*Naked at the Feast*, 102) discusses the sign at Place de l'Opéra; Kühn (*Josephine*, 36) depicts the doll.

49. Baker describes a cruise to South America with Le Corbusier where he appeared in blackface wearing a Baker costume and she dressed as a whiteface clown for the equatorial crossing (Baker and Bouillon, *Josephine*, 81). For a detailed description of the costume party, see also Wood, *Josephine Baker Story*, 198–99.

50. Demay, "Joséphine apprend à voler." See also a photograph of Josephine Baker receiving her pilot's lesson from M. Demay, 1933, file #4° ICO-PER 1326, Bibliothèque de l'Arsenal, Paris. Lahs-Gonzales also reproduces a photograph from this series in

her discussion of Baker as the "new woman," including her flying, golfing, and hunting forays. See Lahs-Gonzales, "Josephine Baker: Modern Woman," 31–51, for that discussion; the photo is on page 32.

51. Hines, "Historic Architecture," 107–8.

52. Hines (ibid., 110) describes Adolf Loos's flamboyant private life and the passion for cabaret culture that attracted him to Baker.

53. Groenendijk and Vollaard, *Adolf Loos*, 30. Paul Groenendijk and Piet Vollaard reproduced and photographed a miniature model based on an axonometric reconstruction of Adolf Loos's plan for Baker's house, depicted in figure 4–7.

54. Ibid., 35.

55. Colomina, "Split Wall," 88–92; Peterson, "Bizarre Charm," 83–86. Colomina (83) argues that Loos's rooms in the Baker house resemble theater loges around the pool and encourage the voyeurism of spectators by using Baker as a theatrical object.

56. Bhabha, *Location of Culture*, 70–75. Although it is important to recognize the crucial role of colonial discourse and popular fantasies in shaping Baker's early image as a dominated and desired object, it is also crucial to acknowledge Baker's own agency and her skill in manipulating contrasting images at various stages of her career.

57. Ibid., 70.

58. Ibid., 72.

59. Fanon, *Black Skin, White Masks*, 126.

Chapter 5: Baker's Scripts

1. Goffman, *Presentation of Self*, 562.

2. Mbembe ("African Modes of Self-Writing," 239) defines self-writing in the context of African national and cultural ideologies. Thomas Turino (*Nationalists, Cosmopolitans, and Popular Music in Zimbabwe*, 48) develops a typology of ideal types of music making that includes live performance, music lyrics, and recordings as styles of self-writing.

3. From 1927 until the end of her life, Baker was constantly engaged in producing autobiographies and collaborative biographies. She signed several contracts with publishers, some of which were not fulfilled. These projects included an unpublished biography with Gerold Frank. Wood, *Josephine Baker Story*, 362.

4. Sauvage, *Les Mémoires* (1927), 32.

5. Guillaume Apollinaire's *Les Peintres cubistes: Méditations esthétiques* (1913) contains critical biographical essays on cubist painters. Apollinaire coined the term "cubism" and described the styles and themes linking the works of the painters. His book served as both a marketing device and a model for criticism. The works of Marcel Sauvage and André Rivollet are continuations of this genre of biographical criticism. All translations of Sauvage and Rivollet appearing in the text are my own.

6. Sauvage, *Les Mémoires* (1927), 34.

7. Ibid., 44–47.

8. P. Rose, *Jazz Cleopatra*, 10.

9. Baker and Chase, *Josephine*, 16–17.

10. Ibid., 17.

11. Sauvage, *Les Mémoires* (1927), 47.

12. Ibid. Baker's statement that her father was Spanish also casts doubt on Eddie Carson's paternity.

13. Ibid., 56. Note that both Sauvage and Rivollet provide phonetic renditions of the name of the theater based on Josephine Baker's account. Sauvage (*Les Mémoires* [1927], 56) refers to "Bascher" Washington Theater, and Rivollet (*Une vie de toutes les couleurs,* 69) calls it "Bocker" Washington Theater. Neither author appears to know who Booker T. Washington was.

14. Ibid., 65–66.

15. Ibid., 91. Note also that in Brian Gibson's 1991 HBO film, Pepito Abatino (played by Rubén Blades) paraphrases this remark, warning Josephine that "dancers don't last."

16. Ibid., 91–92.

17. Ibid., 16.

18. Sauvage (*Voyages et aventures,* 61–71) describes some of the opposition that Josephine encountered on her 1928–29 world tour, but he keeps the tone light and intersperses travelogue descriptions with allusions to the public protests against Baker in Eastern Europe and South America.

19. Sauvage, "Joséphine Baker, cuisinière." On September 26, 1927, the newspaper *Candide* published Josephine's recipes from *Les Mémoires,* presumably as a publicity move. The recipes included dishes served at her nightclub, Chez Joséphine. Sauvage, and later Pepito Abatino, made sure that every activity in which Josephine was involved was covered by the press.

20. Sauvage, *Les Mémoires* (1927), 149–50.

21. Ibid., 81–82. Sauvage's 1927 biography was widely covered by the Parisian press. The newspapers also covered Josephine's disagreements with Sauvage and the legal threat arising from the comment on disabled war veterans (Lazareff, "Pourquoi Joséphine Baker veut intenter un procès à Marcel Sauvage"). Baker claimed that Sauvage misrepresented her comments. The coverage of Baker's disagreement with Sauvage might be compared to contemporary articles on celebrities in the tabloid press.

22. Sauvage, *Les Mémoires* (1927), 97.

23. Lazareff, "Pourquoi Joséphine Baker veut intenter un procès à Marcel Sauvage."

24. Sauvage, *Voyages et aventures,* 63.

25. Ibid., 66–67.

26. P. Rose, *Jazz Cleopatra*, 129.

27. "Un artiste se suicide."

28. Sauvage, *Voyages et aventures*, 71; Haney, *Naked at the Feast*, 149.

29. Sauvage, *Voyages et aventures*, 35–36.

30. Ibid., 95.

31. Baker's letter of apology to the public in Berlin was written in simple German, apparently by her, and was published in a local newspaper. Nenno, "Masquerade," 165. See also Onana, *Joséphine Baker contre Hitler*, 18–19, for a detailed account of the impact of the Munich incident on Baker's performances in Germany.

32. Sauvage, *Voyages et aventures*, 141.

33. Rivollet, "Du jazz hot à 'La Créole,'" 71.

34. Baker, "Preface" in de la Camara and Abatino, *Mon sang*, 5–6 (translation mine). Baker signed the preface "Josephine Baker" without the *accent aigü* in 1931.

35. De la Camara and Abatino, *Mon sang*, 178.

36. The fear of racial mixing in late-1920s Europe was evoked by the "négritude" of Baker's primal performances. Martin and Roueff, *La France du jazz*, 120–21.

37. Sauvage, *Voyages et aventures*, 67.

38. Baker literally bleeds as she learns to incorporate classical ballet into her routines. This sacrifice becomes an integral part of her new persona.

39. *La Tribu arc-en-ciel*, now a rare book, was illustrated in color by Piet Worm and published in a limited edition by Opéra Mundi in Paris in 1957. There is currently no official English translation of this unique children's book.

40. Bonini, *La Véritable Joséphine*, 222.

41. Baker, with Bouillon, *La Tribu*, 30.

42. *La Tribu* has an artisanal quality. There are several misspellings and inconsistencies. For example, Jary's name is spelled that way (page 34) and as "Jari" (pages 37–40). Elsewhere it is also spelled "Jarry." Similar alternate name spellings occur in other descriptions of the Rainbow children by Baker and Bouillon.

43. Baker with Bouillon, *La Tribu*, 46. The punctuation in *La Tribu* is unconventional and includes frequent use of ellipses and exclamation points.

44. Baker and Chase, *Josephine*, 26.

45. Wood, *Josephine Baker Story*, 21.

46. Jo Bouillon's posthumous biography of Baker, first published in French in 1976, contains especially informative materials on the final move to Les Milandes and the founding of the Rainbow Tribe. See Baker and Bouillon, *Josephine*, 192–225. It is based on Josephine's notes and letters. See also "Joséphine Baker se raconte."

47. Baker and Bouillon, *Josephine*, xiii.

48. Ibid., 102.

49. Ibid., 224.

50. Ibid., 221.

51. Hammond and O'Connor (*Josephine Baker,* 287–94) present a comprehensive discography of Baker's works from 1926 through 1975, complete with reproductions of album covers. Bonini (*La Véritable Joséphine,* 349–59) also develops a thorough discography based on independent research and cross-referenced with Hammond's discography. Both sources are excellent compilations.

52. Bonini (*La Véritable Joséphine,* 349–50) dates the first Odéon releases as September 20 and October 5, 1926. Hammond and O'Connor (*Josephine Baker,* 287–88) date these releases as December, 1926. There may have been more than one series released in late 1926.

53. Flanner, *Paris Was Yesterday,* 72–73.

54. Hammond and O'Connor, *Josephine Baker,* 292.

55. Stearns and Stearns, *Jazz Dance,* 146.

56. Williams, *Underneath a Harlem Moon,* 82; see also Gendron, *Between Montmartre,* 115–16.

57. The silent film *La Revue des revues,* based on *La Folie du jour* at the Folies-Bergère, is the earliest surviving film of Josephine Baker's banana dance (Bonini, *La Véritable Joséphine,* 359). This color-tinted black-and-white film, produced by Joé Francis and Alex Nalpas, is now in fragile condition. *Le Pompier des Folies-Bergère* is held in file #FRBNF38939399(11), Bibliothèque Nationale, Paris. It was digitally remastered by Kino International in 2005.

58. Sauvage, *Voyages et aventures,* 59.

59. Derval, *Folies Bergère,* 76–82.

60. Gates and Dalton (*Josephine Baker and La Revue Nègre,* 4) point out that the "cakewalk craze" lasted over a decade and was still popular when Baker began dancing in Paris. Originally a plantation harvest dance, the cakewalk involved a quadrille with strutting imitations of well-to-do plantation masters (Lhamon, *Raising Cain,* 140). Both the cakewalk and the Charleston rapidly spread to large populations, completing a cycle of imitation and assimilation.

61. Martin and Roueff, *La France du jazz,* 32–33.

62. Hammond and O'Connor, *Josephine,* 95. See also J. Jackson, *Making Jazz French,* 114–16.

63. Achille Mbembe ("African Modes," 254–56) describes the dominant narratives of African self-writing as political philosophies and ideologies. Self-writing also consists of actual literary sources deployed as personal biographical and collective identity discourses and narratives.

64. Frantz Fanon (*Wretched of the Earth,* 112) points out the ironies of perceiving oneself in terms of a dominant image and ego-ideal that is not shared. One way out of this dilemma is the transcendence of racial identity through self-sacrifice, which is the hallmark of Baker's Marian motif.

65. In spite of shifting images, the themes and structure of Baker's life narratives

remain consistent. Greimas and Courtés, *Sémiotique*, 242–44; Genette, *Narrative Discourse*, 114.

66. See, for example, Barshak, "Modern 'Primitive' Images"; Nenno, "Masquerade."

Chapter 6: Hues of the Rainbow in a Global Village

1. During the 1960s, as Baker made one comeback after another to save Les Milandes, journalists followed every move and took sides about the value of the undertaking. Bruce Dunning's article "Josephine Baker Makes a Comeback with a Purpose," along with articles in *Le Figaro* and *L'Aurore,* speculated about the role that Bruno Coquatrix might play in helping to save the château and Baker's dream.

2. Maffesoli, *Le Temps de tribus*, 53–54.

3. Fabre, *From Harlem to Paris*, 50–54.

4. Mannheim, *Ideology and Utopia*, 212.

5. Papich, *Remembering Josephine*, 149. In an extended conversation on August 2, 2005, Papich described his experiences at Les Milandes to me. He stated, "Josephine had the best of everything at Les Milandes. We had a great time together."

6. Miller, *Errand into the Wilderness*, 217–20; Davis, "Formal Utopia/Informal Millennium," 17–32; Walzer, *Revolution of the Saints*, 191–92; Marin, "Frontiers of Utopia," 7–16.

7. Corbett, *Through French Windows*, 82.

8. Relf, "Utopia and the Good Breast," 110.

9. Goffman, *Frame Analysis*, 86.

10. MacCannell, *The Tourist*, 22.

11. Bonnal, *Josephine Baker et le village*, 55.

12. Ibid. Another version of the family name on some official documents is Bouillon-Baker. These changes of name reflect the complexities of the adoption process.

13. Haney, *Naked at the Feast*, 269.

14. P. Rose, *Jazz Cleopatra*, 233.

15. Baker's biographers note how quickly plans for the expansion of the Rainbow Tribe changed when Josephine started her quest. Papich, *Remembering Josephine*, 149; Haney, *Naked at the Feast*, 269–70; P. Rose, *Jazz Cleopatra*, 231–38.

16. Kephart and Zellner (*Extraordinary Groups*, 198–239) examine religious movements in which the parental metaphor is used as the basis for establishing a utopian community. The movement of Father Divine (George Baker), founded in New York in 1915, is one such case. In Father Divine's movement, adults, rather than children, constitute the primary family group and believe that their movement will change the world when they enter heaven on earth with their leader.

17. Baker and Chase, *Josephine*, 384.

18. Baker was torn between the obligations of returning to work on tour to support her dream at Les Milandes and providing a sense of love and security for the family. Haney (*Naked at the Feast*, 273) writes, "The children longed to have a real

mother who would stay at home, and their feelings were obvious." When they were very young, some of the children would even throw tantrums every time she left. These incidents highlight the tension between the nuclear family and the composite utopian community in Baker's rainbow experiment as well as between her career and her family life. B. Baker, with Trichard (*Joséphine Baker: Le Regard*, 58–59) describes some of these family tensions in detail as seen from his perspective.

19. Baker and Bouillon, *Josephine*, 194; Haney, *Naked at the Feast*; P. Rose, *Jazz Cleopatra*, 232.

20. On October 6, 2004, I interviewed Albert Jaton and his wife, Juliette Pallas Jaton, in their apartment in Paris. Albert Jaton worked as an assistant at the château and La Chartreuse, backing up many of Jo Bouillon's activities, while Juliette Pallas was a governess for the Rainbow children. The couple met at Les Milandes in the "Deux Amours" Square, and they still hold fond memories of the time that they spent there. My observations in the text about the children are based on a personal communication and a typewritten activity schedule provided by Juliette Pallas Jaton.

21. Baker and Chase, *Josephine*, 340.

22. Papich (*Remembering Josephine*, 151–52) elaborates on the experience of Moïse. B. Baker, with Trichard (*Joséphine Baker: Le Regard*, 60–61) describes a similar experience with Monsieur Nassim, his Islamic tutor with whose ideas he disagreed.

23. Papich, *Remembering Josephine*, 151.

24. Ibid., 156–57; Haney, *Naked at the Feast*, 273–74.

25. In religious and utopian movements, conversion is voluntary, although socialization may involve some element of coercion (see Lofland and Skonovd, "Conversion Motifs"). In the case of the Rainbow Tribe, the children had no choice about their participation, and they did not have a complete grasp of the ideological principles grounding the experiment.

26. Hammond and O'Connor, *Josephine Baker*, 203. B. Baker, with Trichard (*Joséphine Baker: Le Regard*, 56–66) further develops these comments.

27. Bonnal, *Joséphine Baker et le village*, 133.

28. Ibid., 32.

29. Haney, *Naked at the Feast*, 278.

30. Wood, *Josephine Baker Story*, 351.

31. "Jo Bouillon: 'Je ne vieux pas divorcer.'"

32. Hirsch, *Family Frames*, 7.

33. Kuhn, "Remembrance," 23.

34. Jean-Claude Bonnal (*Joséphine Baker et le village*, 56) reproduces this archival photo without a date. Although Stellina is not present, she may have been an infant at the time. The statement that all eleven children are present ("Tous les onze enfants réunis dans la joie!") suggests, however, that everyone is there, which would date the photo to about 1962, before Stellina's arrival.

35. Bonnal, *Joséphine Baker et le village*, 57.

36. Ibid., 63.

37. Ibid., 64.

38. Ibid., 70.

39. Hammond and O'Connor, *Josephine*, 225.

40. Many of the group shots in the community with Josephine, Jo, and the children from 1956 and 1957 are contained in the Collection Diaz of the Departmental Archives of Dordogne (Bonnal, *Joséphine Baker et le village*, 123–30). Later group shots of the children as adolescents with Josephine on tour appear in newspaper coverage in *L'Aurore, Paris-Jour, France-Soir,* and *Le Figaro.* These photographs highlight Josephine's role in promoting the public image and press coverage of the Rainbow Tribe.

41. Hirsch, *Family Frames*, 7.

42. The Rainbow Tribe may be analyzed both with respect to the history of utopian movements in France and in the context of movements for civil rights and minority pride. Claeys, "Utopianism, Property"; Jules-Rosette, *Black Paris*, 240–44.

43. Gilroy, *Black Atlantic*, 186.

44. Sartre, "Orphée noir," xli.

45. Ibid., xliii.

46. On September 18, 1964, Stephen Papich received a nine-page letter in French from Josephine, entitled "The Ideal of Brotherhood in Les Milandes as Seen by Josephine Baker." Papich had the letter translated and he excerpted a large portion of it in his 1976 biography on Baker (Papich, *Remembering Josephine*, 154–55). The letter is a treatise describing Baker's rationale for her experiment in universal brotherhood and discusses the Rainbow Tribe in idealistic terms. The original French letter is not available. Papich explains that Baker preferred to write in French, and as he could not speak the language, he would ask a friend to provide him with translations. Some of this correspondence is reproduced in English as part of his biography.

47. "Coquatrix a peut-être sauvé les Milandes."

48. "Pour sauver Joséphine Baker Bardot payera ce soir de sa personne."

49. De Becker, "La Télévision au secours de orphelins de luxe."

50. Bonini, *La Véritable Joséphine*, 260.

51. Cartier, "L'Un des enfants de Joséphine Baker."

52. "Another Eviction Story for Josephine Baker."

53. Baker found the atmosphere in Monaco to be supportive, and she was able to continue her rainbow experiment there as she watched the children grow up and embark on their own lives. Baker and Bouillon, *Josephine*, 269–70.

Chapter 7: Legendary Legionnaire

1. The best first-hand account of Baker's activities during the war years is Jacques Abtey's *La Guerre secrète de Joséphine Baker.* Baker and Bouillon's biography also con-

tains first-hand descriptions of the war years in chapters 10 and 11. See Baker and Bouillon, *Josephine*, 115–38.

2. Another celebrity autobiography, *Toute ma vie*, was Mistinguett's attempt to reinforce her role as a music-hall avatar long after the pinnacle of her performance. In many respects, this autobiography resembles the collaborative works of Marcel Sauvage and André Rivollet on Baker.

3. After their initial encounter in 1939, Abtey remained at Baker's side as her official connection to the counterintelligence and Resistance forces throughout the war, and he was her staunch friend until her death.

4. Abtey, *La Guerre secrète*, 19–20. See also Onana, *Joséphine Baker contre Hitler*, 55–56, for a description of Baker's first encounter with Commander Abtey.

5. Abtey, *La Guerre secrète*, 20.

6. Baker and Bouillon, *Josephine*, 118.

7. Traimond, personal communication, 2001.

8. Baker and Bouillon, *Josephine*, 116.

9. Ibid., 121.

10. Abtey, *La Guerre secrète*, 91. Onana (*Joséphine Baker contre Hitler*, 70–72) also describes Baker's early period in North Africa.

11. Haney, *Naked at the Feast*, 225; P. Rose, *Jazz Cleopatra*, 196–97.

12. Haney, *Naked at the Feast*, 225.

13. Ibid., 228; P. Rose, *Jazz Cleopatra*, 197; Wood, *Josephine Baker Story*, 296.

14. Haney, *Naked at the Feast*, 230–31. In 1943, after the Allied troops landed in North Africa, Sidney Williams was charged with establishing interracial clubs at which American soldiers could meet during their free time. Baker's performances at the Liberty Clubs led to a series of appearances across North Africa and the Middle East, with Jacques Abtey continuing to serve as her counterintelligence connection.

15. Ibid., 232.

16. Baker's fund-raising efforts during the war included performances, auctions, raffles, and spontaneous gatherings for the soldiers (Haney, *Naked at the Feast*, 235; Baker and Bouillon, *Josephine*, 131–33; P. Rose, *Jazz Cleopatra*, 202–3). During this period, she developed a pattern of fund-raising that she would later use to support her multicultural project at Les Milandes.

17. Haney, *Naked at the Feast*, 237.

18. Schroeder, *Josephine Baker*, 105.

19. Hammond and O'Connor, *Josephine Baker*, 212. See also B. Baker, with Trichard, *Joséphine Baker: Le Regard*, 44–45, for his mother's critique of communication.

20. Baker's decision to travel to the United States was not entirely altruistic. Although she was reluctant to return to the racial difficulties that she had experienced during her 1936 and 1948 visits, Ned Schuyler's lucrative contract convinced her

that the 1951 concert tour would be profitable for her and Les Milandes. Baker and Bouillon, *Josephine*, 171–72; Haney, *Naked at the Feast*, 247–48.

21. Haney, *Naked at the Feast*, 247.

22. An article from *Counterattack*, dated March 23, 1951, and included in Baker's FBI files, used the Willie McGee incident as a basis for establishing Baker's distance from the Communist Party. Baker supported the American Labor Party rally, but refused to attend when she learned who the other participants at the event would be.

23. Baker attempted to broaden her desegregation activities beyond the performance arena to the media and hiring practices for several local and national organizations. P. Rose, *Jazz Cleopatra*, 214–15.

24. Brian Gibson's 1991 HBO special *The Josephine Baker Story*, depicts Jo Bouillon as present at the Stork Club incident. An interview with Jack O'Brian in the film *Chasing a Rainbow* (1986) also refers to Jo Bouillon as present, although he was in France at the time. See Baker and Bouillon, *Josephine*, 181–82.

25. Hammond and O'Connor, *Josephine Baker*, 195.

26. FBI file 62-95834 contains two parts, with cross-references. They document Baker's movements, speeches, and press coverage spanning 1951–68. The FBI concluded that Baker had not engaged in Communist activities and eventually dropped the surveillance. The State Department, however, continued to view Baker as a dangerous personality who could not be relied on to represent U.S. interests abroad. Onana (*Joséphine Baker contre Hitler*, 125–26, 151–55) also discusses the FBI files at length with regard to Baker's political visibility in France and the United States.

27. Haney, *Naked at the Feast*, 259. Baker left the United States in January 1952 for South America, making several short stops during her journey to perform in Mexico City, Uruguay, and other venues in Latin and South America before arriving in Buenos Aires.

28. Haney, *Naked at the Feast*, 262; Dudziak, "Josephine Baker, Racial Protest, and the Cold War" (1994), 558 (Powell quote and FBI file information).

29. Baker and Bouillon, *Josephine*, 188.

30. P. Rose, *Jazz Cleopatra*, 231.

31. Baker and Bouillon, *Josephine*, 190.

32. Dudziak, "Josephine Baker, Racial Protest, and the Cold War" (1994), 566; Dudziak, "Josephine Baker, Racial Protest, and the Cold War" (2000), 179–80.

33. Dudziak, "Josephine Baker, Racial Protest, and the Cold War" (1994), 569.

34. Mel, *Alioune Diop*, 145–46; Jules-Rosette, *Black Paris*, 63.

35. The *Présence Africaine* organizing committee included Josephine Baker, among other artists and celebrities. James Miller and Jerry Watts ("The First Congress of Black Writers") argue that invitations to the First Congress of Black Writers and Artists were limited to conservative African American participants. Although my 1988 interviews with two conference organizers, Christiane Yandé Diop and Jacques

Rabemananjara, did not support this claim, Baker's FBI files show that Présence Africaine and the Congress of Black Writers and Artists were under surveillance. Some invitees, such as W. E. B. DuBois, were unable to attend because of State Department travel restrictions.

36. Although Baker was not an active organizer of the 1966 World Festival of Black Arts in Dakar, her very presence there, along with African American performers and writers such as Katherine Dunham and Langston Hughes, made a public impression (Jules-Rosette, *Black Paris*, 67–70). Baker used international conferences as important arenas in which she performed politics.

37. James Baldwin (*No Name in the Street*, 49) states that he was covering the 1956 congress for the CIA, as well as for *Encounter* magazine. Richard Wright, who was an active participant in the congress, was under FBI and CIA surveillance. Baldwin later claimed that he was interested in intelligence activity because he wanted to write a book on the FBI. Dudziak, "Josephine Baker, Racial Protest, and the Cold War" (1994), 568. See also Onana, *Joséphine Baker contre Hitler*, 136–38, for a discussion of the FBI and U.S. State Department surveillance of Josephine Baker and Présence Africaine.

38. Bonnal, *Joséphine et le village*, 165–78.

39. Ibid., 123.

40. Ibid.

41. Fabre, *From Harlem to Paris*, 338–44; Stovall, *Paris Noir*, 154–55.

42. Baker and Bouillon, *Josephine*, 253.

43. Bonnal, *Joséphine et le village*, 165–78.

44. The protests of students and workers in Paris during May 1968 forced the temporary closing of Josephine's new comeback show at the Olympia. It was during the hiatus that she joined President de Gaulle in his march down the Champs-Elysées in defense of the stability of French traditions. Baker's support of de Gaulle was unflinching, and she viewed her militancy as a continuation of the patriotism of the war years. Baker and Chase, *Josephine*, 394; Wood, *Josephine Baker Story*, 374.

45. Josephine also admired and remained loyal to Robert Kennedy until the end. After her 1968 show at the Olympia, she flew to Robert Kennedy's funeral, taking the Rainbow children with her. They were dressed in identical uniforms with insignia representing France. Baker and Chase, *Josephine*, 394; Wood, *Josephine Baker Story*, 374–75.

46. My only personal glimpse of Josephine Baker was from a distance at the March on Washington.

47. Stephen Papich (*Remembering Josephine*, 210) states that Josephine informed him that she spoke to the crowd at the March on Washington spontaneously for twenty minutes. Haney (*Naked at the Feast*, 284) describes Josephine as briefer and sandwiched in between other, more prominent, civil rights leaders. Schroeder (*Josephine Baker*, 105) describes Baker's speech as one of the most "uplifting" of the day.

48. Papich, *Remembering Josephine,* 210–13.

49. Baker and Chase, *Josephine,* 372.

50. The Collège Universitaire de Fraternité Universelle was planned to be both a college (that is, a secondary school, in French terms) and a university with a curriculum in multicultural studies resembling contemporary departments of ethnic studies at U.S. universities. Baker, however, did not have the professional guidance and support to design a complete curriculum.

51. Haney, *Naked at the Feast,* 282.

52. Baker and Bouillon, *Josephine,* 243.

53. Baker and Chase (*Josephine,* 420) briefly describe a trip made by Josephine and a few of the Rainbow children to Marshal Tito's Adriatic island in Yugoslavia. Brahim stated that he thought that the island was a disappointment, while Baker optimistically visualized how she could improve it. See also Baker and Bouillon, *Josephine,* 272, and Wood, *Josephine Baker Story,* 386–87.

54. Stovall, *Paris Noir,* 287–88. See also Gates, "Interview with Josephine Baker and James Baldwin."

55. Amselle, *Vers un multiculturalisme français,* 178–79.

56. A year following Baker's death, Bouillon published her posthumous biography in French. The press coverage was extensive. Between 1988 and 2000, over a half-dozen published biographies and several masters' theses and doctoral dissertations have appeared. Bryan Hammond's *Josephine Baker* (1988) and Phyllis Rose's *Jazz Cleopatra* (1989) are the best known of the early round of these publications, all of which benefited from renewed public interest in multiculturalism.

57. Goffman, *Frame Analysis,* 128.

58. Ibid., 129.

59. In his version of speech act theory, J. L. Austin (*How to Do Things with Words,* 14–18) analyzes linguistic performance in technical terms. He describes infelicities in performance with reference to circumstances in which individuals do not understand, or lack the competence to complete, actions invoked by performative verbs such as "I promise." This type of performance differs from narrative performance in which subjects act within the parameters of a narrative and fulfill designated roles accordingly.

60. Rob Nixon (*Homelands, Harlem, and Hollywood,* 155–59) describes the international artists' boycott of South Africa and the founding of Artists and Athletes Against Apartheid. This movement, as well as the individual activities of musicians such as Paul Simon and Peter Gabriel, began to frame a new approach to social activism that promoted artists' careers while simultaneously giving them the opportunity to support international causes through their performances, recordings, and videos. The July 2005 Live 8 concerts to benefit African debt relief are another example of celebrity support for international political causes.

Chapter 8: Echoes and Influences

1. Baudrillard, *Simulacres*, 43.

2. Ibid., 124–28. The structure of communication referred to here is based on Baudrillard's notion of the precession of simulacra whereby images are commodified and reproduced as a chain of media representations. An archaeology of knowledge addressing these images as discourses of representation is also a useful method. See also Foucault, *Les Mots et les choses*, 221–24.

3. P. Rose, *Jazz Cleopatra*, 252–53. Information on Carter is also available on the World Wide Web; see http://phantomdragon.com/THELEGEND/carter.htm, accessed January 19, 2006.

4. Barthes, "Introduction to the Structural Study of Narrative," 237.

5. Léopold Senghor's concepts of passion, rhythm, and sonority are the basis of his approach to the aesthetics of négritude (Senghor, "Discours du Président," 513–15). Josephine Baker's négritude is an enactment of these rhythms and emotions through her primal performances.

6. Edmund Husserl (*Ideas*, 287–88) describes this process as neutrality modification, whereby an image or depicted reality is framed and modified in the imagination. Memory operates to retrieve an image that may be framed in realistic, representational, or imaginary terms. Each of Baker's images may be viewed as subject to a neutrality modification or shift in framing.

7. Lange ("Hypermedia and Ethnomusicology," 132–49) argues that hypermedia, including digital and online representations, transform the content, sequencing, and aesthetic quality of the image and interrupt or reconfigure the narrative flow of a presentation.

8. Baudrillard, *Simulacres*, 69–71.

9. Kaplan, *Rocking around the Clock*, 150–51. Kaplan analyzes advertising, film, and television as media that convert the subject into an image within a new universe of communication.

10. Baudrillard, *Forget Foucault*, 98.

11. Appiah, *In My Father's House*, 137–57.

12. Baudrillard, *Simulacres*, 123–28.

13. Ibid., 125.

14. Jameson, *Postmodernism*, 19.

15. Ibid., 79–80. Jameson describes the continual and virtual present created by postmodern images of the past through collage, collision, pastiche, and parody in contrast to the sequential imagery of documentary history.

16. Maffesoli (*L'Ombre de Dionysos*, 82–84) argues that the Dionysian myth, representing a return to naturalism and spontaneity, counterbalances Greek philosophies of

rationalism. He contends that this myth is central to the libertine spirit of modernism and the oppositional aesthetics of postmodernism.

17. Lhamon (*Raising Cain*, 7) argues that minstrelsy involved "complex cultural work" in which black and white performers colluded in the creation of stereotypical imagery. See also Harris, *Colored Pictures*.

18. Njami, "Invention of Memory," 8–9.

19. Baudrillard (*Simulacres*, 125) states, "Every strategy of the universalization of differences is an entropic strategy of the system." This quote suggests that the postmodern sampling of primal images reinforces the images without stimulating a reflection on their social origins and consequences.

20. Foster, *Recodings*, 181.

21. Clifford, *Predicament of Culture*, 197–200.

22. Ibid., 198. Clifford argues that the appropriation of primitivism in modern art marks a specific moment of history that must be interpreted in context. His use of Baker's image, however, creates a postmodern collage that raises further questions about the enduring psychological and cultural meanings and appeal of primal exoticism.

23. Ibid., 199.

24. Willis and Williams, *The Black Female Body*, 102.

25. Ibid., 101.

26. Ibid., 109.

27. In his essay on the postcolonial and the postmodern, Kwame Appiah (*In My Father's House*, 149) argues that the postcolonial and the postmodern are not synonymous. Therefore, recycling Baker's colonialist primal images in "postmodern" pastiche does not remove the original elements of the image's appeal as a primitivist stereotype.

28. Minh-ha, *When the Moon Waxes Red*, 159.

29. Diawara, *In Search of Africa*, 237–39.

30. Kaplan, *Rocking around the Clock*, 90.

31. Diawara, *In Search of Africa*, 246–48.

32. Ibid., 267–70.

33. These identity shifts may be conceived of in terms of what Genette (*Narrative Discourse*, 137) calls an "entangled hierarchical structure" of nested narratives. I am framing these narratives in terms of the progression of identity shifts within each artist's career conceived of as a master narrative.

34. Kaplan (*Rocking around the Clock*, 122) argues that the "patriarchal feminine" image emerges as an exaggerated pastiche, and occasionally a parody, of conventional images of women in postmodern media. These conventional images of the mother, the prostitute, and the *femme fatale* are constructed in relationship to a male gaze and perspective. See also Dijkstra, *Evil Sisters*, 70–71.

35. Greimas and Fontanille (*Semiotics of Passions*, 30) refer to this unveiling process as a "circulation" of simulacra, whereby one appearance is linked to a series of other images in a semiotic chain. This process also explains why fans adopt the clothing or appearance of pop idols as an internalization of the simulacrum, or mediated image, in the semiotic chain.

36. Although Anderson ("En Route," 494) argues that Jones's direct awareness of Baker cannot be established, Goude clearly used Baker's model in fashioning Jones's public image. Whether artists were directly influenced by Baker or merely echoed her image is not the salient fact in a cultural critique. Instead, what is important is how Baker's image is ultimately deployed in the postmodern media.

37. Ibid., 491–512.

38. Goude, *Jungle Fever*, 109.

39. Goude (ibid., 102–7) intentionally occults the facts of Jones's life in order to construct her flamboyant popular image. See also Anderson, "En Route," 493.

40. Anderson, "En Route," 494–96.

41. Patton, "Embodying Subaltern Memory," 84.

42. Gandoulou, *Au Coeur de la sape*, 18–22; Gondola, "Dream and Drama." See also Thomas, "Fashion Matters."

43. Goude, *Jungle Fever*, 102.

44. Ibid., 107.

45. Ibid., 105.

46. Sharpley-Whiting, *Black Venus*, 52–56. Ourika was an African woman offered as a gift to the Duchess of Orléans in the late eighteenth century. Her image was the basis of two novels and a host of journalistic articles and parodies of the negress and the Black Venus during the early nineteenth century.

47. Ibid., 56.

48. Goude, *Jungle Fever*, 102–7. Goude's description of Jones discusses his personal and public relationship to her and the strategies that he used in constructing her popular image.

49. Ibid., 116–17. Stripped naked except for a tail, Jones snarled and growled her way through an erotic, primal performance.

50. Peterson, "Bizarre Charm," 92–93.

51. Kaplan (*Rocking around the Clock*, 117–27) and Schwichtenberg (*Madonna Connection*, 1–11) provide more detailed discussions of Madonna's imagery.

52. Hunt, "Madonna Discography."

53. R. Scott, "Images of Race and Religion," 65–66.

54. hooks, *Outlaw Culture*, 11.

55. Ronald Scott ("Images of Race and Religion," 62) writes, "The recently released HBO special about the life of Josephine Baker . . . illustrates that much of what Madonna brings to music and music videos had already been accomplished by lesser

known artists." On page 75, in a footnote, Scott provides this qualification: "Lesser-known does not mean less talented." Presumably, Scott is referring to Madonna's contemporary public notoriety and its use as a way of reintroducing Baker's image to a new public that has never heard of, or has forgotten, her.

56. Nenno, "Masquerade," 71–96.

57. Kaplan, *Rocking around the Clock,* 162.

58. MacCannell, "Marilyn Monroe Was Not a Man," 123. Here MacCannell argues that Marilyn's cultural transgression can be summed up by the fact that she was not a man, but exhibited both the empowerment and existential dilemmas associated with male heroes.

59. In *The English Roses,* Madonna uses a classic folktale as an inspiration for lessons about race and tolerance.

60. Jackson, with Romanowski, *La Toya,* 304–6.

61. Ibid., 224.

62. Beyala's rapid rise to fame has inspired serious analyses of her work in relationship to feminism and francophone literature. See Gallimore, *L'Oeuvre romanesque de Calixthe Beyla,* 7–33. I have also discussed Beyala's work as part of the literary movement of Parisianism. See Jules-Rosette, *Black Paris,* 170–75; Jules-Rosette, "Identity Discourses," 52–53.

63. For a critical analysis of Beyala's *Comment cuisiner son mari à l'africaine,* see Hitchcott, "*Comment cuisiner.*"

64. By 2000, Beyala had written over a dozen books, including the prize-winning *Les Honneurs perdus* and two open letters. *Lettre d'une Africaine à ses soeurs occidentales* (1995) established Beyala's position as an African feminist in France. *Lettre d'une Afro-française à ses compatriotes* (2000) situated Beyala within French debates on multiculturalism and outlined her project for the inclusion of visible minorities in the French media and public discourse on race.

65. See the discussion in Hitchcott, "Calixthe Beyala."

66. Jules-Rosette, *Black Paris,* 203; interview by Bennetta Jules-Rosette with Calixthe Beyala, July 27, 1990.

67. Minh-ha, *When the Moon Waxes Red,* 158. Minh-ha criticizes the limitations of feminitude as a theoretical stance.

68. Beyala, *Lettre d'une Africaine,* 20–21.

69. Genevoix, "Lire," 18.

70. After receiving the literary Grand Prix from the Académie Française in 1996, Beyala was publicly attacked in an unwarranted debate over the originality of some of the book's passages (Jules-Rosette, *Black Paris,* 170). This debate also coincided with the rise of Beyala's visibility as a public figure in France.

71. Kaplan (*Rocking around the Clock,* 130–42) discusses the tenacity of patriarchal feminine images in the postmodern media. Although these images are modified and restructured on the surface level, their core meanings persist.

72. Kaja Silverman (*Threshold*, 18–20) applies Lacan's notion of the screen to the creation of normative images and the positioning of the viewing subject. She also emphasizes the cultural frames that influence the viewer's gaze. See also Hirsch, *Family Frames*, 101–4.

73. Lacan, *Four Fundamental Concepts of Psycho-Analysis*, 106.

74. Silverman, *Threshold*, 19.

75. Fanon, *Black Skin, White Masks*, 109.

76. Kaplan, *Rocking around the Clock*, 91.

77. Ibid., 90–91. Kaplan describes images projected in cinema and video, but Baker's work also relied on the figurative imagery of song lyrics and the iconic signs reproduced in photography and music-hall tableaux.

78. T. Rose, *Black Noise*, 177.

79. Jameson (*Postmodernism*, 17) argues that in the postmodern media, pastiche is the dominant mode of mimesis and borrowing. He distinguishes pastiche from parody by virtue of the "neutral practice" of mimesis in pastiche. In pastiche, images, or simulacra, are juxtaposed to mime and evoke existing cultural forms and messages rather than to present them ironically in parody.

80. In his discussion of strategic anti-essentialism in popular music, George Lipsitz (*Dangerous Crossroads*, 56–66) develops an incisive analysis of the role of artists in mobilizing to support various causes during the 1980s and 1990s. See also Nixon, *Homelands, Harlem, and Hollywood*, 155–72; Erlmann, *Nightsong*, 306–13.

81. Maffesoli, *La Transfiguration du politique*, 257–58.

82. MacCannell, *Marilyn Monroe Was Not a Man*, 125.

83. Teshome Gabriel ("Ruin and the Other," 214–16) describes the memory work involved in cinematic and televisual images as the recuperation of "ruins," or ephemeral images that recur in a collective cultural imaginary. Baker's primal image is an example of the mnemonic floating signifiers, or ruins, to which Gabriel alludes.

Chapter 9: Eternal Comeback

1. In April 1966, Baker reconnected with Langston Hughes at the World Festival of Black Arts in Dakar. She attempted to persuade him to write her biography, and he discussed this project with his longtime friend Arna Bontemps. Baker was also interested in doing a biography with James Baldwin (Haney, *Naked at the Feast*, 282; P. Rose, *Jazz Cleopatra*, 267). In 1964, Baker had asked Gerold Frank to help with a biography, but the plans never materialized (Wood, *Josephine Baker story*, 362). Baker wanted to have biographies written from multiple perspectives, highlighting her successes in both performance and politics.

2. Haney, *Naked at the Feast*, 296; P. Rose, *Jazz Cleopatra*, 249.

3. Both P. Rose (*Jazz Cleopatra*, 254–57) and Wood (*Josephine Baker Story*, 390–92) describe Baker's spiritual marriage to Robert Brady in Acapulco in September 1973.

4. Baker's comeback performances in the mid-1950s and the 1960s marked a pattern

of vacillating between performance and semi-retirement that she was to continue for two decades. Press clippings for this period are contained in file 40 S.W 1651(1), (2), and (3), Bibliothèque de l'Arsenal, Paris. The Carnegie Hall concert was recorded live by Tele General Studios in a double album. See Hammond and O'Connor, *Josephine Baker,* 294, and Bonini, *La Véritable Joséphine,* 358.

5. Haney, *Naked at the Feast,* 308.

6. Jack Jordan and Howard Saunders pitched the Carnegie Hall performance toward two major audiences: African Americans and the gay community (Bonini, *La Véritable Joséphine,* 307–8; Wood, *Josephine Baker Story,* 387). They emphasized the camp and retro aspects of Baker's appearance as a new selling point, and Baker performed with energy, irony, and good humor.

7. Haney, *Naked at the Feast,* 318, and Wood, *Josephine Baker Story,* 399, both quote Astric.

8. This incident is described by several Baker biographers. See Haney, *Naked at the Feast,* 319; Wood, *Josephine Baker Story,* 400; Bonini, *La Véritable Joséphine,* 320.

9. According to Baker and Chase (*Josephine,* 480), Bodson and Dauzonne were committed to making the Bobino performances both a personal and a professional triumph for Baker. In addition to remodeling the theater and taking care of Baker's accommodations, they attempted to pay off some of her debts so that she could perform in comfort.

10. Bodson and Dauzonne also booked rooms for Baker at the Sheraton Hotel in the fourteenth arrondissement to accommodate her late nights of rehearsal at the theater (Baker and Bouillon, *Josephine* 285–86). No detail was left to chance in preparing the gala 1975 performance at the Théâtre Bobino.

11. The audio recording of *Joséphine à Bobino 1975* made by Festival on March 24, 1975 (FLD 643), has now become a classic album covering fifty years of her performance history. Hammond and O'Connor, *Josephine,* 294; Bonini, *La Véritable Joséphine,* 358–59.

12. Bonini, *La Véritable Joséphine,* 328. See also "Jo Bouillon: 'Je ne veux pas divorcer'" and "Joséphine Baker se raconte."

13. "L'Éternal retour de Joséphine Baker." The author signs this article D.H.

14. Viso K., "Pipi de chat et vieille rosette."

15. Haney, *Naked at the Feast,* 321.

16. Although President Giscard d'Estaing was not present for Baker's performance at the Bobino, his telegram provided official recognition of the importance of this comeback not only for Baker's career but also as a political symbol for France. Haney, *Naked at the Feast,* 322; Wood, *Josephine Baker Story,* 403–4.

17. Baker and Chase, *Josephine,* 483.

18. Whether inadvertently or not, Haney (*Naked at the Feast,* 324) reports that Baker was officially pronounced dead on Friday, April 14, 1975, at 5:00 A.M. However, April

11 was a Friday, and all other official reports list Baker's death as Saturday, April 12, at 5:00 A.M. Errors of fact about Baker's birth, parentage, marriages, and death seem to enhance the mythological character of her life and the narratives that surrounded it.

19. Stovall, *Paris Noir*, 286.

20. Haney, *Naked at the Feast*, 325.

21. Ibid., 327.

22. Gérard Genette discusses how iterative narratives illustrate the passage of real time while remaining timeless kernels, repeated over and over again. He writes, "And in fact, an iterative unit . . . constituted from a series extended over several years, can only very well be narrated in its own successiveness . . . without letting the passage of 'external time' . . . intervene in any way." Genette, *Narrative Discourse*, 140.

23. Baker and Bouillon, *Josephine*, 101.

24. Dudziak supports the domestic exile thesis; see her "Josephine Baker, Racial Protest, and the Cold War" (1994), 569.

25. Haney, *Naked at the Feast*, 294.

26. There is potential for new research on Baker to articulate with multicultural studies of the African diaspora. Gilroy's *Black Atlantic,* Hall's "The New Ethnicities" (esp. 441–49), and Njami's *James Baldwin* are studies that highlight the roles of diasporic figures in constituting transatlantic dialogues. Works on multiculturalism and related paradigms in France are also pertinent; see, for example, Amselle's *Vers un multiculturalisme français* and Maffesoli's *Éloge de la raison sensible.*

27. Costa-Lascoux, "La Nationalité par naissance ou par le choix," 18–22; Jules-Rosette, *Black Paris*, 152–57.

28. Hall, "New Ethnicities," 445.

29. In his discussion of the emergence of new ethnic identities, Stuart Hall ("New Ethnicities," 444) critiques essentialism and unidimensional racial stereotypes structured around the notion of "fixed 'selves.'"

30. Although I have argued that Baker's philosophy does mesh completely with Sartre's 1948 definition of négritude's synthesis as a "society without races," her initial performance of négritude was rooted in the primal image and its exotic panoramas.

31. Stovall, *Paris Noir*, 94–95; Edwards, *Practice of Diaspora*, 161–62.

32. Baker was devoted to transforming her everyday activities into performances (Goffman, *Presentation of Self*, 65). She made her living spaces into stage sets for the public and drew on the successes and failures of her everyday life to create her stage performances.

Bibliography

Abel, Richard. *The Ciné Goes to Town: French Cinema, 1896–1914*. Berkeley: University of California Press, 1994.

———. *French Cinema: The First Wave, 1915–1929*. Princeton, N.J.: Princeton University Press, 1984.

Abtey, Jacques. *La Guerre secrète de Joséphine Baker*. Paris: Siboney, 1948.

Allégret, Marc, director. *Zouzou*. Script by Pepito Abatino and Carlo Rim. Paris: Arys Nissotti and Arys Productions, 1934.

Amselle, Jean-Loup. *Vers un multiculturalisme français: L'Empire de la coutume*. Paris: Aubier, 1996.

Anderson, Carolyn G. "En Route to Transnational Postmodernism: Grace Jones, Josephine Baker and the African Diaspora." *Social Science Information* 32, no. 3 (1993): 491–512.

"Another Eviction Story for Josephine Baker." *International Herald Tribune*. September 30, 1968.

Apollinaire, Guillaume. *Les Peintres cubistes: Méditations esthétiques*. Geneva: Pierre Cailles, Éditeur, Presses de la Plaine du Rhône, 1950. (Originally published, Paris: Eugène Figuière, 1913.)

Appiah, Kwame Anthony. *In My Father's House: Africa in the Philosophy of Culture*. New York: Oxford University Press, 1992.

Austin, J. L. *How to Do Things with Words*. London: Oxford University Press, 1962.

Baker, Brian B., with Gilles Trichard. *Joséphine Baker: Le Regard d'un fils*. Paris: Patrick Robin, 2006.

Baker, Jean-Claude, and Chris Chase. *Josephine: The Hungry Heart*. New York: Random House, 1993.

Baker, Josephine. "Statement about the Nobel Peace Prize." In *The Josephine Baker Story*, by Ean Wood, 384. London: Sanctuary Publishing, 1970.

Baker, Josephine, and Jo Bouillon. *Josephine*. Trans. Mariana Fitzpatrick. New York: Harper and Row, 1977. (Originally published as *Joséphine* [Paris: Robert Laffont–Opéra Mundi, 1976].)

Baker, Josephine, with Jo Bouillon, illustrated by Piet Worm. *La Tribu arc-en-ciel*. Paris: Opéra Mundi 1957.

Baldwin, James. *No Name in the Street*. New York: Dial, 1972.

Barnouw, Erik. *Documentary: A History of Non-Fiction Film*. New York: Oxford University Press, 1974.

Barshak, Jackie. "The Modern 'Primitive' Images of Josephine Baker in Film, Photographs, Illustration and Performance, France 1925–1935." Master's thesis, San Francisco State University, 1994.

Barthes, Roland. *The Fashion System*. Trans. Matthew Ward and Richard Howard. New York: Hill and Wang, 1983. (Originally published as *Système de la mode* [Paris: Seuil, 1967].)

———. "An Introduction to the Structural Analysis of Narrative." *New Literary History* 6, no. 2 (1975): 237–72.

Battersby, Martin. *Art Deco Fashion: French Designers, 1908–1925*. New York: St. Martin's, 1974.

Baudrillard, Jean. *Simulacres et simulation*. Paris: Galilée, 1981.

Baudrillard, Jean, with Sylvère Lotringer. *Forget Foucault*. New York: Semiotexte, 1987. (Originally published as *Oublier Foucault* [Paris: Galilée, 1977].)

Benjamin, Walter. *Angelus Novus*. Frankfurt: Suhrkamp, 1966.

———. "Paris, Capital of the Nineteenth Century. In *Reflections*, trans. Edmund Jephcott, 146–62. New York: Schocken, 1986.

———. "The Work of Art in the Age of Mechanical Reproduction." In *Marxism and Art: Writings in Aesthetics and Criticism*, ed. Berel Lang and Forrest Williams, 281–300. New York: David McKay, 1972. (Originally published in *Illuminations: Essays and Reflections*, by Walter Benjamin [New York: Harcourt, Brace, Jovanovich, 1968].)

Benstock, Shari. *Women of the Left Bank: Paris, 1900–1940*. Austin: University of Texas Press, 1986.

Beyala, Calixthe. *C'est le soleil qui m'a brulée*. Paris: Stock, 1987.

———. *Comment cuisiner son mari à l'africaine*. Paris: Albin Michel, 2000.

———. *Les Honneurs perdus*. Paris: Albin Michel, 1996.

———. Interview by Bennetta Jules-Rosette. July 27, 1990.

———. *Lettre d'une Africaine à ses soeurs occidentales*. Paris: Spengler, 1995.

———. *Lettre d'une Afro-française à ses compatriotes: Vous avez dit racistes?* Paris: Mango, 2000.

———. *Le Petit prince de Belleville*. Paris: Albin Michel, 1992.

———. *Tu t'appeleras Tanga*. Paris: Stock, 1988.

Bhabha, Homi K. "Interrogating Identity." *ICA Documents* 6 (1987): 5–11.

———. *The Location of Culture*. New York: Routledge, 1994.

Blanchard, Pascal, and Nicolas Bancel. *De l'indigène à l'immigré*. Paris: Découvertes Gallimard, 1998.

Bloom, Peter J. "Networks of Empire: The French Colonial Archive, 1889–1933." Ph.D. diss., University of California, Los Angeles, 1996.

Bonini, Emmanuel. *La Véritable Joséphine Baker.* Paris: Pygmalion, Gérard Watelet, 2000.

Bonnal, Jean-Claude. *Joséphine Baker et le village des enfants du monde en Périgord.* Le Bugue, France: PLB Éditeur, 1992.

Borshuk, Michael. "An Intelligence of the Body: Disruptive Parody through Dance in the Early Performances of Josephine Baker." In *Embodying Liberation: The Black Body in American Dance,* ed. Dorothea Fischer-Hornung and Allison Goeller, 41–57. Piscataway, N.J.: Transaction, 2001.

———. "'Queen of the Colonial Exposition': Josephine Baker's Strategic Performance." In *Critical Voicings of Black Liberation: Resistance and Representation in the Americas,* ed. Kimberly L. Phillips, Hermine D. Pinson, Lorenzo Thomas, and Hanna Wallinger, 47–65. Piscataway, N.J.: Transaction, 2003.

Bricktop, with James Haskins. *Bricktop.* New York: Atheneum, 1983.

Bureau de Tourisme. *Château des Milandes: Joséphine Baker.* Touristic Brochure, n.d.

Camard, Jean-Pierre. *Joséphine Baker et Paul Colin* (catalog). Paris: Cabinet d'Expertises Camard, 1992.

Cartier, Jacqueline. "L'Un des enfants de Joséphine Baker: 'Si nous quittons les Milandes, nous poursuivrons notre idéal ailleurs.'" *France-Soir,* May 17, 1968.

Cendrars, Blaise. *Anthologie nègre.* Paris: Buchet-Chastel, 1921.

Césaire, Aimé. *Corps perdu.* Illustrated by Pablo Picasso. Paris: Fragrance, 1950.

Claeys, Gregory. "Utopianism, Property, and the French Revolution Debate in Britain." In Kumar and Bann, *Utopias and the Millennium,* 46–62.

Clifford, James. *The Predicament of Culture: Twentieth-Century Ethnography, Literature, and Art.* Cambridge, Mass.: Harvard University Press, 1988.

Colin, Paul. *Le Tumulte noir.* Paris: Success, 1927.

"Collection of Photos and Press Clippings of Josephine Baker," 1927–62. File 4° ICO-PER 1326. Bibliothèque de l'Arsenal, Paris.

"Collection of Press Clippings," 1968. File 4° S.W 1651 (1) and (2). Bibliothèque de l'Arsenal, Paris.

"Collection of Press Clippings on *Sirène de tropiques,*" 1926–27. File Rf 56254. Bibliothèque de l'Arsenal, Paris.

"Collection of Press Clippings of Josephine Baker," 1970–74. File 4° S.W 4754 (1). Bibliothèque de l'Arsenal, Paris.

"Collection of Press Clippings of Josephine Baker," 1975. File 4° S.W 4754 (2) and (3). Bibliothèque de l'Arsenal, Paris.

Colomina, Beatriz. "The Split Wall: Domestic Voyeurism." In *Sexuality and Space,* ed. Beatriz Colomina, 73–128. New York: Princeton Architectural Press, 1994.

"Comment le docteur-escroc Prieur offrit un cabaret de nuit à Joséphine Baker." *Paris-Midi,* December 12, 1926. File R.87448. Bibliothèque de l'Arsenal, Paris.

"Coquatrix a peut-être sauvé les Milandes." *Paris-Jour,* May 6, 1968. File 4° S.W 1651 (2). Bibliothèque de l'Arsenal, Paris.

Corbett, James. *Through French Windows: An Introduction to France in the Nineties.* Ann Arbor: University of Michigan Press, 1994.

Costa-Lascoux, Jacqueline. "La Nationalité par la naissance ou par le choix." *Hommes et Migrations* 1178 (July 1994): 18–22.

Covarrubias, Miguel. *Negro Drawings.* New York: Knopf, 1927.

Cripps, Thomas. *Black Film as Genre.* Bloomington: Indiana University Press, 1978.

Dakou, Yves. "La Quête identitaire, dans 'j'appartiens au grand jour' de Paul Dakeyo: Approche sémiolinguistique." Ph.D. diss., Université de Toulouse, Le Mirail, 1988.

"Danseuse et couturier." *Cyrano,* June 12, 1927.

Davis, Fred. *Fashion, Culture, and Identity.* Chicago: University of Chicago Press, 1992.

Davis, J. C. "Formal Utopia/Informal Millennium: The Struggle between Form and Substance as Context for Seventeenth-Century Utopianism." In Kumar and Bann, *Utopias and the Millennium,* 17–31.

de Baroncelli, Jacques, director. *Fausse alerte.* Script by Michel Duran. Paris: Flag Films, 1940.

de Becker, Raymond. "La Télévision au secours des orphelins de luxe." *Arts,* June 10, 1964.

de Labarre, Angélique. *Le Château des Milandes.* Bordeaux: Sud Ouest, 2006.

de la Camara, Félix, and Pepito Abatino. *Mon sang dans tes veines.* Preface by Josephine Baker. Paris: Isis, 1931.

Demay, M. "Joséphine apprend à voler." *Excelsior,* May 11, 1935. File R.99287. Bibliothèque de l'Arsenal, Paris.

de Pawlowski, G. "*Paris qui remue.*" *De la Revue,* 1930, 5–6.

Derval, Paul. *The Folies Bergère.* Trans. Lucienne Hill. London: Methuen, 1955. (Originally published as *Les Folies-Bergère* [Paris: Éditions de Paris, 1954].)

des Cars, Jean, and Pierre Pinon. *Paris-Haussmann.* Paris: Pavillon de l'Arsenal, 1991.

Desproges, Pierre. "C'était la dernière star rétro." *L'Aurore,* April 14, 1975.

Diawara, Manthia. *In Search of Africa.* Cambridge, Mass.: Harvard University Press, 1998.

Dijkstra, Bram. *Evil Sisters: The Threat of Female Sexuality in Twentieth-Century Culture.* New York: Henry Holt, 1996.

Diop, Alioune. "L'Artiste n'est pas seul au monde." *Présence Africaine,* 2d ser., 10–11 (1951): 5–8. Special Issue: *L'Art nègre.*

Dudziak, Mary L. "Josephine Baker, Racial Protest, and the Cold War." *Journal of American History* 81, no. 2 (1994): 543–70.

———. "Josephine Baker, Racial Protest, and the Cold War." In *Global Critical Race Feminism*, ed. Adrien Katherine Wing, 170–91. New York: New York University Press, 2000.

Dunning, Bruce. "Josephine Baker Makes a Comeback with a Purpose." *International Herald Tribune*, April 4, 1968.

Eco, Umberto. *A Theory of Semiotics*. Bloomington: Indiana University Press, 1979.

Edwards, Brent Hayes. *The Practice of Diaspora: Literature, Translation, and the Rise of Black Internationalism*. Cambridge, Mass.: Harvard University Press, 2003.

Erlmann, Veit. *Nightsong: Power, Performance, and Practice in South Africa*. Chicago: University of Chicago Press, 1996.

Etiévant, Henri, and Mario Nalpas, directors. *La Sirène des tropiques*. Script by Maurice Dekobra. Paris: Centrale Cinématographique, 1927.

Ezra, Elizabeth. *The Colonial Unconscious: Race and Culture in Interwar France*. Ithaca, N.Y.: Cornell University Press, 2000.

Fabre, Michel. *From Harlem to Paris: Black Writers in France, 1840–1980*. Urbana: University of Illinois Press, 1991. (Originally published as *La Rive noire: De Harlem à la Seine* [Paris: Lieu Commun, 1985].)

Fanon, Frantz. *Black Skin, White Masks*. Trans. Charles Lam Markmann. New York: Grove Wiedenfeld, 1967. (Originally published as *Peau noire, masques blancs* [Paris: Seuil, 1952].)

———. *The Wretched of the Earth*. Trans. Constance Farrington. New York: Grove Wiedenfeld, 1963. (Originally published as *Les Damnés de la Terre* [Paris: François Maspero, 1961].)

Farcaros, Dana, and Michael Pauls. *Dordogne and the Lot*. Guilford, Conn.: Globe Pequot Press, 2001.

Federal Bureau of Investigation (FBI). BuFile 62-95834, parts 1 and 2, 1951–68 (declassified September 2, 1982). Federal Bureau of Investigation, Washington, D.C.

———. "Josephine Baker Won't Support Communist Fronts." Letter 200, March 23, 1951. *Counterattack*, 1952.

———. "Subject: First Congress of the Présence Africaine." FBI file 100-15-7464, May 18, 1956. Federal Bureau of Investigation, Washington, D.C.

Fiennes, Peter, ed. *Time Out Paris Guide*. London: Time Out Magazine, 1992.

Flanner, Janet. *Paris Was Yesterday, 1925–1939*. New York: Viking, 1972.

"La Foire à la brocante." *Le Parisien*, March 4, 1976.

Folies-Bergère. *Le Pompier des Folies-Bergère*. Film clip, no director listed. File FRBNF38939399(11), 1928. Bibliothèque Nationale, Paris. Remastered by Kino International, 2005.

Foster, Hal. *Recodings: Art, Spectacle, Cultural Politics*. Seattle, Wash.: Bay Press, 1985.

Foucault, Michel. *Les Mots et les choses: Une archéologie des sciences humaines.* Paris: Gallimard, 1966.

Francis, Joé, and Alex Nalpas, director. *La Revue des revues.* Film clip. (Also known as *La Folie du jour.*) Paris: Alex Nalpas Productions, 1927.

Francis, Terri Simone. "Embodied Fictions, Melancholy Migrations: Josephine Baker's Cinematic Celebrity." *MFS Modern Fiction Studies* 51, no. 4 (2005): 824–45.

———. "Under a Paris Moon: Transatlantic Black Modernism, French Colonialist Cinema, and the Josephine Baker Museum." Ph.D. diss., University of Chicago, 2004.

Fry, Edward F. *Cubism.* Trans. Jonathan Griffin. London: Thames and Hudson, 1966.

Gabriel, Teshome H. "Ruin and the Other: Towards a Language of Memory." In *Otherness and the Media,* ed. Hamid Naficy and Teshome H. Gabriel, 211–19. Chur, Swit.: Harwood Academic Publishers, 1993.

Gallimore, Rangira Béatrice. *L'Oeuvre romanesque de Calixthe Beyala.* Paris: L'Harmattan, 1997.

Gandoulou, Justin-Daniel. *Au Coeur de la sape: Moeurs et aventures de Congolais à Paris.* Paris: L'Harmattan, 1989.

Gates, Henry Louis, Jr. "An Interview with Josephine Baker and James Baldwin." *Southern Review* (Summer 1985): 594–602.

Gates, Henry Louis, Jr., and Karen C. C. Dalton. "Introduction." In *Josephine Baker and La Revue Nègre: Paul Colin's Lithographs of Le Tumulte noir in Paris, 1927,* by Gates and Dalton, 4–12. New York: Harry N. Abrams, 1998.

Geertz, Clifford. "Deep Play: Notes on the Balinese Cockfight." *Daedalus* 101 (1972): 1–37.

———. *The Interpretation of Cultures.* New York: Basic Books, 1973.

Gendron, Bernard. *Between Montmartre and the Mudd Club: Popular Music and the Avant-Garde.* Chicago: University of Chicago Press, 2002.

Genette, Gérard. *Figures of Literary Discourse.* Trans. Alan Sheridan. New York: Columbia University Press, 1982. (Originally published as *Figures I* and *Figures II* [Paris: Seuil, 1969].)

———. *Narrative Discourse: An Essay in Method.* Trans. Jane E. Lewin. Ithaca: Cornell University Press, 1980. (Originally published as *Figures III* [Paris: Seuil, 1972].)

Genevoix, Sylvie. "Lire." *Figaro Madame,* July 1993, p. 18.

George, G. L. "Joséphine Baker revient à l'écran." *Paris-Jour.* September 27, 1934.

Gibson, Brian, director. *The Josephine Baker Story.* HBO Pictures in association with RHI Entertainment, Inc., and Anglia Television, Ltd., docudrama produced by John Kemeny with script by Ron Hutchins and Michael Zagor. New York: HBO Video, 1991.

Gilroy, Paul. *The Black Atlantic: Modernity and Double Consciousness.* Cambridge, Mass.: Harvard University Press, 1993.

Goffman, Erving. *Frame Analysis: An Essay on the Organization of Experience.* New York: Harper and Row, 1974.

————. *The Presentation of Self in Everyday Life.* Garden City, N.Y.: Doubleday Anchor, 1959.

Gombrich, Ernst H. *Art and Illusion.* New York: Pantheon, 1960.

Gondola, Ch. Didier. "Dream and Drama: The Search for Elegance among Congolese Youth." *African Studies Review* 42, no. 1 (1999): 23–48.

Goude, Jean-Paul. *Jungle Fever.* Ed. Harold Hayes. New York: Xavier Moreau, 1981.

Greimas, A. J., and Joseph Courtés. *Sémiotique: Dictionnaire raisonné de la théorie du langage.* Paris: Hachette, 1979.

————. *Sémiotique: Dictionnaire raisonné de la théorie du langage, Tome 2.* Paris: Hachette, 1986.

Greimas, Algirdas Julien. *Du Sens: Essais sémiotiques.* Paris: Seuil, 1970.

————. *Sémantique structurale: Recherche de méthode.* Paris: Larousse, 1966.

————. *Structural Semantics: An Attempt at Method.* Trans. Daniele McDowell, Ronald Schleifer, and Alan Velie. Lincoln: University of Nebraska Press, 1983.

Greimas, Algirdas Julien, and Jacques Fontanille. *The Semiotics of Passions: From States of Affairs to States of Feelings.* Trans. Paul Perron and Frank Collins. Minneapolis: University of Minnesota Press, 1993. (Originally published as *Sémiotique des passions: Des états des choses aux états d'âme* [Paris: du Seuil, 1991].)

Gréville, Edmond T., director. *Princesse Tam-Tam.* Script by Pepito Abatino and Yves Mirande. Paris: Arys Nissotti and Arys Productions, 1935.

Groenendijk, Paul, and Piet Vollaard. *Adolf Loos: House for Josephine Baker. Architectural Models,* no. 7. Rotterdam: Uitgeverij, 1985.

Hall, Stuart. "New Ethnicities." In *Stuart Hall: Critical Dialogues in Cultural Studies,* ed. David Morley and Kuan-Hsing Chen, 441–49. New York: Routledge, 1996.

Hammond, Bryan, and Patrick O'Connor. *Josephine Baker.* London: Jonathan Cape, 1988.

Haney, Lynn. *Naked at the Feast: A Biography of Josephine Baker.* New York: Dodd, Mead, 1981.

Hansen, Arlen J. *Expatriate Paris: A Cultural and Literary Guide to Paris of the 1920s.* New York: Little, Brown, 1990.

Harris, Michael D. *Colored Pictures: Issues of Race and Visual Representation.* Chapel Hill: University of North Carolina Press, 2003.

Hines, Thomas S. "Historic Architecture: Adolf Loos in Paris." *Architectural Digest* 48, no. 4 (1991): 104–12.

Hirsch, Marianne. *Family Frames: Photography, Narrative, and Postmemory.* Cambridge, Mass.: Harvard University Press, 1997.

Hitchcott, Nicki. "Calixthe Beyala: Black Face(s) on French TV." *Modern and Contemporary France* 12, no. 4 (2004): 473–82.

———. "*Comment cuisiner son mari à l'africaine:* Calixthe Beyala's Recipes for Migrant Identity." *French Cultural Studies* 14, no. 2 (2000): 211–20.

hooks, bell. *Outlaw Culture: Resisting Representations.* New York: Routledge, 1994.

Hoskins, Janet. *Biographical Objects: How Things Tell the Stories of People's Lives.* New York: Routledge, 1998.

Houze, Rebecca. "Fashionable Reform Dress and the Invention of 'Style' in Fin-de-Siècle Vienna." *Fashion Theory* 5, no. 1 (2001): 29–55.

Howard, Donald R. *Writers and Pilgrims: Medieval Pilgrimage Narratives and Their Posterity.* Berkeley: University of California Press, 1980.

Howell, Georgina. *In Vogue.* London: Condé Nast, 1975.

Huet, Maurice. "Joséphine." *Petit Parisien,* December 23, 1926.

Hunt, Matthew. "Madonna Discography." Online, http://www.matthewhunt.com/madona.html, accessed September 17, 2004.

Husserl, Edmund. *Ideas: General Introduction to Pure Phenomenology.* Trans. W. R. Boyce Gibson. London: Collier, 1962. (Originally published in German as *Ideen au einer reinen phänomenologie und Phänomenologischen Philosophie,* 1913.)

Jackson, Jeffrey H. *Making Jazz French: Music and Modern Life in Interwar Paris.* Durham, N.C.: Duke University Press, 2003.

Jackson, La Toya, with Patricia Romanowski. *La Toya.* New York: Penguin, 1992.

Jameson, Fredric. *Postmodernism, or the Cultural Logic of Late Capitalism.* Durham, N.C.: Duke University Press, 1991.

Jamin, Jean. "Objects trouvés des paradis perdus: A propos de la mission Dakar-Djibouti." In *Collections Passion,* ed. Jacques Hainard and Roland Kaehr, 69–100. Neuchâtel, France: Musée d'Ethnographie, 1982.

Jardin, Maïté, director. *Dans mon village.* Sixty-minute video. Sarlat, France: Kinéma Production, TV 10 Anger, and the Association Joséphine Baker of Castelnaud La Chapelle, 1999.

Jaton, Albert, and Juliette Pallas Jaton. Interview by Bennetta Jules-Rosette, Paris, October 6, 2004.

"Jo Bouillon: 'Je ne veux pas divorcer.'" *L'Aurore,* July 3, 1957.

Jonas, Raymond A. "Sacred Tourism and Secular Pilgrimage: Montmartre and the Basilica of Sacré-Coeur." In *Montmartre and the Making of Mass Culture,* ed. Gabriel P. Weisberg, 94–119. New Brunswick, N.J.: Rutgers University Press, 2001.

Jorgefélice, C. "*La Sirène des tropiques.*" *Presse,* October 18, 1927.

"Joséphine Baker aviatrice." 1935. In "Collection of Photos and Press Clippings of Josephine," file 4° ICO-PER 1326. Bibliothèque de l'Arsenal, Paris.

"Josèphine Baker et le champion Al Brown." 1931. In "Collection of Photos and Press

Clippings of Josephine Baker." File 4° ICO-PER 1326. Bibliothèque de l'Arsenal, Paris.

"Joséphine Baker—Les Adieux à Bobino." Château des Milandes. Postcard, Ref. M15. Dordogne: Château des Milandes, 1970.

Josephine Baker's African Village at Les Milandes. Château des Milandes Publicity Brochure. Dordogne: Château des Milandes, 1992.

"Joséphine Baker se raconte." *France-Soir,* July 13, 1976.

"Joséphine-Zouzou." *Paris-Jour,* September 19, 1934.

Jules-Rosette, Bennetta. *Black Paris: The African Writers' Landscape.* Urbana: University of Illinois Press, 1998.

———. "Black Paris: Touristic Simulations." *Annals of Tourism Research* 21, no. 4 (1994): 679–700.

———. "Identity Discourses and Diasporic Aesthetics in Black Paris: Community by Formation and the Translation of Culture." *Diaspora* 9, no. 1 (2000): 39–58.

———. "Josephine Baker: Inventing the Image and Preserving the Icon." In Lahs-Gonzales, *Josephine Baker,* 3–28.

———. "Josephine Baker and Utopian Visions of Black Paris." *Journal of Romance Studies* 5, no. 3 (2005): 33–50.

———. "Two Loves: Josephine Baker as Icon and Image." *Emergences* 10, no. 1 (2000): 55–77.

Jules-Rosette, Bennetta, Cristin McVey, and Mark Arbitrario. "Performance Ethnography: The Theory and Method of Dual Tracking." *Field Methods* 14, no. 2 (2002): 123–47.

Kalinak, Kathryn. "Disciplining Josephine Baker: Gender, Race, and the Limits of Disciplinarity." In *Music and Cinema,* ed. James Buhler, Caryl Flinn, and David Neumeyer, 316–35. Hanover, N.H.: Wesleyan University Press and the University Press of New England, 2000.

Kaplan, E. Ann. "Madonna Politics: Perversion, Repression, or Subversion? Or Masks and/as Master-y." In Schwichtenberg, *The Madonna Connection,* 149–65.

———. *Rocking around the Clock: Music Television, Postmodernism, and Consumer Culture.* New York: Methuen, 1987.

Kephart, William M., and William W. Zellner. *Extraordinary Groups: An Examination of Unconventional Lifestyles.* 6th ed. New York: St. Martin's, 1998.

Kirshenblatt-Gimblett, Barbara. *Destination Culture: Tourism, Museums, and Heritage.* Berkeley: University of California Press, 1998.

Kuhn, Annette. "Remembrance." In *Family Snaps: The Meaning of Domestic Photography,* ed. Jo Spence and Patricia Holland, 17–25. London: Virago Press, 1991.

Kühn, Dieter. *Josephine: Aus der öffentlichen Biografie der Josephine Baker.* Frankfurt: Suhrkamp, 1976.

Kumar, Krishan, and Stephen Bann, eds. *Utopias and the Millennium*. London: Reaktion Books, 1993.

Lacan, Jacques. *Four Fundamental Concepts of Psycho-Analysis*. Trans. Alan Sheridan. New York: Norton, 1978.

Lahs-Gonzales, Olivia, ed. *Josephine Baker: Image and Icon*. St. Louis: Reedy Press and Sheldon Art Galleries, 2006.

———. "Josephine Baker: Modern Woman." In Lahs-Gonzales, *Josephine Baker*, 31–53.

Lange, Barbara Rose. "Hypermedia and Ethnomusicology." *Ethnomusicology: Journal of the Society for Ethnomusicology* 45, no. 1 (2001): 132–49.

Lazareff, Pierre. "Pourquoi Joséphine Baker veut intenter un procès à Marcel Sauvage." *Paris-Midi*, November 2, 1927, p. 5.

Lemarchand, Henri (lyrics), and Francis Lopez (musical score). "Dans mon village." Paris: Salabert, 1953.

"L'Éternel retour de Joséphine Baker." *L'Express*, April 14, 1975.

Lhamon, W. T. *Raising Cain: Blackface Performance from Jim Crow to Hip Hop*. Cambridge, Mass.: Harvard University Press, 1998.

Lindfors, Bernth, ed. *Africans on Stage: Studies in Ethnological Show Business*. Bloomington: Indiana University Press, 1999.

Lipsitz, George. *Dangerous Crossroads: Popular Music, Postmodernism, and the Poetics of Place*. London: Verso, 1994.

———. *The Sidewalks of St. Louis*. Columbia: University of Missouri Press, 1991.

Lofland, John, and Norman Skonovd. "Conversion Motifs." *Journal for the Scientific Study of Religion* 20, no. 4 (1981): 373–85.

Loos, Adolf. "Ornament and Crime." [1908.] Trans. Wilfried Wang. *The Architecture of Adolf Loos*. London: Arts Council of Great Britain, 1985.

Loti, Pierre. *Le Roman d'un spahi*. Paris: Calmann-Lévy, 1881.

Lynam, Ruth, ed. *Paris Fashion: The Great Designers and Their Creations*. London: Michael Joseph, 1972.

Lyon, Janet. "Josephine Baker's Hothouse." In *Modernism, Inc.: Body, Memory, Capital*, ed. Jani Scandura and Michael Thurston, 29–47. New York: New York University Press, 2001.

MacCannell, Dean. "Marilyn Monroe Was Not a Man." *Diacritics* 17, no. 2 (1987): 114–27.

———. *The Tourist: A New Theory of the Leisure Class*. New foreword by Lucy R. Lippard; new epilogue by the author. Berkeley: University of California Press, 1999.

Madonna. *The English Roses*. Illustrated by Jeffrey Fulvimari. New York: Viking, 2003.

Maffesoli, Michel. *Éloge de la raison sensible: Essai*. Paris: Bernard Grasset, 1996.

———. *L'Ombre de Dionysos: Contribution à une sociologie de l'orgie*. Paris: Méridiens/Anthropos, 1982.

———. *Le Temps des tribus*. Paris: Méridiens Klincksieck, 1988.

———. *La Transfiguration du politique: La Tribalisation du monde*. Paris: Bernard Grasset, 1992.

Mannheim, Karl. *Essays on the Sociology of Knowledge*. Ed. Paul Kecskemeti. London: Routledge and Kegan Paul, 1952.

———. *Ideology and Utopia: An Introduction to the Sociology of Knowledge*. Trans. Louis Wirth and Edward Shils. New York: Harcourt, Brace, and World, 1936.

Maran, René. *Batouala, véritable roman nègre*. Paris: Albin Michel, 1921. (Published in English as *Batouala: A True Black Novel*. Trans. Barbara Beck and Alexandre Mboukou [Washington, D.C.: Black Orpheus Press, 1972].)

Marcus, Sharon. *Apartment Stories: City and Home in Nineteenth-Century Paris and London*. Berkeley: University of California Press, 1999.

Marin, Louis. "The Frontiers of Utopia." In Kumar and Bann, *Utopias and the Millennium*, 7–16.

Martin, Denis-Constant. "Du jazz band au zazous: L'Invention du jazz français (1900–1945)." Paper presented at the African Americans and Europe Conference, Université de Paris III, February 5–9, 1992.

Martin, Denis-Constant, and Olivier Roueff. *La France du jazz: Musique, modernité et identité dans la première moitié du xxe siècle*. Marseille: Parenthèses, 2002.

Mbembe, Achille. "African Modes of Self-Writing." *Public Culture* 14, no. 1 (2002): 239–73.

Mel, Frédéric Grah. *Alioune Diop: Le Bâtisseur inconnu du monde noir*. Abidjan, Côte d'Ivoire, and Paris: Presses Universitaires de Côte d'Ivoire and ACCT, 1995.

Miller, James, and Jerry Watts. "The First Congress of Black Writers and Intellectuals in Paris, 1956." Paper presented at the African Americans and Europe Conference, Université de Paris III, February 5–9, 1992.

Miller, Perry. *Errand into the Wilderness*. Cambridge, Mass.: Harvard University Press, 1964.

Minh-ha, Trinh T. *When the Moon Waxes Red: Representation, Gender, and Cultural Politics*. New York: Routledge, 1991.

———. *Woman, Native, Other: Writing Postcoloniality and Feminism*. Bloomington: Indiana University Press, 1989.

Mistinguett. *Toute ma vie*. Paris: René Julliard, 1954.

Moret, Frédéric. "Images de Paris dans les guides touristiques en 1900." *Le Mouvement Social* 160 (July–September 1992): 79–98.

Nenno, Nancy Pauline. "Masquerade: Woman, Naure, Modernity." Ph.D. diss., University of California, Berkeley, 1996.

Nixon, Rob. *Homelands, Harlem, and Hollywood: South African Culture and the World Beyond*. New York: Routledge, 1994.

Njami, Simon. "The Invention of Memory: Birth and Evolution of Contemporary

African Art." Colloquium presented in the Department of Art History, UCLA, April 14, 1993.

———. *James Baldwin ou le devoir de violence.* Paris: Seghers, 1991.

Onana, Charles. *Joséphine Baker contre Hitler: La star noire de la France libre.* Paris: Duboiris, 2006.

Papich, Stephen. Personal communication, Los Angeles, August 2, 2005.

———. *Remembering Josephine.* Indianapolis: Bobbs-Merrill, 1976.

"*Paris qui remue.*" *Ami du Peuple,* October 22, 1930.

Patton, Cindy. "Embodying Subaltern Memory: Kinesthesia and the Problematics of Gender and Race." In Schwichtenberg, *The Madonna Connection,* 81–105.

Peterson, Jessica Kristen. "The Bizarre Charm of This Music: Stereotypes in Images of Josephine Baker, 1925–1935." Master's thesis, University of California, Riverside, 1996.

Phantom Dragon. Web page about Lynne Carter. http://phantomdragon.com/THE-LEGEND/carter.htm, accessed January 19, 2006.

"Pour sauver Joséphine Baker Bardot payera ce soir de sa personne." *Le Figaro,* June 4, 1964.

Price, Sally. *Primitive Art in Civilized Places.* Chicago: University of Chicago Press, 1989.

Propp, Vladimir. *Morphology of the Folktale.* Trans. Laurence Scott. Bloomington: American Folklore Society and Indiana University Press, 1968.

Ralling, Christopher, director. *Chasing a Rainbow: The Life of Josephine Baker.* Documentary film with narration by Oliver Todd. London: Csáky Productions, Channel Four, United Kingdom, 1986.

Reichenbach, François, director. *Olympia Story.* 1987. Film. File FRBNF38160905 (10). Bibliothèque Nationale, Paris.

Relf, Jan. "Utopia and the Good Breast." In Kumar and Bann, *Utopias and the Millennium,* 107–28.

Rivollet, André. "Du Jazz hot à 'La Créole.'" Lecture at Neuilly. *Conferencia,* July 1, 1935, 65–71. File R.99287. Bibliothèque de l'Arsenal, Paris.

———. *Une Vie de toutes les couleurs.* Grenoble: B. Arthaud, 1935.

Rose, Phyllis. *Jazz Cleopatra: Josephine Baker in Her Time.* New York: Vintage, 1989.

Rose, Tricia. *Black Noise: Rap Music and Black Culture in Contemporary America.* Hanover, N.H.: Wesleyan University Press, 1994.

Roueff, Olivier. "L'Acclimation du jazz en France et la question de la négritude: De l'Amerique mécanisée à l'Afrique sauvage (1917–1932)." Paper presented at the Conference on Africa, France, and the United States, CÉAN, Bordeaux, May 22, 1997.

Said, Edward W. *Orientalism.* New York: Vintage, 1978.

Sartre, Jean-Paul. "Orphée noir." In *Anthologie de la nouvelle poésie nègre et malgache de langue française,* ed. Léopold Sédar Senghor, ix–xliv. Paris: Presses Universitaires de France, 1948. Excerpted in *Présence Africaine,* 1st ser., 6, 1st trimester (1949): 9–14.

Sauvage, Marcel. "Joséphine Baker, cuisinière." *Candide,* September 26, 1927.

———. *Les Mémoires de Joséphine Baker.* Paris: Kra, 1927.

———. *Les Mémoires de Joséphine Baker.* Recueillis et adaptés par Marcel Sauvage. Paris: Kra, 1947.

———. *Voyages et aventures de Joséphine Baker.* Paris: Marcel Seheur, 1931.

Schlumberger, Eveline. "Georges-Henri Rivière: Homme-orchestre des musées du 20e siècle." *Connaissance des arts* (December 1974): 100–106.

Schroeder, Alan. *Josephine Baker.* New York: Chelsea House, 1991.

Schwartz, Vanessa R. "Museums and Mass Spectacle: The Musée Grévin as a Monument to Life." *French Historical Studies* 19, no. 1 (1995): 7–26.

———. *Spectacular Realities: Early Mass Culture in Fin-de-Siècle Paris.* Berkeley: University of California Press, 1998.

Schwichtenberg, Cathy, ed. *The Madonna Connection: Representational Politics, Subcultural Identities, and Cultural Theory.* Boulder, Colo.: Westview Press, 1993.

Scott, James C. *Domination and the Arts of Resistance: Hidden Transcripts.* New Haven: Yale University Press, 1990.

Scott, Ronald B. "Images of Race and Religion in Madonna's Video *Like a Prayer.*" In Schwichtenberg, *The Madonna Connection,* 57–77.

Senghor, Léopold Sédar. "Discours du Président Léopold Sédar Senghor." In *Le Critique africain et son peuple comme producteur de civilisation: Colloque de Yaoundé, 16–20 avril, 1973,* ed. Société Africaine de Culture, 513–15. Paris: Présence Africaine, 1977.

Shack, William A. *Harlem in Montmartre: A Paris Jazz Story between the Great Wars.* Berkeley: University of California Press, 2001.

Sharpley-Whiting, T. Denean. *Black Venus: Sexualized Savages, Primal Fears, and Primitive Narratives in French.* Durham, N.C.: Duke University Press, 1999.

Silverman, Kaja. *The Threshold of the Visible World.* New York: Routledge, 1996.

Stearns, Marshall, and Jean Stearns. *Jazz Dance: The Story of American Vernacular Dance.* New York: Macmillan, 1968.

Steele, Valerie. *Paris Fashion: A Cultural History.* New York: Oxford University Press, 1988.

Stovall, Tyler. "Freedom, Community, and the Paris Jazz Age: Josephine Baker and the World of Black Montmartre." In Lahs-Gonzales, *Josephine Baker,* 55–68.

———. *Paris Noir: African Americans in the City of Light.* New York: Houghton Mifflin, 1996.

Strother, Zoe S. "Display of the Body Hottentot." In *Africans on Stage: Studies in Ethnological Show Business,* ed. Bernth Lindfors, 1–61. Bloomington: Indiana University Press, 1999.

Thomas, Dominic. "Fashion Matters: *La Sape* and Vestimentary Codes in Transnational Contexts and Urban Diasporas." *MLN* 118, no. 4 (2003): 947–73.

Tournès, Ludovic. *New Orleans sur Seine: Histoire du jazz en France.* Paris: Arthème Fayard, 1999.

Traimond, Bernard. Personal communication, Bordeaux, France, 2001.

Turino, Thomas. *Nationalists, Cosmopolitans, and Popular Music in Zimbabwe.* Chicago: University of Chicago Press, 2000.

Turner, Victor, and Edith Turner. *Image and Pilgrimage in Christian Culture: Anthropological Perspectives.* New York: Columbia University Press, 1978.

"Un artiste se suicide aux pieds de Joséphine Baker." *Liberté,* September 7, 1928.

Urbain, Jean-Didier. "The Tourist Adventure and His Images." *Annals of Tourism Research* 16 (1989): 108–18.

Vincour, John. "At 64, Josephine Baker Looks at Black Power." *International Herald Tribune,* August 31, 1970.

Viso K., André. "Pipi de chat et vieille rosette." *Libération,* April 5, 1975.

Vogel, Susan. *Art/Artifact.* New York: Center for African Art and Prestel, 1988.

Vreeland, Diana. "Introduction." In *Inventive Paris Clothes, 1909–1939: A Photographic Essay,* by Irving Penn, with text by Diana Vreeland, 8–13. New York: Viking, 1977.

Walzer, Michael. *The Revolution of the Saints: A Study in the Origins of Radical Politics.* New York: Atheneum, 1968.

Whitaker, Charles. "The Real-Life Josephine Baker: What the Movie Didn't Tell You." *Ebony,* June 1991, 25–30.

Williams, Iain Chambers. *Underneath a Harlem Moon: The Harlem to Paris Years of Adelaide Hall.* New York: Continuum, 2002.

Willis, Deborah, and Carla Williams. *The Black Female Body: A Photographic History.* Philadelphia: Temple University Press, 2002.

Wolff, Janet. "The Invisible *Flâneuse:* Women and the Literature of Modernity." *Theory, Culture, and Society* 2, no. 3 (1985): 37–46.

Wood, Ean. *The Josephine Baker Story.* 2nd ed. London: Sanctuary, 2002.

Zdatny, Steven, ed. *Hairstyles and Fashion: A Hairdresser's History of Paris, 1910–1920.* Oxford: Berg, 1999.

Discography

The following selected songs recorded by Josephine Baker are discussed in the text. Within each year, the song or LP title is followed, where known, by the name of the composer and/or lyricist, the month of the recording, the orchestra name, and the record label and catalog number. Unless noted otherwise, the recordings were made in Paris, in the same year they were issued. Data in this discography draws on information in Hammond and O'Connor, *Josephine Baker,* 287–94; Bonini, *La Véritable Joséphine Baker,* 349–59; and the Bibliothèque de l'Arsenal files.

1926

"I Want to Yodel." Jack Palmer and Spencer Williams. September 20. Odéon 49.180.

"Always." Irving Berlin. October. Odéon 49.224.

"I Found a New Baby." Jack Palmer and Spencer Williams. October. Odéon 49.226.

"I Love My Baby." Warren/Green. October. Odéon 49.225.

"Feeling Kind of Blue." Wohlman/Ruby/Cooper. October. Odéon 49.182.

"Brown Eyes." Unidentified composer. October. Odéon 49.183.

"Skeedle Um." Unidentified composer. October. Odéon 49.227.

"You're the Only One for Me." Monaco/Warren. December. Odéon 49.181.

1930

"La Petite Tonkinoise." Géo Koger, Henri Varna, and Vincent Scotto. October. Melodic-Jazz du Casino de Paris. Columbia DF229.

"J'ai deux amours." Géo Koger, Henri Varna, and Vincent Scotto. October. Melodic-Jazz du Casino de Paris. Columbia DF229. Sheet music published by Francis Salabert (Paris: Éditions Salabert, 1930).

"Voulez-vous de la canne à sucre?" Léo Lelièvre, Henri Varna, and Georges Paddy. October. Melodic-Jazz du Casino de Paris. Columbia DF228.

"Dis-moi Joséphine." Leo Lelièvre, Henri Varna, Marc Cab, and Bela Zerkowitz. October. Melodic-Jazz du Casino de Paris. Columbia DF228.

1932

"Sans amour." A. Farel and Charles Borel-Clerc. November. *La Joie de Paris.* Recorded by the orchestra of Josephine Baker. Columbia DF1071.

"Si j'étais blanche!" Henri Varna, L. Lelièvre, and L. Falk. November. *La Joie de Paris*. Recorded by the orchestra of Josephine Baker. Columbia DF1070.

"Les Mots d'amour." Henri Varna, Pierre Paul Fournier, and Virgilio Ranzato. November. *La Joie de Paris*. Recorded by the orchestra of Josephine Baker. Columbia DF1070.

1934

"C'est lui." R. Bernstein and Georges Van Parys. November. From the film *Zouzou*. Jazz du Poste-Parisien, directed by Al Romans. Columbia DF1623.

"Haïti." Géo Koger and Vincent Scotto. November. From the film *Zouzou*. Jazz du Poste-Parisien, directed by Al Romans. Columbia DF1623.

1935

"Sous le ciel d'Afrique (Neath the Tropic Blue Skies)." André de Badet and Jacques Dallin. September 1935. From the film *Princesse Tam-Tam*. Columbia DF1814. Also released in limited edition in the United States.

"Le Chemin de bonheur (Dream Ship)." André de Badet and Jacques Dallin. October. From the film *Princesse Tam-Tam*. Recorded in New York for radio in 1935 as "Dream Ship" and by Totem Records, 1977, for radio broadcast. No catalog number available.

1936

"La Conga blicoti." A. Oréfiches and André de Badet. November. From the film *Princesse Tam-Tam*. Recorded by Josephine Baker and the Lecuona Cuban Boys. Columbia BF30.

1953

"Dans mon village." Henri Lemarchand and Francis Lopez. Recorded in Germany by Pierre Dreuder and his orchestra. Bertelsmann, Columbia CL9475.

1959

"Don't Touch My Tomatoes." Henri Lemarchand and Jo Bouillon. Performed live under the name of Jo Duval and his orchestra. RCA 76321.

1961

Joséphine Chante Paris, including a rerecording of "J'ai deux amours." Guy Lafarge and Jean Claudric. RCA 430.058.

1966

Joséphine Baker en La Habana. Tony Taño and his orchestra. Havana, Cuba. Egrem 3213.

1973

The Incredible Return of Josephine Baker, Recorded Live at Carnegie Hall. Karl Hampton Porter, musical director, with an introduction by Ada Smith (Bricktop). June 5. New York. Tele General Studios JB-001.

1975

Josephine à Bobino 1975. March 24. Pierre Spiers and his orchestra. Festival FLD 643.

1975

Homage à Joséphine Baker: Disque du centennaire. Twenty-seven remastered pieces from 1930–53. Sepia 1065.

Index

of children by, 190–91, 194; biography of Baker by, xx, 55, 68, 85, 101,
157, 171–73, 293, 310n46, 314–15n1,
318n56; and Château des Milandes, 35,
38, 41–42, 172–73, 197–99, 202–3, 223,
314n40, 316n24; departure of, 198–99;
divorce proceedings of, 194, 198–99,
304n44, 313nn27–31; and film, 118–20,
182, 197–98; and his band, 236, 342; as
Jo Duval, 198; marriage to Baker, 25, 27,
29, 35, 41–42, 70, 108, 112, 116–29, 173,
188, 189, 190, 194–99, 220, 221, 290,
304n44
Bouillon, Koffi (adopted son), 190, 194,
200, 201, 204. See also Rainbow Tribe
Bouillon, Luis (adopted son), 111, 169, 190,
193, 200, 208. See also Rainbow Tribe
Bouillon, Mara (adopted son), 190, 193,
194, 200–201, 204. See also Rainbow
Tribe
Bouillon, Marianne (adopted daughter),
108, 111, 170, 182, 190, 194, 199, 200–
201, 204, 233. See also Rainbow Tribe
Bouillon, Maryse (sister of Jo Bouillon), 197
Bouillon, Moïse (adopted son), 111,
169–70, 190, 193–96, 200, 202. See also
Rainbow Tribe
Bouillon, Noël (adopted son), 119, 190,
194–95, 199, 200. See also Rainbow Tribe
Bouillon, Stellina (adopted daughter), 190,
195, 199, 200, 204, 313n34. See also
Rainbow Tribe
boulevard des Batignolles, 16
Bourbon monarchy, 17
Bourgeois, Jeanne, 134. See also Mistinguett
Bowie, David, 262
Brady, Robert (Baker's spiritual husband),
269, 323n3
Brescia, 238. See also Fedrigolli, Bruno
Breton, André, 138
Brialy, Jean-Claude (actor and director),
270, 271, 274; and Levasseur, 271, 293
Bricktop (Ada Smith), 61, 137, 301n19. See
also cabarets, of African Americans
Brioni Island, 239, 318n53. See also Tito,
Marshal
Brown, Alfonso Teofilo, 140, 288, 306n21
"Brown Eyes" (song recorded by Baker),
174, 341

Brussels, Baker's tours and performances in,
19, 253
Buchanan, Bessie (performer and politi-
cian), 223–24
Buenos Aires, Baker's tours and perfor-
mances in, 164, 214
Bullard, Eugene (cabaret owner), 61
Bunche, Ralph, 223, 291
Buñel, Luis, 76
Bureau of Counterespionage, 107, 215–16

Cab, Marc (composer), 174, 341
cabarets: of African Americans, 16, 61, 62,
135–37, 150, 156, 158, 162, 268, 287;
in Berlin, 105, 106, 107, 160; culture of,
73, 138; in New York, 70, 105, 160, 276;
in Paris, 17, 70, 74, 105, 106, 107, 160,
268, 276
caged bird (from Zouzou), 89–90, 91
Cairo, Baker's tours and performances in,
219
cakewalk craze, 61, 96, 179, 301n18,
311n60. See also Walker, George; Williams, Bert
Calder, Alexander, sculptures of Baker by,
135, 136, 280, 288
Camard, Jean-Pierre, 298n25, 307n46
caricatures: of Baker, 130, 157, 161; and
caricaturists, 17, 130, 161; and cartoons,
17, 47, 133
Carnegie Hall, 244; Baker at, 235, 269–70,
271, 293, 324n6
Carpentier, Jules (engineer), 73
Carson, Eddie, 53, 159, 187, 287; Baker's
paternity by, 53, 159, 187, 309n12
Carter, Lynne (female impersonator), 244,
262; at Carnegie Hall, 244
Cartier, Jacqueline (journalist), 105, 108,
157, 171, 208, 314n51
Casablanca, Baker's tours and performances
in, 70, 218, 290
Casino de Paris, 21, 22, 23, 62, 63, 65, 67,
138, 145–46, 165, 174, 175, 216–17, 220,
271, 288, 289, 290, 298n20; Baker's bid
to return to, 271
Castaldi, Francesca, xviii
Castelnaud, 1, 35, 203, 234; Lord of, 35.
See also Association Joséphine Baker;
Château des Milandes

Le Jour, 80, 94
Journal lumineux, 18, 40. See also wax
    museums
Judaism, Baker and, 71, 193–94, 195–96,
    225, 226
Jules-Rosette, Benjamin (actor and film
    director), xviii, xix
Jules-Rosette, Bennetta, 299–300n49,
    304n38, 314n42, 317n36, 322n66,
    325n27
Jungle Fever (Goude), 252–54, 321nn36–39

Kahn, Gus (composer), 161
Kalinak, Kathryn, 303n30
Kaplan, E. Ann, 245, 252, 257, 263, 264,
    265, 319n9, 320n34, 321n51, 322n71,
    323n77
Kemeny, John (producer), 110
Kennedy, Franz, xix, 279
Kennedy, Robert, 235, 317n45
Kephart, William, 312n16
Khoikhoi (Hottentot) Venus. See Baartman,
    Sartjee
Kiki (Baker's pet snake), 148
King, Martin Luther, Jr., 39, 71, 235, 236,
    237
King Hassan of Morocco, 239
Kino International, 74, 75, 76, 78, 178
Kiranine (actor), 76
Kirshenblatt-Gimblett, Barbara, 19, 298n18
kitsch, 17, 40. See also souvenirs; tourism
Koger, Géo (composer), xxi, 62, 174, 176,
    341, 342
Kott-Kott (character in La Tribu arc-en-ciel),
    167–71
Kuhn, Annette, 313n33
Kühn, Dieter, 300–301n8
Ku Klux Klan, 104, 256

Lacan, Jacques, 264, 323n72
Lahillonne, André (prefect of Dordogne),
    188
Lahs-Gonzales, Olivia, xviii, xx, 295,
    307–8n50
La Madeleine, 276, 284. See also Baker,
    Josephine, funeral services of
La Madone des sleeping (Dekobra), 73
laminated adumbration (in art and life),
    155. See also Goffman, Erving
Lamy, Adrien (performer and singer), 174

Larquey, Pierre (actor), 81
l'art nègre, 140, 248. See also African art
Lascaux, caves of, 169
L'Aurore, 198, 273
Lazareff, Pierre, 309n21
League Against Racism and Anti-Semitism,
    226, 292. See also Judaism, Baker and
Lebanon, Baker's tours and performances
    in, 219
Le Corbusier (Charles-Edouard Jeanneret),
    131, 148, 307n49
Lederer, Hugo (fashion designer), 307n46
Léger, Fernand, 130, 248, 249
Légion d'Honneur, 39, 71, 107, 192, 232,
    233, 276, 292. See also Baker, Josephine,
    awards and medals of
Leiris, Michel, 228
Lelièvre, Lé (composer and theater pro-
    ducer), 145, 174, 341, 342
Lemarchand, Henri (composer), xxi, 176,
    177, 291, 342. See also Bouillon, Jo;
    "Dans mon village"
Leslie, Earl (choreographer), 145
Lettre d'une Africaine à ses soeurs Occiden-
    tales (Beyala), 260, 322n64
Lettre d'une Afro-française à ses compatriotes
    (Beyala), 260, 322n64
Levasseur, André (set designer and theater
    director), 109, 269, 270, 272, 273, 293
Lévy-Bruhl, Lucien, 138
L'Express, 273
Lhamon, W. T., 311n60, 320n17
Libération, 273
Liberty Clubs, 108, 116, 122, 218, 219,
    315n14
Like a Prayer (Madonna, 1989), 256, 257,
    294
Like a Virgin (Madonna, 1984), 256
Lincoln Elementary School (St. Louis) , 53
Lindfors, Bernth, 129, 305n5
linear narrative. See narrative, linear
linguistic performance, 241–42, 318n59.
    See also discourse, and expressive
    coherence
L'Intransigeant, 157
Lion, Jean, 70, 290, 292
lioness pose, 20, 21, 105
Lipnitzki, Haim (Boris), 21–22, 140
Lipsitz, George, xviii, 53, 323n80
Live 8 concert, 256, 318n60

Sartre, Jean-Paul, 5, 206, 228, 314nn44–45, 325n30

Saudé, J. C. (artist), 131

Saunders, Howard (theater producer), 269, 324n6

Sauvage, Marcel, Baker biographies by, xxi, 2, 53, 111, 137, 142, 156, 157, 159, 160–62, 164, 167, 181, 182, 214, 224, 244, 260, 272, 277, 279, 287, 288, 300n7, 306n26, 309n13, 309n19–22, 309n24, 310nn28–29, 310n32, 310n37

Sauvage, Paulette, 157

savage dancer, 2, 3, 48, 72, 78, 99, 110, 113, 122, 123, 128, 129, 135, 153, 166, 179, 188, 244, 287; and animal imagery, 20. See also Baker, Josephine, and drama; danse sauvage

Scandinavia, Baker's tours and performances in, 162

scenodrama, 43. See also Baudrillard, Jean

Schlumberger, Eveline, 306n20

Schroeder, Alan, 220, 315n18, 317n47

Schuyler, Ned (nightclub owner), 221, 315–16n20

Schwartz, Vanessa: and wax museums, 298n12, 299n47; and cinema, 302n6. See also cinema; wax museums

Schwarzenegger, Arnold, 254

Schwichtenberg, Cathy, 321n51

Scott, Hazel (vocalist and performer), 226

Scott, Ronald, 321–22n55

Scotto, Lélia, 276

Scotto, Vincent, xxi, 62, 145, 146, 174, 176, 177, 341, 342

sculpture, 134, 135, 136, 138. See also African art; Chouski

Secessionism, 144, 145

Secret Service, 70. See also Bureau of Counterespionage

Selassie, Haile, 219

self-sacrifice motif, 31–35, 167, 182, 183, 188, 311n64

self-writing: and Baker's narratives, 7, 8, 52, 167, 241, 274; and primal images, 180–83, 280, 311n63; styles and symbolic elements of, 156. See also Baker, Josephine, writings of; narrative

semiography, 5–7

semiotics: and performance, 49, 88, 123,

240, 251, 252, 284; and narrative, 8, 301n9, 311n65; and semiography, 5–7; and sociosemiotics, 5

Sénégal, Baker's tours and performances in, 229; plight of soldiers from, 185

Senghor, Léopold: and négritude, 140, 142, 206, 319n5; and Présence Africaine, 228

Seniors, Paula Marie, xviii

Senufo, figure of, 134. See also African art

sexualized savage, 128

Shack, William A., 305n16

Sharpley-Whiting, T. Denean, 98, 253, 303n29, 304n34, 305n.3, 321n46, 321n57

Sheldon Art Galleries, xviii, 295

Shuffle Along, 55, 56, 57, 60, 105, 129, 145, 160, 177, 272, 287

"Si j'étais blanche!" (song by Varna, Lelièvre, and Falk), 63–64, 174, 289, 301n291, 342

silent film. See film, silent

Silva, Romeo (musician), 179

Silverman, Kaja, 103, 264, 304n37, 323n72

Simon, Paul, 318n60

simulacra, 252, 321n35. See also Baudrillard, Jean

simulation: and simulacra, 252, 321n35; touristic, 42, 43, 299–300n49. See also Baudrillard, Jean; Greimas, A. J.

La Sirène des tropiques (1927), 8, 19, 45, 64, 72–73, 74, 75, 76–79, 102, 106, 164, 165, 283, 288, 302n1

Sissle, Noble (composer and musician), 55, 56, 57, 58, 105, 129, 145, 160, 177, 178, 272, 287. See also Blake, Eubie; Chocolate Dandies; Shuffle Along

Sixteen Baker Boys, 179

Sixteen Jackson Girls, 145

"Skeedle Um" (song by Berlin), 173–74, 341

Slave to Rhythm (Jones, 1987), 254

Smith, Ada, 61, 137, 301n19. See also Bricktop

Société Africaine de Culture (SAC), 142, 228–29, 231, 232, 283, 293, 306n24

"Sous le ciel d'Afrique" (song by de Badet and Dallin), xxi, 99–101, 176, 180, 289, 342

South Africa: Baker's tours and perfor-

BENNETTA JULES-ROSETTE is professor of sociology and director of African and African-American studies at the University of California, San Diego. She is an expert in sociosemiotic studies and has published eight books, including *The Messages of Tourist Art: An African Semiotic System; Terminal Signs: Computers and Social Change in Africa;* and *Black Paris: The African Writers' Landscape.* She has served as consulting editor for *African Arts* and *Revue Noire* magazines and has published numerous articles in such journals as *American Anthropologist, African Studies Review, American Journal of Semiotics, Cahiers d'Études Africaines,* and *Semiotica.* Professor Jules-Rosette has served as president of the Semiotic Society of America (1988–89) and of the Association of Africanist Anthropology (2004–6). She has also been on the board of the National Museum of African Art, Smithsonian Institution (2005–8).

The University of Illinois Press
is a founding member of the
Association of American University Presses.

Composed in 10/13.5 Berkeley Oldstyle
by Barbara Evans
at the University of Illinois Press
Designed by Paula Newcomb
Manufactured by Thomson-Shore, Inc.

University of Illinois Press
1325 South Oak Street
Champaign, IL 61820-6903
www.press.uillinois.edu